Clint Eastwood: Interviews
Revised and Updated

Conversations with Filmmakers Series
Gerald Peary, General Editor

Clint Eastwood
INTERVIEWS
REVISED AND UPDATED

Edited by Robert E. Kapsis and Kathie Coblentz

University Press of Mississippi / Jackson

www.upress.state.ms.us

The University Press of Mississippi is a member of the Association of American University Presses.

Copyright © 2013 by University Press of Mississippi
All rights reserved
Manufactured in the United States of America

First printing 2013
∞
Library of Congress Cataloging-in-Publication Data

Eastwood, Clint, 1930-
 Clint Eastwood: interviews / edited by Robert E. Kapsis and Kathie Coblentz. — 2nd ed., rev. and updated.
     p. cm.
 Includes filmography and index.
 ISBN 978-1-61703-662-0 (cloth: alk. paper) — ISBN 978-1-61703-663-7 (pbk.: alk. paper) — ISBN 978-1-61703-664-4 (ebook) 1. Eastwood, Clint, 1930– 2. Motion picture actors and actresses—United States—Interviews. 3. Motion picture producers and directors—United States—Interviews. I. Kapsis, Robert E. II. Coblentz, Kathie. III. Title.
 PN2287.E37A3 2012
 791.4302'8092—dc23
 [B]
                    2012021757

British Library Cataloging-in-Publication Data available

Contents

Introduction   ix

Chronology   xxiii

Filmography   xxxi

No Tumbleweed Ties for Clint   3
    Rex Reed / 1971

Eastwood on Eastwood   7
    Stuart M. Kaminsky / 1971

Eastwood Direction   20
    Richard Thompson and Tim Hunter / 1976-77

Director Clint Eastwood: Attention to Detail and Involvement for the Audience   40
    Ric Gentry / 1980

Eastwood: An Auteur to Reckon With   53
    Charles Champlin / 1981

Cop on a Hot *Tightrope*   57
    David Thomson / 1984

"Whether I Succeed or Fail, I Don't Want to Owe It to Anyone but Myself": From *Play Misty for Me* to *Honkytonk Man*   72
    Michael Henry Wilson / 1984

Clint Eastwood: The *Rolling Stone* Interview   93
    Tim Cahill / 1985

Eastwood on Eastwood   106
    Christopher Frayling / ca. 1985

Flight of Fancy   112
    Nat Hentoff / 1988

Interview with Clint Eastwood   119
    Michel Ciment / 1990

Interview with Clint Eastwood   131
    Thierry Jousse and Camille Nevers / 1992

Any Which Way He Can   142
    Peter Biskind / 1993

America on the Brink of the Void   156
    Henri Béhar / 1993

Q & A with a Western Icon   163
    Jerry Roberts / 1995

"Truth, Like Art, Is in the Eyes of the Beholder": *Midnight in the Garden of Good and Evil* and *The Bridges of Madison County*   168
    Michael Henry Wilson / 1998

A Conversation with Clint Eastwood about *Mystic River*   178
    Charlie Rose / 2003

Mystic River: Eastwood, without Anger or Forgiveness   189
    Samuel Blumenfeld / 2003

Staying Power   193
    Amy Taubin / 2005

Eastwood's *Letters from Iwo Jima*   206
    Terry Gross / 2007

The Quiet American   219
    Geoff Andrew / 2008

Do You Feel Lucky, Monk?   226
    Nick Tosches / 2008

Clint Eastwood, America's Director: The Searcher   230
    Scott Foundas / 2008

Eastwood on the Pitch: At Seventy-Nine, Clint Tackles Mandela in *Invictus*   234
    Scott Foundas / 2009

Interview with Clint Eastwood: First, Believe in Yourself   245
    Michael Henry Wilson / 2010

With *J. Edgar*, Eastwood Again Flexes His Freedom   252
    Scott Bowles / 2011

For Further Reading   257

Index   259

Introduction

The present volume is the second edition of *Clint Eastwood: Interviews*; the first edition came out in 1999. In the years since, Eastwood's thirty-year career as a filmmaker has become a more than forty-year career, and his twenty-plus feature films as director have become more than thirty. The introduction that follows was originally written for the first edition. Like the contents of this volume, it has been revised and expanded.

Clint Eastwood achieved international stardom in the mid-1960s with an unlikely acting project, a trio of European-made Westerns. Back in the U.S., he embarked on a career as a filmmaker that is practically unparalleled. For four decades, as a film star of iconic status, he appeared almost exclusively in films he produced or co-produced himself, and ever more frequently under his own direction. He has directed himself in a leading role twenty-three times, a figure no other contemporary actor-director has approached, except for Woody Allen. He has also become one of the more prolific active directors. His 2011 project *J. Edgar* is his thirty-third feature as director since 1971. Along the way, he has attained wide recognition for a directorial style that is coolly classical and yet adamantly personal. A Hollywood insider, he retains an outsider's perspective through his refusal to heed cultural and aesthetic trends in film production. "I trust my instinct and I make the films that I believe in," he told Michael Henry Wilson in 1984.

As a star, Eastwood is often recalled chiefly for two early roles: the "Man with No Name" in the three European Westerns that launched his career, and "Dirty" Harry Callahan, the uncompromising San Francisco cop who spoke softly and carried a big gun in five movies. All but one of these were directed by others (not without input from Eastwood, as several of our interviews document). As a director, however, Eastwood has created a more varied body of work. Notably, his films have examined the artist's life (*Honkytonk Man, Bird, White Hunter, Black Heart*); called into question the ethos of masculinity and his own star image

(*The Gauntlet, Bronco Billy, Tightrope, Heartbreak Ridge, Unforgiven, Gran Torino*); and explored the Western, the most traditional American film genre, as an eloquent medium of personal expression (*High Plains Drifter, The Outlaw Josey Wales, Pale Rider, Unforgiven*). In recent years, other themes have surfaced as well, such as the traumas of childhood and the loss of innocence (*A Perfect World, Mystic River, Changeling, Hereafter*); the nature of heroism (*Heartbreak Ridge, Flags of Our Fathers, Letters from Iwo Jima, Gran Torino*); and the "plight of women in a profoundly imperfect patriarchal world," as Geoff Andrews expressed it (*Unforgiven, The Bridges of Madison County, Million Dollar Baby, Changeling*).

As a producer-director, Eastwood has maintained a rare degree of independence within the Hollywood system. His star status and his long-standing reputation as an economical and efficient filmmaker are financial guarantees for the studio distributing his works. Frank Wells, former president of Warner Bros., told Peter Biskind in 1993, "You'd make the deal and not see him again until the preview—of an under-budget movie. We always did what he wanted to do." Still going strong in his sixth decade in films, Eastwood continues to select his projects on the basis of the only criterion he has cited repeatedly to interviewers: the story is something he himself would want to see on screen.

"So I directed this picture and I'm editing it myself and I think it's damn good."

Eastwood's 1971 comment to Rex Reed about his directorial debut, *Play Misty for Me*, manifests a singular self-confidence for a first-time director. By then, however, he had seventeen years in the television and film industry behind him. He had first come to fame as the second lead in a TV Western series, *Rawhide*. Over its long run (1959–65), he gained invaluable experience in acting for the camera and observing how films are made. It was on location for *Rawhide*'s endless cattle drive, as he states in several interviews, that his first directorial ambitions surfaced, only to be thwarted by the show's producers.

Rawhide led to his real breakthrough, in 1964, when an unknown Italian director named Sergio Leone looked for a convincing cowboy to star in a low-budget Western-style remake of Kurosawa's *Yojimbo*, to be shot in Rome and Spain. *Rawhide*'s clean-cut young trailhand decided to take a chance on the odd project. *Per un pugno di dollari* (*A Fistful of Dollars*) became an unexpected hit across Europe and started a new genre, the "spaghetti Western."

Eastwood's and Leone's accounts differ regarding their respective contributions to the appearance and nature of the mysterious gunslinger Eastwood played in *Fistful* and its successors, *For a Few Dollars More* and *The Good, the Bad and the Ugly*. It seems beyond dispute that Eastwood, against Leone's initial protests, cut back drastically on the exposition in the original film's script, depriving the character of a background and his deeds of a ready explanation—like many of his later films' protagonists. Eastwood related this anecdote to Tim Cahill of *Rolling Stone*: "I kept telling Sergio, 'In a real A picture, you let the audience think along with the movie; in a B picture, you explain everything.'"

Leone's openness to his star's suggestions gave Eastwood his first real experience in collaborating in the filmmaking process, although, as he complained to Stuart Kaminsky, the director "would never give me any credit for the style of a film I'd been in with him." More importantly, the "Dollars" trilogy made Eastwood an international star, with the power such status entailed.

The release of the trilogy was delayed in the U.S. until early 1967, when *Fistful* opened, followed within a year by its two successors. All were huge audience hits. Still, it is startling to find Eastwood, that same year, dictating to United Artists the terms by which he would make his first domestic starring appearance. He proposed the project (the modest but thematically challenging Western *Hang 'Em High*), imposed his choice of director (Ted Post), and proceeded to collaborate with Post on script revisions during the shoot. In order to serve as de facto co-producer in this fashion, Eastwood established his own production company: Malpaso. For now, it was a corporate convenience for his studio deals, but by 1970 it would become, within the studio structure, the independent filmmaking concern he has employed ever since, to assure that the ultimate control of his projects resides with Eastwood himself.

Hang 'Em High was a success, and Eastwood's singular career was underway. At first he would alternate low-profile, low-budget productions (retaining some control, through Malpaso, over script, director, and casting) with the kind of big-budget project that could garner him sufficient prestige, as well as money, to ensure he could function independently in the industry. To begin with, there were three films directed by Don Siegel: *Coogan's Bluff*, *Two Mules for Sister Sara*, and *The Beguiled*.

Eastwood's encounter with the veteran action director Siegel was a career milestone. Both found quickly they were on the same filmmaking wavelength. Eastwood told Patrick McGilligan (in an interview not included in the present edition), "[Siegel]'s a very lean kind of director—he usually knows what he wants and goes in and shoots what he has intended to shoot, and doesn't protect himself like a lot of guys." Siegel's way of making movies, in fact, neatly accorded with Eastwood's own views, often expressed in similar terms: know what you want, shoot fast, and move on as soon as you have it. Siegel, moreover, was open to collaboration; as he told Stuart Kaminsky, "I found Clint very knowledgeable about making pictures, very good at knowing what to do with the camera.... He started to come up with ideas for camera set-ups.... And even if I decided not to use them they invariably gave me another idea." To Kaminsky, Eastwood praised Siegel in turn, "Don ... kind of breeds an atmosphere of participation."

This was the opposite of the atmosphere on his three other films from those years, *Where Eagles Dare*, *Paint Your Wagon*, and *Kelly's Heroes*. The waste of time, resources, and money on these shoots infuriated him, and he was frustrated by having little input beyond his own performance. He was now even more determined to take charge of his career through Malpaso, and from this point on he was, in effect, his own producer.

But next, Eastwood persuaded Siegel to direct him in their fourth film together, one that would prove a different kind of career milestone: *Dirty Harry* (1971). In a politically polarized era, *Dirty Harry* touched a sore spot because of its blatant anti-Miranda/Escobedo stance and its sympathetic portrayal of Eastwood's eponymous rogue cop, who exercised brutality towards the presumed guilty, contempt for bureaucratic constraint, and total disregard for the letter of the law. Some called Inspector Callahan a "fascist." Audiences, however, embraced the movie, which became Eastwood's highest-grossing film to that date and spawned four sequels. The consequences for his future were twofold: as a performer, he had now attained superstar status, but for years afterward he would be considered *persona non grata* by many influential liberal critics and other cultural arbiters for the perceived politics of *Dirty Harry*.

Eastwood has often responded brusquely to the political charges against the film, dismissing them as misdirected or groundless; he and Siegel were not making a political statement but simply "telling a story." If pressed, he defended Harry as a before-his-time champion of victim's rights, at a moment when champions of the rights of the accused dominated the public debate. In several interviews, he characterized Harry's adherence to a "higher morality" as, in fact, "the opposite of fascism."

In later decades, Eastwood sometimes dismissed such attacks as characteristic of the rhetoric of their era. But in 1993, he directed another film (*A Perfect World*) in which a lawman shoots a kidnapper without remorse and against orders. By then, Eastwood's sympathies were clearly against the shooter, and he was willing to concede (in an interview not included here, in *Positif*, March 1994) that *"Dirty Harry* provided simple solutions to horribly complicated problems."

Dirty Harry was Eastwood's first film for Warner Bros. It marked the beginning of an informal near-exclusive relationship, to the mutual benefit of both the studio (Eastwood's pictures were generally very profitable) and the producer-director-star (who would be granted an almost entirely free hand with his projects). Moreover, Warners willingly assisted Eastwood in his ambition to become a respected filmmaker, helping him attain prestigious media exposure and supporting his international promotional tours and film festival entries. Eastwood appeared to return the favor to Warners via his Malpaso releases: for every "personal" film with little commercial potential that Eastwood directed, he would direct or star in a project more clearly aimed at a mass audience and high grosses. However, Eastwood denies that this is a "conscious process," asserting that he never tries to guess the potential audience for a film. He told *Cahiers du cinéma* in 1992, "If you're constantly thinking about what the audience's reaction is going to be, you stop thinking in terms of how the film should look"—and even in his "commercial" vehicles it is not difficult to locate his personal themes and stylistic markers.

In the year of *Dirty Harry*, Eastwood also took the firmest step towards total career control by becoming his own director for *Play Misty for Me*. Don Siegel signed his Director's Guild card. Judging from remarks he made at the time of *Misty*'s release, Eastwood did not realize how fundamentally the fact that he had become a director would affect his career. As late as 1976, he told McGilligan, "I don't intend to direct every picture I make. In fact, I'd like to lay off a bit, directing. It's a terribly mind-fatiguing job to be both actor and director." Eastwood did continue to alternate films he directed with films he only appeared in. But he would show an increasing reluctance to work with directors over whom he could not exercise some measure of control, such as his long-time Malpaso associates James Fargo and Buddy Van Horn. Indeed, he has shown an increasing reluctance to be directed by anyone else at all. In the decade after *Misty*, he appeared in seven films directed by others, but since then, only in five. *Trouble with the Curve*, released in 2012, is his first in nearly twenty years.

Malpaso remains a small and orderly operation, optimally suited to turning out the reasonably priced, efficiently produced features Eastwood favors. The company's small scale also makes it possible for the control of the entire operation to rest conveniently in one man's hands, and there has seldom been any doubt that that man is Eastwood. On two occasions, when a director proved incapable of realizing a film as Eastwood envisioned it, that director was made to feel the consequences, and both films, done Eastwood's way, would prove to be among his most successful of the respective decade.

In 1975, Eastwood dismissed the screenwriter-director Philip Kaufman and took over himself as director of *The Outlaw Josey Wales*. Eastwood told David Thomson, "I . . . didn't want it to be done the way he was going to interpret it. And he didn't want to do it the way I wanted to do it." The Directors Guild reacted by promulgating a rule (the "Eastwood rule") forbidding the replacement of a DGA member engaged for a film by anyone working in any capacity on the same film.

In 1983, that rule would prevent Eastwood from formally replacing Richard Tuggle as director of *Tightrope*. The screenwriter and first-time director reportedly came to the set uncertain of what he wanted and unprepared for the technical demands of shooting the film—both cardinal sins to the ever-focused and efficient Eastwood. Tuggle received the directorial credit, and Eastwood has never expressly disavowed it. But the full story was told in Richard Schickel's 1996 *Clint Eastwood*: "A compromise was worked out. The writer would stay on, contribute what he could in a collaborative way and receive directorial credit, while [Eastwood], literally, called most of the shots."

Though Eastwood insists on maintaining the ultimate control over his projects, many who have worked with him describe him as a benevolent chief who exercises this control in a cooperative spirit; Peter Biskind's profile in *Premiere* includes several such testimonies. Eastwood achieves the results he seeks by choosing collaborators he can trust to work freely within the parameters of his vision, and by keeping his ideas about a film supple enough to incorporate creative suggestions from all the participants. This applies both to actors, who have often praised the calm and the lack of pressure on his sets, and to his crew, many of whom have stayed with him for years or even decades. He dislikes the word "auteur," preferring to liken his role in the ensemble to that of "the leading force," or the "lieutenant to the platoon," and his films never begin with his own name, but with that of his production company: "A Malpaso Company Film," "A Malpaso Production."

For a long time, Eastwood's popularity as a film star overshadowed his directorial achievements, particularly in the popular press, where interviewers tended to concentrate on his on-screen persona. As for the serious critics, many dismissed him as the "politically incorrect" co-creator of the *Dirty Harry* series. Since the late seventies, with a half-dozen films as director to his credit, Eastwood has courted the approval of those who could boost his reputation as a filmmaker, expounding on his body of work in interviews with cinema journals and film trade publications. Several of these are included here: *Film Comment, Millimeter, American Film, Sight & Sound, Daily Variety*. In these sessions he frequently points out often-overlooked features of his films such as their consistent employment of strong female characters, or he notes how his macho image has been subject to scrutiny in many roles he has played, like *Tightrope*'s sexually troubled cop, or *Bronco Billy*'s hero, who endures an unavenged humiliation for the sake of loyalty to a member of his troupe. Such statements are reflected in the works of critics who were in the vanguard of the reevaluation of Eastwood's reputation, beginning in the early eighties.[1]

In 1980, Eastwood took *Bronco Billy* to the American Film Festival in Deauville, France, his first appearance at a European festival. Since then he has regularly included European publicity tours in the promotional strategy for his most prestigious films. European critics have often been quicker than their American counterparts to recognize artistic merit in filmmakers who probe genre boundaries and express a personal aesthetic in movies directed at a popular audience. In Eastwood's case, the effect was pronounced.

In 1985, Paris's Cinémathèque française honored him with a four-week retrospective, while the first homage paid him by a major American cultural institution was a one-day 1980 tribute at New York's Museum of Modern Art. Interviews with him abound in European film journals. France's *Cahiers du cinéma* has published eight over the years, and its archrival *Positif* has published fifteen. Three of Eastwood's films, *Pale Rider, Bird*, and *White Hunter, Black Heart*, had competed at the Cannes Film Festival by 1990 (*Mystic River* and *Changeling* would follow in the 2000s), and in 1992, his Oscar-winning *Unforgiven* was received perhaps even more enthusiastically in Europe than in the U.S—it was a cover story for at least nine European film journals. In this period, Eastwood's directorial efforts regularly met with more widespread critical approval abroad than at home. In December 1992, Camille Nevers of *Cahiers du cinéma* flatly called Eastwood "at present, the greatest American filmmaker," a judgment Serge Toubiana of *Cahiers* repeated in September 1995. In March 1998, in the Paris daily *Le Monde*, Jean-Michel Frodon called Eastwood's 1997 *Midnight in the Garden of Good and Evil*, which was widely disliked in the U.S., "his richest, most complex, and most courageous work."

Eastwood was appreciative. In his 1992 *Cahiers* interview, he said,

"Actually, the Europeans encouraged me much more from my first film as director, *Play Misty for Me*, than the Americans, who had a hard time convincing themselves I could be a director because they already had a hard time recognizing me as an actor."

When we were preparing the first edition of this book, we found that European interviewers tended to ask more penetrating questions about Eastwood's filmmaking style and practices than their American counterparts. American interviewers often focused on Eastwood's status as one of the most popular movie stars of his day rather than on his directorial achievements. Indeed, in 1999, many in the U.S. still perceived Eastwood as primarily an iconic actor who dabbled in directing, despite the more than twenty feature films he had directed. Even *Unforgiven*'s four Academy Awards had done little to change that perception. Accordingly, ten of the twenty-two interviews included in the original edition were from European sources such as *Sight & Sound*, *Positif*, *Cahiers*, *Le Monde*, and Cologne's maverick film journal *Steadycam*.

But in recent years things have begun to change, in part because it has become increasingly the exception rather than the rule for Eastwood to appear in the films he directs, but also because of his greatly enhanced reputation as a director in his native country. In the thirteen years since the first edition, Eastwood has directed eleven more films (another is still in the planning stages at this writing). These films have garnered a total of seven Academy Awards as well as dozens of other critics' and industry awards. Eastwood now has two Oscars as Best Director and two Best Picture Oscars to his personal credit, and he ranks among the most highly honored living filmmakers in the U.S. as well as in Europe. Therefore this edition could be more heavily weighted towards American sources, reflecting the increased recognition of Eastwood's directorial achievements in the U.S.

We have retained five of the original ten European pieces, among them a key interview in *Positif* in which Eastwood relates the philosophy of the John Huston–like character he plays in *White Hunter, Black Heart* to his own ideas about filmmaking. Of the twelve original American selections we have retained ten. There are eleven new interviews and profiles. Seven of these are from U.S. publications, making up about two-thirds of the new material by length. Four others are from European sources, including a 2008 Eastwood tribute in *Sight & Sound* that ran with the cover line "The greatest living American director?"

All but one of the pieces added in the new edition focus primarily on Eastwood's work since 1999. The volume thus spans the more than four decades of his career. As before, it concentrates on practical filmmaking issues and Eastwood's philosophy of filmmaking, though we have also sought out material that explores Eastwood's engagement with political and social issues.

The variety of subject matter in the films Eastwood has released since the first edition is striking. They do include two fairly conventional crime dramas starring himself, *True Crime* and *Blood Work*, but both allowed him to appear as a weaker and more flawed figure than his earlier "cop movie" vehicles. But we also find a comedy about a crew of superannuated astronauts (*Space Cowboys*); an ambitious psychodrama about the scars of violence in the lives of three working-class former childhood friends (*Mystic River*); a boxing drama with a tragic ending and a profoundly felt subtext of a father-daughter love story (*Million Dollar Baby*); and two World War II dramas (*Flags of Our Fathers* and *Letters from Iwo Jima*), the second of which came into being because of research Eastwood undertook for the first. They are respectively the true-life story of the "flag raisers" in the iconic photograph from one of the decisive battles of the war, and the story of the same battle from the Japanese point of view, which Eastwood had come to believe was also worth telling.

His last three films in the 2000s were a true-life period drama about a mother's fight to recover her abducted son (*Changeling*); a contemporary film about an aging, bigoted war veteran in a desolate Detroit suburb and the young Asian neighbors he reluctantly befriends (*Gran Torino*); and *Invictus*, which relates how Nelson Mandela helped reconcile the racial factions in post-apartheid South Africa by uniting blacks and whites in support of South Africa's World Cup team in the formerly abhorred "white" sport of rugby. He has now begun the 2010s with an international drama with supernatural elements, *Hereafter*, and a biopic about one of the most complicated figures in recent American public life, *J. Edgar*. His next directorial project is to be a musical version of the classic showbiz story *A Star Is Born*. "It's closer to Wellman's version than Cukor's," he told Michael Henry Wilson, who again interviewed him for *Positif* in 2011. But first, he is once again starring in a film directed by another (his longtime Malpaso associate Robert Lorenz in his directorial debut), the baseball-themed *Trouble with the Curve*. "Like *Million Dollar Baby*," as he told Wilson, "it's the story of a father and daughter, but not as depressing!"

A number of the new selections in this edition explore how Eastwood's thematic concerns have changed and deepened with the years—notably, his views on heroism and his take on the pervasive role of violence and gender discrimination in American life (see, for instance, Taubin 2005). We have also included several recent profiles that offer glimpses of Eastwood at work (see the two pieces by Scott Foundas), as well as interviews that include in-depth discussions of Eastwood's best work from the past decade—see Rose 2003 (*Mystic River*); Taubin 2005 (*Million Dollar Baby*); Gross 2007 (*Flags of Our Fathers* and *Letters from Iwo Jima*); Andrew 2008 (*Changeling*); and Wilson 2011 (*Hereafter*).

Yet another extraordinary facet of Eastwood's career has been his increasing involvement with the scores of his films. One lengthy study that could not be included here, Lillian Ross's *New Yorker* profile (March 24, 2003), emphasizes Eastwood's passion for music and discusses his work on the *Piano Blues* documentary, concluding with a look at Eastwood working out the score for *Mystic River*: "I was improvising one melody and fooling around with another. . . . Then Dina came into the room to listen to what I was playing, and she said she liked the first one. . . . I put it in the picture. . . . If I had to describe it, I'd say it's something bittersweet. It's like life, where you're constantly adjusting to everything. It's all improvisation." This is a trend that goes back to the eighties and the themes Eastwood wrote for *Tightrope* and *Pale Rider*, but it has become more pronounced; he now regularly contributes at least one or two themes and sometimes the whole score, often working with his son, the jazz musician Kyle Eastwood. It is one more way in which he puts his personal stamp on his projects. For a glimpse of Eastwood as a music aficionado and musician, see Tosches 2008.

As an interview subject, Eastwood has occasionally reminded his interviewers of his silent and indomitable film characters. David Thomson reported, "You don't have to be too imaginative to see the rock against which some of your questions break. It is startling and intimidating when an actor has so little need of your love, and not much softened if he still wants your respect." He evidently prefers to maintain close control of his interview sessions, and he sometimes seems to be answering another, more comfortable question, rather than the one the interviewer has asked. He may deflect questions he considers inappropriate, for instance on aspects of his private life, with curt replies—or his trademark stare. He can be equally recalcitrant about perceived shifts in his political views. Still, most interviewers have reported him relaxed and quite willing to talk about a variety of topics. Those who have concentrated on his work as a filmmaker and questioned him knowledgeably have usually been rewarded with knowledgeable and detailed replies concerning the technical means he employs to achieve the results he seeks and the philosophical and stylistic precepts that guide his practical course.

Through the interviews collected here, it is possible to outline some of the elements of Eastwood's filmmaking philosophy, what Pascal Mérigeau (in a profile omitted in this edition) called the "Eastwood touch":

On the director's role: "You have to have the picture there in your mind before you make it. And if you don't, you're not a director, you're a guesser." (Gentry 1980)

On the importance of the story: "I try to concentrate above all on the story, because it's there that it's all tied up.... Then I try to see how the image can best agree with the story, what form I want the story to appear in, with what emotions, what sonorities." (Jousse and Nevers 1992)

On spontaneity: "Sometimes the imperfection of things is what makes them real.... So I tell everybody to just rehearse quietly, and I'll have the camera running. You get some marvelous little pieces because everybody's just doing it, they're not just sitting there thinking about acting in front of the camera. They're doing it for real." (Hentoff 1989)

On the role of the audience: "They must participate in every shot, in everything. I give them what I think is necessary to know, to progress through the story, but I don't lay out so much that it insults their intelligence. I try to give a certain amount to their imagination." (Thompson and Hunter 1978)

On ambiguity: "There's a tendency in moviemaking to treat the audience as if they won't stay with you unless you explain every little thing along the way.... I like it, personally, in movies when there's something left to think about. I'm attracted to that sort of thing.... Without using ambiguity to the point where it's boring, if sometimes something is left unsaid, it's much more picturesque in the person's mind than something that's drawn out for you which could be disappointing 'cause you wish it were something else." (Taubin 2005)

On lighting: "The use of light and darkness in film, for me, is very important.... I try to design the light and the color to go with the drama." (Taubin 2005)

On how easy it all is: "I believe that when you're making a film, you've got everything in mind, in an almost subliminal way, and that all you have to do is make all that become reality on screen." (Mérigeau 1998, not included in the present edition)

Eastwood has been in the public eye for more than fifty years, and the volume of material available on him is overwhelming. It was difficult to select from among the dozens of interviews we considered worthy for inclusion here originally, and even more difficult to settle on a representative selection from the last decade for the new edition. If we have emphasized interviews from film periodicals and the film trade press, that is where we found the most extensive and interesting material on Eastwood *as a director*. We regret there was no room for several early profiles in the popular press in which he made sure interviewers realized how deeply he was involved in the production of his films, even when he did not direct them. For Judy Fayard's *Life* cover story (July 23, 1971), he granted the interview on a night he was actually directing himself in a scene in Siegel's *Dirty Harry*. Fayard watched him "climbing on and off a crane, fistfighting in a stunt scene six stories above the ground, and crawling on a window ledge on his hands and knees" for several hours. She reports that the sound man observed, "He'll make a hell of a good director."

For Chris Hodenfield's July 1979 *Look* profile, Eastwood saw to it that part of the interview was conducted in the sound laboratory where he was supervising the final mix for Siegel's *Escape from Alcatraz* (Siegel was working on another film). Hodenfield was duly impressed: "On the screen flickered the same ten-minute reel of film, over and over, until every gurgle and clank sounded just right.... Clint Eastwood has by now directed six pictures. And he meddles freely.... Eastwood even follows the final cut of a film right into the processing laboratory, so he can sit with the man who times the development. Eastwood likes the print a little dark, so he makes sure."

Eastwood summed up his commitment to filmmaking in an article for *Action*, the magazine of the Directors Guild (March/April 1973), which concluded, "I love acting and intend to continue doing it. But I must admit that the satisfaction of directing goes deeper than any other facet of film making.... But I suppose my involvement goes even deeper than acting or directing. I love every aspect of the creation of a motion picture, and I guess I'm committed to it for life."

As we write, Eastwood has completed around forty films as producer, director, or star—most often all three—since that declaration was published. Like the character he played in *The Bridges of Madison County* (1995), he might well reply, when asked whether he loves his work, "Yeah—I'm obsessed by it, really."

There is inevitably some repetition in this anthology. Eastwood's views on directing have changed little over the years, and so he often repeats the same thoughts and anecdotes about specific films and specific aspects of filmmaking. As with other books in the Conversations with Filmmakers series, the interviews are presented in chronological order and unabridged, with the exception of Rose 2003, where we omitted several minutes from the end of the program for reasons of space. In a few cases, the interviewer's introduction has been omitted. Some obvious errors of fact have been corrected.

The editors would like to express their gratitude to all those who granted us their permission to make this material available. In addition, we would like to thank the colleagues and friends who assisted us on the first edition, notably Amy Stoller, for her unflagging professionalism and versatility, Stephan Müller, for his aid in researching Eastwood's European reception, and Seetha Srinivasan, Elizabeth Young, and Anne Stascavage of the University Press of Mississippi. For the present edition, we would like to add thanks to Leila Salisbury, Valerie Jones, and Walter Biggins of the Press for their guidance and support, and a particular word of thanks to the series editor, Gerald Peary, for his many helpful suggestions. We are grateful to Queens College for providing much-needed financial support. Finally, we dedicate this volume to Peter Brunette, recently deceased, who as general editor of the Conversations with Filmmakers series originally offered us this project in 1998, and to Mary Lea Bandy, formerly of the Museum of Modern Art, for her kind help on the first edition.

Translator's note: All interviews were originally conducted in English or through interpreters. In preparing translations of those first published in French, I have tried to stay close to the published texts, while maintaining a colloquial tone consistent with Clint Eastwood's voice as we know it. Inevitably some distortion has occurred, however, and we apologize for it. Michael Henry Wilson (who also writes in French as Michael Henry) generously allowed us to use the English versions of two of his interviews that were included in his book *Eastwood on Eastwood*.

REK
KC
July 2012

Notes

1. For discussion, see Robert Kapsis, "Clint Eastwood's Politics of Reputation," *Society* 30, no. 30/6 (September/October 1993): 70.

Interviews Not Retained from the First Edition:

McGilligan, Patrick. "Clint Eastwood." *Focus on Film*, no. 25 (Summer-Fall 1976): 12-20.

Pavlović, Milan. "Clint Eastwood interviewed by Milan Pavlović." Translation of an extended version of "'Kein Popcorn-Film.'" *Steadycam*, no. 10 (Fall 1988): 18-20.

Abbott, Denise. "Clint Eastwood: Dirty Harry Is No Rookie When It Comes To Directing." *American Cinemeditor* 41, no. 1 (winter 1991): 14-15.

Béhar, Henri. "Portrait of the Gunslinger as a Wise Old Man: Encounter with Clint Eastwood." Translation of "Portrait du flingueur en vieux sage: rencontre avec Clint Eastwood." *Le Monde*, September 3, 1992.

Verniere, James. "Clint Eastwood Stepping Out." *Sight & Sound* 3, no. 9 (September 1993): 6-9.

Blair, Iain. "Clint Eastwood: The Actor-Director Reflects on His Continuing Career and New Film, *Absolute Power*." *Film & Video* 14, no. 3 (March 1997): 70-78.

Mérigeau, Pascal. "Eastwood in His Carmel." Translation of "Eastwood en son Carmel." *Le Nouvel observateur*, March 5, 1998, 50-52.

Chronology

Dates following film titles are U.S. release dates unless otherwise noted. Unless another director is noted, the director is Eastwood; if other actors are not named, the film stars or co-stars Eastwood.

1930	Clinton Eastwood Jr. is born on May 31 in San Francisco.
1930–40	The Eastwood family moves around California as Clinton Sr. takes what jobs he can find during the Depression.
1940–48	The Eastwoods settle in Piedmont, California; Eastwood attends school in Piedmont and Oakland.
1946	Hears Charlie Parker for the first time in Oakland. Begins playing jazz piano informally at the Omar Club in Oakland.
1948	Graduates from Oakland Technical High School; moves with his family to Seattle.
1948–51	Works at several jobs in the Pacific Northwest: lifeguard, lumberjack, paper mill worker, steelworker, etc.
1951	Applies to Seattle University, intending to major in music, but is drafted; stationed at Fort Ord on the Monterey Peninsula. Nearly lost at sea when the two-man plane he is in goes down; swims three miles to shore.
1951–53	Army service at Fort Ord.
1953	Discharged; meets and marries Maggie Johnson; enrolls at Los Angeles City College. Attends drama classes; his teachers include the Michael Chekhov disciple George Shdanoff.
1954–55	Accepted into Universal-International Studios' talent program. Assigned minor roles in seven Universal films before leaving the program in late 1955.
1956–58	Small parts in three more films and the second lead in a minor Western, *Ambush at Cimarron Pass* (Jodie Copelan, 1958); occasional television work; digs swimming pools to supplement his income.

1959–66	Appears as second lead in most of the 217 episodes of the Western series *Rawhide*. The Eastwoods settle in Carmel-by-the-Sea, near Fort Ord.
1964	Stars for Sergio Leone in a Western filmed in Spain and Italy. Released in Italy as *Per un pugno di dollari* (*A Fistful of Dollars*), it unexpectedly becomes a hit across Europe. Birth of daughter Kimber (with Roxanne Tunis).
1965–66	Stars in two more films for Leone: *For a Few Dollars More* and *The Good, the Bad and the Ugly*, also hits in Europe.
1966	Directed by Vittorio de Sica in a segment of *The Witches* (Italy, 1967). United Artists acquires U.S. rights to the Leone films.
1967–68	The three Leone films open in the U.S.; all are huge hits.
1967	Establishes his own production company, Malpaso, to share in the production of his first U.S. starring vehicle, the Western *Hang 'Em High* (Ted Post, 1968), shot for UA in New Mexico. Signs three-picture deal with Universal, later extended (films made through 1975 are Malpaso productions for Universal unless otherwise noted). First collaboration with Don Siegel, the cop drama *Coogan's Bluff* (1968), shot in New York City and the Mojave Desert.
1968	In Austria and London for MGM's World War II thriller *Where Eagles Dare* (Brian G. Hutton, 1969). Birth of son Kyle. In Oregon for Paramount's Western-themed musical *Paint Your Wagon* (Joshua Logan, 1969). *Hang 'Em High* and *Coogan's Bluff* released; both are hits.
1969–70	Shoots two more films with Don Siegel: the Western *Two Mules for Sister Sara* (1970) and the Civil War drama *The Beguiled* (1971), respectively in Mexico and near Baton Rouge, Louisiana.
1969	Shoots MGM's World War II adventure *Kelly's Heroes* (Brian G. Hutton, 1970) in Yugoslavia; the last film he will work on in which Malpaso is not involved, except for 1993's *In the Line of Fire*.
1970	Death of Eastwood's father. Shoots his first film as director in Carmel and vicinity, *Play Misty for Me* (1971) about a disc jockey (Eastwood) stalked by a crazed female fan.
1971	Shoots the controversial cop picture *Dirty Harry* in San Francisco for Don Siegel and Warner Bros., beginning what will become a near-exclusive relationship with Warners. *Play*

	Misty for Me opens; a modest success. Shoots the Western *Joe Kidd* (John Sturges, 1972) in New Mexico. *Dirty Harry* is released; despite some sharply negative critical reaction owing to its perceived political message, it is Eastwood's biggest audience success to date.
1972	Birth of daughter Alison. Shoots his first Western as director, *High Plains Drifter* (1973), at Mono Lake, California. Named to the National Council for the Arts. Directs William Holden in the romance *Breezy* (1973).
1973	Named Quigley Publications' Number One Box-Office Star for 1972; the first of five times he heads the list (1973–74, 1984–85, 1994). Stars in the first "Harry" sequel *Magnum Force* (Ted Post, 1973). Stars in Michael Cimino's debut feature, the caper/buddy drama *Thunderbolt and Lightfoot* (1974; UA).
1974	Directs himself and does his own mountain climbing stuntwork in the espionage yarn *The Eiger Sanction* (1975), shot in Monument Valley and the Swiss Alps.
1975	Moves Malpaso from Universal to Warner Bros. (Subsequent films are Warners releases unless otherwise noted.) Shoots the epic Western *The Outlaw Josey Wales* in Arizona, Utah, and California; replaces director Philip Kaufman after a week, taking over as director himself. The Directors Guild reacts with the "Eastwood rule," forbidding the replacement of a DGA member engaged for a film by anyone working on the same film.
1976	*The Outlaw Josey Wales* released; mixed reviews including some of his best to date. *The Enforcer* (James Fargo), another "Dirty Harry" sequel, partners Harry with a woman (Tyne Daly).
1977	Directs himself and Sondra Locke in the cop movie/romantic comedy *The Gauntlet*; shot in Nevada and Arizona.
1978	Shoots his most popular film to that date, the orangutan buddy picture *Every Which Way but Loose* (James Fargo), in the San Fernando Valley and elsewhere in the West. Last collaboration with Siegel, *Escape from Alcatraz* (1979), shot for Paramount on the prison island in San Francisco Bay.
1979	Separates from Maggie. Shoots *Bronco Billy* (1980), a Capraesque comedy, in the Boise, Idaho area.
1980	At the Deauville (France) American Film Festival with Bron-

	co Billy. Retrospective at New York's Museum of Modern Art (MoMA).
1981	Shoots the cold war thriller *Firefox* (1982) partly in Vienna.
1982	Shoots the Depression-era saga *Honkytonk Man*, his most "personal" project from this period, in central California; on release it "fails to find an audience" but attracts favorable critical attention, particularly in Europe.
1983	Shoots *Sudden Impact*, his only "Dirty Harry" film as director; highest-grossing of the series. Shoots the troubled cop/serial killer story *Tightrope* in New Orleans; composes a theme for the soundtrack, a practice he will continue in several subsequent films. Takes over the direction from Richard Tuggle, who however receives directorial credit because Eastwood is forbidden by the DGA's "Eastwood rule" from replacing him. Options David Webb Peoples's 1976 Western screenplay, *The Cut-Whore Killings*.
1984	Divorce from Maggie becomes final. Shoots his third Western as director, *Pale Rider*, in Idaho. *Tightrope* opens the Montreal Film Festival; favorably reviewed on its U.S. release.
1985	Retrospectives at the Paris Cinémathèque française, Germany's Filmmuseum and Britain's National Film Theatre. Made a Chevalier de l'ordre des arts et des lettres in France; delivers Guardian Lecture in London. First appearance at Cannes Film Festival with *Pale Rider*. Malpaso produces Sondra Locke's debut film as director, *Ratboy* (1986). Directs episode of Steven Spielberg's television series *Amazing Stories* ("Vanessa in the Garden").
1986–88	Elected Mayor of Carmel; serves a single two-year term. Birth of son Scott and daughter Kathryn (with Jacelyn Reeves).
1986	Directs himself in *Heartbreak Ridge* as an aging Marine sergeant facing separation from the Corps.
1987	Following extensive research to acquire original musical materials, shoots the Charlie Parker biopic *Bird*.
1988	Cecil B. DeMille Lifetime Achievement Award at the Golden Globes. Executive producer for *Thelonious Monk: Straight No Chaser* (Charlotte Zwerin), a documentary on the jazz pianist. Shoots the last "Dirty Harry" film, *The Dead Pool* (Buddy Van Horn). At Cannes with *Bird*: Forest Whitaker named Best Actor for his portrayal of the title role; the film wins a Technical Grand Prize. Private U.S. premiere of *Bird*

	at MoMA, marking the establishment of the Clint Eastwood Cinema Collection there. *Bird* shown at the New York Film Festival; receives generally good reviews, but will play to small audiences.
1988–90	Shoots two "commercial" films, the comedy-adventure *Pink Cadillac* (Buddy Van Horn, 1989) and the cop drama *The Rookie* (1990); both fare poorly at the box office.
1989	*Bird* wins Eastwood a Golden Globe as Best Director. Shoots *White Hunter, Black Heart*, in which he plays a John Huston–like film director, in London and Africa.
1990	At Cannes with *White Hunter, Black Heart*, which will open in the U.S. to mixed reviews and scanty audiences.
1991	Directs and stars in *The Cut-Whore Killings*, now retitled *Unforgiven*, shot mostly in remote areas of Alberta, Canada.
1992	*Unforgiven* released to Eastwood's best reviews to date and excellent box office; rejected for the Venice Film Festival, it is shown in Deauville. Stars in the thriller *In the Line of Fire* (Wolfgang Petersen, 1993) for Castle Rock and Columbia. *Unforgiven* wins numerous year-end critics' awards.
1993	*Unforgiven* wins the Best Director Golden Globe and Directors Guild of America award for Outstanding Directorial Achievement in Motion Pictures. Nominated for nine Oscars, it wins four, including Directing and Best Picture. Directs and plays a supporting role in the prison escape/road movie *A Perfect World*, shot in rural Texas, starring Kevin Costner. Birth of daughter Francesca Ruth (with actress Frances Fisher). Tribute to Eastwood at MoMA; retrospective of his films. *In the Line of Fire* a hit. *A Perfect World* reviewed well but performs poorly in the U.S.; does very well abroad.
1994	Produces *The Stars Fell on Henrietta* (James Keach, 1995), filmed in Texas, starring Frances Fisher. President of the jury at the Cannes Film Festival. Made a Commandeur de l'ordre des arts et des lettres. Directs himself and Meryl Streep in the mid-life romance *The Bridges of Madison County*, based on Robert James Waller's bestseller, in Iowa.
1995	Receives the Irving G. Thalberg Memorial Award at the Oscar ceremony for his body of work as a producer. *Bridges* opens in the U.S. to generally favorable reviews and respectable box office; later shown at Deauville.
1996	American Film Institute Lifetime Achievement Award. Mar-

ries Dina Ruiz, a television journalist. Film Society of Lincoln Center tribute. Shoots the political thriller *Absolute Power* for Castle Rock and Columbia, starring himself as a gentleman thief who witnesses a murder. "Eastwood After Hours" concert at Carnegie Hall; a tribute to his love of jazz and its use in his films. Birth of daughter Morgan.

1997 *Absolute Power* released to generally poor reviews; the closing-night feature (out of competition) at Cannes. Shoots *Midnight in the Garden of Good and Evil*, based on John Berendt's bestseller and starring Kevin Spacey and John Cusack, in Savannah, Georgia; released to mixed reviews. Both films fare poorly at the box office.

1998 Receives honorary César Award from the French Academy of Cinema Arts and Techniques. Awarded Lifetime Achievement Award in Motion Pictures at the Producers Guild of America's Golden Laurel Awards. Directs himself as a disreputable reporter in the death-row thriller *True Crime*.

1999 *True Crime* released to generally poor reviews and box office. Directs himself, Tommy Lee Jones, Donald Sutherland, and James Garner in the comedy-adventure *Space Cowboys*, about a crew of aged astronauts on a mission to save Earth.

2000 *Space Cowboys* released to generally favorable reviews and good box office; opens the Venice Film Festival, where Eastwood is awarded a career Golden Lion; also shown at Deauville. Named a Kennedy Center Honoree.

2001 Directs himself as a heart transplant patient hunting a killer in *Blood Work*, based on a Michael Connelly thriller.

2002 *Blood Work* released; a critical and box-office failure. Receives Screen Actors Guild Life Achievement Award. Directs Sean Penn and Tim Robbins in *Mystic River*, based on Dennis Lehane's South Boston psychological thriller; also composes the score.

2003 *Mystic River* shown at Cannes; Eastwood receives the Golden Coach Award as director. Directs "Piano Blues" for Public Television's documentary mini-series *The Blues*. *Mystic River* opens the New York Film Festival; released to excellent reviews and good box office; wins numerous critics' awards.

2004 Penn and Robbins take the top acting awards at both the Golden Globes and Academy Awards. *Mystic River* wins César for Best Foreign Film. Directs himself, Hilary Swank, and

	Morgan Freeman in the boxing drama *Million Dollar Baby*, which he calls a father-daughter love story; also composes the score. On release, the film is controversial for its mercy killing theme, but is well received by critics and audiences.
2005–10	Executive producer for four Bruce Ricker documentaries, on director Budd Boetticher and the musicians Tony Bennett, Johnny Mercer, and Dave Brubeck. Executive producer and narrator for a documentary on Warner Bros.
2005	*Million Dollar Baby* wins two Golden Globes (Best Director; Best Actress, Drama for Swank) and four Oscars (Director and Best Picture; Actress for Swank, Supporting Actor for Freeman). Also wins the DGA Outstanding Directorial Achievement award and awards for Best Foreign Film from the French and Italian film academies (César and David di Donatello), followed in 2006 by the Japan Academy Prize for Best Foreign Film. Shoots the World War II epic *Flags of Our Fathers*, about the men in the famous Iwo Jima photograph, on Iwo Jima and in Iceland and the U.S. (Paramount); also composes the score.
2006	Eastwood's mother dies at ninety-seven. Receives the Directors Guild of America Lifetime Achievement Award. Shoots companion piece to *Flags* to show the battle from the Japanese point of view; *Letters from Iwo Jima* is filmed in Japanese, on Iwo Jima and in Iceland and California (Paramount). The two Iwo Jima films are released weeks apart; neither draws large audiences, though *Letters* is critically praised and wins several year-end awards.
2007	*Flags* wins Japan Academy Prize for Best Foreign Film. *Letters* wins Best Foreign Language Film at the Golden Globes; nominated for four Academy Awards, it wins only for Sound Editing. Made Chevalier de la Légion d'Honneur by the President of France. Composes a new score for *Grace Is Gone* (James C. Strouse) after the film's Sundance screening. Directs Angelina Jolie in *Changeling* (Universal), based on a true story about child abduction and police corruption in 1920s Los Angeles; also composes the score.
2008	*Letters* wins Japan Academy Prize for Best Foreign Film. Directs himself in *Gran Torino*, about a bigoted Detroit area retired auto worker who learns to appreciate his Hmong neighbors. *Changeling* premieres at Cannes (Eastwood wins a

	"Special Prize Ex-aequo") and is later shown at Deauville and the New York Film Festival. Reviews are mixed and audiences disappointing. *Gran Torino*, released at year's end, is well reviewed and becomes Eastwood's highest-grossing film.
2009	*Gran Torino* wins Best Foreign Film awards from the French (César), Italian (David di Donatello), and Japanese academies. Receives an honorary Palme d'Or for lifetime achievement from the Cannes Film Festival. Made Commandeur de la Légion d'Honneur. Directs Morgan Freeman and Matt Damon in *Invictus*, about Nelson Mandela's championing of the "white" sport rugby to defuse racial tensions in post-apartheid South Africa. The film opens to generally good reviews but poor box office.
2009–10	Directs Matt Damon in *Hereafter*, a three-part story involving a psychic, a near-death experience, and a young boy's bereavement, shot in Paris, London, San Francisco, and Hawaii; also composes the score.
2010	Complete retrospective of his directorial work by the Film Society of New York. *Hereafter* premieres at the Toronto International Film Festival and the New York Film Festival. Reviews are sharply mixed; box office is poor.
2011	*Hereafter* wins a David di Donatello Award as Best Foreign Film. Directs and scores the biopic *J. Edgar*, starring Leonardo DiCaprio as FBI director Hoover. Plans are announced for a musical remake of *A Star Is Born*, to star Beyoncé Knowles. When this project is postponed, announces plans to star in a baseball-themed movie, *Trouble with the Curve*, to be directed by his Malpaso associate Robert Lorenz, marking the first time in two decades he has worked for another director. *J. Edgar* released to mixed reviews and poor box office; it will fare better with critics in Europe. Comprehensive retrospective at the Cinémathèque française.
2012	Narrates a Super Bowl commercial for Chrysler Corporation, "Halftime in America," whose message about "job growth and the spirit of America" proves politically controversial. Eastwood reports that he and his wife Dina helped compose the copy and that his fee was donated to charity. Shoots *Trouble with the Curve* for Lorenz for a fall release. Continues pre-production work on *A Star Is Born*, now planned for a 2013 release.

Filmography

As Director

THE BEGUILED: THE STORYTELLER (1971)
A twelve-minute short on Don Siegel that is sometimes listed as Eastwood's directorial debut.

PLAY MISTY FOR ME (1971)
Malpaso / Universal
Producer: Robert Daley
Director: **Clint Eastwood**
Screenplay: Jo Heims, Dean Riesner
Director of Photography: Bruce Surtees
Editor: Carl Pingitore
Art Director: Alexander Golitzen
Music: Dee Barton
Cast: **Eastwood** (Dave), Jessica Walter (Evelyn), Donna Mills (Tobie), John Larch (Sergeant McCallum)
Technicolor, 102 minutes

HIGH PLAINS DRIFTER (1973)
Malpaso / Universal
Executive Producer: Jennings Lang
Producer: Robert Daley
Director: **Clint Eastwood**
Screenplay: Ernest Tidyman
Director of Photography: Bruce Surtees
Editor: Ferris Webster
Art Director: Henry Bumstead
Music: Dee Barton
Cast: **Eastwood** (The Stranger), Verna Bloom (Sarah Belding), Mariana

Hill (Callie Travers), Mitchell Ryan (Dave Drake), Jack Ging (Morgan Allen)
Technicolor, Panavision, 109 minutes

BREEZY (1973)
Malpaso / Universal
Executive Producer: Jennings Lang
Producer: Robert Daley
Director: **Clint Eastwood**
Screenplay: Jo Heims
Director of Photography: Frank Stanley
Editor: Ferris Webster
Art Director: Alexander Golitzen
Music: Michel Legrand
Cast: William Holden (Frank Harmon), Kay Lenz (Breezy), Roger C. Carmel (Bob Henderson), Marj Dusay (Betty), Joan Hotchkis (Paula)
Technicolor, 109 minutes

THE EIGER SANCTION (1975)
Malpaso / Universal
Executive Producers: Richard D. Zanuck, David Brown
Producer: Robert Daley
Director: **Clint Eastwood**
Screenplay: Hal Dresner, Warren B. Murphy, Rod Whitaker; based on the novel by Trevanian
Director of Photography: Frank Stanley
Editor: Ferris Webster
Art Directors: George Webb, Aurelio Crugnola
Music: John Williams
Cast: **Eastwood** (Jonathan Hemlock), George Kennedy (Ben Bowman), Vonetta McGee (Jemima Brown), Jack Cassidy (Miles Mellough), Heidi Bruhl (Mrs. Montaigne)
Technicolor, Panavision, 129 minutes

THE OUTLAW JOSEY WALES (1976)
Malpaso / Warner Bros.
Producer: Robert Daley
Director: **Clint Eastwood**
Screenplay: Phil Kaufman, Sonia Chernus; based on the novel *Gone to Texas* by Forrest Carter

Director of Photography: Bruce Surtees
Editor: Ferris Webster
Production Designer: Tambi Larsen
Music: Jerry Fielding
Cast: **Eastwood** (Josey Wales), Chief Dan George (Lone Watie), Sondra Locke (Laura Lee), Bill McKinney (Terrill), John Vernon (Fletcher)
DeLuxe, Panavision, 135 minutes
Academy Award Nomination: Music (Original Score), Fielding

THE GAUNTLET (1977)
Malpaso / Warner Bros.
Producer: Robert Daley
Director: **Clint Eastwood**
Screenplay: Michael P. Butler, Dennis Shryack
Director of Photography: Rexford Metz
Editors: Ferris Webster, Joel Cox
Art Director: Allen E. Smith
Music: Jerry Fielding
Cast: **Eastwood** (Ben Shockley), Sondra Locke (Gus Mally), Pat Hingle (Josephson), William Prince (Blakelock), Bill McKinney (Constable)
DeLuxe, Panavision, 109 minutes

BRONCO BILLY (1980)
Warner Bros., [Malpaso[1]], Second Street Films / Warner Bros.
Executive Producer: Robert Daley
Producers: Dennis E. Hackin, Neil Dobrofsky
Director: **Clint Eastwood**
Screenplay: Dennis E. Hackin
Director of Photography: David Worth
Editors: Ferris Webster, Joel Cox
Art Director: Gene Lourie
Music Supervision: Snuff Garrett
Cast: **Eastwood** (Bronco Billy), Sondra Locke (Antoinette Lily), Geoffrey Lewis (John Arlington), Scatman Crothers (Doc Lynch), Bill McKinney (Lefty LeBow)
DeLuxe, 117 minutes

FIREFOX (1982)
Warner Bros., [Malpaso[1]] / Warner Bros.
Executive Producer: Fritz Manes

Producer: **Clint Eastwood**
Director: **Eastwood**
Screenplay: Alex Lasker, Wendell Wellman; based on the novel by Craig Thomas
Director of Photography: Bruce Surtees
Editors: Ferris Webster, Ron Spang
Art Director: John Graysmark, Elayne Ceder
Music: Maurice Jarre
Cast: **Eastwood** (Mitchell Gant), Freddie Jones (Kenneth Aubrey), David Huffman (Buckholz), Warren Clarke (Pavel Upenskoy), Ronald Lacey (Semelovsky)
DeLuxe, Panavision, 136 minutes

HONKYTONK MAN (1982)
Warner Bros., [Malpaso[1]] / Warner Bros.
Executive Producer: Fritz Manes
Producer: **Clint Eastwood**
Director: **Eastwood**
Screenplay: Clancy Carlile, based on his novel
Director of Photography: Bruce Surtees
Editors: Ferris Webster, Michael Kelly, Joel Cox
Production Designer: Edward Carfagno
Music Supervision: Snuff Garrett
Cast: **Eastwood** (Red Stovall), Kyle Eastwood (Whit), John McIntire (Grandpa), Alexa Kenin (Marlene), Verna Bloom (Emmy)
Technicolor, 122 minutes

SUDDEN IMPACT (1983)
Warner Bros., [Malpaso[1]] / Warner Bros.
Executive Producer: Fritz Manes
Producer: **Clint Eastwood**
Director: **Eastwood**
Screenplay: Joseph C. Stinson
Story: Earl E. Smith, Charles B. Pierce
Director of Photography: Bruce Surtees
Editor: Joel Cox
Production Designer: Edward C. Carfagno
Music: Lalo Schifrin
Cast: **Eastwood** (Harry Callahan), Sondra Locke (Jennifer Spencer),

Pat Hingle (Chief Jannings), Bradford Dillman (Captain Briggs), Paul Drake (Mick)
Technicolor, Panavision, 117 minutes

TIGHTROPE (1984)
Malpaso / Warner Bros.
Producers: **Clint Eastwood**, Fritz Manes
Director: Richard Tuggle*
Screenplay: Richard Tuggle
Director of Photography: Bruce Surtees
Production Designer: Edward Carfagno
Music: Lennie Niehaus
Eastwood composed "Amanda's Theme"
Cast: **Eastwood** (Wes Block), Genevieve Bujold (Beryl Thibodeaux), Dan Hedaya (Detective Molinari), Alison Eastwood (Amanda Block), Jennifer Beck (Penny Block), Marco St. John (Leander Rolfe)
Technicolor, 114 minutes
*Credited to Tuggle, directed by **Eastwood**. See Introduction

PALE RIDER (1985)
Malpaso / Warner Bros.
Executive Producer: Fritz Manes
Producer: **Clint Eastwood**
Director: **Eastwood**
Screenplay: Michael Butler, Dennis Shryack
Director of Photography: Bruce Surtees
Editor: Joel Cox
Production Designer: Edward Carfagno
Music: Lennie Niehaus
Eastwood composed "Megan's Theme"
Cast: **Eastwood** (Preacher), Michael Moriarty (Hull Barret), Carrie Snodgress (Sarah Wheeler), Christopher Penn (Josh LaHood), Richard Dysart (Coy LaHood), Sydney Penny (Megan Wheeler)
Technicolor, Panavision, 116 minutes

VANESSA IN THE GARDEN (Television series AMAZING STORIES) (1985)
Amblin Entertainment / NBC

Executive Producer: Steven Spielberg
Producer: David E. Vogel
Director: **Clint Eastwood**
Screenplay: Steven Spielberg
Director of Photography: Robert Stevens
Editor: Jo Ann Fogle
Production Designer: Rick Carter
Music: Lennie Niehaus (after themes by John Williams and Richard Wagner)
Cast: Harvey Keitel (Byron Sullivan), Sondra Locke (Vanessa), Beau Bridges (Ted)
Color, 25 minutes

HEARTBREAK RIDGE (1986)
Jay Weston Productions, Malpaso / Warner Bros.
Executive Producer: Fritz Manes
Producer: **Clint Eastwood**
Director: **Eastwood**
Screenplay: James Carabatsos; and Joseph C. Stinson, uncredited
Director of Photography: Jack N. Green
Editor: Joel Cox
Production Design: Edward Carfagno
Music: Lennie Niehaus
Eastwood composed "How Much I Care"
Cast: **Eastwood** (Highway), Marsha Mason (Aggie), Everett McGill (Major Powers), Moses Gunn (Sgt. Webster), Eileen Heckart (Little Mary), Mario Van Peebles (Stitch)
Technicolor, 130 minutes
Academy Award Nomination: Sound, Dick Alexander, Les Fresholtz, William Nelson, Vern Poore

BIRD (1988)
Malpaso / Warner Bros.
Executive Producer: David Valdes
Producer: **Clint Eastwood**
Director: **Eastwood**
Screenplay: Joel Oliansky
Director of Photography: Jack N. Green
Editor: Joel Cox

Production Designer: Edward C. Carfagno
Music: Lennie Niehaus; with original music by Charlie Parker
Cast: Forest Whitaker (Charlie "Bird" Parker), Diane Venora (Chan Parker), Michael Zelniker (Red Rodney), Samuel E. Wright (Dizzy), Keith David (Buster Franklin), Anna Levine* (Audrey) *Billed as "Anna Thomson" in *Unforgiven*
Technicolor, 160 minutes
Academy Award: Sound, Dick Alexander, Willie D. Burton, Les Fresholtz, Vern Poore

WHITE HUNTER, BLACK HEART (1990)
Malpaso, Rastar / Warner Bros.
Executive Producer: David Valdes
Producer: **Clint Eastwood**
Director: **Eastwood**
Screenplay: Peter Viertel, James Bridges, Burt Kennedy; based on the novel by Viertel
Director of Photography: Jack N. Green
Editor: Joel Cox
Production Designer: John Graysmark
Music: Lennie Niehaus
Cast: **Eastwood** (John Wilson), Jeff Fahey (Pete Verrill), George Dzundza (Paul Landers), Alun Armstrong (Ralph Lockhart), Marisa Berenson (Kay Gibson), Boy Mathias Chuma (Kivu)
Technicolor, 112 minutes

THE ROOKIE (1990)
Malpaso / Warner Bros.
Producer: Howard Kazanjian, Steven Siebert, David Valdes
Director: **Clint Eastwood**
Screenplay: Boaz Yakin, Scott Spiegel
Director of Photography: Jack N. Green
Editor: Joel Cox
Production Designer: Judy Cammer
Music: Lennie Niehaus
Cast: **Eastwood** (Nick Pulovski), Charlie Sheen (David Ackerman), Raul Julia (Strom), Sonia Braga (Liesl), Tom Skerritt (Eugene Ackerman)
Technicolor, Panavision, 121 minutes

UNFORGIVEN (1992)
Malpaso / Warner Bros.
Executive Producer: David Valdes
Producer: **Clint Eastwood**
Director: **Eastwood**
Screenplay: David Webb Peoples
Director of Photography: Jack N. Green
Editor: Joel Cox
Production Designer: Henry Bumstead
Music: Lennie Niehaus
Eastwood composed "Claudia's Theme"
Cast: **Eastwood** (William Munny), Gene Hackman (Little Bill Daggett), Morgan Freeman (Ned Logan), Richard Harris (English Bob), Jaimz Woolvett (The "Schofield Kid"), Saul Rubinek (W. W. Beauchamp), Frances Fisher (Strawberry Alice), Anna Thomson* (Delilah Fitzgerald) *Billed as "Anna Levine" in *Bird*
Technicolor, Panavision, 131 minutes
Academy Awards: Best Picture, **Eastwood**; Directing, **Eastwood**; Actor in a Supporting Role, Hackman; Film Editing, Cox. Academy Award Nominations: Actor in a Leading Role, **Eastwood**; Art Direction–Set Decoration, Bumstead, Janice Blackie-Goodine; Cinematography, Green; Sound, Dick Alexander, Les Fresholtz, Vern Poore, Rob Young; Writing (Screenplay Written Directly for the Screen), Peoples

A PERFECT WORLD (1993)
Malpaso / Warner Bros.
Producers: Mark Johnson, David Valdes
Director: **Clint Eastwood**
Screenplay: John Lee Hancock
Director of Photography: Jack N. Green
Editors: Joel Cox, Ron Spang
Production Designer: Henry Bumstead
Music: Lennie Niehaus
Eastwood composed theme "Big Fran's Baby"
Cast: Kevin Costner (Butch Haynes), **Eastwood** (Red Garnett), Laura Dern (Sally Gerber), T. J. Lowther (Phillip Perry), Keith Szarabajka (Terry Pugh)
Technicolor, Panavision, 138 minutes

THE BRIDGES OF MADISON COUNTY (1995)
Amblin, Malpaso / Warner Bros.
Producers: **Clint Eastwood**, Kathleen Kennedy
Director: **Eastwood**
Screenplay: Richard LaGravenese, based on the novel by Robert James Waller
Director of Photography: Jack N. Green
Editor: Joel Cox
Production Designer: Jeannine C. Oppewall
Music: Lennie Niehaus
Eastwood composed theme "Doe Eyes"
Cast: **Eastwood** (Robert Kincaid), Meryl Streep (Francesca Johnson), Annie Corley (Carolyn), Victor Slezak (Michael), Jim Haynie (Richard)
Technicolor, 135 minutes
Academy Award Nomination: Actress in a Leading Role, Streep

ABSOLUTE POWER (1997)
Castle Rock Entertainment, Malpaso / Columbia Pictures
Producers: Karen Spiegel, **Clint Eastwood**
Director: **Eastwood**
Screenplay: William Goldman, based on the novel by David Baldacci
Director of Photography: Jack N. Green
Editor: Joel Cox
Production Designer: Henry Bumstead
Music: Lennie Niehaus
Eastwood composed "Power Waltz" and "Kate's Theme"
Cast: **Eastwood** (Luther Whitney), Gene Hackman (President Richmond), Ed Harris (Seth Frank), Laura Linney (Kate Whitney), Scott Glenn (Bill Burton), Judy Davis (Gloria Russell) Technicolor, Panavision, 121 minutes

MIDNIGHT IN THE GARDEN OF GOOD AND EVIL (1997)
Malpaso, Silver Pictures / Warner Bros.
Executive Producer: Anita Zuckerman
Producers: **Clint Eastwood**, Arnold Stiefel
Director: **Eastwood**
Screenplay: John Lee Hancock, based on the book by John Berendt
Director of Photography: Jack N. Green
Editor: Joel Cox

Production Designer: Henry Bumstead
Music: Lennie Niehaus, featuring songs by Johnny Mercer
Cast: Kevin Spacey (Jim Williams), John Cusack (John Kelso), Jack Thompson (Sonny Seiler), Irma P. Hall (Minerva), Jude Law (Billy Hanson), Alison Eastwood (Mandy Nicholls), The Lady Chablis (Chablis Deveau)
Technicolor, 155 minutes

TRUE CRIME (1999)
The Zanuck Company, Malpaso / Warner Bros.
Executive Producer: Tom Rooker
Producers: **Clint Eastwood**, Richard D. Zanuck, Lili Fini Zanuck
Director: **Eastwood**
Screenplay: Larry Gross, Paul Brickman, Stephen Schiff; based on the novel by Andrew Klavan
Director of Photography: Jack N. Green
Editor: Joel Cox
Production Designer: Henry Bumstead
Music: Lennie Niehaus
Eastwood composed "Why Should I Care"
Cast: **Eastwood** (Steve Everett), Isaiah Washington (Frank Beechum), Dennis Leary (Bob Findley), Lisa Gay Hamilton (Bonnie Beechum), Diane Venora (Barbara Everett), Bernard Hill (Luther Plunkitt), James Woods (Alan Mann), Francesca Fisher-Eastwood (Kate Everett)
Technicolor, 127 minutes

SPACE COWBOYS (2000)
Malpaso, Mad Chance Productions, Village Roadshow Pictures, Clipsal Films / Warner Bros.
Executive Producer: Tom Rooker
Producers: **Clint Eastwood**, Andrew Lazar
Director: **Eastwood**
Screenplay: Ken Kaufman, Howard Klausner
Director of Photography: Jack N. Green
Editor: Joel Cox
Production Designer: Henry Bumstead
Music: Lennie Niehaus
Eastwood composed "Espacio"
Cast: **Eastwood** (Frank Corvin), Tommy Lee Jones (Hawk Hawkins),

Donald Sutherland (Jerry O'Neill), James Garner (Tank Sullivan), James Cromwell (Bob Gerson), Marcia Gay Harden (Sara Holland)
Technicolor, Panavision, 130 minutes
Academy Award Nomination: Sound Editing, Alan Robert Murray, Bub Asman

BLOOD WORK (2002)
Malpaso / Warner Bros.
Executive Producer: Robert Lorenz
Producer: **Clint Eastwood**
Director: **Eastwood**
Screenplay: Brian Helgeland, based on the novel by Michael Connelly
Director of Photography: Tom Stern
Editor: Joel Cox
Production Designer: Henry Bumstead
Music: Lennie Niehaus
Cast: **Eastwood** (Terry McCaleb), Jeff Daniels (Buddy Noone), Wanda De Jesús (Graciella Rivers), Tina Lifford (Jaye Winston), Paul Rodriguez (Detective Ronaldo Arrango), Anjelica Huston (Dr. Bonnie Fox)
Technicolor, Panavision, 110 minutes

PIANO BLUES (Documentary; television series THE BLUES) (2003)
Road Movies Filmproduktion, Vulcan Productions, Cappa Productions, Jigsaw Productions / PBS
Series Executive Producers: Martin Scorsese, Ulrich Felsberg, Paul G. Allen, Jody Patton
Producers: **Clint Eastwood**, Bruce Ricker
Director: **Eastwood**
Director of Photography: Vic Losick
Editors: Joel Cox, Gary Roach
With: Marcia Ball, Pinetop Perkins, Dave Brubeck, Jay McShann, Ray Charles, Dr. John, **Eastwood**
Color, black and white, 92 minutes

MYSTIC RIVER (2003)
Malpaso, Village Roadshow Pictures, NPV Entertainment / Warner Bros.
Executive Producer: Bruce Berman
Producers: Robert Lorenz, Judie G. Hoyt, **Clint Eastwood**
Director: **Eastwood**

Screenplay: Brian Helgeland, based on the novel by Dennis Lehane
Director of Photography: Tom Stern
Editor: Joel Cox
Production Designer: Henry Bumstead
Music: **Eastwood**
Cast: Sean Penn (Jimmy Markum), Tim Robbins (Dave Boyle), Kevin Bacon (Sean Devine), Laurence Fishburne (Whitey Powers), Marcia Gay Harden (Celeste Boyle), Laura Linney (Annabeth Markum)
Technicolor, Panavision, 138 minutes
Academy Awards: Actor in a Leading Role, Penn; Actor in a Supporting Role, Robbins; Academy Award Nominations: Actress in a Supporting Role, Harden; Writing, Adapted screenplay, Helgeland; Director, **Eastwood**; Best Picture, Lorenz, Hoyt, **Eastwood**

MILLION DOLLAR BABY (2004)
Malpaso, Lakeshore Entertainment / Warner Bros.
Executive Producers: Gary Lucchesi, Robert Lorenz
Producers: **Clint Eastwood**, Albert S. Ruddy, Tom Rosenberg, Paul Haggis
Director: **Eastwood**
Screenplay: Paul Haggis, based on stories from *Rope Burns* by F. X. Toole
Director of Photography: Tom Stern
Editor: Joel Cox
Production Designer: Henry Bumstead
Music: **Eastwood**
Cast: **Eastwood** (Frankie Dunn), Hilary Swank (Maggie Fitzgerald), Morgan Freeman (Eddie Scrap-Iron Dupris), Anthony Mackie (Shawrelle Berry), Jay Baruchel (Danger Barch), Lucia Rijker (Billie "The Blue Bear")
Technicolor, Panavision, 132 minutes
Academy Awards: Actor in a Supporting Role, Freeman; Actress in a Leading Role, Swank; Directing, **Eastwood**; Best Picture, **Eastwood**, Ruddy, Rosenberg; Academy Award Nominations: Actor in a Leading Role, **Eastwood**; Film Editing, Cox; Writing (Adapted Screenplay), Haggis

FLAGS OF OUR FATHERS (2006)
Malpaso, Amblin Entertainment / DreamWorks, Warner Bros.
Producers: **Clint Eastwood**, Steven Spielberg, Robert Lorenz
Director: **Eastwood**

Screenplay: William Broyles, Jr., Paul Haggis; based on the book by James Bradley, Ron Powers
Director of Photography: Tom Stern
Editor: Joel Cox
Production Designer: Henry Bumstead
Music: **Eastwood**
Cast: Ryan Phillippe (John "Doc" Bradley), Jesse Bradford (Rene Gagnon), Adam Beach (Ira Hayes), John Benjamin Hickey (Keyes Beech), John Slattery (Bud Gurber), Barry Pepper (Mike Strank)
Technicolor, Panavision, 132 minutes
Academy Award Nominations: Sound Editing, Alan Robert Murray, Bub Asman; Sound Mixing, John Reitz, Dave Campbell, Gregg Rudloff, Walt Martin

LETTERS FROM IWO JIMA (2006)
Malpaso, Amblin Entertainment / DreamWorks, Warner Bros.
Executive Producer: Paul Haggis
Producers: **Clint Eastwood**, Steven Spielberg, Robert Lorenz
Director: **Eastwood**
Screenplay (Japanese): Iris Yamashita
Story: Yamashita, Haggis; based on the book *Picture Letters from the Commander in Chief* by Tadamichi Kuribayashi
Director of Photography: Tom Stern
Editors: Joel Cox, Gary D. Roach
Production Designers: Henry Bumstead, James J. Murakami
Music: Kyle Eastwood, Michael Stevens
Cast: Ken Watanabe (General Kuribayashi), Kazunari Ninomiya (Saigo), Tsuyoshi Ihara (Baron Nishi), Ryo Kase (Shimizu), Shidou Nakamura (Lieutenant Ito)
Technicolor, Panavision, 141 minutes
Academy Award: Sound Editing, Alan Robert Murray, Bub Asman; Academy Award Nominations: Directing, **Eastwood**; Best Picture, **Eastwood**, Spielberg, Lorenz; Writing (Original Screenplay), Yamashita, Haggis

CHANGELING (2008)
Imagine Entertainment, Malpaso, Relativity Media / Universal
Executive Producers: Tim Moore, Jim Whitaker
Producers: **Clint Eastwood**, Brian Grazer, Ron Howard, Robert Lorenz
Director: **Eastwood**

Screenplay: J. Michael Straczynski
Director of Photography: Tom Stern
Editors: Joel Cox, Gary D. Roach
Production Designer: James J. Murakami
Music: **Eastwood**
Cast: Angelina Jolie (Christine Collins), John Malkovich (Rev. Gustav Briegleb), Jeffrey Donovan (Captain J. J. Jones), Michael Kelly (Detective Lester Ybarra), Colm Feore (Chief James E. Davis), Jason Butler Harner (Gordon Northcott), Amy Ryan (Carol Dexter)
Technicolor, Panavision, 142 minutes
Academy Award Nominations: Actress in a Leading Role, Jolie; Art Direction, Murakami, Gary Fettis; Cinematography, Stern

GRAN TORINO (2008)
Double Nickel Entertainment, Malpaso, Village Roadshow Pictures / Warner Bros., Matten Productions
Executive Producers: Jenette Kahn, Adam Richman, Tim Moore, Bruce Berman
Producers: **Clint Eastwood**, Robert Lorenz, Bill Gerber
Director: **Eastwood**
Screenplay: Nick Schenk
Story: Dave Johannson, Schenk
Director of Photography: Tom Stern
Editor: Joel Cox, Gary D. Roach
Production Designer: James J. Murakami
Music: Kyle Eastwood, Michael Stevens
Eastwood composed "Gran Torino"
Cast: **Eastwood** (Walt Kowalski), Bee Vang (Thao), Ahney Her (Sue), Christopher Carley (Father Janovich), John Carroll Lynch (Barber Martin)
Technicolor, Panavision, 116 minutes

INVICTUS (2009)
Malpaso, Spyglass Entertainment, Revelations Entertainment, Man Company / Warner Bros.
Executive Producers: Morgan Freeman, Tim Moore, Gary Barber, Roger Birnbaum
Producers: **Clint Eastwood**, Lori McCreary, Robert Lorenz, Mace Neufeld
Director: **Eastwood**

Screenplay: Anthony Peckham, based on the book *Playing the Enemy* by John Carlin
Director of Photography: Tom Stern
Editors: Joel Cox, Gary D. Roach
Production Designer: James J. Murakami
Music: Kyle Eastwood, Michael Stevens
Cast: Morgan Freeman (Nelson Mandela), Matt Damon (Francois Pienaar), Tony Kgoroge (Jason Tshabalala), Julian Lewis Jones (Etienne Feyder), Adjoa Andoh (Brenda Mazibuko)
Technicolor, Panavision, 134 minutes
Academy Award Nominations: Actor in a Leading Role, Freeman; Actor in a Supporting Role, Damon

HEREAFTER (2010)
Malpaso, Amblin Entertainment / Warner Bros.
Executive Producers: Steven Spielberg, Frank Marshall, Peter Morgan, Tim Moore
Producers: **Clint Eastwood**, Kathleen Kennedy, Robert Lorenz
Director: **Eastwood**
Screenplay: Peter Morgan
Director of Photography: Tom Stern
Editors: Joel Cox, Gary D. Roach
Production Designer: James J. Murakami
Music: **Eastwood**
Cast: Matt Damon (George Lonegan), Cécile de France (Marie Lelay), Jay Mohr (Billy), Bryce Dallas Howard (Melanie), George McLaren (Marcus/Jason), Frankie McLaren (Marcus/Jason)
Technicolor, Panavision, 129 minutes
Academy Award Nomination: Visual Effects, Michael Owens, Bryan Grill, Stephan Trojansky, Joe Farrell

J. EDGAR (2011)
Imagine Entertainment, Malpaso / Warner Bros.
Executive Producers: Tim Moore, Erica Huggins
Producers: **Clint Eastwood,** Brian Grazer, Robert Lorenz
Director: **Eastwood**
Screenplay: Dustin Lance Black
Director of Photography: Tom Stern
Editors: Joel Cox, Gary D. Roach
Production Designer: James J. Murakami

Music: **Eastwood**
Cast: Leonardo DiCaprio (J. Edgar Hoover), Naomi Watts (Helen Gandy), Judi Dench (Annie Hoover), Armie Hammer (Clyde Tolson), Josh Lucas (Charles Lindberg)
Technicolor, Panavision, 137 minutes

A STAR IS BORN (planned for 2013; tentative credits)
Malpaso, Thunder Road Pictures, Wonderful Films / Warner Bros.
Producers: Basil Iwanyk, Jon Peters, Bill Gerber, **Clint Eastwood**
Director: **Eastwood**
Screenplay: Will Fetters, Pamela Gray
Director of Photography: Tom Stern
Editor: Joel Cox
Production Designer: James J. Murakami
Cast: Beyoncé Knowles

As Actor Only

TELEVISION

Eastwood's first television appearance was on a Steve Allen special, *Allen in Movieland* (1955). He appeared in one episode each of the following TV series: *Highway Patrol*, *Death Valley Days* (1956); *West Point*, *Navy Log* (1957); *Maverick* (1959); *Mister Ed* (1962).

RAWHIDE (217 episodes) (1959–65)
CBS
Series Executive Producer: Charles Marquis Warren
   Producers: Warren, Vincent M. Fennelly, Endre Bohem, and others
Writers: Louis Vittes, John Dunkel, Charles Larson, and others
Directors: Thomas Carr, Ted Post, Christian Nyby, and others
Cinematography: John M. Nickolaus Jr. and others
Editors: George A. Gittens and others
Cast: Eric Fleming (Gil Favor), **Clint Eastwood** (Rowdy Yates), Paul Brinegar (Wishbone), Steve Raines (Jim Quince), James Murdock (Mushy)

FEATURE FILMS

At the beginning of his career Eastwood played small parts in ten films, which we list briefly; all are for Universal-International, unless otherwise noted.

Revenge of the Creature (Jack Arnold, 1955): **Eastwood** (uncredited) as Jennings

Francis in the Navy (Arthur Lubin, 1955): **Eastwood** as Jonesey

Lady Godiva (Arthur Lubin, 1955): **Eastwood** (uncredited) as First Saxon

Tarantula (Jack Arnold, 1955): **Eastwood** (uncredited) as jet squadron leader

Never Say Goodbye (Jerry Hopper, 1956): **Eastwood** (uncredited) as Will

Star in the Dust (Charles Haas, 1956): **Eastwood** (uncredited) as a ranch hand

Away All Boats (Joseph Pevney, 1956): **Eastwood** (uncredited) as a sailor

The First Traveling Saleslady (Arthur Lubin; RKO, 1956): "And introducing **Clint Eastwood**" as Jack Rice

Escapade in Japan (Arthur Lubin; RKO, Universal-International, 1957): **Eastwood** as rescue plane pilot

Lafayette Escadrille (William A. Wellman; Warner Bros., 1957): **Eastwood** as George Moseley

STARRING / CO-STARRING ROLES

AMBUSH AT CIMARRON PASS (1958)
Regal / 20th Century-Fox
Producer: Herbert E. Mendelson
Director: Jodie Copelan
Screenplay: Richard G. Taylor, John K. Butler
Director of Photography: John M. Nickolaus Jr.
Editor: Carl L. Pierson
Art Director: John Mansbridge.
Music: Paul Sawtell, Bert Shefter
Cast: Scott Brady (Sgt. Matt Blake), Margia Dean (Teresa), **Clint Eastwood** (Keith Williams)
Black and white, RegalScope, 73 minutes

PER UN PUGNO DI DOLLARI / A FISTFUL OF DOLLARS (1964; U.S., 1967)
Jolly Film, Constantin, Ocean Film / United Artists
Producers: Arrigo Colombo (as Harry Colombo*), Giorgio Papi (as George Papi*)
Director: Sergio Leone
Screenplay: Leone, Duccio Tessari, Victor A. Catena, G. Schock

Director of Photography: Massimo Dallamano (as Jack Dalmas*)
Editor: Roberto Cinquini (as Bob Quintle*)
Art Director: Carlo Simi (as Charles Simons*)
Music: Ennio Morricone (as Dan Savio*)
Cast: **Clint Eastwood** (Joe, the Stranger), Gian Maria Volonté (as Johnny Wels*) (Ramón Rojo), Marianne Koch (Marisol), José Calvo (Silvanito), Wolfgang Lukschy (John Baxter), Josef Egger (as Joe Edger*) (Piripero)
*Several participants were credited under "American" pseudonyms
Technicolor, Techniscope, 96–100 minutes

PER QUALCHE DOLLARO IN PIÙ / FOR A FEW DOLLARS MORE (1965; U.S., 1967)
Produzioni Europee Associate, Constantin, Arturo Gonzales / United Artists
Producer: Alberto Grimaldi
Director: Sergio Leone
Screenplay: Luciano Vincenzoni, Sergio Leone
Director of Photography: Massimo Dallamano
Editors: Giorgio Serralonga, Eugenio Alabiso
Art Director: Carlo Simi
Music: Ennio Morricone
Cast: **Clint Eastwood** (Manco, the Stranger), Lee Van Cleef (Colonel Douglas Mortimer), Gian Maria Volonté (Indio), Klaus Kinski (Hunchback), Josef Egger (Prophet)
Technicolor, Techniscope, 128–130 minutes

IL BUONO, IL BRUTTO, IL CATTIVO / THE GOOD, THE BAD AND THE UGLY (1966; U.S., 1968; restored, extended version, 2003)
Produzioni Europee Associate / United Artists
Producer: Alberto Grimaldi
Director: Sergio Leone
Screenplay: Age [Agenore Incrocci], [Furio] Scarpelli, Luciano Vincenzoni, Sergio Leone; English version: Mickey Knox
Director of Photography: Tonino Delli Colli
Editors: Nino Baragli, Eugenio Alabiso
Art Director: Carlo Simi
Music: Ennio Morricone
Cast: **Clint Eastwood** (Blondie, the Good), Eli Wallach (Tuco, the Ugly), Lee Van Cleef (Angel Eyes, the Bad), Aldo Giuffré (Northern

Officer), Rada Rassimov (Maria), Mario Brega (Corporal Wallace)
Technicolor, Techniscope, 180 minutes (Italy), 161 minutes (US); extended version, 179 minutes

LE STREGHE / THE WITCHES (1967; not commercially released in the U.S.)
Dino de Laurentiis Cinematografica, Productions Artistes Associés / United Artists
Executive Producer: Alfredo De Laurentiis
Producer: Dino De Laurentiis
Director of Photography: Giuseppe Rotunno
Art Directors: Mario Garbuglia, Piero Poletto
Music: Piero Piccioni, Ennio Morricone
Technicolor, 106 minutes
Part Five, "Una sera come le altre" / "An Ordinary Evening"
Director: Vittorio De Sica
Screenplay: Cesare Zavattini, Fabio Carpi, Enzo Muzii
Editor: Adriana Novelli
Cast: Silvana Mangano (Giovanna), **Clint Eastwood** (Carlo)
25 minutes

HANG 'EM HIGH (1968)
Leonard Freeman Productions, Malpaso / United Artists
Producer: Leonard Freeman
Director: Ted Post
Screenplay: Freeman, Mel Goldberg
Directors of Photography: Richard Kline, Leonard South
Editor: Gene Fowler, Jr.
Art Director: John Goodman
Music: Dominic Frontiere
Cast: **Clint Eastwood** (Jed Cooper), Inger Stevens (Rachel), Ed Begley (Captain Wilson), Pat Hingle (Judge Fenton), Bruce Dern (Miller), Dennis Hopper (Prophet)
DeLuxe, 115 minutes

COOGAN'S BLUFF (1968)
Malpaso / Universal
Executive Producer: Richard E. Lyons
Producer: Donald Siegel
Director: Siegel

Screenplay: Herman Miller, Dean Riesner, Howard Rodman
Director of Photography: Bud Thackery
Editor: Sam E. Waxman
Art Directors: Alexander Golitzen, Robert C. MacKichan
Music: Lalo Schifrin
Cast: **Clint Eastwood** (Coogan), Lee J. Cobb (Lt. McElroy), Susan Clark (Julie), Tisha Sterling (Linny Raven), Don Stroud (Ringerman)
Technicolor, 94 minutes

WHERE EAGLES DARE (1969; U.K., 1968)
Winkast Film Productions / Metro-Goldwyn-Mayer
Producers: Elliott Kastner, Jerry Gershwin
Director: Brian G. Hutton
Story and Screenplay: Alistair MacLean
Director of Photography: Arthur Ibbetson
Editor: John Jympson
Art Director: Peter Mullins
Music: Ron Goodwin
Cast: Richard Burton (Smith), **Clint Eastwood** (Schaffer), Mary Ure (Mary), Patrick Wymark (Turner), Michael Hordern (Rolland), Ingrid Pitt (Heidi)
Metrocolor / Panavision, 155 minutes

PAINT YOUR WAGON (1969)
Paramount
Producer: Alan Jay Lerner
Director: Joshua Logan
Screenplay, Lyrics: Lerner
Adaptation: Paddy Chayefsky
Director of Photography: William A. Fraker
Editor: Robert C. Jones
Production Designer: John Truscott
Music: Frederick Loewe, André Previn
Cast: Lee Marvin (Ben Rumson), **Clint Eastwood** ("Pardner"), Jean Seberg (Elizabeth), Ray Walston ("Mad Jack" Duncan), Harve Presnell ("Rotten Luck Willie")
Technicolor, Panavision, 166 minutes
Academy Award Nomination: Score of a Musical Picture Original or Adaptation, Nelson Riddle

TWO MULES FOR SISTER SARA (1970)
Malpaso, Sanen Productions / Universal
Producers: Martin Rackin, Carroll Case
Director: Don Siegel
Screenplay: Albert Maltz
Story: Budd Boetticher
Director of Photography: Gabriel Figueroa
Editors: Robert F. Shugrue, Juan José Marino
Art Director: José Rodríguez Granada
Music: Ennio Morricone
Cast: Shirley MacLaine (Sara), **Clint Eastwood** (Hogan), Manolo Fábregas (Colonel Beltran), Alberto Morin (General LeClaire)
Technicolor, Panavision, 114 minutes

KELLY'S HEROES (1970)
The Warriors Company / Metro-Goldwyn-Mayer
Producers: Gabriel Katzka, Sidney Beckerman
Director: Brian G. Hutton
Screenplay: Troy Kennedy Martin
Director of Photography: Gabriel Figueroa
Editor: John Jympson
Production Designer: Jonathan Barry
Music: Lalo Schifrin
Cast: **Clint Eastwood** (Kelly), Telly Savalas (Big Joe), Don Rickles (Crapgame), Carroll O'Connor (General Colt), Donald Sutherland (Oddball)
Metrocolor, Panavision, 145 minutes

THE BEGUILED (1971)
Jennings Lang, Malpaso / Universal
Producer: Donald Siegel
Director: Siegel
Screenplay: Albert Maltz (as John B. Sherry), Irene Kamp (as Grimes Grice); based on the novel by Thomas Cullinan
Director of Photography: Bruce Surtees
Editor: Carl Pingitore
Production Designer: Ted Haworth
Art Director: Alexander Golitzen
Music: Lalo Schifrin

Cast: **Clint Eastwood** (John McBurney), Geraldine Page (Martha), Elizabeth Hartman (Edwina), Jo Ann Harris (Carol), Mae Mercer (Hallie), Pamelyn Ferdin (Amy)
Technicolor, 105 minutes

DIRTY HARRY (1971)
Malpaso / Warner Bros.
Executive Producer: Robert Daley
Producer: Don Siegel
Director: Siegel
Screenplay: Harry Julian Fink, Rita M. Fink, Dean Riesner
Director of Photography: Bruce Surtees
Editor: Carl Pingitore
Art Director: Dale Hennesy
Music: Lalo Schifrin
Cast: **Clint Eastwood** (Harry Callahan), Harry Guardino (Bressler), Reni Santoni (Chico), Andy Robinson (Killer/Scorpio), John Larch (Chief), John Vernon (The Mayor)
Technicolor, Panavision, 103 minutes

JOE KIDD (1972)
Malpaso / Universal
Executive Producer: Robert Daley
Producer: Sidney Beckerman
Director: John Sturges
Screenplay: Elmore Leonard
Director of Photography: Bruce Surtees
Editor: Ferris Webster
Art Directors: Alexander Golitzen, Henry Bumstead
Music: Lalo Schifrin
Cast: **Clint Eastwood** (Joe Kidd), Robert Duvall (Frank Harlan), John Saxon (Luis Chama), Don Stroud (Lamarr), Stella Garcia (Helen Sanchez)
Technicolor, Panavision, 88 minutes

MAGNUM FORCE (1973)
Malpaso / Warner Bros.
Producer: Robert Daley
Director: Ted Post

Screenplay: John Milius, Michael Cimino
Director of Photography: Frank Stanley
Editor: Ferris Webster
Art Director: Jack Collis
Music: Lalo Schifrin
Cast: **Clint Eastwood** (Harry Callahan), Hal Holbrook (Lt. Briggs), Mitchell Ryan (McCoy), David Soul (Davis), Felton Perry (Early Smith)
Technicolor, Panavision, 123 minutes

THUNDERBOLT AND LIGHTFOOT (1974)
Malpaso / United Artists
Producer: Robert Daley
Director: Michael Cimino
Screenplay: Cimino
Director of Photography: Frank Stanley
Editor: Ferris Webster
Art Director: Tambi Larsen
Music: Dee Barton
Cast: **Clint Eastwood** (Thunderbolt), Jeff Bridges (Lightfoot), George Kennedy (Red Leary), Geoffrey Lewis (Goody), Catherine Bach (Melody)
DeLuxe, Panavision, 115 minutes
Academy Award Nomination: Actor in a Supporting Role, Bridges

THE ENFORCER (1976)
Malpaso / Warner Bros.
Producer: Robert Daley
Director: James Fargo
Screenplay: Stirling Silliphant, Dean Riesner
Story: Gail Morgan Hickman, S. W. Schurr
Director of Photography: Charles W. Short
Editors: Ferris Webster, Joel Cox
Art Director: Allen E. Smith
Music: Jerry Fielding
Cast: **Clint Eastwood** (Harry Callahan), Tyne Daly (Kate Moore), Harry Guardino (Lt. Bressler), Bradford Dillman (Capt. McKay), John Mitchum (DiGeorgio), Albert Popwell (Mustapha)
DeLuxe, Panavision, 97 minutes

EVERY WHICH WAY BUT LOOSE (1978)
Malpaso / Warner Bros.
Producer: Robert Daley
Director: James Fargo
Screenplay: Jeremy Joe Kronsberg
Director of Photography: Rexford Metz
Editors: Ferris Webster, Joel Cox
Art Director: Elayne Ceder
Music Supervision: Snuff Garrett
Cast: **Clint Eastwood** (Philo Beddoe), Sondra Locke (Lynn Halsey-Taylor), Geoffrey Lewis (Orville), Beverly D'Angelo (Echo), Ruth Gordon (Ma)
DeLuxe, 115 minutes

ESCAPE FROM ALCATRAZ (1979)
Malpaso / Paramount
Executive Producer: Robert Daley
Producer: Donald Siegel
Director: Siegel
Screenplay: Richard Tuggle, based on the book by J. Campbell Bruce
Director of Photography: Bruce Surtees
Editor: Ferris Webster
Production Designer: Allen Smith
Music: Jerry Fielding
Cast: **Clint Eastwood** (Frank Morris), Patrick McGoohan (Warden), Roberts Blossom (Doc), Jack Thibeau (Clarence Anglin), Fred Ward (John Anglin), Paul Benjamin (English), Larry Hankin (Charley Butts)
DeLuxe, 112 minutes

ANY WHICH WAY YOU CAN (1980)
Warner Bros., [Malpaso[1]] / Warner Bros.
Executive Producer: Robert Daley
Producer: Fritz Manes
Director: Buddy Van Horn
Screenplay: Stanford Sherman
Director of Photography: David Worth
Editors: Ferris Webster, Ron Spang
Production Design: William J. Creber
Music Supervision: Snuff Garrett

Cast: **Clint Eastwood** (Philo Beddoe), Sondra Locke (Lynne Halsey-Taylor), Geoffrey Lewis (Orville), William Smith (Jack Wilson), Harry Guardino (James Beekman), Ruth Gordon (Ma)
DeLuxe, 115 minutes

CITY HEAT (1984)
Malpaso, Deliverance / Warner Bros.
Producer: Fritz Manes
Director: Richard Benjamin
Screenplay: Blake Edwards (as "Sam O. Brown"), Joseph C. Stinson
Director of Photography: Nick McLean
Editor: Jacqueline Cambas
Production Designer: Edward Carfagno
Music: Lennie Niehaus
Cast: **Clint Eastwood** (Lt. Speer), Burt Reynolds (Mike Murphy), Jane Alexander (Addy), Madeline Kahn (Caroline Howley), Rip Torn (Primo Pitt), Irene Cara (Ginny Lee)
Technicolor, 97 minutes

THE DEAD POOL (1988)
Malpaso / Warner Bros.
Producer: David Valdes
Director: Buddy Van Horn
Screenplay: Steve Sharon
Director of Photography: Jack N. Green
Editor: Ron Spang
Production Designer: Edward C. Carfagno
Music: Lalo Schifrin
Cast: **Clint Eastwood** (Harry Callahan), Patricia Clarkson (Samantha Walker), Liam Neeson (Peter Swan), Evan C. Kim (Al Quan), Jim Carrey (as James Carrey) (Johnny Squares)
Technicolor, 91 minutes

PINK CADILLAC (1989)
Malpaso / Warner Bros.
Executive Producer: Michael Gruskoff
Producer: David Valdes
Director: Buddy Van Horn
Screenplay: John Eskow
Director of Photography: Jack N. Green

Editor: Joel Cox
Production Designer: Edward C. Carfagno
Music: Steve Dorff
Cast: **Clint Eastwood** (Tommy Nowak), Bernadette Peters (Lou Ann McGuinn), Timothy Carhart (Roy McGuinn), John Dennis Johnston (Waycross), Michael Des Barres (Alex), Jim Carrey (as James Carrey) ("Elvis" Lounge Entertainer)
Technicolor, 121 minutes

IN THE LINE OF FIRE (1993)
Apple/Rose, Castle Rock Entertainment / Columbia Pictures
Executive Producers: Wolfgang Petersen, Gail Katz, David Valdes
Producer: Jeff Apple
Director: Wolfgang Petersen
Screenplay: Jeff Maguire
Director of Photography: John Bailey
Editor: Anne V. Coates
Production Designer: Lilly Kilvert
Music: Ennio Morricone
Cast: **Clint Eastwood** (Frank Horrigan), John Malkovich (Mitch Leary), Rene Russo (Lilly Raines), Dylan McDermott (Al D'Andrea), Gary Cole (Bill Watts), Fred Dalton Thompson (Harry Sargent)
Technicolor, Panavision, 128 minutes
Academy Award Nominations: Actor in a Supporting Role, Malkovich; Film Editing, Coates; Writing (Screenplay Written Directly for the Screen), Maguire

TROUBLE WITH THE CURVE (2012)
Malpaso / Warner Bros.
Executive Producer: Tim Moore
Producers: **Clint Eastwood**, Robert Lorenz, Michele Weisler
Director: Lorenz
Screenplay: Randy Brown
Director of Photography: Tom Stern
Editors: Joel Cox, Gary Roach
Production Designer: James J. Murakami
Music: Marco Beltrami
Cast: **Eastwood** (Gus Lobel), Amy Adams (Mickey), Justin Timberlake (Johnny Flanagan), John Goodman (Pete Klein), Matthew Lillard, Scott Eastwood (Billy Clark)

As Producer Only

THE STARS FELL ON HENRIETTA (1995)
Malpaso / Warner Bros.
Producers: **Clint Eastwood**, David Valdes
Director: James Keach
Screenplay: Philip Railsback
Director of Photography: Bruce Surtees
Editor: Joel Cox
Production Designer: Henry Bumstead
Music: David Benoit
Cast: Robert Duvall (Mr. Cox), Aidan Quinn (Don Day), Frances Fisher (Cora Day), Brian Dennehy (Big Dave), Billy Bob Thornton (Roy)
Technicolor, Panavision, 110 minutes

TONY BENNETT: THE MUSIC NEVER ENDS (Documentary; television series AMERICAN MASTERS) (2007)
Rhapsody Films, RPM Music Productions, Thirteen/WNET New York / PBS, Red Envelope Entertainment
Executive Producer: Ted Sarandos
Producers: **Clint Eastwood**, Bruce Ricker
Director: Ricker
Writers: Nick Tosches, Ricker
Directors of Photography: Scott Sinkler, Jerry Hogrewe
Editor: Joel Cox
Narrator: Anthony Hopkins
Color, black and white, 87 minutes

Other Documentaries

Eastwood was credited as executive producer for the following documentary features, which we list briefly. Except for *Thelonious Monk: Straight No Chaser*, all also include Eastwood as a participant.

Thelonious Monk: Straight No Chaser (Charlotte Zwerin; Warner Bros., 1988)
Monterey Jazz Festival: Forty Legendary Years (William Harper; MJF Productions, 1998)
Budd Boetticher: A Man Can Do That (Television) (Bruce Ricker; Rhapsody Films / Turner Classic Movies, 2005)
You Must Remember This: The Warner Bros. Story (Television miniseries,

in series *American Masters*) (Richard Schickel; narrator: **Eastwood**; Lorac Productions, Thirteen/WNET New York / PBS, Warner Bros., 2008)

Johnny Mercer: The Dream's on Me (Television) (Bruce Ricker; Rhapsody Productions / Turner Classic Movies, BBC Arena, 2009)

Dave Brubeck: In His Own Sweet Way (Television) (Bruce Ricker; Rhapsody Productions / Turner Classic Movies, BBC Arena, 2010)

Additionally, the following are respectively "A Malpaso Production" and produced largely with Malpaso personnel:

RATBOY (1986)
Malpaso / Warner Bros.
Producer: Fritz Manes
Director: Sondra Locke
Screenplay: Rob Thompson
Director of Photography: Bruce Surtees
Editor: Joel Cox
Production Design: Edward Carfagno
Music: Lennie Niehaus
Cast: Sondra Locke (Nikki Morrison), Robert Townsend (Manny), Christopher Hewett (Acting Coach), S. L. Baird (Ratboy)
Technicolor, 105 minutes

RAILS & TIES (2007)
Warner Bros. / Warner Bros.
Producers: Robert Lorenz, Peer J. Oppenheimer, Barrett Stuart
Director: Alison Eastwood
Screenplay: Micky Levy
Director of Photography: Tom Stern
Editor: Gary D. Roach
Production Design: James J. Murakami
Music: Kyle Eastwood, Michael Stevens
Cast: Kevin Bacon (Tom Stark), Marcia Gay Harden (Megan Stark), Miles Heizer (Davey Danner)
Technicolor, Panavision, 101 minutes

As Composer Only

GRACE IS GONE (2007)
Plum Pictures, New Crime Productions / The Weinstein Company

Executive Producers: Paul Bernstein and others
Producers: John Cusack, Grace Loh, Galt Niederhoffer, Celine Rattray, Daniela Taplin Lundberg
Director: James C. Strouse
Screenplay: Strouse
Director of Photography: Jean-Louis Bompoint
Editor: Joe Klotz
Production Design: Susan Block
Music: **Clint Eastwood**
Cast: John Cusack (Stanley Phillips), Shélan O'Keefe (Heidi Phillips), Gracie Bednarczyk (Dawn Phillips)
Technicolor, 85 minutes

Notes

1. The five Eastwood films released between 1980 and 1983 were issued without the Malpaso name but were filmed with the usual Malpaso personnel. Most filmographies include them as Malpaso productions.

Clint Eastwood: Interviews
Revised and Updated

No Tumbleweed Ties for Clint

Rex Reed / 1971

Published in *Los Angeles Times*, April 4, 1971. Reprinted by permission of the author.

He was on the phone, talking about the matrix and the looping and all the other things directors talk about when they call the Coast. "The sound is twenty frames ahead of the music and the color processing is wrong on the work print." Hitchcock? Minnelli? Well, don't snicker. Would you believe Clint Eastwood?

He was in New York to publicize his new movie, *The Beguiled,* a Gothic Civil War horror film in which a group of predatory females feed him poison mushrooms because he steps on a little girl's turtle. But it was clear that his real interests lay in another film called *Play Misty for Me,* which marks his debut as a director.

"After seventeen years of bouncing my head against the wall, hanging around sets, maybe influencing certain camera setups with my own opinions, watching actors go through all kinds of hell without any help, and working with both good directors and bad ones, I'm at the point where I'm ready to make my own pictures. I stored away all the mistakes I made and saved up all the good things I learned and now I know enough to control my own projects and get what I want out of actors. So I directed this picture and I'm editing it myself and I think it's damn good.

"In my starving days, I knew a girl who went around knocking on doors trying to get a job as a writer while she worked as a secretary. She wrote a sixty-page treatment about a small-town disc jockey who meets a girl in a saloon one night and even after he goes back to his real girl, this chick turns psychotic, starts haunting him, murders his maid and turns his life into a nightmare.

"It's got a lot of action and suspense and I used a small crew and a low budget of only $800,000, but I think I got more than $800,000 on the screen. At least I know that if it's a failure it's my own fault and not somebody else's. I've been in enough bombs that were somebody else's fault."

For an actor some people consider a cut-out from the old Hollywood mold known as "cowboy star, Gary Cooper voice, 6-foot-4, suitable for framing," the attitude seems startling. But when you talk to Clint Eastwood you begin to discover that his head and his heart are not tied to a tumbleweed.

Until now, his career hasn't been taken very seriously by the judges and juries who draw the lines between marketable movie stars and practitioners of serious art. But at least he's honest about it. "Whatever success I've had is a lot of instinct and a little luck," he says. "I just go by how I feel."

It's made him a whacking good living, women mob him everywhere, he turns down ten scripts a week and—honor of honors—there are Clint Eastwood imitators popping up like ragweed wherever you look. He grins a boyish grin, throws his legs and arms over the sides of the cushy furniture in his suite at the Regency Hotel, bites into a chicken sandwich, and philosophizes.

"Hollywood is strange. Everyone is looking for a formula. One year it's two guys on a motorcycle, the next year it's a girl dying of cancer and they flood the market with imitations. For years I bummed around trying to get a job and it was the same old story—my voice was too soft, my teeth needed capping, I squinted too much, I was too tall—all that constant tearing down of my ego was bound to turn me into either a better person or a complete jerk.

"And I know that if I walked into a casting office right now and nobody knew I was Clint Eastwood, I'd get the same old thing. My voice is still too soft, my teeth still need capping, I still squint, and I've been compared to a small redwood tree. But after the westerns I did in Spain I was suddenly Clint Eastwood and now the other guys who are too tall and squint too much are the ones cursing me! You go figure it out."

Actually, he was on his way before the Sergio Leone westerns. He had loped into Hollywood to attend college on the GI Bill after two years at Ft. Ord where he wafted through basic training teaching swimming. He had been a lumberjack in Oregon and had worked at a variety of odd jobs, from the steel mills to Boeing Aircraft.

At Los Angeles City College, he met a photographer who talked him into doing a screen test and he got a contract with Universal. "I was always the prison guard who brings the guy in to see the D.A. I got seventy-five dollars a week for forty weeks a year and I got kicked out after a year and a half, but by then I was determined to do something about a career. I got kicked around the unemployment offices a lot, but I finally got into TV and played a lot of motorcycle hoods and lab assistants, but all that time I never played anyone in a business suit.

"I was very close to quitting when *Rawhide* came along. I was visiting a friend at CBS and an executive saw me drinking coffee in the cafeteria and came over and asked me to test. It was a fluke. It lasted seven and a half years. In the sixth year, I had exhausted everything I could do on a horse, so I took a hiatus and went to Spain to make *Fistful of Dollars*. I had nothing to lose. I had a job waiting in TV and I knew if it was a flop nobody would ever see it anyway."

Oh, but they did. *Fistful of Dollars*, *A Few Dollars More*, and *The Good, the Bad and the Ugly*—better known as "the paella trilogy"—became camp institutions. "They weren't movies you got acclaim for," says Eastwood with a straight face, "but they were harder to do than a lot of the better roles I've had lately. I look back on them as satire, which was difficult to do without lapsing over into slapstick—and I also learned from watching the Italians how to make only a few dollars look like ten times that much on the screen."

The Italian westerns were remakes of Japanese samurai epics, made in Spain with Americans by an Italian director, but they were the bricks that formed the foundation of the box-office phenomenon known as Clint Eastwood. For a Hollywood symbol, he had oddly enough never made a film there. Out of twelve films, ten were made on location and the remaining two used only partial interiors on sound stages. Nor does he live the Hollywood life.

Shyly, he hides away on a cliff overlooking the San Fernando Valley when in Los Angeles or a cliff overlooking the sea in a small rustic house in Carmel with his wife Maggie and their son Kyle, two and a half. "I've been married to the same chick for seventeen years. I'd better check my pulse. She's lived through all the changes in me, and she hasn't thrown me out, so I think I'll hang around. I'm just now beginning to find out who I am and what I can do. I know I'll never be a Laurence Olivier.

"With my physical type and my legato personality, I'll never play certain parts. But I still can do things that have some quality. I have never studied acting. Life is a study, film-making in general is a study. There are two kinds of actors—one sits in a dressing room waiting for his call and the other gets out into the business and polishes his craft by absorbing everything. I don't know enough, I'll never learn everything I need to learn. When a guy thinks he's already learned it, he can only go backwards."

Clint Eastwood unhooks his tree-trunk legs from around the dainty chair he's been sitting on and smiles that chuck-wagon smile that has made him a star. "I thought Geraldine Page was out of my league, being a big star on the Broadway stage and all, but when we started *The Beguiled* she told me she was a big fan of mine on *Rawhide*. I've got no regrets, man, no regrets at all."

Eastwood on Eastwood

Stuart M. Kaminsky / 1971

Published as chapter 7 in Stuart M. Kaminsky, *Clint Eastwood* (New York: New American Library, 1974), 80–100. Reprinted by permission.

Clint Eastwood moves quickly. I had been at Universal Studios, where Eastwood's Malpaso Production Company is headquartered, for three weeks before I could catch up with him. A few nights before I made my third try to catch him at his Universal bungalow, I had seen a preview of *Play Misty for Me*, Eastwood's first attempt at directing.

I got through to Eastwood's producer and associate Bob Daley, who called across to Eastwood and asked if he could squeeze me in before he got in his Sting Ray and headed back to Carmel, where he lives. The interview was set for six-thirty that night.

Eastwood's name is not on Bungalow 64, which is about thirty yards from his friend Siegel's bungalow. The outer office is covered with pictures of Eastwood from his movies and a large Eastwood poster showing him in a Sergio Leone picture. There is also a picture of Don Siegel in his role as a bartender in *Misty*.

Eastwood, wearing a blue pullover T-shirt, greeted me by name, and we went into his office. He is a nonslouching six-foot-four, as soft-spoken in life as in his movie roles.

His office is large—comfortable executive conference table at one end, sofa against one wall, large desk across the carpeted room. On the wall above the sofa was a huge poster in Italian for *Where Eagles Dare*. Another wall contained a slashed portrait of Eastwood, which figures in the plot of *Misty*.

Popular disc jockey Dave Garver (Eastwood) finds himself at loose ends when his girl friend, Tobie Williams (Donna Mills), unexpectedly leaves town. One night, while drinking at his favorite bar, Eastwood meets Evelyn Draper (Jessica Walter), an attractive brunette who suggests a visit to her apartment and then informs him that she is the girl who regularly phones his radio station to request that he play the song "Misty." By morning, however, it becomes apparent to Eastwood that what he thought was a one-night stand is really a romantic obsession on Evelyn's part; openly pursuing him, she begins dropping in at his home uninvited, at one point disrupting him while he and his co-worker Al Monte are preparing a presentation for station owner Madge Brenner. Further, when Tobie returns and Eastwood resumes their relationship, Evelyn becomes uncontrollably jealous, spying on them during their romantic walks and even cutting her wrists in a desperate effort to win Eastwood's attention and concern. After entrusting Evelyn to the care of Frank Dewan, a doctor friend, Eastwood leaves to discuss a job offer with Madge; but Evelyn interrupts their luncheon and so hysterically insults the older woman that the deal is permanently squelched. Arriving back home, Eastwood finds his cleaning woman, Birdie, almost slashed to death with a razor, his apartment wrecked, and a dazed Evelyn being questioned by Police Sergeant McCallum. With Evelyn removed to a sanitarium, Eastwood sees Tobie again and learns that she has taken a new roommate named Annabelle. But before long, Evelyn phones Dave at the station to tell him that she is cured and on her way to Hawaii—and would he please play "Misty" for her? Then late that night, awakened by the sound of "Misty" coming from his stereo, Eastwood finds Evelyn standing at the foot of his bed. Suddenly lunging, she makes an unsuccessful knife attack and then runs off. A few days later, Eastwood recalls that Evelyn once quoted two lines from Poe's "Annabelle Lee" to him over the phone; remembering that Tobie's new roommate is named Annabelle, Eastwood calls McCallum and asks him to rush to Tobie's apartment. When Eastwood gets there, McCallum is lying dead with a pair of scissors in his chest, Tobie is bound and gagged on the bed, and the deranged Evelyn is once more poised with a knife. In staving off her violent attack, Eastwood hurls Evelyn across the terrace, and stumbling backward, she falls off the edge, plummeting to her death on the jagged rocks below. As Eastwood unties Tobie and helps her from the apartment, "Misty" once more begins to play on the radio.

With darkness coming over the San Fernando mountains beyond the bungalow, the actor and, now, director sat and talked for a few hours over a couple of beers.

Kaminsky: You've done four pictures with Don Siegel as your director. He appears as an actor, the only time he has done so, in the first movie you directed, *Play Misty for Me*. The only other thing you have directed is a short, the subject of which was Don Siegel. What is there about the man that you obviously like so much?

Eastwood: It's a mutual-admiration thing. He likes a lot of my ideas, and I like his. I like his attack on directing. He's very straightforward. His films always have energy. He has that energy as a person. He moves briskly and tries to get right to the point in directing. I've been involved with some directors who are wishy-washy, don't know what they want. Don never starts rolling until he has an attack. We change a lot of things in the middle, but even the changes are positive, forward. I think that's what I like: his forward momentum is always there. He never gets bogged down, even in disaster. I think he's fantastic. We have worked a lot together, and probably will in the future. I feel he is an enormously talented guy who has been deprived of the notoriety he probably should have had much earlier because Hollywood was going through a stage where the awards went to the big pictures and the guys who knew how to spend a lot of money. As a result, guys who got a lot of pictures with a lot of effort and a little money weren't glorified. So Don had to wait many years until he could get to do films with fairly good budgets. He's the kind of director there's not enough of. If things don't go as planned, he doesn't sit down and cry and consider everything lost, as some directors do.

Kaminsky: How does working with Siegel compare to working with Sergio Leone?

Eastwood: Don likes to hear ideas. He has an ego like everyone else, but if a janitor comes up with something, he won't turn it down. He'll take from anybody. He kind of breeds an atmosphere of participation. Sergio Leone, whom I respect very much, would never give me any credit for the style of a film I'd been in with him. Don would and does. This is true even though Sergio and I would hash out ideas together, toss them back and forth. I want to make it clear that I like Sergio, liked working with him. Filmmaking is ensemble work. A director who can have a clear focus in a film, a clear idea of the style he's moving toward, and still draw creative things out of everybody working with him has an atmosphere which will make superior movies in the long run. The director is still the leading force, the captain.

Kaminsky: Did your outlook change when you became a director? Do you appreciate the problems of a director more now, after *Misty*?

Eastwood: No, I knew what I was getting into. I've been in front of a camera for a lot of hours in the last eighteen years. In TV, I saw so much that I *wouldn't* do as a director. I felt prepared.

Kaminsky: In *Misty*, I know the first scene you did was the one in which Don Siegel had his acting debut. Did you do that purposely to put him on a spot?
Eastwood: Actually, it just worked out that way. I tell everybody I did it that way because it was my first day on the set, and I wanted somebody to be more nervous than I was, but actually I just started with that sequence because I wanted to start with something moderate, not too rough. We had three days scheduled for it, since it was Don's first acting job, but we did it in a little over a day. He was very nervous during the first few takes, but by the second morning, he was an old pro.

Kaminsky: When you work as a director, do you feel you're working the way he does, or some other director, or what?
Eastwood: No, I work my own way, although I've certainly been influenced by the directors I've worked with over the years. Siegel has had influence on my directing, but so has Sergio, and so has Ted Post [*Hang 'Em High*]. And so have other guys from the television years, as well as directors whose work I've seen though I've never met them.

Kaminsky: What other directors do you admire?
Eastwood: Well, I used to love Hitchcock, some of that earlier stuff.

Kaminsky: Why did you decide to do *The Beguiled*, which was so different from everything you'd done earlier?
Eastwood: The studio owned the property, and I was intrigued by it. It's a wild story. I told Don about it and told him I thought it was the kind of thing that could go right to the roof—or right down the toilet. He eventually read it and liked it, and then I had doubts. He was kind of the leading force in getting me to do, it, as it wound up. He said: You can always be in a Western or adventure, but you may never get a chance to do this type film again. The studio wanted to do it, so we did it.

Kaminsky: Did you think you were taking a chance because it was different from what you had been doing?
Eastwood: Only in the sense that it wasn't a typical commercial film, but we thought it could be a very good film, and that was important.

Kaminsky: How would you compare it with the other ones you've done?
Eastwood: I think it was a very well-executed film, the best-directed film Don's ever done, a very exciting film. Whether it's appealing to large masses or not, I don't know.

Kaminsky: How did you come to do *Two Mules for Sister Sara*?
Eastwood: I had read the script, which was given to me by Elizabeth Taylor when I was doing *Where Eagles Dare* with her husband. We wanted to do it together, and the studio approved of the combination, but she was going through some deal where she didn't want to work unless it coincided with Richard's working, so we had it set up to do in Mexico while Richard was working there on something else, but then there were some other problems, and I think the studio kind of leaned toward Shirley MacLaine, because they had such high hopes for *Sweet Charity* at that time. It required some writing, and the casting of Shirley stretched the imagination a bit. It would have been ideal for Sophia Loren.

Kaminsky: Would you comment on the different styles of Leone and Siegel?
Eastwood: Leone is a very good film editor, and has a good way of making things important. When you build up to an action scene, it's pow! exciting, and then it's back to being very leisurely. Don is a little more impatient. American people are used to shorter films. Don is more direct, though *The Beguiled* was a little more leisurely. It was very smooth; everything sort of folded over nicely.

Kaminsky: Do you feel that about particular sequences or the whole film?
Eastwood: The whole film, because it was different. Don usually does those detective-type films. *Dirty Harry* will need Don's kind of energy; it will be very important to that film. I don't think it will be the most exciting I've ever been in, but I do have good feelings about it.

Kaminsky: *Dirty Harry* has so little dialogue.
Eastwood: It's a very physical-moving film. I'm anxious to see the first cut. Don usually makes the first cut and then we run it together and sit and play around with it, and then after he's picked any ideas he has off me, we kick it around, try it and see how it looks, and then tell the studio that's it.

Kaminsky: Let's talk about *Play Misty for Me* now. First, why did you stick with the particular song "Misty," since you had so much trouble getting it?

Eastwood: The problem with a new song would have been that you had to play it a lot in the film, and the way the script was designed, you couldn't play the song a lot. I couldn't use it as an underscore. The script was designed by Bob Daley and myself to have most of the music from a source. Now, I needed a song that was not so old that the present generation would say: Gee, I never heard of that. It had to be an old-new song, something that everyone from eighteen on would recognize. The studio wanted me to use "Strangers in the Night," which they own, but it's not a classic, though it was a hit, and there's that dooby-dooby-do at the end. I just thought it wouldn't work. Also, it had already been used once in a movie, and I just didn't like the title "Strangers in the Night" for the movie. It was a square hit song, you know.

Kaminsky: Your relationship in the movie with the black d.j. was interesting. At one point, I thought you were going to take him into your confidence and get him to help you with your problem with the girl. The point when I realized this wouldn't happen was when you were sitting at the turntable talking to him while he was getting high in the dark, unseen—was that intentional?

Eastwood: No, though maybe I had underlying thoughts of it that way. I just thought that visually and emotionally it made more sense that the guy is contemplating out loud, he's got somebody to talk to. It was just so much better to take the other d.j. off than to cut back and forth. Dave, the character I play, just talks freely, thinks out loud. How do you do that when you're looking at somebody? The other guy is there and listening, but he won't help. Of course, he doesn't realize how serious the problem is, since Dave only takes him into his confidence to a certain degree. If he had taken him into his confidence more and been offered some profound advice, I would have brought the other guy into the scene more. Remember, Dave never tells the other guy any of the jazz about the suicide and homicide attempts.

Kaminsky: The only comment the friend makes as he leaves is a joke, a sexual innuendo: "He who lives by the sword, dies by the sword." You do pretty nearly die by the sword [or a knife, technically] in *Misty*.

Eastwood: Well, I wrote that line. I did it years ago. There was this friend of mine who was hung up over a chick and trying to get her an abortion, and he was asking me for advice on the telephone. I told him what I thought he should do, and then he said: He who lives by the sword shall die by the sword. And I incorporated it into the film.

Kaminsky: How did you come by that game business you did with Don Siegel in the bar scene?
Eastwood: It was made up by the writer, Dean Riesner. The moves were just improvised. I had brought in Dean Riesner, incidentally, to work with my role, which was a little soft in an earlier version. The character was apologizing to his girl for things, and he didn't pick up the other girl in the saloon. She picked him up. I just didn't think it was natural. I thought the problems with his girl friend needed some motivation, perhaps the fact that he gets hung up with a fan now and then—you know, d.j.'s in small towns are somewhat big fish in a small pond, and they do get a lot of activity. I thought it would be better if he thinks he's making a deal with the girl in the bar. Anyway, Riesner made up the game. It was certainly an interesting thing. The game does not exist in reality: it was just something Dave and the bartender made up to intrigue women to come over and watch.

Kaminsky: How did you come to choose Jessica Walter as the psychopath?
Eastwood: Over the studio's dead body. No, I was looking at film on different gals, and I was looking at this film *The Group*, a movie made in 1965, which happened to have in it about three girls who were being pushed by their agents for *Misty*. One was Jessica Walter. She was very good in that film. She plays a frigid gal who talks about sex but is really turned off—and she's with this German guy who's trying to put the make on her and she starts this turn-off, and he just hauls off and slaps the shit out of her. And the look on her face, the transition she makes, the story on her face made me want to get her. I talked to the studio and they named a couple of people who were more well-known, people they could get deals on because business was slow, and I said: I don't want deals, I just want someone who is right for the part. Jessica has certain characteristics as an actress that just made me have a hunch that she would be right. I thought she was very good in *Misty*.

Kaminsky: What was Dave's motivation for going in the door at the end after he sees the dead cop?
Eastwood: Well, I think the motivation is justified because the girl

friend is in there, and he thinks: Geez, if this is what happened to the cop, what has happened to this chick?

Kaminsky: When the maid is slashed up by the psychotic girl, I expected her to die. Why did you have her live?
Eastwood: Well, if she [Jessica Walter] had killed someone, it would have been just too much that she was released. We'd have to make up some other reason for her getting on the loose again, and we just preferred release to, say, escape. Things like that do happen: there was a case in Palo Alto where a guy went up to a door and just stabbed the girl who answered. She lived, he was put away for treatment for about six months, then released, and the girl was not told. One day he accidentally ran into her at a supermarket, and she really freaked out.

Kaminsky: It's interesting that the psychotic girl has no background.
Eastwood: I was advised by lots of people to put in background, but you know, we in the audience meet her the same time the protagonist meets her, and we see her unfold as he does. I didn't see any reason for a scene in which we find out that the mother treated her wrong, the father ran off, etc. When a person finds out that someone is screwed up, knifing maids and things, unless he's very interested in psychiatry he's not interested in why she's screwed up; he just wants to get out. I think that audiences are smarter than a lot of producers think they are, and I think the audience will draw with you.

Kaminsky: Did you want to feel that the protagonist was somehow being paid back for his selfish sexual behavior in the past by being stuck with her?
Eastwood: No, I don't think he's being chastised by divine scrutiny. It's just that he's been in some situations, and just when he tries to straighten his life, this comes as a sort of ironic thing. He probably could have handled the situation better if this other girl hadn't come back just at that time. The problems for him are complicated by the one showing up all the time when he wants to be with the other girl.

Kaminsky: Did you purposely hold off on your physical confrontations with Jessica Walter? The only physically violent thing you do is hit her once, near the end, and of course it works, because the audience is so worked up against her too.
Eastwood: At the sneak preview, guys in the audience were saying:

"Hit her, hit her." They were also with it throughout, saying things like: "Don't go in that door." That's very satisfying, but, yes, to answer the question, that's just the final thing. Here she is, she's killed a cop and is working him over—I mean, this is it.

Play Misty for Me was taken from a true story. The suicide attempt, the cutting up of the clothes, the attempt on Dave's life during the night all were taken from actual incidents (not the knifing of the maid, though, or the killing of the cop or the becoming roommates with the girl). The roommate part was stimulated by the fact that the woman in the real series of incidents would dress up, put on wigs, and go into saloons where the guy was drinking and keep an eye on him and see if he was trying to pick up someone.

Kaminsky: Was this a story you knew or read or what?
Eastwood: Jo Heims, who wrote the story, worked it up, fictionalizing it. What appealed to me about the script is that there are incidents like this in everyone's life, to some degree, this whole thing of interpretation of commitment, or misinterpretation of commitment. A girl may say: Sure, I feel the same way; I don't want any part of marriage. But then next week, slowly, there's that kind of throwing a blanket over a person.

Kaminsky: The constriction comes through very well.
Eastwood: It's a very important part of the film, because that's the thing that makes it personal to the audience as opposed to just a horror movie. If you've had any kind of experience in your life where somebody has just tried to move in too fast, or has just held on too hard; I think everybody has had something like that. It's something that could happen.

Kaminsky: Yes, a psychological distortion of something we all feel.
Eastwood: A lot of times, with stories about psychotic people, there's no identification factor. In a picture like *Psycho*, the real highlights of the film are strictly the shock and the suspense. It was of course fabulous to have that scene where she sees the skeleton in the basement, but then they almost destroyed everything later with all that unnecessary exposition. Of course, that was eleven years ago, and they used more exposition then.

Kaminsky: Obviously your picture will be compared to *Psycho*, and you yourself have just made one comparison. Were you thinking of comparisons when you made the film?

Eastwood: No, I certainly wasn't trying to duplicate *Psycho* in any way. I never saw it that way myself, other than the attacks. Those attacks could be sprung upon the audience with the same kind of suspense and energy as Hitchcock used, I thought, but other than that, I saw it as a story of constriction, the blanket thrown over one, the things we talked about before, the bound-in feeling, the frustration of trying to solve it and not being able to, of having to sit down and calm the person you want to escape from.

No exposition after that is necessary. I heard one person say that he thought the explanation about Tony Perkins by the psychiatrist at the end of *Psycho* was because they didn't want to make it seem like the lead had any homosexual motivation. Nowadays you wouldn't care.

Kaminsky: The cutting in and out of the seascape and cliffs, which sort of work into the end—were they part of the original conception?
Eastwood: Well, L.A. has a hundred disc jockeys and stations. So, in the first place, I know that area where we shot. I live up there, and I knew a disc jockey up there. Disc jockeys know everybody in a small town. They're big stars in their areas. So here's a guy who is quite successful working for a small station in a small town, and he has ambitions to do television and better things, and this is all destroyed because of this relationship, too.

Kaminsky: What about the seascapes, specifically? In editing, you keep coming back to sea, birds, and cliffs.
Eastwood: It's just because the sea is so much a part of the whole thing, not just because it was the place of the conclusion of her life [Jessica Walter].

Kaminsky: The movie contains two breaks. First, when Jessica Walter goes to the hospital, there is that love sequence with the other girl, followed by the jazz-festival sequence. Both, I assume, are used to show passage of time, yet both go on longer than would be necessary just to show passage of time. Was it that you liked the sequences, or were you trying to make us forget about the mentally disturbed girl, or what?
Eastwood: A little of both. The real motive was temporarily to take us away from Evelyn [Jessica Walter]. People were also suggesting that the part of the other girl, Tobie, needed strengthening and there should be some sort of love scene. Well, I hated the idea of a dialogue sort of love scene, bullshit dialogue, and I was trying to look for a visual way to show

life was really falling into place for these two people. I heard this song, "The First Time," going to work one day, on this FM station, and I said: God, that just tells the whole story, so I went out and bought the song, not just the song but the whole record and just took the master tape and played it, and I edited the scene to that, because I thought it told the whole story. There was nothing else around, no human life, aircraft, automobiles, etc. in that sequence. It showed that things were really working well for them. That was the only non-source music I used. Then we went to the jazz festival and back into his profession with a little bit of music, music which was more into the rhythm of the film, and then I figured: boom, I could go back to the station and the phone call. Bingo, here's this little fairy tale with a wrench stuck in the wheels.

Kaminsky: There's one shot in there which is one of the most beautiful I've ever seen, and that is the orange-ish sea with the sun going down. But as far as plot in those two sequences, all we know is that Dave's girl has a new roommate.
Eastwood: Well, it's just a thing that grates on the guy. It was a very tough thing to set up that roommate thing without setting up so much that you tip it off. If you talk too much about it, you tip it off. So there has to be a first discussion of it, and then you meet one of them, and then there is the jazz festival, which is the last time roommates are mentioned. I had to do that in a very brief way. I don't doubt that a good percentage of the audience did guess what would happen.

Kaminsky: I think the normal reaction is that when Tobie calls to the roommate and says, "Annabelle," what you expect is nobody to come out because Evelyn has killed Annabelle, but this isn't what happens. Evelyn walks out and is accepted as Annabelle.
Eastwood: Yes, that's when everybody starts lighting up their cigarettes.

Kaminsky: I came into the movie cold, not knowing what it was about. Do you think that publicity and word of mouth will hurt the picture, and did you think of this in making the movie? The critics of course will screw things up too by giving away the plot and direction.
Eastwood: Yes, I have to hope that there's just enough entertainment value there regardless. If it is effective, even if they know what is going to happen, people will stay with it.

Kaminsky: *Psycho* is an example of this: everybody knows what will happen, and it's exciting anyway.
Eastwood: Yes, the first thing everyone talks about is the shower sequence.

Kaminsky: I was watching your knifing scenes closely, and you actually show a couple of slashes, unlike *Psycho*, though the feeling of revulsion and pain is similar.
Eastwood: Well, I just preferred to make it a little more . . . maybe I'm not as subtle as Hitchcock is.

Kaminsky: How long did it take you to make the film?
Eastwood: We shot it in four and a half weeks. We had a five-week schedule. We were two and a half days under schedule.

Kaminsky: Would you say it was expensive or inexpensive?
Eastwood: Inexpensive. We shot it completely away from the studio, 100 percent natural locations. We just rented houses, moved in, and shot. We rented a house for Dave, for example, and decorated it some, because there was stuff that had to be carved up and broken. Bob Daley is a very sharp guy on costs, and he didn't let too many false charges stack up. The studio would have liked it to have been even more expensive, but we were trying to prove something: that we could make something of entertainment value without exorbitant fees tacked on. I did have complete freedom on the picture, so if it doesn't work, it's my fault, and that's fine. I was given a chance to fail or do it right.

Kaminsky: Do you do what Don tries: go for a usable take the first time?
Eastwood: Well, I do rehearse. I use a different technique than Don, a Video West technique. We used Panavision equipment, which goes through the same lens as the camera, and I can go back and look at the scene afterwards. Jerry Lewis uses a similar method, a TV camera which goes parallel with the movie camera. My method is superior in that even the focus is the same, so even if the focus operator misses the shot, you can see it. It's black and white, but you can see how the scene will be set up. It's terrific on zoom shots.

Kaminsky: I also noticed that you use a lot of the people that Don Siegel uses, for example Carl Pingitore was your editor, Dean Riesner your writer, Bruce Surtees your cameraman.

Eastwood: Well, as far as Bruce goes, I'd worked with him three times as an operator, and Don and I promoted him for *The Beguiled*, which he did, but even before he did *The Beguiled*, Bruce was set for *Misty*: we had talked about it and he'd read the story.

Kaminsky: You directed several sequences of *Dirty Harry*. Was that your first real experience of directing?

Eastwood: No, I had directed *Misty* first and also a short subject on Don Siegel. Actually, I can't take as much credit for directing the latter. The editor/writer was more or less the brains behind the thing. I thought it was pretty good. We slapped it together in about a day. Had to use still pictures and everything.

The reviews of *Play Misty for Me* were among the best Eastwood had received as an actor, and his debut as a director was generally admired, though there were strong dissenters.

Andrew Sarris in *The Village Voice* called the film "a surprisingly auspicious directorial debut for Clint Eastwood . . . one of the most effectively scary movies of this or any year."

Joseph Gelmis said in *Newsday*: "Eastwood's first crack at directing is remarkably effective. . . . Throughout, Eastwood resists overreaching [and] keeps his cool very nicely on both sides of the camera."

Most critics did complain about the idyllic sequence in which Eastwood and Miss Mills roamed about to the music of "The First Time Ever I Saw Your Face." Ironically, the song, which was several years old at the time, became a top hit of 1971 and 1972 after *Play Misty for Me* reintroduced it.

Eastwood Direction

Richard Thompson and Tim Hunter / 1976–77

Published as "Clint Eastwood, Auteur" in *Film Comment* 14, no. 1 (January/February 1978): 24–32. Reprinted by permission of the authors.

(This interview was conducted in the summer of 1976 and in December 1977. Jack Shafer generously contributed key suggestions. Dick Guttman arranged the interviews. The authors are grateful to both.)

Q: How did you start directing?
A: I first got interested when I was doing *Rawhide*. We were shooting a stampede on location, three thousand head of cattle, and I was riding right in the middle of it, dust flying, really dramatic looking. I went to the director and said, "Look, give me a camera. There's some great stuff in there that you're not getting because you're way out here on the periphery." I got all kinds of static about union problems. As usual, everybody's afraid to try something new. Finally, they threw me a bone: I directed some trailers. I was so disappointed with the whole damn thing that I let it drop.

Q: What made directing so important to you?
A: It's a natural progression, if you're interested in films. The overall concept of a film was more important to me than just acting. I'd done second unit work for Don Siegel and enjoyed it—not so I'd want to do it in every picture, but whenever one came along that stuck in my mind when I read it.

Q: You have a remarkable sense of your own material, more objective than most stars have.
A: You mean: which ones to act in?

Q: To act in, and which ones of those to direct yourself in.
A: Just instinct. If I thought about it too long, I'd probably change my mind and do something wrong. I try to think about it in terms of the end, not in terms of the character I play. Hopefully, the story takes over and brings you into it, as you want it to do for the audience. If I have a virtue, it's decisiveness: I make decisions very fast, right or wrong.

Q: Do you get your shots with few takes?
A: I'm always trying to get it on the first take—a Don Siegel technique. After directing awhile, you get an instinct about it, but you have to be able to trust your own feelings. Invariably, two-thirds of the way through a film, you say, "Jeezus, is this a pile of crap! What did I ever see in it in the first place?" You have to shut off your brain and forge ahead, because by that time you're getting so brainwashed. Once I commit myself to a film I commit myself to that ending, whatever the motivations and conclusions are.

Q: Do you have a main flaw as a director?
A: Tons of 'em, probably. Sometimes I slough myself too much when I'm acting a scene. It's difficult to make the changeover from directing the scene to stepping into it as an actor.

Q: You're at the center of the challenge to the hero in this decade: what do you think about heroes?
A: I was one of the people who took the hero further away from the white hat. In *A Fistful of Dollars*, you didn't know who was the hero till a quarter of the way through the film, and then you weren't sure; you figured he was the protagonist, but only because everybody else was crappier than he was. I like the way heroes are now. I like them with strengths, weaknesses, lack of virtue . . .

Q: And humor?
A: Yeah. And a touch of cynicism at times. In the old days, with Hays Office rules, you never drew until drawn upon. But if some guy is trying to kill the character I'm playing, I shoot 'em in the back.

Q: Pauline Kael has tossed you some antimacho barbs.
A: Well, she's out of line there. Some of the points she made I agree with, about the changes of movies over the years, and Vietnam. She goes on and on about the need for showing the weaknesses of men, and that's

all right—there's a place for that. But why isn't there a place for escaping into the era of some would-be person you'd like to have the ingenuity of?

She's obsessed by something else; you see it in the films she likes. I've talked with her about it. Her image is being outspoken, so she has to be outspoken about something. She picked macho-ism, because that's the name of the moment. In the sixties, it was racism; who knows what it'll be next. It doesn't bother me, because my films don't do any less well because of what she's talking about. *Josey Wales* will outgross *Nashville*.

Q: John Milius claimed Pauline Kael was in love with him because she kept talking about him all the time.
A: Oh, I said that. Just for laughs, I called a psychiatrist and read him the article. He said, "That's what you call 'reaction formation,' a defense mechanism. She wants to fuck you." And I said, "I don't believe that." And he said, "Well, it may not be the case, but it's fun to think about, anyway."

Q: Macho is very much under fire now.
A: Oh, yeah. The way Jack Nicholson plays the guy in *Cuckoo's Nest*: Super macho. One of the guys she praises—and he's terrific in it. It's the style. She'll go on to something else in a couple months. In a year or two, everybody'll look back and say, "God, sure wish we had one of those films again." Obviously, I'm not like those characters. I'm not shooting people down in the streets.

Q: What's left for that hero now?
A: I don't know. Take Josey: unlike the High Plains Drifter or those other characters who come and go, picking up their vengeance or motivation along the way, you see what makes him the way he is, gradually growing. But I don't think of it in terms of the hero—I think of it in terms of person. He *becomes* heroic, as heroic as I've presented him to be.

Q: Anthony Mann said that the audience liked to see someone accomplish something; they didn't like to see someone fail.
A: I think that's true. The one picture I failed in was *The Beguiled*. It was good for me personally, critically well-received, but it was very poor for the company that spent the money to produce it. Maybe it couldn't have been successful, because the hero failed. He tried to do everything through the back door. He wasn't such a bad person; he was just trying to exist. It showed the sicknesses of war, and what war does to people.

I think people still like the guy who accomplishes. I just think that nowadays they want him to accomplish it in a different way, maybe not so pseudo-virtuous, if there is such a word.

Play Misty for Me (1971), Eastwood's first film as director, shows a remarkable sense of place, an eye for interesting interior design—especially modern—and an ability to fix characters through visual description of an environment. His talent for tailoring landscape to fit a film's mood and theme is unsurpassed among recent American directors. His films are also superbly paced: unhurried; cool; and giving a strong sense of real time, regardless of the speed of the narrative.

Eastwood's pictures come from the male point of view, but this very one-sidedness gives them a certain truth and conviction beyond politics. Of all his films, *Play Misty for Me* best reveals Eastwood's need to test and compromise his own image, pushing it toward the limit of personal honor.

The movement of the plot is simple: as Eastwood tries to win back *fair lady* Donna Mills (a woman with whom he can be satisfied without putting out a lot of emotion), spurned *dark lady* Jessica Walter goes crazier and crazier, finally plotting to kill him. Eastwood sees the story as being about "misinterpretation of commitment," and his character as essentially victimized—but *Play Misty for Me* works on darker levels.

Walter is the exact opposite of Eastwood: impulsive where he is controlled, passionate where he is complacent. Consequently, we admire her a little, sensing some justice in her attack at the base of his self-satisfied life. She is nearly his alter-ego, a projection of his suppressed furies and fear of love—a pull toward death and self-destruction that he must battle and exorcise within himself. In this sense, *Play Misty* is a companion piece to Siegel's *The Beguiled* (in which the anti-hero surrenders to dark passion and does die). They are Eastwood's two sexual meditations; both films show women archetypically as Innocent or as Corruptor. In *Play Misty for Me*, violence is equated with sex, and women with life (pulling man out of his isolation) or death. The film plugs into the main stream of the male American romantic tradition and exerts a fascination well beyond the limits of the plot. If *Play Misty* benefits from these subconscious implications, it is finally satisfying because Walter is such a wonderful villainess: a personal devil for Eastwood to fight equalled only by Andy Robinson's prime psycho in Siegel's *Dirty Harry*. Regarding alter egos, one remembers how that film and its ad campaign stressed the similarities between hero and villain; in *Play Misty for Me*, as in all his films, good triumphs in the fight with evil—but rarely has the devil lived so close to home. —R.T. & T.H.

Q: You can work with a fine range of directors. How do you pick the films you want to direct?
A: I had optioned *Play Misty for Me* as a treatment. It was written by [Jo Heims,] a gal I knew in the old days when she was just a secretary and I was an actor. I couldn't sell it. Couldn't get UA to do it: David Picker didn't think it was commercial. Tried Gordon Stulberg, at CBS-Studio Center; tried Fox, who said, "No, we're doing something too much like this with Liza Minnelli"—which I didn't see was like it at all, but that was their reason. I went away, lost the option, and forgot about it. Somewhere in there, Universal bought it.

Then I started thinking about what had happened to it. But I didn't know any directors particularly; Don Siegel was busy. Anybody could have done it, with a lot of different concepts. It was a small enough picture, small cast, not overly difficult—not like starting out with a massive thing.

So I went to Universal and told them I'd like to develop this picture and act in it. Then I went to Don Siegel and said, "I have a pretty good idea of what I want to do with this; I want to direct it. What's your advice?" He said, "Yeah, do it, I'll sign your DGA card." I told Universal—I had a three-picture deal with them—and they said, "OK, if you'll do it for nothing." So I said OK. As it turned out, they're paying more than if they'd hired me at straight salary, because the film did all right.

Q: When you knew you were going to direct it, how did you prepare?
A: I worked on the script: I got Dean Riesner, a guy I'd worked with before. I wasn't going to get a big name cast: without overhead costs, the picture was only about $740,000, maybe a little more. I came in quite a bit under that. I compared all the shots in my mind, laid everything out, made notes to myself, looked at film, cast Jessica—the key role—cast the other people, went to the jazz festival and got permission to shoot at no cost. Just normal preparation, following logical sequence. Coming from acting to directing, you're used to working on a set with lots of people, whereas writers or editors turning director are used to working by themselves. Gives me an edge on problem solving.

Q: Interesting that you optioned *Misty* so long before you made it; what was it about the story you related to?

A: The idea of suffocation. I'd seen a lot of psychotic films, like *Psycho*. But if you think of *Psycho*, you never think of its story. You think about the tremendous scenes: where Marty Balsam got it on the stairway, or Janet Leigh in the shower. If you ask people about the plot line, they have a hard time telling it.

This was an opportunity to do a film that had that kind of element and at the same time a story which everyone knows—it's not polarized one sexual way or another; it could be man against woman or woman against man—about suffocation, that misinterpretation of commitment. One person's casually dating the other, who's saying, "Forever and ever." I thought a lot of people would identify with that. It happened to me when I was younger, not quite to that degree. This girl who wrote it took it from a real person. That person didn't commit homicide, but did everything else that was in the picture plus other things. She'd dress up in wigs, disguise herself, and go to saloons hoping this guy'd walk in so she could catch him with another gal. She cut all his clothes up in the closet. Really insane things.

Q: Did studio people tell you it wouldn't go because it was so uncharacteristic for you at the time?
A: The studio first said, "Who the hell wants to see Clint Eastwood play a DJ?" I said, "Who the hell wants to see him play anything? It just seems like a good idea to me." They said, "Why would you want to do a part in a picture where the woman has the best part?" "I don't give a crap," I said; "I'll look out for me. The guy is the subject of what's going on, so what difference does it make?"

Q: The scene in the outdoor restaurant, when she comes in and makes trouble, totally blew my mind. Until then, you know it's rational, it can be solved by communication; that's the scene where you think, "Oh, Christ, she's never gonna let him out."
A: You just can't believe it. The guy I played couldn't, and the audience couldn't believe there were people that far off. That combination made an interesting idea for me to tackle, plus I thought I could do the film all on location without ever setting foot in the studio, which I didn't.

Q: How did you pick jazz arranger Dee Barton for the music?
A: I just happened to hear him and ask him if he'd like to interpret some old music that MCA owned—we had to use all their standards in order to get by, budget-wise; the only big expense was paying for Errol Garner.

I had to fight Universal on that too. They wanted to call the film *Strangers in the Night*, because they owned that tune. But it had already been used in a film [*A Man Could Get Killed*], and it hadn't been a success then. I needed a standard that bridged several generations. I didn't want to use "Stardust": it goes too far back and doesn't hit the newer generations. I finally crammed "Misty" down their throats.

Q: Did you go through a formal process like storyboarding for *Play Misty*?
A: I just have the shots down, marking in my script what I want. The only board I have is the scheduling board of the assistant director's.

Q: About visual composition. Do you draw sketches?
A: I have a pretty good idea what I want, but it always has to adjust to what's happening. Sometimes you get out there and say, "Jesus, the light's lousy," and you want to change it around the other direction to get it backlit. There's a million different reasons why you might have to change it. So I go out and line it up in my mind, just looking around to get the general idea. Then if an actor has a hangup about moving to that side, I can adjust. I've found that if you explain to the actors what you're trying to do, you never have any problem with anybody. I keep them abreast of what I'm trying to accomplish as a movie.

The real inspiration of *High Plains Drifter* (1973) is its conception of the town, a sparkling clean main street that looks as much like a new condominium in Northern California as it does the movie western towns of the past. This town, built on an oasis-like lake in the middle of a scorched desert, ably serves the allegory of the film. Both it and Eastwood's man-with-no-name hero appear completely cut off from the world.

This is Eastwood's best revenge picture, and the most skillful thing about it is that we never really know why he's taking revenge, even after the picture's over. The people in the town are so corrupt, though—worthy of Brecht and Weill's *Mahagonny*—that one can take special pleasure watching Eastwood get most of them killed. The overtones of Sodom and Gomorrah are deliberate, as is the devil quality of Eastwood's anti-hero—not to mention the film's homage to Japanese ghost-revenge melodramas.

The contrast of dark brown interiors and blinding white light exteriors added to the strikingly different look of the town, gives *High Plains Drifter* a stylized visual originality that goes beyond the expressionistic CinemaScope shots influenced by Sergio Leone and Don Siegel. The pacing casually makes the most of the action. Of all the films he's directed, *High Plains* has the best stylization of violence, with a laconic shooting from a bathtub especially memorable. —R.T. & T.H.

Q: When *Breezy* came out, I was booking a college film society. Picking up prints at a Universal exchange one day, the people there told me how much they loved the film and how pissed off they were at the head office for not pushing it. I don't know if you knew the little people were behind you.
A: I knew it—you could just tell. That's one of the reasons I'm not at Universal for every picture. They didn't push *Play Misty* either, but it took off in spite of them. I'd get calls from execs saying, "Goddamn, that picture's doing well." I'd say, "Why shouldn't it do well?" They'd say, "Well, I don't know, it isn't a western and you're not a cop." Their eyes were really channeled.

Q: Did the rep *Play Misty* built improve your bargaining position when you came around to direct a second picture?
A: Yeah, on the second picture they left me completely alone. But it was a western, *High Plains Drifter*. They argued with me very little. Their first suggestion was that we make it on the back lot—they always do, because Universal owns the back lot. With smog. So I say, "Nope, we're gonna go away and build this very inexpensive western town, looking sparse." So Ferris Webster [Eastwood's house editor] and I went up to Mono Lake and did it, even did initial editing there; we did final editing back in L.A.

Q: Did you know then that *High Plains* would be the second film you'd direct?
A: No. That came to Universal as a nine-page treatment called *Mesa* or something. I made a deal with Ernest Tidyman to make a script out of it.
  I wanted to get an off-look to it rather than a conventional western look. It was written for a typical, middle-of-the-desert, Monument Valley town. I was trying to find someplace on the water: I looked at Lake Powell, Pyramid Lake, and Mono Lake. Mono Lake has a weird look to it, a lot of strange colors—never looks the same way twice during the day. And it has such a high saline content, nobody'll put a boat in it, so you don't have to worry about waterskiers in the background.
  I picked a spot up there and we built a little town, interiors, exteriors, all together. Shot the picture in five weeks.

Q: An abstract-looking town: no railroad, no industry, no reason for the town to be there.
A: Just that it's fresh water, and most towns would be on water as opposed to the conventional western where the town is out in the middle of someplace nobody'd want to live.

Q: People felt your film was an homage to Leone.
A: No, I don't think so. I didn't shoot it like he does; I used a different style. The character might resemble his hero.

Q: Did you work out the style ahead of time? What style did you want?
A: I just saw the film clearly. That's why I decided to direct it. I had two westerns in preparation at that time, *High Plains* and *Joe Kidd*. I didn't particularly like the story on *Joe Kidd*, so I let somebody else [John Sturges] direct it—it had some pretty good elements to it, but I didn't visualize it as strongly as *High Plains*. I visualized *High Plains* so strongly I figured I'd better do it, just to make sure; you hate to hire someone and then impose a total concept on them, it's not fair to them. I've found that out since then.

Q: Do you collect images, ideas for shots?
A: You mean prior to having a story? Sometimes. For instance, I was in a barn the other day, showing my kid a chicken ranch. There were chickens pecking away, zero space in between. I thought, God, what a great shot. I don't know what to do with it, but someday I'll need the shot and have to go into that chicken barn.

Q: *High Plains* reminds me of Japanese ghost-story films, particularly the way you leave the door open for that reading at the end, when the hero rides out of town and the midget sidekick asks him who he is. Did you ever make a decision in your own mind as to who he was?
A: Yeah, to me he was the brother. But I presented him . . . [trails off, pauses]. The way the whole town was, no children, kind of strange: it's a weird situation. As far as me justifying the role, he was the brother. But as far as the audience is concerned, if they want to draw him as something a little more than that, that's fine.

Breezy (1973) is the only film Eastwood has directed in which he didn't star; its commercial failure minimizes the possibility for another directing-only project. Following *High Plains Drifter*, *Breezy* is again an allegory, with Eastwood still concerned with the hypocrisies and failed values of middle-class society—in this case, L.A.'s idle *nouveau riche*. Directly, effortlessly, Eastwood conveys (and satirizes) the impotence of this *dolce vita* cocktail set, and this lack of equivocation gives his simple tender love story a special grace quite different from the cold new crop of romances released since *Breezy*.

Breezy has the biting, moralistic wit of this period in Eastwood's work; one feels that here, in *High Plains*, and in *Play Misty*, Eastwood enjoys stripping the mystique from the leisure class. *Breezy* evokes the spirit of his home ground, Carmel, more than it does the Laurel Canyon-Hollywood-West L.A. setting of the story. The use of the setting is rich. William Holden's elegant but lonely house—natural woods, rough boulder walls, indoor/outdoor jungle—is the perfect mirror of his soul in the balance. The *mise-en-scène* is so transparently simple, closest in style to *Play Misty for Me*, that *Breezy* overtly becomes an actor's showcase. Probably because he wasn't starring in the film, Eastwood gives freer rein to his sentimental streak; one of the many pleasures of the film is the degree of self-pity allowed the Holden character as well as the unabashed hippy corniness of Kay Lenz's Breezy. —R.T. & T.H.

Q: What attracted you to the story?
A: It was written by Jo Heims, who wrote *Play Misty*. She wrote the man and woman's characters so well I thought, I don't know if I'm going to act in it, but I'd sure like to make it. I liked the whole comment on the rejuvenation of a cynic, living around L.A., divorced, making good dough but hating it, then finding out about life through a seventeen-year-old. She teaches him more about it than he teaches her. It's a mutual exchange, but it doesn't go on forever and ever, and she doesn't die of some exotic disease. It's just deciding to exist and see what happens. What's wrong with existing?

Breezy was a big risk at the time, in the sense that I knew I was making it at Universal, who were doing me a favor in letting me make it. It wasn't an expensive film, so they didn't have that much to lose; but they didn't feel it was commercial, subject-wise. It cost $725,000 direct, then they tacked on the overhead. They're not very adept at promoting films, especially that kind. I think here, at Warner Bros., the film might have had a chance. When we four-walled the picture, it seemed to do well; word of mouth was good, people liked it. Universal was writing it off before they even released it, as they occasionally do.

Q: How was Holden?
A: Terrific. Technically very astute as an actor, he understood the role completely, so it was easy for him to play. After he'd signed for the part—I'd just met him—he told me, "You know, I've been this guy." And I said, "Yeah, I thought so." A lot of people have been this guy at one time or another in their lives. The actress, Kay Lenz, was young, so I had to work a little more with her. Holden was very, very gentle with her, even during the screen test. I tested ten gals, and he shot all the tests; most guys would say, "Get some kid." Holden's a snap.

Q: The scale of the production was perfect for the material—it's an actor's film.
A: It was. There's nothing in it to overshadow the people. The main thing for the director to do is set up an atmosphere to work in, move on, and keep everybody involved with the plot. Some scenes I'll rehearse quite a bit, if they're technically complicated, but others I'll improvise. Depends on the actor or actress, too: Jessica Walter liked to improvise and shoot the first take. The big advantage of film is that you can always reshoot it if it's wrong. But if it's just right in rehearsal and you didn't shoot that, you may not see it for awhile, six-eight-ten takes down the road, if ever. Through the years, I've seen too many good takes left on the rehearsal floor.

Q: Now, *The Eiger Sanction*: Did you get to do it with the condition that you would star in it?
A: The studio had it and they offered it to me. I said I'd try to make a script of it; then the agents couldn't agree on a price, so it went to another director. He couldn't get a script together either, and it came back to me.

When I began planning it, I went out climbing. When you get into mountain climbing, you realize there's just no room for a crew hanging around—literally no space on the mountainside. So I figured I had to at least do the climbing sequences.

I didn't totally visualize *Eiger Sanction*. It was difficult to place the way the story should be told—whether to go completely outlandish like James Bond, or to go for the middle line. There was tremendous room for the adventure part, which was the big challenge as far as I was concerned. I got wrapped up in wanting to be the first guy to shoot totally on the side of a mountain, not papier-mâché rocks—outside of documentaries, that is. We did everything, dangling two thousand feet over the first splatter.

Q: That's some shot where you fall into the frame and are jerked short by your safety rope.
A: We hung off the cliff and built a ladder out from it for the downshot. I had to cut myself loose. That was a psychologically damaging thing to do.

Q: Why psychologically?
A: It's just against your nature. You do it and for three days afterward, you're just staring off. You don't say much.

Part of Eastwood's strong appeal is that he seems too large for society. He embodies a dream: that a man can rise above the treadmill of bureaucracy and act on his own law. But the price of this independence is isolation. Eastwood's films often focus on this theme, as if to say that good can triumph in the world only when set apart from it.

Leone and Siegel nurtured Eastwood's image as a cutthroat anti-hero who could play dirtier than anyone as long as his motives justified his means. Treading the line between hero and devil in the characters he plays, Eastwood selects stories about bounty hunters, policemen, and revengers—all subjects where character motivation turns murky and paradoxical. With all moral values so compromised, Eastwood has only to maintain a tiny edge of purity so that the audience can identify with the self-righteousness that allows him to set himself above the rest of the world and act on his own predatory impulses. Regardless of director, the movement in all his best films is toward a dichotomy between the Eastwood character and, at the opposing pole, everybody else.

His recent films have moved toward softening this polarity, testing it through wider interaction with other characters and a continued belief in the potential of romance. From all indications, Phil Kaufman would have made a more sincerely communal *Josey Wales* than the one Eastwood finally made, one which would have incorporated Eastwood more completely into the whole. The crisis undoubtedly arose because Eastwood, conscious of "shorting" himself when he directs, felt he wasn't being covered well. The final version points up the standard dichotomy of his films even more than those which play off it more overtly. Close-ups of Eastwood as Josey Wales are less well blended into the style of the overall film than usual. An increasingly abstracted stylization of violence doesn't quite mesh with the theme of the film and its desire to be a tapestry or Breughel scene of the West. Despite a certain lack of tension, *Josey Wales* is an admirable attempt at broadening his scope and—no puns intended—the best thing about this visually sumptuous movie are the remarkable Panavision master shots, and an ease with the medium that gains in assurance as it looks for new challenges and directions in choice of subjects. —R.T. & T.H.

A: Every picture takes on its own style. I get into the film and then I get the look of it as it comes, rather than having a constant style that goes through each film, putting a mark on it. I think each picture should have its own mark.

Q: How did you become involved in *The Outlaw Josey Wales*?
A: This one was a book submitted to me. It was written by a Cherokee Indian who had never written a book before but who was a well-known poet in Indian circles. My associate, Bob Daley, was so taken by his cover letter that he took the book home to read and couldn't put it down. It was written in a very honest fashion. The character seems like he's destined to become a loser. It's an episodic kind of story. It just read beautifully—even the dialogue jumped off the page.

It's fun to do a saga-type film: introduce a lot of people . . . hope the audience will get to like them and miss 'em when they're gone. When the kid dies, I think people are genuinely lost for a minute, as the Wales character is, riding through the forest of vines and drizzle.

Q: How long did *Josey* take to shoot?
A: About eight and a half weeks. *Josey* was difficult in the sense that we shot in Utah, two different locations in Arizona, and in California—we had to move a lot on that one, 'cause it's a saga—you have to feel the travelling in the land.

Q: Playing against conventional expectation in scenes is a strategy throughout the film. For instance, when the bounty hunter comes through the door and you say, "Look, it doesn't have to be this way," and he goes back out the door.
A: That was all the book, very intelligently written. My favorite line in the movie is when one of the bounty hunters says, "Man's got to do *some-*

thing for a living these days," and Josey answers, "Dyin' ain't much of a living." He [Forrest Carter, the novelist] understands the guy completely.

A lot of guys have done Quantrill and the Missouri guerrillas on film, but nobody's ever done the Kansas Redlegs, who were a lot like carpet baggers. When the winning side of the war came, they were always seen as heroic, even though they were just as much renegades as Quantrill.

Q: As the director, you play yourself as actor down to give Chief Dan George the focus in quite a few scenes. He's very funny, wry.
A: Like when you think the Indian girl is Josey's, and then she and the Chief become involved instead. Our hero just keeps losing out all the way. Not that he wants to get involved; he even says, later in the picture, trouble just follows him. Chief was very good in those scenes.

When I read the book, I knew Chief Dan George was the only person to play that character. He's got a face you never get tired of looking at. You put a camera on it and you just can't do wrong. One minute he looks like a puppy dog and the next minute he looks like a very aristocratic king. Magnificent face. I love the last scene where he comes up to Josey; all he says is, "You're up kind of early," but he knows Josey is leaving, he reads the whole situation. A lot of pro actors can't move you that way. He gives you gold. He says the simplest thing and it sounds like an important statement; everything has importance.

(Sondra Locke, who played in the film, and was present during this part of the interview, said: "I was commenting on how I didn't have any dialogue in the film and Bruce Surtees [the cinematographer] said, 'Well, it's much better to be that way. You notice the Chief talks so slowly that you listen very closely to hear his next word, because you don't know when it's going to come. Same thing with you: if you don't talk, they'll be waiting for a word.'")

A: I did that for fourteen pictures, then finally I had to utter one and blew the whole thing.

Q: We understand that Phil Kaufman was set to direct and even began shooting *Josey*.
A: Yeah, he shot a week of it. He did marvelous work on the script. It was just a matter of how the shooting was going down, so I just took it over and re-shot stuff. I hated it; it was the worst moment of my life. I've never

fired anybody. It was just a disagreement. . . . He did some really good writing. I'd seen his first two films [*The Great Northfield Minnesota Raid* and *The White Dawn*] and thought he'd be terrific directing *Josey*; but it was larger, less documentary, and more episodic, a very difficult film for a person who's done a lot of films, much less a few. It was my fault: I should have prepared and done it myself, but after *Eiger*, I was kind of weak, mentally, and wanted to get somebody else to do it. Then, as I got into it, I began to visualize it differently.

Q: You've worked with Bruce Surtees, the cinematographer, on five films [*The Beguiled, Play Misty for Me, Dirty Harry, High Plains Drifter, The Outlaw Josey Wales*]; what made you use him on this one?
A: I used Surtees in this picture because his photography has a hard light effect and I wanted that. I wanted to backlight the whole movie; a lot of guys are afraid to do it.

Q: He'll shoot very dark, too; darker than most.
A: Yeah, I didn't want to pump light in the faces. That's the conventional thing to do, but I wanted to backlight it. It's very easy to do if you shoot in the fall. It's the best time to shoot a western: the sun stays low and you've got cross-light; it's not overhead and flat all the time.

Q: It takes the star quality out of the film when you can't see features—when faces aren't lit and made up for glamor.
A: You lean forward to get into them rather than having them bombarding out at you. I love that cross-lighting; in November, the sun stays low all the time, never really gets overhead. It rained every time I wanted it to—I willed it. Especially for the opening montage of the war, I didn't want any sunlight. It gives it a much more sombre effect. The first part of the film showed a kind of idyllic light; then all of a sudden it goes to a very sombre tone. Then it gradually gets to a nicer tone as his life gets better when he gets to the ranch and starts winning—going from a loser to a winner. That was the way it was planned, and fortunately The Head Gaffer Up Above stayed with us.

Q: We're struck by the boldness of your widescreen composition and your free-and-easy construction of sequences.
A: I felt good with it. It has a lot of scenes with two people, and then it has a lot of scenes with things going on in towns. The easiest thing is to shoot long shots and close-ups; the hard part is in between, the connec-

tive tissue. It's how you connect the scenes with the camera, how you tie it all up.

I shoot reverse masters: masters one way, masters the other way. Drives 'em crazy sometimes, but I like to flop between masters and not worry, where a lot of older directors are afraid to flop people from side to side in the frame; for them, everybody starts out on one side of the camera and they stay there, unless they cross during a shot. But I'll jump around, go through here, then go right through there, reverse this way, break the composition up. And in my coverage, there are the kind of mistakes that if you make on purpose are OK—if you make them *without* knowing it, you get yourself in a corner, painted in tight.

One of the most important things on this film, after it was all over, was the lab timing, which Spanky Surtees doesn't sit in on. I sit in on it with the lab to make sure that I have a very good timer. There are so many light changes between shots. You have to make the light change evenly and then balance it up. In the old days, guys like George Stevens would wait around a year till the light was perfect. I can't afford a year, wouldn't want a year. Nine weeks is OK, eight weeks is terrific, six weeks is even better 'cause I like to be moving.

Q: It seemed to us that the film in some ways is more democratic than your other films. You've tried to share it more with your other characters, although you are the main focus.
A: I know what I can do and what I can carry, I think; but at the same time, it's the ensemble and all that periphery—those little characters, even the ones that come and go, like the river rats—that make for a rich tapestry as opposed to just a quickie, where you do the plot and get out of it. I like the other people in *Josey Wales*.

Q: Also, more people save your life in this film than usual.
A: Exactly.

Eastwood has just directed *Gauntlet*, which is a Christmas release (as were *Dirty Harry*, *Magnum Force*, and *The Enforcer*). It's a couple-on-the-run, paranoid chase film. At $5 million—including overhead—it's his most expensive to date, and his most technically complex: $1.25 million for special effects. The cast includes Eastwood, Sondra Locke, Pat Hingle, and Bill McKinney.

Judging from the production stills, *Gauntlet* moves away from the elegant visual style—post-genre painting, with a bow to the Brandywine School—of *Josey Wales*, to locate itself within a contemporary L.A. art tendency involving kinetic, environmental, and event art ideas, in which domestic icons are transformed by barrage violence, a movement obviously taken from demolition derbies. The point of this sort of art is not to exhibit the finished object, but for the viewers to witness the progressive cruelty visited upon the subject until it is, indexically, finally exhausted of surface/textural potential to absorb any more. This process is preserved on film as the only significant record of the art work, as Tinguely's work has been, or that of many other event artists.

In *Gauntlet*, two of these events are:

1. Police surround a bungalow and lavish so many rounds on it that it implodes, leaving only a cubic yard of fresh barkdust (the idea that the house becomes its own negative space).

2. A Greyhound SceniCruiser runs a downtown Phoenix gauntlet of officers until it becomes a *Guinness Book of Records* item (how many heavy-caliber bullet holes can one bus contain?).

Eastwood was kind enough to take time out from preparing a release version of the film for the lab to discuss *Gauntlet* in a phone call; the film had not yet been screened.

Q: *Film Comment* wants to run the interview. They're gonna put your kisser on the cover.
A: Great balls of flame!

Q: Did you have Dean Riesner work over the script?
A: No. It was written by Dennis Shryack and Michael Butler. It was in very good shape. There was a minor amount of rewriting, a lot of it deletions; I did it myself.

A cop starts out to fly an extradited witness from Vegas back to Phoenix for trial. Everything goes wrong—there's this group of people who don't want him to get back. She's a hooker, and he's a cop who hates hookers, but they grow together as they go—via car, via foot, via motorcycle, via train, via bus, you name it. They're just on the run. It's a strong woman's role like in the old days, *It Happened One Night*. The gal stands up to the guy, and because of that, it makes both characters more interesting.

Q: Do they both live through the film?
A: Yeah, we both make it.

Q: You seem to avoid making the same type of film twice.
A: Right. This isn't like anything I've directed before. It's a detective story, but very unlike the [Dirty] Harry Callahan character. This guy, Ben Shockley, has the same determination as Harry, but he isn't as all-knowing. There's a vulnerability factor in *Gauntlet* that isn't there in the Callahan hero. Well, there is some in Callahan, very subtly.

Q: His grim commitment to victims and little people?
A: Yeah. There's a sadness about him, about his personal life, about his smart-alecky fight with the bureaucracy: that's a lot of fun, but there's a lot of sadness behind it, too.

Ben Shockley in *Gauntlet* is a guy who's never had the big cases Callahan's had. The big case is happening to him right during the movie; that's where they're different characters. Shockley fumbles through a few situations that Callahan would have handled much slicker.

What attracted me to the story was that it was a good relationship story. It's an action picture with a ton of action, but at the same time, great relationships. The girl's part is a terrific role, not just token window-dressing like in so many action films. Her part is equal to the male part, if not even more so. It's in *The African Queen* tradition: a love-hate thing that turns out to be a love story. It's a bawdy adventure, too.

Q: All your films have major women's roles, in which the hero-heroine relationship is used to define each character.
A: Good ladies' roles are always important; *Play Misty, Breezy* . . . it's a nice way to define characters.

Q: What did you want to emphasize about the characters?
A: There are little moments, gestures between them as they grow together, that become symbolic—but they're not overt gestures. He never goes to bed with her even though she plays a hooker, and that would have been the obvious thing to do. It's a relationship built on another plane. A cop who's had a lot of disappointments, never had a personal life that reached any heights—it becomes a very pure love affair, with great friendship, great regard for one another.

Q: Do they become partners in the fight for survival?
A: Yes. And they have this dream, very idealistic discussions of what their lives should be together. They go on this suicidal mission which

they don't think they're going to come out of; then, you don't know what they go on to—they could go their separate ways, you know.

Q: Do you consciously choose to protect certain private areas of your characters' lives from the audience?
A: Oh, sure, definitely. I do that consciously: it's much more interesting for the audience to write with you, to draw with you. In *High Plains Drifter*, they could draw in many endings. At the end of *Josey Wales*, who knows what's going to happen? The audience is rooting for him to go back, but you don't show him going back into the arms of the girl he's left. He's just riding off in that direction, into the sunrise rather than the sunset. Hopefully, it gives you the feeling. The audience is willing him to go back there. That's their participation.

Q: When you plan a film, how do you think about the place of the audience?
A: I think they must participate in every shot, in everything. I give them what I think is necessary to know, to progress through the story, but I don't lay out so much that it insults their intelligence. I try to give a certain amount to their imagination. I try to play straight across with the audience.

I don't like expository scenes, unless they have an important payoff. I hate to have the scene where you take a break, sit down, and tell the audience what's been done up to that point because they're not smart enough to understand it. That's playing down to the audience. As a rule, I always shy away from exposition.

Q: Do you have a dream film you'd like to direct, if you could do anything at all, no restrictions?
A: No. I wouldn't know it till I read it. I wish I had the talent to sit down and say, "I'll write this, and that, and that," but I can't do it.

Q: What is the gauntlet?
A: They run the gauntlet at the end. Their bus travels down through town and is just ripped to shreds. Hence the title.

Q: Is this the strategy of displacing violence against people with violence against expensive objects such as cars that television took up a few years ago?

A: Yeah. This isn't a terribly violent film in the sense of gruesome violence. There's a lot of action, but not a lot of killing per se.

Q: When you began planning *Gauntlet*, did you have a particular visual look you wanted?
A: Yeah, but it wasn't one I could compare with anything else. We had a lot of night shooting, and one thing I knew I didn't want was a lot of forced shooting. In the night sequence in the cave, when we weren't in light, I wanted the screen black—*real* black. With forcing, it's all grey: they low-key light, they force-develop, and then it all comes out milky.

Q: You've been spoiled by Bruce Surtees.
A: Yeah, he likes hard light. Frank Stanley, on the other hand, likes soft light, which is OK, and which worked well for a film like *Breezy*—I liked that look. For *Josey*, the hard light worked much better. I wanted it very natural, for the sets to be unlit looking.

When I build a film, I build a lot for the sound, too. I'm always conscious when I'm shooting of how it's going to sound. I'm not sitting around like a lab technician, saying "Oh God, the color's off, the light's too low, you're not going to be able to see enough of the scene, nobody'll know what it's about." Well, they're gonna hear and they're gonna feel it—there's a lot of other elements that are not limited to just photographing a blank shot. You always picture the end result while you're doing it.

Director Clint Eastwood: Attention to Detail and Involvement for the Audience

Ric Gentry / 1980

Published in *Millimeter*, December 1980, 127–33. Reprinted by permission.

"Making a good movie takes a good cast, a good story, and everything else," Eastwood begins. "But what it comes down to, whether it's going to be any good or not, is how disciplined you are in keeping the overall concept through the assembling. And it's tough to do because you look at the film over and over again, and you have to go back to your original instinct in making subsequent decisions."

And that's the primary reason Clint Eastwood likes to work fast once he begins a film, to minimize the duration between the "original instinct" and the final cut. The second reason is, of course, economic, and the combined momentum of both factors allows him to finish *every* project ahead of schedule and under budget. So an Eastwood budget is low—while the returns are extremely high. The comparatively scant $3.5 million needed to produce *Every Which Way but Loose*, for example, spawned over $87 million, and the $6.5 million for *Bronco Billy* has already made $28 million and still is rising, as it circulates to accolades overseas.

More than Eastwood's implicit box-office magnetism goes into the success of his work and his production company, Malpaso Films (recently Robert Daley Productions, for legal reasons). Cost-effective filmmaking is one part of it. The other is having a sense of what the public wants. "You have to trust your instincts to be in sync with the audience," he says.

Eastwood is largely an intuitive thinker, as that comment and his working methods might imply. When he directs a film or chooses a project to appear in, he has very firm "emotions"—not reasons—for knowing how to proceed. Working quickly keeps these emotions intact.

"Because half-way through every movie you always say to yourself, 'Gee, I wonder if I should do this?' or even, 'Do I like this?' But you have to grab yourself and say, 'No, this is what my first feelings were about it. I'm committed to this ending and this development of the story and I'm going to stick with it.' Because you're dealing in an emotional art, a visual medium which has its own logic, and so you're telling a story in a way that accords with that. Film is mostly an expression of how we feel and think. So if you sit and analyze *why* you're having these thoughts, then you're distancing yourself from the emotions. You just have to go with those first emotions."

When Eastwood reads a script he visualizes it, both in terms of shots and composition. But pre-eminent is the *mood* gleaned from the material, the overall sensuous texture of environments and movements that have implicit emotional resonances. Thus, he does not transfer his impressions into a shooting script, an intermediary repository of those impressions which could tempt a reconsideration of the mental pictures, while intricately plotting them.

Instead, Eastwood first seeks a confirmation of the mood, or the nearest approximation of it, in an appropriate location. It is no coincidence, then, that one of his salient features as a director is his penchant for landscape, the widest concentricity of a dramatic center. Moreover, his intimate knowledge of the topographical United States, particularly the West, contributes to his distinction as a director of certified American tastes.

"I scout locations in different ways," he explains. "*High Plains Drifter* I scouted by myself, just me and a pick-up truck, hauling around through Oregon and back down through Nevada and California . . . But you have to find spots that read into the story. Sometimes you just have to keep looking because there's always a million other places you could do a picture, some maybe better, some maybe not. The location just has to correspond with the concept of the film, to the atmosphere created by the story."

For *Play Misty for Me*, his first film as a director in 1971, Eastwood chose the irregular and diverse territory of Carmel and Monterey, California, the area near his home, to suit the unstable psychology of the characters. In *The Outlaw Josey Wales* (1975), it was northern Arizona and southern Utah that communicated the sombre, sometimes Gothic tones of the post–Civil War saga. For *Bronco Billy* (1980), the story of a modern-day Wild West Show entrepreneur, his most recent directorial venture, he situated the production in Idaho for several reasons.

"It was written for Oklahoma or Kansas," he explains, "but if you're familiar with that area you know everything's the same. And I'd been through Boise, Idaho, and Ontario, Oregon, that area, and up in the mountains nearby while vacationing in McColl. As I drove through it, going through the eastern Oregon plains, there, which were only a few miles away, I saw that it was the same kind of country as middle America. And then with the mountains nearby, I chose Boise as the central location because it gave us a lot of variation within a few miles. Though it was West, it could have been anywhere in middle America, the plains of Kansas or Illinois or Oklahoma."

Boise was first of all practical, enabling the backdrops to change as they needed to change to conjure the wayfaring of the traveling show. But another reason was thematic, for the open spaces reflect the protagonist's need for freedom, Billy's escape from the one-room tenement in New Jersey where in an earlier life he was a discontented shoe salesman.

Another crucial factor in establishing mood for Eastwood is, of course, cinematography. But unlike most directors, he does not choose a cinematographer for a specific style, but rather an able and creative technician who is as adaptable as Eastwood is as a director. "I try to get the cinematographer involved with the story, I tell him what I want to accomplish and try to convey a feeling for what I think it should look like, because the style grows out of the material, and so the style changes really with each picture."

Consequently, Eastwood will keep the same cinematographer for several films. David Worth for example, who shot the lush, sometimes piquant colors for *Bronco Billy*, is reportedly doing something much different for *Any Which Way You Can*, the sequel to *Every Which Way but Loose* (to be released shortly) which Buddy Van Horn is directing.

An even better example is perhaps Eastwood's five-film relationship with Bruce Surtees, which produced some extraordinary visual diversities and innovations, all of which marry the cinematography to the respective stories with such distinction that no two even resemble each other. *The Beguiled*, directed by Don Siegel with Eastwood in the lead, is composed of almost Expressionistic distortions of color, with red the overriding tint. In *Dirty Harry*, another Siegel film, Surtees strips the look of all stylization to better view the harsh realism of the story.

It is with *Josey Wales*, however, that Eastwood and Surtees teamed up to do some of their most imaginative work. "Bruce came up with a suggestion that I thought was very innovative," Eastwood recalls. "At that time they were going to stop manufacturing a certain film stock, a much slower stock than is used presently. We were scheduled to begin shooting in the fall of the year, which is a great time to shoot a Western because the sun stays low in the sky, though you do run the risk of an early winter setting in. But Bruce said, 'Why don't we use this slow stock? We'll have to use a little more light for certain scenes, but for outdoors it gets richer blacks. The only trouble is they're running out of it.'

"Now, I love rich blacks in a film. I can't stand it when the blacks go grey and come out milky. In fact, I worked with one cinematographer who wanted to force everything, but I didn't have the patience for the way the blacks would curdle and go milky. But Bruce doesn't do that. He has a hard light effect and I wanted to backlight the whole movie. He knew what I liked, the blacks and the contrast, and he wanted to use this stock. So I said, 'OK, let's buy up enough stock to use for this picture.' So we did." They bought the stock they needed and stored it in the basement of Eastwood's office on the Burbank lot. "It was the last of the old speed," he says. "If you were to duplicate that look now, you'd have to do it through an entirely different technique."

But there was still another problem on *Josey Wales*. "We got to the final sequence of the picture and the scene was to be shot at dawn, the scene where Josey has his final encounter with the Cherokee chief (Chief Dan George) before he rides off at sunrise. Bruce said, 'Maybe we should just shoot it in portions, do a piece of it at dawn every day.' And I said, 'That's just prohibitive. In the first place, when I'm in a sequence I want to stay in sequence. And secondly, I don't have that much to fill up the rest of the day.' So I said, 'Here's what I want you to do. I've never seen a film shot day-for-night that looked like night. At best, it looked like dawn. So I want you to shoot that sequence as if you were shooting it for night, just like a day-for-night sequence, and it'll come out dawn.' So that's the way we did it."

Similarly, Eastwood shot another scene, where Josey has a final confrontation with the bounty hunter who's been pursuing him throughout the film, "at sunset as if it were sunrise. At sunset you get that very heavy cross light and it was like the first light of the day. I just did it out of order, so the sun would be at a certain angle at a certain time, which is very tricky and requires preparation because it happens so fast and the shadows get longer rather than shorter."

Another practical habit Eastwood has is to designate scenes that require bad weather and then withhold them until they actually happen—breaking the continuity of the shooting schedule at that point to accommodate the inclemency. For *Bronco Billy* there is a scene early in the film where rain is needed to bolster the humor and the pathos of an argument Billy has with his five cohorts in the show, along the roadside in the middle of nowhere. "All along I wanted to play with this rain sequence," he recalls, "and on that day it was just colder than a well-digger's ass. Every actor in the scene was just praying that he wasn't going to be the one to forget his lines so we'd have to start over. But we shot it real quick, with one camera, moving from set-up to set-up as fast as we could.

"I laid it out, shot by shot, as a cover set, as you would normally on a day for rain, setting it aside so that when it did rain we could shoot the scene. It was raining, but very lightly, and we added to it from a creek we found nearby in order to have it pouring. We just went and threw a lot of water on it, but the light was consistent because it really was an overcast day, so the lighting is flat. It was wet in depth. The highways were slick in the distance and not just wet around the camera. Everything worked to our advantage that way. And it's a good position to be in, to have a sequence where you want bad weather, because inevitably you get some. We just continued along until it looked like a storm was brewing."

Once the mood is established, Eastwood works extensively with the script, "until you see the total picture, and all the perspectives of the character." In *The Gauntlet* he rewrote several scenes, and in *Bronco Billy* he added an entire sequence. Wearing his sharpshooter six guns, Billy is in line to cash what is surely a meagre check when two masked men suddenly enter to hold up the bank. One of them knocks over a little boy who drops his own savings to the floor. And it's then that Billy takes action, preventing the robbery and becoming an instant local hero.

"I felt the script needed that because of the sequence later on where the sheriff humiliates Billy when he's trying to bail his friend out of jail. Because the sheriff taunts him about who's quicker on the trigger, you've got to know that Billy can be very cool and quick-witted and good with the guns so that the audience is really rooting for Billy to blow the sheriff away. It's important that he doesn't, though, because he's more interested in his friend than in his own pride at that point. To be more commercial, you would have had him draw on the sheriff. But as far as the statement of the movie goes, it wasn't appropriate. Clint Eastwood fans are maybe saying, 'Yeah, take 'im out.' But in terms of the statement, what that scene has a lot to do with, loyalty and sacrifice, Billy couldn't do that. The main thing he had to do, no matter how the sheriff humiliated him, was to get his friend out of jail."

More often than not, however, Eastwood subtracts from the script rather than adds. One of the primary strategies of his films is to minimize the background information about the characters and to let gesture transmit the nature of the character to the audience. The less revealed, he contends, the greater is the participation of the audience. The technique originated with his creation of "The Man with No Name" in the Sergio Leone film *A Fistful of Dollars*, the film that gained Eastwood his international status.

"Originally it was written with just pages of dialogue," he points out, "all of it explaining the background of the character. But I wanted to play it with an economy of dialogue and to build a whole feeling through attitude and movements. So I said to Sergio, 'Let's keep the mystery of the character and just allude to what happened in the past.' Sergio argued with me, though he did agree in a way, but it was just much harder for the Italian mentality to accept. They're just used to so much more exposition and I was throwing that out. Finally he accepted it, but then the producers thought something was really awry. They said, 'Christ, this guy isn't doing anything. He isn't saying anything. He doesn't even have a name! And that cigar is just sitting there burning.' They just didn't know what the hell was going on. But when they saw it all assembled, they realized what it was, and then how it went over on the public. The 'No Name' guy soon became a very imitated character."

And the mystique transfers to narrative structure, for just as all but the most pertinent exposition is deleted, so is the final destiny of Eastwood's characters. The action finishes, the dramatic elements are resolved, but there is still the sense of the protagonist still at large. "I like to leave them that way," he says, "still in the process of finding their way. You're not ending with a person's demise and you're not telling a life story. It's the nature of films maybe. In a Scott Fitzgerald novel you might do an entire life span, almost start with a flashback and then bring it up to the present and proceed from there. But these movies are really incidents. *Dirty Harry* was just an incident in one man's life. *Josey Wales* is more of a saga, covering a longer period, but you felt that he was going back to the group he collected along the way."

Eastwood recalls an argument he had with his editor regarding the open-ended conclusion of *Josey Wales*. "He felt that I should literally show him returning to the girl and the group after he has that final talk with the chief. And I said, 'No, you don't need to show him going back. You see him riding off at sunrise and that's enough.' He said, 'Yeah, but how will the audience know that he's going back to the girl and the others?' And I said, 'Because they're *willing* him to go back there. The audience is taking him back there.' It's the audience's imagination and participation that makes a film work. You don't have to tell them everything."

Perhaps the most vivid demonstration of excluding expository material to heighten audience participation is *High Plains Drifter*. The film begins with one of Eastwood's most dazzling visual flourishes. A lone rider emerges from the desert through a dance of lights and haze that, through the use of an extreme telephoto lens and the mirage-effect of the wavering heat, renders the impression that he is gliding through the sky. It is the virtual arrival of an Apocalyptic Horseman. As he reaches the isolated town of Lago, he gradually subjugates the populace to his authority and finally wreaks havoc upon them for reasons we never really learn. The Drifter then leaves as mysteriously as he arrived, crossing the desert once more and disappearing.

"It was originally written that the Drifter was the brother of the murdered sheriff, but I played it as if it could have been some apparition. You're not quite sure, but you know that he has a strong interest in making this town suffer for their sins and that it ties in with their complacency with the murder. But the only clue is when the Drifter lies down (later in the hotel) and has this dream of the sheriff being whipped to death, and you know from there that he's tied in some way, but you're not sure how. That way you keep the mystique and the whole atmosphere is mysterious. To me, if the Drifter comes to town and immediately says, 'I'm the brother of the murdered sheriff,' right away you draw the conclusions. Instead, once he takes the town and humiliates them through his own methods, you're asking, '*Who* is he? *Why* is he doing this?'

"The traditional way of doing it," Eastwood continues, "was to just lay everything out. You know, right away, as the guy rides into town—using the Western as an example, but it could be any kind of film—he rides into town and sees a man beating a horse. He interferes with it, punches the guy out, so you know immediately that's the antagonist with whom the hero is going to resolve a conflict later on. Then he sees the school marm on the porch and she gives him a stare or whatever, and you also know that they're going to be romantically involved. And you can almost draw the ending right there, in the first five minutes. The audience should never be able to anticipate that far ahead where it's going, because otherwise they sit there waiting for the movie to catch up with them."

High Plains Drifter, basically a morality play, also benefits considerably, if not definitively, by the location, the Mono Lake district of northeastern California. The story was originally situated in Monument Valley, the grandiose site of so many John Ford films, but, Eastwood says, "that wouldn't have provided the same mood I got from the story. I needed a place that would correspond with that mood and Mono Lake is what I finally found. It's a dead lake. It has some very interesting outcroppings and the colors almost change moment by moment, so it gave the film an elusive quality.

"The visuals at the beginning were to set up the mood of the rider. I took a piece of the heat wave out of the corner of the shot and blew it up so it was the same texture in the whole frame. As it was initially, I couldn't get back far enough with the lens to get the rider out of sight, so I just started with a blank screen and dissolved through it. With the heat wave you don't notice the dissolve. Things like that just set the tone for the film, but from the very beginning I saw the film very clearly. It was the reason I decided to direct it."

Again working with Bruce Surtees, Eastwood shot *Drifter* with unusually wide apertures to intensify the outdoor brightness, so that everything in the town appears visibly scorched by the light, almost flaming. (And the effect precipitates the later incident when the Drifter coerces the people to paint their whole town red and re-title it "Hell.") By contrast, the interiors are composed of deep browns, sienna, and burnt orange, with a proclivity for underexposure to render a sense of decay.

Eastwood describes the difficulties—and the importance—of establishing a continual spatial relationship between the indoors and the outdoors, and vice-versa. "It was part of the elusiveness again, because you never felt stable with what you saw. The colors changed, the clouds changed, and the exposures jumped at you. In one instance we started with the Drifter in the saloon, a very dark room, and then had him walk out the door into the light, so there's a huge exposure change. As you get to the front door you have to start changing it for the outside or you just get a giant flare. It's not unusual, but it was a bit tricky, and in the film it worked quite effectively."

In addition to narrative vacancies and character distillations, Eastwood also strives to include the audience within a complete use of space to focus on the action. He has no compunction about breaking the 180° rule for camera placement, a visual stylistic that only Japanese directors are really comparable to. "I'm not afraid to reverse master shots, to shoot on both sides of the actors. A lot of older, more traditional directors would never do it. For them, the camera stays on one side of the actors in a scene unless they cross during a shot. But I like to break up the composition. I think you involve the audience more by changing perspective freely, not binding them to their seats that way. One reason I like location shooting is that you don't have to worry which side of the actors you're on at any point, and are not limited to a set, which dictates where the camera goes."

And he does fully exploit the advantages of being on location, availing himself of stimulations in the environment and improvising when inspired. In *Bronco Billy*, the pivotal moment in the film involves a scene where Billy decides to single-handedly rob a diesel train. The absurdity is self-evident as the train goes roaring by and Billy gives chase, but the moment is not only the culmination of his frustrations with the struggling Wild West show, it's also the clearest example of his commitment to the romantic ethos of his cowboy fantasies. So the scene itself, as Eastwood suggests, had to be very carefully constructed and sufficiently understated. "It can be very dangerous in a scene like that," he says, "because if it isn't done correctly, you can just blow the whole momentum of the picture." The scene had to make you laugh and evoke your sympathies at the same time.

But instead of playing it safe, Eastwood added something which more than summarized the thematic intentions while it jolted our perspective of the scene. It occurred to him about a half-hour before he did it. "What happened was that it was cold outside," he explains. "It was real sunny, but it was real cold. I was on the train with the extras and I saw this little kid, a kind of extroverted little guy and his mother was sitting there. He was asking her a lot of questions and I started thinking that I should get a point of view from the train. So I just made up this little deal. I said, 'You just look out there when I come riding up, and say "Cowboys and Indians."' So I got him real excited about it and then had the mother take the opposite tack, of 'Uh, yeah, OK,' as if she's hardly paying him any attention. But it just gave the ultimate irony to the whole thing, because his imagination is going wild just like Billy's. They're both intrigued by this thing with the Old West because, after all, Billy's like a kid himself."

It has been suggested by Sondra Locke, now in her fifth film with Eastwood, that in directing actors, he communicates motive for character through the position and angle of the camera rather than through effusive verbal cues. "I'll let the actors create their own roles," he says, "find what it is in the material that means something to them, what connects for them emotionally. Casting, though, is already a designation of character. And I've worked with almost all these people before, so I know what they can do.

"But camerawork is like penmanship; there is as much expressed in the way you write as in what you write about. And so the camera works *with* the actors for a cumulative effect. The camera is not a neutral eye, and the actors aren't the whole scene either." What is the scene more than anything else is the moment of its articulation, when the whirr of the camera heightens the activity like adrenalin, and the long nurtured sense for mood is brought into focus with the greatest discrimination.

"I think that directing a film is *seeing* it, when you see it there live, when it's happening right there in front of you. The guy walks in and then the girl walks in and the scene just goes, right at the first instance of the first take. A lot of times it's a shock. You say, 'Jesus, that worked terrific.' But you have to be able to say, 'That's what I want,' and walk away. And if it's not working, you have to work until it *does* happen, even if it's the tenth time. But if it works immediately, you've got to have enough wherewithal to say, 'That's it. That's good. That's what I want.' You have to have the picture there in your mind before you make it. And if you don't, you're not a director, you're a guesser."

Significantly, Eastwood's films are extremely well paced—unrushed, relaxed—with a strong sense for real time, regardless of the force of the action or the speed of the narrative. He ascribes much of this to the "proper punctuation" of scenes during the cutting, but it would also suggest a faithfulness to the rhythm of things as they were experienced during the shooting—so that the editing is in accord, not manipulative of the moment of visual record.

Obviously, style is a result of technical mastery, the implicit use of the elements of production to cohere with one's vision of the material. Eastwood was never content to express himself solely as an actor, and as a regular on the TV series *Rawhide* some twenty years ago, he strove to increase his creative contribution. The channels proved limited, however, and the most he was permitted to direct were some trailers. But working on the show from week to week gave him the opportunity to acquaint himself with the technology and then to think *with* the director, weighing his decisions and considering his strategies. "I would always ask myself, 'How would I do it?' If it was something impractical I would make a point of never getting myself into that position, but rather than second guessing, just disagreeing with what he was doing, I tried to come up with a viable alternative, a real solution and not just a complaint.

"But I think you pick things up from people just as you pick up your own ideas as you go along. I've always said that you learn something from almost everybody you work with—every director, actor, or actress, you always learn something. They do something particularly interesting or well that you've never seen before and you always remember it. And on the other side of the scale, you see a director do something that impresses you negatively and you always remember that too. You think, 'Shit, don't ever do that.'"

Eastwood is specifically critical of directors who are either hyper-meticulous in their methods or, for lack of decisiveness and therefore virtually without methods, those who repeat a single set-up to the exhaustion of the actors and the energy of the film. Furthermore, such counter-productive habits, which he sees advancing to epidemic proportions today, skyrocket costs and infringe on the potential for other features. "Anybody can make a film if you shoot forty or fifty takes on everything. If you run off enough footage you can put all that together and get something out of it. But whether it's any good or not, has any soul to it, is another thing again. It's like firing a shotgun. You can hit a lot more things with that than you can with a rifle, but it takes a lot less skill and it has a lot less impact.

"There was a thing in the *Hollywood Reporter* recently, in that regular feature they run about things happening forty years ago on this date, that just shows you the irony implicit with all these guys doing all these takes and exposing a million feet of film per picture. It said that John Ford had just finished *The Grapes of Wrath* and he had exposed the least amount of film for a feature up to that time, which was something like 37,000 feet. Now here's a guy who makes a classic, that people want to see forever. Long after the man's dead people will be running it, for years and years, and he did it with a record low of exposed film for that time, and that's because Ford knew exactly what he wanted and knew when he had it. He didn't go out there for six or eight months or a year and do fifty takes on everything. When he saw the prints that he liked he went off to the next thing. . . . *The Grapes of Wrath* had tremendous energy and it's a classic on every score. What makes you think you're going to make any more of a classic by exposing fifty times the amount of film he did? It just doesn't make any sense."

Another way that Eastwood facilitates the celerity and economy of the production is to have a crew that is compatible with quick decisions and set-up changes. "You have to be able to move and have everybody move with you," he says. "But most of the people I work with are in sync with it." He has worked with virtually the same crew for the last five films. Moreover, and no doubt recalling his years as a stifled talent on *Rawhide*, Eastwood is highly receptive to their suggestions on the set. In fact, all the outward signs of either authority or star status are removed in order to encourage camaraderie and equality. There are no director's chairs, no extravagant preferential treatment for the actors, nor any exclusive cliques to stratify the community, which a full production unit implicitly comprises.

"It's definitely a democracy," says Eastwood. "If I have any qualities that work as a director, it's that I try to stimulate everybody to be as creative as they possibly can. I like them to contribute to the film and not just do their jobs by rote. It makes for a better atmosphere and ultimately for a better film. If I come in and play big shot and say, 'This is the way I want it and you guys just do this. You do the slate. You run the sound. And I don't want to hear anything but what I tell you,' I mean, that's so shortsighted. I think that's what a lot of people think auteur directing is. But there's no such thing as 'auteur' in my mind. It's an ensemble. Somebody leads the ensemble, there's a lieutenant to the platoon or something, but that doesn't mean all the other people aren't being innovative. Rather than just having them pick up a brick and laying it in, they're all being creative with the design in a certain way. And as long as that doesn't deviate too far, that's great, because I turn down as many suggestions as I accept, but I do take some good ones." And similarly, no one in the industry can be said to have provided so many new talents with opportunities to advance their careers. Michael Cimino, Philip Kaufman, Bruce Surtees, John Milius, writer Jo Heims, David Worth, and numerous others from within his own production ranks have benefited from Eastwood's trust and encouragement. Veteran stunt coordinator Buddy Van Horn is making his debut as a director on the upcoming *Any Which Way You Can*, a step forward that led to other offers before the film was even started.

But all of this coincides with Eastwood's philosophy of choosing roles and material for himself. "You've got to take chances. You've just got to. If I don't take chances, then I don't deserve to be where I am to some degree because what's the point of getting into a position where you can make certain films and not make others? I could sit and go through scripts and say, 'Now that's not commercial,' or 'That's not what I built as an image.' When I went to make *Every Which Way but Loose*, my agent, my attorney, and a lot of people were against it. They said, 'This isn't Clint Eastwood.' And I said, 'What do you mean it isn't me? None of these other guys are me either.' There are elements maybe, but you do it for different reasons. You can do a picture with the idea of doing it for straight entertainment, but then, I've proven I can make pictures that make a buck here and there. But there's other things I've got to prove in my life, too, just to myself as a person, to make comments that are of other natures." He even goes on to say that he would consider projects adverse to his own political position or of highly controversial nature if they offered both a relevant alternative to a public issue and a generally accessible story.

"You've got to keep stretching out and trying other stuff," he adds. "I could have chosen a lot of scripts that were different than *Bronco Billy*, that were less of a challenge. But *Bronco Billy* was just worth trying. If it doesn't work, it doesn't work, but it's worth trying." The receipts on *Billy*, one of Eastwood's most unusual and complex films, would certainly indicate that it does work. But more than that, the plethora of critical writing that the film has inspired would also suggest that it's a film that will be looked at for a long time to come.

"I hope so," he concluded. "It's really gratifying to make a film like *Josey Wales* or *High Plains Drifter*, that people have a long-range interest in. I get a whole lot of cinema groups who want to talk about those films. And I really enjoy that, when they want to come back and go into it years down the line, to learn what made it tick and how it evolved. It means you did something right. But you've got to trust yourself, trust your instincts."

Eastwood: An Auteur to Reckon With

Charles Champlin / 1981

Published in *Los Angeles Times*, January 18, 1981. Copyright © 1981. Los Angeles Times. Reprinted with Permission.

Success begets power, but power does not necessarily beget more success in turn, or corporate life would be very dull. The question of what the successful will do with their powers is somehow more suspenseful in the movies than anywhere else because the answers are so visible—ponderous failures or daring and imaginative leaps to further success.

Clint Eastwood, in his deceptively low-keyed and laid-back way, has used the star power generated initially in other people's pictures to build an independent production company with a success record that is probably second to none in its return on investment.

By electing to do what he wants to do, Eastwood has, it turns out, done exactly what his public wants him to do, sometimes confounding his critics, the local man included.

Having been a laconic man of action, he became a good-hearted slapstick man of action, feeding second-banana lines to an orangutan in *Every Which Way but Loose*, a loose-jointed farce the public clasped to its bosom in a frenzy of pleasure. In last year's *Bronco Billy*, he took the comedy a long step further and played a sweet-hearted and gentle idealist, a man so in love with the heroic myth of the West and a man of such goodness that he would not even seek revenge on the corrupt and nasty sheriff who had humiliated him.

By an irony that did not escape Eastwood for a minute, it was the critics, who had previously been as eager to scoff as to praise, who now embraced *Bronco Billy* in a frenzy of admiration. It was the customers who initially weren't so sure (possibly put off by an artful but ambiguous ad campaign). But virtue triumphed in the end and *Bronco Billy* has done nice, steady business ($15 million gross domestically so far) and is, Eastwood calculates, safely into profit.

Any Which Way You Can, the sequel to *Every Which Way but Loose*, is one of a handful of runaway box-office successes of year-end. At last count it had taken in something more than $50 million at the box office. It is the same Eastwood, but a new and younger orangutan. "Two years in the life of an orangutan is a lot," Eastwood said the other day. The original had grown as if aspiring to be King Kong, no longer pal-sized.

The script of *Every Which Way but Loose* had been around for a long time, rejected by everyone, Eastwood says. The script itself was dog-eared and food-stained. "Most sane men were skeptical about it; there were conflicts about it in my own group. They said it was dangerous. They said it's not *you*. I said, it *is* me. Nothing on the screen yet has been me. It's a left-handed compliment when people say, 'That's him.' If you make people think that, you've done a lot."

Bronco Billy came in over the transom on a friend's recommendation, not from an agent. Eastwood was going to send it back to writer Dennis Hackin but was caught by the title, glanced at a couple of pages and couldn't put it down.

"My first thought was that Frank Capra or Preston Sturges might have done it in their heyday. It had some values that were interesting to explore in contrast to the sixties, Vietnam and Watergate and so on.

"Here was a guy who was a loser but who wouldn't acknowledge it and who was a holdout against cynicism. It wasn't old-fashioned but in a way it was.

"The guy was fun to play because he had to be stripped bare of all his dignity, like the character in *It's a Wonderful Life*, to make the transition and end up all right."

There was nervousness, not to say dissension, within the ranks of Eastwood's Malpaso Co. about *Bronco Billy*, particularly about the unavenged humiliation.

"I knew it wasn't a commercial attempt," Eastwood says. "There were suggestions we add more action and some sex, but I stuck to the writer's intent. If that's what we had to do to be a slam-bang commercial success, I didn't want to. I don't have to prove my commercial value at this point in my career. I didn't pay off the bad sheriff. I suppose a 'normal' Clint Eastwood picture would have."

If the budget had been $12 million, Eastwood admits, that would have been another matter; he is not a spendthrift with his own money or anyone else's. But he brought *Bronco Billy* in for a dirt-cheap, by present standards, $5 million.

"When I started directing in 1970, whoever would've said $5 million would be a very modest budget?" he asks.

The spiraling cost cycle, however, is one Eastwood has seen before. Watching *Paint Your Wagon* swell to $20 million as far back as 1969, Eastwood decided it needn't be and started his Malpaso production company to do it more efficiently.

"*Bronco*," Eastwood says, "wasn't hard or expensive to make in this day of overblown budgets and jaded regard for the financiers. I always think, what would Jack Warner say in this situation? You can say what you will, those guys watched the store, and they pulled the plug when it ought to be pulled. I'm told that the production costs get out of hand because some of the executives know other things but not film making. What I ask is, if they don't know film making, what is their function?"

Eastwood keeps Malpaso small and loose. "Nobody looks at you sideways if you make a suggestion or argue about a point. Just tell the truth is all I ask."

He has developed a sort of repertory company of supporting players, like the marvelous veteran Scatman Crothers who played the ringmaster in *Bronco Billy* and who entertained the crowd extras in Boise so Eastwood could film reaction shots. Geoffrey Lewis, another expert farceur, is also an Eastwood regular, and Sondra Locke is Eastwood's costar onstage and off.

What Eastwood would most like to do now is another Western. His *The Outlaw Josey Wales* seems to have been the last really successful Western—excepting, perhaps, *Blazing Saddles*, which was a bit off-trail as Westerns go. The recent fate of Westerns is not encouraging, but then again they have not had Eastwood and they have not had the mythic quality that classic Westerns have had and that Eastwood as the laconic loner carries with him like a saddle blanket.

But if the Western is alive in his mind (a script is being developed, one of three projects he has in the works), Dirty Harry is dead.

"I'm not sure what you could do with Dirty Harry now," Eastwood says. "I don't know where else to take him. You could do one for commercial satisfaction, maybe, not for personal satisfaction. That's why I'd like to do a Western; I'd love the challenge of people saying you can't do it."

One of Eastwood's first acting jobs was as one of the flyers in William

Wellman's *Lafayette Escadrille* (Tab Hunter and Tom Laughlin were others). His regret, as an intense lifelong film buff, is that he didn't get to work with Raoul Walsh, King Vidor, William Wyler and other great directors. "I came along just a bit too late," he says.

His own career, he has no doubt, will ultimately be as a director. He directed *Play Misty for Me* and had a grand time. "One of the executives at Universal said, 'Who the hell wants to see you play a disc jockey?' I said, 'Who the hell wants to see me play anything?'" Eastwood liked the double duty and says, "I was talking to George Lucas about some things the other day and I know he does not like directing. He said that just before *Star Wars* he was thinking of getting out of that part of it altogether. But I kinda thrive on it. It leaves you zapped, but it's worth it."

Now Eastwood has had the honor of a retrospective tribute at the Museum of Modern Art. "Usually it's some great Yugoslav director. This time it was a commercial, or sometimes commercial, director. And it was *Bronco* that pushed them over the hill into doing it."

A young audience one afternoon went crazy over *Misty*, Eastwood reports. "Those kids analyze everything we took for granted in our day. They can dazzle you with their information and their questions. They can also read in more than there is there, as the critics did on *Dirty Harry*. But the young people are into movies, and that's something."

Eastwood learned directing from watching, reading about and then working with masters, of whom Don Siegel in Eastwood's book is one. "Other directors will say, let's try it once. Don always said, 'I'm never trying for the second time. I'm always trying to make it right the first time.' De Sica would say cut in the middle of a speech. He had enough; he knew what he needed. He'd say, I'll allow you a little lead-in when we do the other shot."

Not long ago, in a "Forty Years Ago" column, Eastwood read that John Ford had shot just 36,000 feet of film on *The Grapes of Wrath*, an astonishingly small amount. "I then thought about the two million feet Mike Cimino did on *Heaven's Gate*. I gave Mike his first feature chance on *Thunderbolt and Lightfoot* and I thought he did a very good job. But one's a director, the other's a guesser."

Eastwood plays his hunches about what he wants to do and what he thinks will work and enjoys the power to play the hunches, but he is not a guesser and in his quiet way he has become an auteur to reckon with.

Cop on a Hot *Tightrope*

David Thomson / 1984

Published in *Film Comment* 20, no. 5 (September/October 1984): 64–73. Reprinted by permission of the author.

Clint Eastwood keeps the same old bungalow at Warners, with subdued light and brown décor, where he can stretch out on a sofa in a T-shirt, jeans, and sneakers, yarning away for a couple of hours about doing his movies. It's all kept at an amiable, easy-going, unpretentious, and unalarming level—hey, come on in, let's talk. Yet Eastwood is more likely to extend that invitation to Norman Mailer than to *Time* or *Newsweek*. In the last two years, Clint was covered by Mailer for *Parade*, and he was the subject of a lengthy article in the *New York Review of Books*. Something in the long, lean loner hankers after respectability.

You don't have to look too far ahead to see him getting an Oscar for overall career excellence, or even the AFI's Life Achievement Award. Meanwhile he has to get along with being the most famous and successful movie star of the last twenty years. There is word at Warners, coaxed out of the discreet woodwork by Joe Hyams, an executive "with special responsibility for keeping Clint happy," that $800 million in rentals have come in on Clint's name since *The Outlaw Josey Wales*. Eastwood is too cool to be counting, though there are stories of him putting on his spectacles at the end of every day to go through the books ("Make my day—show me an error").

And if counting counts, then you'd have to add in the Universal period (with *Dirty Harry, High Plains Drifter, Play Misty for Me*, and *Thunderbolt and Lightfoot*) plus the spaghetti Westerns (and Clint had ten percent of *The Good, the Bad and the Ugly*), not to mention the durability of his films on TV reruns and his newfound supremacy on video-cassette. Nearly all of his work has been done for his company, Malpaso, meaning "bad step—like if it looks like you're going to trip over something."

57

Eastwood has always explained Malpaso as a way of making his own mistakes. But it has been the knife to cut out a fat share of the rentals.

What is he like?

Let Norman Mailer answer that, in the talking-to-himself format of his *Parade* article:

"Do you like him?

"You have to. On first meeting, he's one of the nicest people you ever met. But I can't say I know him well. We talked a couple of times and had a meal together. I liked him. I think you'd have to be around for a year before you saw his ugly side, assuming he has one.

"It would take that long?

"Well, he's very laid-back. If you don't bother him, he will never bother you. In that sense, he is like the characters he plays in his films."

Mailer needs heroes. I think disillusion might come a little quicker, like 364 days quicker. You *have* to like Eastwood: he has Magnum charm, he is very impressive physically—as he nears fifty-five, the beauty hardens; it is edged with frost now, instead of suntan. He is very natural, very strong; his mind is very made up. You don't have to be too imaginative to see the rock against which some of your questions break. It is startling and intimidating when an actor has so little need of your love, and not much softened if he still wants your respect.

Eastwood runs a small, tight unit at Malpaso, and I doubt if there are too many screw-ups or too much Latin tolerance for them. Over the years, there have been reports of his regular gang, headed by producers Bob Daley and Fritz Manes, looking at new young directors as if to say "Prove yourself." It is equally legendary that Eastwood does not rehearse and favors first takes—all of which contribute toward the economy of his operation (*Honkytonk Man* was shot in five weeks for $2 million in below-the-line costs).

The most evident streak of Eastwood's hardness, and his greatest limitation as a screen presence, is his unwillingness to push beyond his own gut reactions. If it felt right to Clint, a director might have a tough time going for more takes. Moreover, his briskness onscreen sometimes imparts a feeling that he is not bothering to think too much about a moment or a situation, but just wants to get it done. Equally, the famous narrowing of the eyes, the hiss of the voice—call it intensity or sudden impact—is a mode that fends off subtlety as surely as the squelching one-liners. Eastwood *can* be ironic about his act, but he keeps going back to it.

Whether from boredom, recklessness, creativity, or the insolence of confidence, he keeps on testing the limits of his own antiheroism. *Bronco Billy* and *Honkytonk Man* were considerable extensions of the self-mockery that emerged in *Josey Wales* and the orangutan pictures. They showed Clint as a self-destructive fraud, and *Honkytonk Man* proved his greatest failure as well as the spur to *Sudden Impact*, which reconfirmed him as number one to all those who want number ones. All of that aside, he is still the most interesting tycoon in Hollywood today, still hidden after all these years.

The penchant for taking risks perseveres. While he has his eye on the box-office target this December with *City Heat*, with Burt Reynolds (originally a Blake Edwards project reassigned to Richard Benjamin after Eastwood stepped in), Eastwood did a dark variation on Dirty Harry Callahan in *Tightrope*, released in August. It was a hit-and-miss movie, made too fast and too sketchily for the good of its own material. Written and directed by Richard Tuggle (who wrote *Escape from Alcatraz*), *Tightrope* is often disturbing. No other big star, I think, would have risked it. For it's about a New Orleans cop on the track of a sex killer who is himself subject to many of the same contorted, violent urges that might make a man lately divorced (like Eastwood) into such a killer. Moreover, the role of the cop's eldest daughter, played by Alison Eastwood, is one of the most ambiguous things in its stripping of a star persona.

Tightrope may have shocked some Eastwood purists. It could have frightened anyone, and with a more searching script and a greater readiness to explore its characters' depths, it could have been far better— along the lines of *In a Lonely Place*. Eastwood's problem could be that the comfort of keeping the Malpaso gang around doesn't stretch him enough. He has made remarkable excursions into vulnerability. But the pictures are put together in such a sure-fire mood of confidence and efficiency, Eastwood is kept from the rawness of his characters. It would require a very forceful director, and very good material, but Eastwood could play a greater range than he has ever attempted, even without the slightly brutal detachment that he maintains toward his films. He is a cautious conservative, but Harry Callahan is a hero in whom our fantasies about lone sufficiency turn into psychosis—not really that far from Gary Gilmore in *The Executioner's Song*, a role Mailer realized Eastwood was made for.

Q: What do you think happens to the central character, Wes Block, in *Tightrope* after the film ends?
A: Well, you can draw in lots of little subplots. But I assume he continues

his relationship with this girl [Genevieve Bujold]. She's the first woman that he has felt something more than just a passing, sexual night kind of thing, like he comes across so many times, in the seamy atmosphere of his work as a New Orleans police officer. I think he wants the stability. And hopefully he can soothe the trauma in his two daughters and go on with someone in a normal life.

Q: Was Wes involved with prostitutes during his first marriage? Could that have had anything to do with the break-up?
A: It might have, but he states in the script that he never had those kinds of friends until just after his wife left. I think the marriage disappointed him a lot. I think he placed a lot of himself emotionally in the marriage. And when it went sour—for whatever reasons—he became very disappointed and he just reached out to whatever's around. Being in the type of work he was in, he ran across a lot of bizarre ladies.

Q: But he has feelings for them that are perverse or strange. And clearly there is a moment in the film where he wonders whether he could be a sex killer. And there are even moments where you're not totally sure he isn't the killer.
A: We definitely wanted that. I stressed that even more in the film than in the screenplay. But I always liked that aspect: is this guy, or isn't he? How does he fit in? I even looped the lines of the actor who played the killer at the beginning, though I changed the voice slightly. Not that I wanted to play all the roles, but I just wanted a little bit of the thing, "Is that Eastwood? Is that him?" You can tell it isn't me, but on the other hand there's just enough familiarity to tie in with the shoes and just kinda getting it going that way. And then later on, when you know it isn't him . . .

Q: . . . You also know it could have been.
A: Yes. It could very well have been him, and even his thoughts about the cop when he talks about him one time, it's like, "This guy is as screwed up as I am." Who knows what happens? He's got involved with enough of these gals that maybe he felt like it.

Q: I'm sure the audience will say, "Clint Eastwood couldn't be the villain." But I wonder to what extent Clint Eastwood is intrigued with teasing the audience? It's a brave film in a lot of ways. Some of your hardcore fans may be shocked.

A: The hardcore fans, I could just bombard them with the same kind of character for the rest of my career. But that wouldn't be as interesting. I think the more astute fans—I hope some of them are astute—will find this provocative. Because in contrast to the obsessed cop, Dirty Harry, Wes has these other emotions. Not just solving the thing he's obsessed about, and the inequities of the legal profession, the courts, and all that. He just does a job and does it the best he can, and he's got all these sideline characters.

Q: Did you think it would be brave or risky, compared with *Sudden Impact*?
A: Yeah. I think if on the surface you gave the studio these two, one in each hand, they'd say *Sudden Impact*. That's a lot of money. But I thought it was bold. If it's exciting and bold, that's fine; if it's bold and dull, that's another thing. Hopefully, those people who like suspense and action films will be intrigued by the climax . . . but along the way they're going to have to bear with this character.

Q: You've also let yourself look bleaker in this film than ever before.
A: Well, that didn't come out of any particular makeup or anything, it just came out of the attitude. It *should* look that way. If I sat there and thought, "What do I look like?" then I'm thinking about the wrong things. I've got to think of the character. You've got to donate yourself to the character. You can't say, "Jeez, will I look as sharp as I have in some films?" Like in *Honkytonk Man*, I'm playing a consumptive—like you're purposefully putting on a type of Kabuki makeup. But I don't usually wear makeup in films, so the character in *Tightrope* is just that way out of his feelings and attitudes.

Q: *Tightrope* is the most extreme case, but there have been others in recent years in which you might have been saying to your fans, "Well, don't fantasize about being Clint Eastwood too much. He gets old, he has personal problems, he doesn't conduct his life like Harry. He's beaten sometimes." How conscious are you of doing that with your fans?
A: Well, I don't know if I'm conscious of doing it. I think it evolves out of love for the story. The story's given to me, and I like the character and feel it's a challenge. I can't just do—regardless of some fans—the mysterious kind of character who has everything under control. That's fun to play, but I've done it a lot. I'll do it again, probably, but I have to broaden the scope.

But it's been successful. Everybody in the world advised me against doing *Every Which Way but Loose*. They said, "That isn't a Clint Eastwood film: the girl dumps you, you give up the fight, and you've got this silly orangutan," that sort of thing. I said, "Yeah, but it's kinda interesting." It's comedic, and yet it's different. And if I hadn't felt in a broadening mood, I might have said, "Yeah, you're right, that isn't me. I'd better do another Harry, or a cowboy." Which is fun—I like to do that. But you have to broaden out.

Sometimes it doesn't work. *The Beguiled*, years ago, wasn't a success. It disappointed people. It was unfortunately sold to appeal to people who liked another kind of Clint Eastwood. *Tightrope*, I hope, will sustain the fans—because he does win out at the end—but it's a tougher win for him than it is for Dirty Harry. This guy isn't inept, he's just more vulnerable. His personal life has affected him more.

Q: Did you want the *Dirty Harry* admirers to think again about him? I wondered how far the obsessiveness in the Harry character has to do with him having virtually no sex life.
A: Yeah, Harry's wife is dead. Several of those films touch lightly on his disappointments in romance, and he's definitely a loner and a lonely character. But Wes is lonely because of the shallowness of his existence, though he loves his daughters. He succumbs to a lot of things in the evening, and he gets involved with a lot of girls Dirty Harry wouldn't be involved with. Not that Harry's asexual or anything, but they're not the kind of gals he'd go for. He'd find some nice secretary, or whatever, and date her, or somebody—a working or professional gal. But this guy doesn't know what he wants.

Q: Was there ever a moment in the planning of this film where someone said, "Suppose we did make him the killer?"
A: No, I never thought of that, but if you'd read the first screenplay we definitely indicated more. [Richard] Tuggle wrote it and then had second thoughts about it. I liked the parallel between him and the killer, and I liked the not knowing. And I felt the more we could lead the audience to think that maybe this was it, the more it gives them somewhere to go. They live with his insecurity and his strife, but at the end there it's okay, enough of all this, now *do* this, get the guy. He becomes as determined as Dirty Harry is normally.

Q: Years ago—this must have been just after *Coogan's Bluff*—Don Siegel

said that he had never met anyone with such an obsession to be an antihero. Is it still true?
A: I think so. In *Dirty Harry*, after shooting the guy, actually torturing the confession out of him—that was my idea—and his feeling was that most actors conscious of a certain image would be afraid to do that. But I felt it as the *immediacy* of the character. At this point, I don't care about his motivation.

And if there is any secret to my success—and I've never sat down and tried to be analytical about it—I think it's that the audience rides along with me. They either sit forward in their seat as to what you're doing, and the intensity with which you're doing it—or, if the audience senses that you're throwing out to them, almost looking to the camera, then they sit back. I've always felt that they're just at the window. Now, I don't want my aunt in Des Moines to think I'm a sadist. I give her credit for being intelligent enough to know I'm an actor playing a part. If they're not that smart, if they think it's really me, then obviously there's something wrong with them.

Q: You give less sense of wanting the public to love you than most actors.
A: Yeah. That's what intrigued Don.

Q: Do you want them to dislike you?
A: I don't want them to dislike me, overall, but a certain aspect of the character. In *Tightrope*, maybe Clint Eastwood wouldn't do some of the things this character would do. I'm just an actor portraying a role.

Q: You give the impression onscreen of being a lot more secure than other actors.
A: That's the way I feel. I don't approach it thinking, What are they going to think behind the camera, or in the theater? I approach it by thinking, What do I have to do *here*? I'm not smart enough to be aware of all these things at once. I'm not that diverse in my concentration. I have to do what the role has to do.

Q: If five or six films in a row went wrong and no one wanted to make Clint Eastwood films, would it trouble you?
A: No, it wouldn't trouble me.

Q: Would it trouble you if you couldn't direct?
A: It would trouble me not to *work* again. But I feel that . . . audiences are

smarter than most people give them credit for. Though sometimes they don't always respond in the way you'd like 'em to. For instance, the two times I've died in films, *Beguiled* and *Honkytonk Man*, the audience has never really enjoyed it. And though I knew in *Honkytonk Man* it was going to be very, very risky, because the other time that happened it didn't work out that well—it didn't work out that well there either! But in certain countries, certain viewers, France, they treated it kindly. Still, nobody ran to it, like they ran to *Dirty Harry* or any of the other films. And I don't know about *Tightrope*, either.

Q: I felt about a year and a half ago, in *Bronco Billy* and *Honkytonk Man* you'd tried to do different things, and in its way *Firefox* was different—you'd never done a special effects film. Those three pictures marked a faltering in your box office. Have you been under pressure to do another Dirty Harry film? Is that what happened with *Sudden Impact*?
A: *(Chuckles.)* Well . . . not really. *Firefox* did pretty well. There was sort of a consensus that *Bronco Billy* wasn't a success, but it was a very inexpensive film and I loved the story, loved making it. I think it's one of the best films I've made. It was one of the more enjoyable ones. It did pretty good, it just wasn't in the league following *Every Which Way but Loose*.

Q: You have the reputation in the business of being very cost-conscious, even downright stingy. Are you proud of that?
A: Yeah. I don't consider it stingy, though. We pay pretty decent. It's just that we try to organize the films and make them in the least amount of time. We're talking about an industry where there's so much waste, and so much faith put in people who have very little experience. Even in the executive strata, not too many of them have the film knowledge of the past generations. Once they've made the deal they turn it over to a film person, and maybe he's experienced, maybe not.

Q: But the budgets on your films are startlingly low.
A: I think so, but that's to do with planning. We use the very best people, who are philosophically aligned at getting the most for the money. If a picture cost $5 million, I hope it looks like $10 million on the screen. If it cost $5 million and it looks $3 million on the screen, then that's a failure to me. There's an awful lot of pictures that cost $20–30 million that look to me like $6–7 million.

Q: Is it also part of your wish not to seem soft?

A: I don't know. Maybe it's a certain pride in workmanship or respect for someone who's going to put his money up and who I do right by. A studio like Warner Bros. will do *Honkytonk Man*. They know Clint Eastwood's not hunching around or shooting up. They're still putting in faith that I'll make the best picture I can. So I try to show them some respect. It's easy to fall into the pattern, I've seen it happen, once you're sucked into a movie it's too late. Jack Warner would have said, "Get back on schedule."

Q: Have you ever been in a situation, as actor or director, where you got a notion for a whole new scene not in the script?
A: Oh, yeah. I change pictures as I go. I just use a script as a framework. A lot of times I'll send out page changes on a script.

Q: Do you think you're a reasonable actor now for other people to direct, or do you notice you have ideas and can't keep quiet about them?
A: I've done so many of my own films I haven't had that situation you're talking about. But I'll offer suggestions, and if the person doesn't like them it doesn't make any difference to me—they're just suggestions. If I'm working with a director and there's something that needs to be added to the script, I'll try to clarify it before we ever shake hands to do the thing. So that there's no surprises. I don't want some guy to turn around and say, "Now you play some transvestite!" I'll have ideas along the way and hopefully that's all hashed out. On *City Heat*, Richard Benjamin seemed to like the contributions. Don Siegel loves participation.

Q: What determines now whether you direct a film or only act in it?
A: It's just a mood thing. Some films I see them kind of vividly, either a story I like very much and want to direct, or I see it clearly and I don't want to have to work with another guy and explain to him. Then there's other scripts where I say, "Well, someone else can have just as good a tack on this." Maybe there's a production problem. On *Every Which Way but Loose* and *Any Which Way You Can* I needed to work out and train up a lot, I just didn't want to take on the job. I wanted somebody there to act as captain of the ship, and I could work with the animals and whatever needs to be done.

Q: What happened on *Josey Wales* with Phil Kaufman?
A: Well, I had . . . I liked him as a writer. I bought this book and owned it myself, and I had my own money in the project, and he liked it when I

gave it to him, and I thought it would be interesting to have him direct. And he did bring some very good contributions to transferring the book into the screenplay. We were both in sync all the way down the line on that. But when it came to shooting, he just had a little bit different ideas of the style of the film. And I did have my own money in it, and I bought the book from scratch, and I just felt I didn't want to see it portrayed that way. So it was strictly a point of view. Nobody will ever know, but for all we know his ideas might have been the best. I just had a line on it and loved the project and didn't want it to be done the way he was going to interpret it. And he didn't want to do it the way I wanted to do it. There wasn't any animosity or disrespect for him in any way, shape, or form.

Q: Can you put your style into words, your way of telling a story and directing?
A: Well, there is no particular way. Most of my films have a different look, depending upon what the film calls for. It's a combination of pace and an eye for composition. I can't explain exactly what it is, because there isn't as much a style to my films—an individualistic style—as there is to those of Don Siegel. Mine vary. *Play Misty* varies greatly from *Breezy*, from *Josey Wales*, from *Bronco Billy*.

I think what has happened these days is that an awful lot of people direct movies in a style they'd direct commercials in. Where they just kind of float around all over the place. Being an actor has one advantage—you don't need to make your presence known. Your presence is already there. So I'm not trying to feature any tricks as a director. I'd say a director who is pretty straight on is Sidney Lumet or Martin Ritt. Guys who never try to intrude themselves. They try to feature the story, because directing is an interpretative art, as opposed to writing, the creative art. Those are guys who've told the story very well.

Q: When you first saw the Sergio Leone films, was there a big shock? Or did you know they'd be so stylized?
A: Yeah, I think I played my character in sync with the style. I spun off Sergio, and he spun off me. I think we worked well together. I like his compositions. He has a very good eye. He wasn't a real experienced director. He'd only done one movie, a thing called *Colossus of Rhodes*. And if you look at that, it doesn't have any of his style. I liked him, I liked his sense of humor. I can't speak for him, but I feel it was mutual. He liked dealing with the kind of character I was putting together. The character was written quite a bit different. I made it much more economical.

Much less expository. He explained himself a lot in the screenplay. My theory to Sergio was, "I don't think you have to explain everything. Let the audience imagine with us." I'd sort of coerce him into going for it on that level, like a B picture. But he did go for it. He wasn't really coerced, he liked the style.

I think the producers of the film were a bit shocked. They didn't know what was going on. They said, "Jeez, this guy doesn't do anything, doesn't say anything, just stands there with the cigar." They were used to Italian films—*Divorce Italian Style*, flamboyant, a lot of things happening. But Sergio, he kinda stayed with it, and he embellished it as he went along over the three films.

He's offered me other films since *The Good, the Bad and the Ugly*, but at that point I felt like he was looking for a different thing in films than I was. I was looking for more character development and maybe a smaller film, and he was looking for more panorama, a David Leanesque kind of thing. So we just drifted, though it was very amicable.

Q: Did he ever ask if you were interested in *Once Upon a Time in America*?
A: Yeah. He started thinking about that project back when we did *The Good, the Bad and the Ugly*. And he had this idea about doing a gangster movie. He said, "What about Irish gangsters? You could play an Irish gangster." Long before *The Godfather* and all these things came out. But he never developed it. It was always just there, hanging there. And a lot of times Sergio would just want to go with an idea. But through the years of television I'd been reading the story too much. Though I did sort of go along with *The Good, the Bad and the Ugly* on a treatment.

But as time went on I didn't think it was a wise thing to do, with him or anyone else. I like to know the joke. I don't want someone to tell me a joke and not give me the punch line. I like to know where I'm going; and I'll improvise, and be as crazy as anyone wants, but I just want to have a clear line on where I'm headed. But he talked to me about doing *Once Upon a Time in the West* and what became *Duck, You Sucker*, but they were just repeats of what I'd been doing. I didn't want to play that character anymore. So I came back and did a very small-budget picture, called *Hang 'Em High*, which had a little more character. Maybe it was time, too, to do some American films, because even though these films were very successful, the movie business for some reason was still thinking of me as an Italian movie actor. I can remember the field guys at Paramount years ago said they'd talked about using me but all they got was, "He's just a TV actor." I wasn't marked to be accepted. There were a lot of other actors who were marked to succeed more than me. Same with the press. I wasn't marked in their estimation. I was never a darling of that group.

Q: These days people go from one lot to another. For eight years you've been Warners' most successful product. They're anxious to keep you, and you look comfortable here. It's a little like the thirties.
A: I wouldn't have been happy with that, as far as being an actor is concerned. Those guys were contract players and they had to do many films they didn't want to do. You couldn't step back for two years. And you had no control over it. The reason I started Malpaso in the first place was I saw a lot of inefficiencies, and I thought I can screw up as good as the next person. I'd rather be the cause of my own demise.

Q: But you also like to keep a settled team.
A: Yeah, I do. I like working with the same people. I've done a lot of films with other people along the way, and sometimes I'll use actors I've used three or four times. Like *Bronco Billy*—everybody in it I'd used before. And it was great fun. Behind the camera, too, a lot of the people have been with me a long time. It's very relaxing to know that certain people are very, very good at their job. A lot of that aspect of the old days I like. Everybody moved at a good clip. Studio heads were tough and obstinate, but they knew about film. But there was no competition then. All movies made money, more or less. A movie actor today is making a tremendous competition.

Q: Do you think the public sees you as an actor playing parts or as a fantasy figure called Clint Eastwood?
A: I think the public understands that you're playing different characters. But there is a fantasy in this era of bureaucracy, of complicated life, income tax and politicizing everything, that there's a guy who can do certain things by himself. There'll always be that fantasy. I think there's an admiration for it. Maybe certain groups will try to suppress it or advocate against it. But that fantasy will always exist.

Q: You hold that fantasy yourself?
A: Yeah, I think so. I like individuality. I think I enjoy people who are individuals.

Q: As history goes on, do you think people like that are going to triumph or be beaten?

A: Who knows? It may become more of a fantasy as it succumbs to civilization and the mass amount of people. If you were in Orwell's 1984 and you looked at one of my pictures, you'd die of shock.

Q: There is an argument that the fantasy figure you represent teaches people that strength, force, and reductions like "Make my day" is a way of getting through life.
A: Well, I think the appeal may be there. Everybody would like to do that, to come up with that kind of saying. But it's absurd—a person comes up and tells you how many bullets he might have fired and do you feel lucky? Everybody would like to be that cool at some point. How many times has someone said something smart to you and half an hour later you've thought of the perfect answer? "My God, I wish I could have nailed him." But you don't, so the fantasy character does that. He has the right saying. And the right act for the right moment. Sure it's a fantasy, and I think people need it. At the same time, he's advocating that there is hope for the individual.

Q: I'm not sure that all the audience sees the absurdity, and I think I prefer the greater doubt and vulnerability of, say, *Josey Wales*.
A: Well, that happens to be one of my favorites. I have such feelings myself, obviously, or I would never have attacked something like *Tightrope*. I could have said it could be altered, we'll make him Dirty Harry, a little more confident, add a few "Make my days," or similar type squelches, and then you're off and running. That would be commercial. On *Honkytonk Man*, somebody said, "Why don't you make him live?" But self-destruct—that's the way that guy is, and you can't make a sudden change at the last frame. Hopefully, it's what the kid learns from it. *Bronco Billy*, it was suggested that I go back and get the sheriff (who humiliates him for standing by his man) and somehow one-up him *à la Superman II*, where the guy goes in and punches him out at the end. That isn't true to the story. That diminishes the scene where he takes the humiliation to get this guy off the hook. And that would be impure.

Q: These tags that become so important in some of your films, like "Make my day," do you think up some of those?
A: That particular one came from the screenwriter, came from Joe Stinson. The only thing I did is I reprised it at the end—that's my contribution. I saw the line as a goodie, so I said let's throw it in right here. Much like we did with *Dirty Harry* and, Did he fire six shots or five . . . ? "To tell

you the truth I've forgotten in all this excitement. But seeing this is a .44 Magnum . . ." And so I thought, let's do it at the very end, let's close with it. Because it's obviously going to be something special. And I told Don [Siegel], I said I can play it looser, with humor, to begin with, so there's a certain irony, but at the end I can play it with a whole different attitude. With a certain, absolutely peak velocity. But that was written in there originally by Harry Julian Fink, in the screenplay. When I read the screenplay it jumped right out and I thought, "Oh, yeah, this'll be quite unusual." You can feel them. "Smith & Wesson and me," I made up. "Who's this 'we'? It's Smith & Wesson and me."

Q: Why did you move so much as a kid?
A: Well, those were the thirties, and jobs were hard to come by. My parents and my sister and myself just had to move around to get jobs. I remember we moved from Sacramento to Pacific Palisades just to be a gas station attendant. It was the only job open. In fact, everybody was in a trailer, one with a single wheel on the end, and the car, and we were living in a real old place out in the sticks. People were actually living in chicken houses. And it was good: you saw a certain side of life that you don't see now unless you're . . . The opportunities are so much more now. My dad was a hard-working guy, and he'd been brought up under the ethic, "Nothing comes from nothing." You get what you give. And you work for what you get. Old-fashioned ethics. Passed down through his family.

Q: Did your family settle eventually?
A: Well, we just moved, but we were close. Then a good portion of the time I was in high school both my parents worked. We moved back to Oakland. My mother worked out at IBM. We should have bought the stock then! Then my dad worked at Bethlehem Steel and they'd go off in two old cars, '31 Chevy and a '32 Chevy, and they made ends meet that way. We lived in a fairly decent neighborhood in Oakland. That was during the forties, war years, and there was a lot more work. That gas station still exists, on the corner of Highway 101 and Sunset Boulevard. There's a Spanish-style roof station there. I have pictures of my dad in that station.

Q: You admired him pretty much?
A: Yeah, yeah. You look back as an adult and you see the struggles both of them went through and you think they put out a lot for us.

Q: You had real poverty.

A: It wasn't like a lot of people suffer. I don't mean to make it sound Dustbowl. There are people in that situation today, and let's hope they'll pull out of it. My father would have pulled his way out of it eventually because he was that sort of person. He would have been a winner eventually. And in the late forties he got with a corporation and worked his way up and became well thought of. He played a little guitar and he sang, and he had a small group. And he liked theatrics. When I did *Rawhide*, he said, "It's very nice you've made a few dollars while you're young."

"Whether I Succeed or Fail, I Don't Want to Owe It to Anyone but Myself": From *Play Misty for Me* to *Honkytonk Man*

Michael Henry Wilson / 1984

Published as "Entretien avec Clint Eastwood" by Michael Henry in *Positif*, no. 287 (January 1985): 48–57; in English in Michael Henry Wilson, *Eastwood on Eastwood* (Paris: Cahiers du cinéma, 2010), 24–52. Reprinted by permission of the author; translated from the French by KC and MHW. Interview conducted on November 19, 1984.

Q: What do you think you've learned from filmmakers you collaborated with before you became a director?
A: I learned a lot, but wouldn't be capable of distinguishing the contribution of each one. The films of Don Siegel, like those of Sergio Leone, were models of economy. They never went over their allotted budget. That was my school. I've made very few pictures where the money was spent without counting, and even when it was, the lesson was useful because I learned what not to do. Each of the filmmakers I worked with taught me something new, or at least helped me to define myself.

Q: When others were directing you, were you conscious of the production work that was going on around you?
A: I don't think I was conscious of it, but I suppose my subconscious assimilated it all. I recall that since the time of *Rawhide* I have wanted to try my hand at directing. My contract with CBS even provided that I would direct several episodes of the series. But after they had some trouble on other series where some actor-directors went over their budgets,

CBS changed policies from one day to the next. It didn't do me any good to make a fuss—at the time I didn't have a choice. They never honored their contract. I did trailers and a few little things here and there, and I fumed, but I convinced myself to wait for a better chance.

Q: Let's go back, if we may, to your first steps in film production. Under what circumstances did you form the Malpaso company at the end of the 1960s?
A: I had come back from Italy, where I had just filmed *The Good, the Bad and the Ugly*. My agent was urging me to do *Mackenna's Gold*, a big, spectacular western, but this wasn't the kind of thing I was looking for. I aspired to something more mature, more probing. That was when *Hang 'Em High* came along, a much more modest project. I liked the idea of weighing the pros and cons of capital punishment in the setting of a western. That gave me the idea of starting my own company to share in the production of this small film.

Q: Were you already thinking of directing films? Wasn't the formation of Malpaso a step towards directing yourself?
A: Not really . . . or maybe subconsciously. After *Hang 'Em High* I acted in several pictures without being actively involved in their production. Then I found myself making my directorial debut directing the second unit on a picture of Don Siegel's, *Dirty Harry*.[1] Don had the flu and I replaced him in the sequence where Harry tries to convince the would-be suicide not to jump from the roof. That turned out OK, because, for the lack of space on the window ledge, the only place to perch me was on the crane. I shot this scene, then another one, and I began to think more seriously about directing. One of my friends, Jo Heims, had written a script I was fond of, *Play Misty for Me*. I'd even taken out an option on it. I had just been offered *Where Eagles Dare* when she called me to ask for my advice. Universal was offering to buy her script and she had scruples about dealing with them, although I wasn't in the position to renew the option. Of course, I encouraged her to sell them her script. And it was only some years later, after I had a contract with Universal, for three movies, that I could tell them, "By the way, you have a project on your shelf that I would like to do. I also want to direct it." Because it wasn't a very costly production, I got the green light.

Q: Why choose this project in particular for your first movie?
A: It was the subject. I had lived through a similar experience, though it

was less dramatic. The character played by Jessica Walter, which was suggested to Jo Heims by an acquaintance of hers, was also familiar to me. It's someone who fantasizes a love relationship. For my character, the disc jockey, it's a one-night stand, but for her it's a devouring passion. This misunderstanding interested me: exactly when do you become involved in a love affair? To what extent are we responsible for the relationship we establish?

Q: Weren't the people you were talking to at Universal surprised that you chose a story in which the dominant character is a woman?
A: Yeah, sure. They kept asking me, "Why are you so eager to make a picture where the woman has the best part?" Their second argument was that the situation wouldn't be believable: "How could a big strong guy like you be threatened physically by a weak young woman?" I thought, on the contrary, that the obsessive dimension of the relationship would only make the dynamic between the two more interesting and would actually work out better. Besides, it is a type of behavior that you can observe in either sex. I've known men who were as possessive as women about the object of their passion.

Q: Was the story originally situated in Carmel and Monterey? Or was it your personal attachment to this region that dictated your choice of locations?
A: In the script, the setting was in Los Angeles, but a friend of mine, who had some features in common with my character, was a disc jockey for a Carmel radio station. And in a small town like Carmel, a disc jockey is more likely to become a celebrity than in Los Angeles. Besides, this region is spectacular, and I happen to live here and be familiar with it.

Q: Did this first experience present any technical problems for you?
A: No, none, except for the challenge of directing oneself while also taking charge of the whole production. The most nervous person was Don Siegel. I had cast him in the role of the bartender and he kept saying, "You've made a big mistake, you should have gotten a real character actor. I'll never be up to it." To which I answered, "Don, you'll be sensational. And it will give you a better appreciation for what actors go through. Besides, if something goes wrong, I'll have a director on hand to get me out of it." In fact, that night after the first day of filming, Don confessed to me that he had had a terrible case of stage fright and would have been completely incapable of helping me out!

Q: How did you prepare for your directorial debut? Did you draw storyboards before filming?
A: No, *Firefox* [1982] is the only picture on which I used storyboards. The last fifteen minutes required some special effects and I made a set of sketches, which I gave to a professional designer for retouching.

Q: Visually, some of your action shots imply a complex choreography. Even in those cases you didn't draw your shots beforehand?
A: I hate to be the prisoner of a diagram. The best ideas come to me when the camera is in place, ready to shoot. That's when I am all wound up. Of course, I have a general idea of the sequence, but I try to remain as flexible as possible, always try to leave an actor the latitude to modify one of his movements if he has a good reason. If I am doing exterior shots, I always take into account the light and the way it evolves during the day, because it might entail changing camera positions.

Q: Visually and thematically, *High Plains Drifter* evokes Sergio Leone's westerns, but I suspect that you wanted to go even further into excess and cruelty.
A: In the Leone films, the story was more fragmented. It was a series of vignettes that were rather loosely linked. In *High Plains Drifter* all the elements overlap, even though there are several sub-plots. Everything is related to the lynching that haunts the protagonist. And there's a moral perspective that only appeared episodically in the Leone films. I am thinking of the scene in *A Fistful of Dollars*, where the hero helps the family get away and pays for this rare moment of compassion with a beating . . . after which he's got to return to take his revenge on the town.

Q: *High Plains Drifter* is a baroque allegory that shatters all the rules of the classic western.
A: I decided to do it on the basis of a treatment of only nine pages. It's the only time that happened to me. The starting point was: "What would have happened if the sheriff in *High Noon* had been killed? What would have happened afterwards?" In the treatment by Ernest Tidyman, the sheriff's brother came back to avenge the sheriff and the villagers were as contemptible and selfish as in *High Noon*. But I opted eventually for a somewhat different approach: you would never know whether the brother in question is a diabolic being or a kind of archangel. It's up to the audience to draw their own conclusions. Tidyman wrote the script from this perspective, but a certain number of elements were missing

and I rewrote it with the help of Dean Riesner, who had collaborated several times with Siegel.

Q: You like characters that form part of the system, or at least appear to form part of it, but don't play by its rules and end up by revealing its corruption. The Stranger of *High Plains Drifter* exerts his power in a subversive way, like a Caligula of the West.
A: I'm aware that this type of character attracts me. Why? Maybe because I have always hated corruption within the system, no matter what it is. In this respect, *High Plains Drifter* goes further than *High Noon*. When the hero helps them get organized, the townspeople believe they can control and manipulate him. As soon as he leaves, they fall back into the error of their ways. Their failure is obvious, their villainy hopeless. In the end, they've learned nothing, but they're forever traumatized. In *Pale Rider*, the western I've just finished, the situation is similar, but this time the hero is really an archangel. He helps the small community of miners to organize themselves against a trust; he inspires them with the courage to resist and defend their rights.

Q: Do you feel affinities with a filmmaker like Kurosawa?
A: I like his films a lot, especially those of his earlier period, from *Seven Samurai* to *Red Beard*. It was *Yojimbo*, as you know, that prompted me to make *A Fistful of Dollars*.

Q: There is a hellish quality to the palette of *High Plains Drifter*, a tonality of blood, fire, and scorched earth.
A: That's due in part to the place where we filmed it, Mono Lake in California. The town in the script was situated in the middle of the desert, like in most westerns, but this convention bothered me because, even in the West, a city couldn't develop without the presence of water. I discovered Mono Lake by chance, while I was driving around, and I was immediately taken with the strangeness of the site. The saline content is so high that no vessel can venture a trip on its waters. I spent two hours walking around in the area. Not a boat, not a living soul, only the natural noises of the desert. From the nearest town I immediately called my art director [Henry Bumstead] and had him jump on the first plane. When he arrived, he blurted out, "You'd think you were on the moon!" And I replied, "It's a weird place, but that's exactly what I want this story to be."

Q: The cinematography of Bruce Surtees was extremely elaborate, especially the chiaroscuro for the night scenes. How did he become one of your faithful collaborators?
A: He'd been the camera operator on several of Siegel's pictures, particularly *Coogan's Bluff*. When we were filming *Two Mules for Sister Sara* in Mexico, Don recruited him because he had communication problems with Gabriel Figueroa [his director of photography]. Figueroa's forte is lighting; Bruce's is composition. His help proved invaluable. So one evening, Don and I resolved that we would promote him to director of photography as soon as the opportunity came up.

Q: At what stage of the preparation do you discuss the style of the cinematography?
A: In general, I only give Bruce a script when it is finished. Then I explain to him what I want. For instance, the light and the colors of autumn were the determining factors in *The Outlaw Josey Wales* and again in *Pale Rider*. I have a predilection for exteriors; I feel more at ease there than in a studio. There's nothing like the atmosphere of a real location to inspire you and your crew. That's where we make most of our decisions.

Q: With *Breezy* you probably surprised a number of your fans. You couldn't conceive a film more remote from the type of movie the public at large identifies you with. Is this a project that was hard to put across?
A: No, not especially. It was a very inexpensive picture and shot on location [in Los Angeles]. I liked a lot the script by Jo Heims, her second I believe. It was about the regeneration of a cynic, an older man, divorced, who's a successful professional but doesn't have an emotional life any more. It's about how he's rejuvenated, thanks to a naive teenager who proves to be not so naive after all.

Q: You feel a particular sympathy, it seems, for those of your characters who learn something in the course of their adventure.
A: The audience follows a story by adopting the point of view of one of the protagonists, whether it's an adult or a child And if this protagonist learns something, you'll identify with him even more when you feel that you're maturing with him. In *Breezy* I wanted to say that even a middle-class man of substance has something to learn from someone who doesn't have anything. This girl hasn't got much of anything, but actually, she has a lot. She sees and feels what he's stopped seeing and feeling, all those things in life he doesn't take time to enjoy. It's a very

simple fable and it's true everywhere. All of us go past something and fail to appreciate all the colors of the prism.

Q: In *The Eiger Sanction*, friendship is stronger than the corruption of the system. Indeed, it's the only value that survives in a world of Machiavellian schemes and plots. Your character and that of George Kennedy make up in the end, foiling the Agency. In *The Outlaw Josey Wales*, the friendship that binds you to John Vernon appears in spite of everything to be stronger than partisan passion.
A: Yes, it's an important value, friendship, especially a friendship that doesn't have any other basis than friendship for its own sake. In *The Eiger Sanction* the pressures of the Agency compromise it, while in *The Outlaw Josey Wales* it succumbs to the psychoses of the war. Josey Wales is like a haunted man. The ghosts of his past, even when he thinks he's starting a new life, beset him. Even the wounded soldier and the women in *The Beguiled*, who are consigned to the periphery of the war, don't escape from this corruption of feelings.

Q: Isn't the strangeness of *The Eiger Sanction* the result of the odd structure of the plot? It develops in three distinct stages, nearly independent of each other.
A: There were, in fact, three stories in one, and it was a very difficult picture to make. It was a good thing that our gadgets were limited in number; we were running the risk of heading in the direction of the James Bond movies. And the mountaineering sequences, especially, posed enormous problems. We had to shoot with two crews: one crew of technicians and one crew of mountain climbers. Every morning we had to decide, depending on the weather report, which one to send up the mountain. The three actors and myself had to undergo intensive training. On the seventh day of filming we lost one of our mountaineers, and believe me, I asked myself repeatedly if it was worth it.

Q: Once again, in *The Eiger Sanction*, you short-circuit genre conventions by means of black humor.
A: The humor was frankly sardonic, but I believe it was inherent in the story. I couldn't have considered handling it otherwise.

Q: But on the other hand, this type of humor is nearly absent in *Firefox*. The film would probably have benefited from a tongue-in-cheek treatment.

A: *Firefox* was more "square," more traditional. It wasn't about bad guys with pink eyes, but ordinary characters faced with an impossible mission.

Q: By its naturalism, *Firefox* also contrasts with *The Eiger Sanction*, which has the baroque, flamboyant quality one finds in *High Plains Drifter* and *The Outlaw Josey Wales*.
A: I probably stand somewhere between the two. I don't believe you can label me, pigeonhole me in one style or another. My films all have a different "look." It depends on the story, on its structure, on the relationships that develop among the protagonists, and probably also on the way I feel about the subject.

Q: When Josey Wales says, "We all died a little in that damn war," one can't help thinking about a contemporary war, Vietnam.
A: You can interpret it like that, but it's a feeling that isn't specific to today's wars. In the case of the Civil War, there had to be something particularly traumatic there. Americans were fighting other Americans. You had one people, but split in half. And according to the state or the county where you were living, you were recruited to join one camp or the other. It is the same absurdity today in Northern Ireland, where a single community is killing itself in the name of God and religion.

Q: You took over the direction from Phil Kaufman after a few days. What happened?
A: I was the one who'd hired him to rewrite the script and direct it. His work as a writer was excellent, but when it came to shooting it, it turned out that our points of view were completely different. I had invested my own money to buy the rights to the book, I'd spent a lot of time developing this project, and I'd conceived a precise vision of what the film had to be. Phil's approach was probably solid, maybe it was better, but it wasn't mine, and I would have been angry with myself if the result hadn't corresponded to what I'd hoped for.

Q: Josey Wales, like the "archangel" of *High Plains Drifter*, sympathizes only with the marginal, the underprivileged, the disenfranchised . . .
A: The irony is that Josey Wales inherits a family. After he has fled from everything he was tied to because everything he ever loved has been destroyed, he finds himself picking up these outcasts along his way: the Indian, the grandmother and her granddaughter, some Mexicans, and

even a stray dog. And soon this heterogeneous group becomes a kind of community.

Q: In *The Gauntlet* the relationship is even more unexpected. For the cop, the discovery of human solidarity happens by way of his prisoner, who also happens to be a prostitute. Was it the improbability of this romance that attracted you?
A: It was that aspect and the contrast with the *Dirty Harry* series. Inspector Callahan was always on top of the situation and he was in permanent conflict with the bureaucratic system. The cop of *The Gauntlet* is a guy who just follows routine, not very sharp, easy to manipulate. All he expects from life are simple things: to do his job well, find a wife, settle down. And when he confesses his longings, it happens that he is talking to a woman he would have ordinarily treated like a whore, but who is much cleverer than him. She is the one who opens his eyes, because he is too regimented to understand what is going on. He can't imagine that his superiors could deceive him deliberately.

Q: In *The Gauntlet*, which is a film noir, you were reworking the theme of betrayal that was already at the heart of *High Plains Drifter*, *The Eiger Sanction*, and *The Outlaw Josey Wales*.
A: Betrayal is everywhere, isn't it? And it's universal. Since Judas, hasn't this been one of the great themes of literature and most kinds of drama?

Q: You declined the part played by Martin Sheen in *Apocalypse Now*, a film that explored that very theme in a provocative way. Why?
A: Mostly, I didn't want to spend month after month on location. I liked the character and everything that was connected to Conrad's book, *Heart of Darkness*. There were impressive action scenes. But I wasn't sure that it would justify my spending two years shooting in the jungle of the Philippines. No film would justify that. It would have to be the most beautiful screenplay, the most beautiful book ever written, and even then . . . I don't like long shoots. I like to work hard and fast, without letting up, twenty hours a day if needed, but over a period of six weeks rather than six months. It's when you have an adrenaline rush that you give your best. Otherwise, you rack your brains, you doze off, and there is a strong chance that the audience will be doing the same in the theater.

Q: Is it possible to see in *Bronco Billy* a commentary on your activities and responsibilities as a filmmaker?

A: I had a really good time. When Dennis Hackin sent me the script, at first I thought it was about Bronco Billy Anderson, the silent movie star. I devoured it in one sitting and immediately thought it was the kind of film Capra would do today if he were still making movies.

Q: Once again, there was this micro-society we were talking about . . .
A: Yes, but in a contemporary version. Of course, you could also say that in a certain way these misfits belong to a bygone era. There aren't a lot of people who are really interested in a "Wild West Show" today.

Q: Bronco Billy allows his fellow players to interpret the role of their choice in a world of illusions, to express their truth by becoming whatever they choose to be. The circus tent is like a metaphor of filmmaking . . . or even of Malpaso Productions?
A: I hadn't ever thought of it from this angle, but maybe you're right: after all, it isn't so different from the movies! I'm always moving on, and I can't analyze what I do as consciously or objectively as an observer who's outside the project.

Q: You supervise the casting very closely. You often say that it's the key moment in your preparation.
A: If the script is good and the casting is right, you've only got to stay on course. On the other hand, if the casting is wrong, you don't have a chance to achieve your goal. I don't mean that there's only one way to cast a role, but I have too much respect for actors, I'm too sensitive to the particular dimension they can give a part, not to control the casting myself from beginning to end.

Q: *Bronco Billy* gives the impression of being a film of family and friends. You're celebrating a certain lifestyle.
A: The actors had almost all worked with me before, many times. They formed a very homogeneous group. The fact that we had this common experience meshed well with the story. The relationships of the characters with Bronco Billy were not very different from those the actors had with me. I think this helped the film. On the other hand, for *Escape from Alcatraz*, we took the opposite approach: we hired only people who had never worked with us. On some films, I surround myself with my family; on others, I search for new faces.

Q: In *Bronco Billy*, as in *Honkytonk Man*, you offer us splendid scenes of provincial life, but the picture is often ambivalent: this rural America is far from being idyllic; it, too, is badly tainted by corruption. Let's take, for example, the episode with the vicious sheriff in *Bronco Billy*.

A: When we were shooting the sequence, someone suggested, "Why not add a scene where Billy returns to town and takes vengeance on the sheriff?" I answered, "You can't do that. It would be another movie." Billy endures the sheriff's insults in order to get his young team member out of jail. This voluntary humiliation says everything about his character. Maybe it's even the message of the picture. If he returns to take vengeance, you're going back to *Dirty Harry*.

Q: How involved are you in establishing the definitive script for your films?

A: Formerly, I'd often make changes during the filming itself. Now, I try to make them beforehand in order not to waste time and be completely organized. If the original writer isn't available, I do the work myself. But on *Pale Rider*, for instance, the screenwriters [Dennis Shryack and Michael Butler] wanted to be involved until the end and they took care of the modifications I asked for. For *Bronco Billy*, I added a number of scenes myself—for instance, the holdup at the bank. I'd attended a fight with Muhammad Ali, and after his victory, while reporters were bombarding him with questions like, "How did you place that lightning left hook in the last round?" all he would say was, "I just want to say hello to my pals. And I'm eager to thank my father, my uncle, the reverend so and so, etc." That gave me the idea of the sequence where Billy is asked about the holdup [which he stopped], but his only thought is to promote his circus. I also wanted to show that this anti-hero was still capable of accomplishing a heroic action.

Q: In your selection of projects, you seem lately to be observing a rule of alternation: a small, intimate, personal film that challenges your image, and a more important production with an assured commercial potential. Thus, after *Bronco Billy* you turned to *Firefox*, and after *Honkytonk Man* to *Sudden Impact*.

A: Maybe that's only a coincidence. I don't believe it's a conscious process. Even if I had been certain that they wouldn't be big successes, nothing would have stopped me from making *Bronco Billy* and *Honkytonk Man*.

Q: What attracted you to *Firefox*? Of all your films it's the one where the confusion of values and ideologies is least marked.

A: I liked the story and the script. It started out like a classic spy movie, but then there were some pertinent reflections on the arms race and the imbalance of strengths caused by new technological advances. What worried me a little were the special effects. Luckily, they came up only in the last part of the film. The problem, in particular, was that these special effects played out against a background of the atmosphere of our planet, and not in some faraway galaxy off in the future. I must confess, I'm not crazy about special effects. I prefer a thousand times over to have to deal with human beings and their problems.

Q: It's often been said that the film drew on the Cold War climate that followed President Reagan's taking office.
A: It was only a hypothesis: "What would happen if . . . ?" I don't believe we manipulated the public's paranoia. We only noted that the Cold War was there. And even if it hadn't been there, you need an antagonist or a certain kind of conflict. And as for conflicts, if it isn't the one that opposes the United States and the USSR, there are enough of them everywhere on the planet.

Q: The hero doesn't call into question either his mission or the system. Not even when he discovers that the Russian dissidents must sacrifice their life for him.
A: He's a professional, and he doesn't have any idea, before he goes over there, of what his mission implies for the dissidents. He doesn't know anything about the behind-the-scenes political machinations. And over there, he doesn't have a single moment when he's at ease. Except when he takes command of the prototype, because then, at last, he's in his element.

Q: You suggest a possible friendship between the American pilot and his Soviet counterpart, a friendship of two technicians as opposed to the infamous games of politicians.
A: It's a little like *The Outlaw Josey Wales*: these two men could have been friends in other circumstances, if they hadn't belonged to different types of society.

Q: In logistical terms, was *Firefox* as difficult as *The Eiger Sanction*?
A: Yes and no. We had to find a substitute for the Soviet city—Vienna, as it turned out. The Russian base was set up in the Austrian Alps. The London scenes were shot here, and so forth. The shot when I head to the hangar was filmed in Austria, but the reverse angle shot was done here,

because we weren't about to transport the contraption from one continent to another.

Q: *Honkytonk Man* is the only one of your movies, other than *The Beguiled*, where you die at the end. Did you have any difficulties pitching to Warner Bros. a project that contradicted your traditional image so decidedly?

A: No, none at all. It was a small inexpensive picture, but since *The Beguiled*, I knew exactly what kind of risk I was taking. I liked the story and thought it deserved to be told. I hoped that the audience would sympathize enough with the young boy to be interested in it. There is a big part of my public that expects heroic actions from me, and perhaps they were disappointed with *Honkytonk Man*. I can't make all my pictures for a specific segment of society, nor can I defend the same values constantly. A filmmaker worth his salt can't keep making the same picture all the time. I need some new variations, or some completely new themes. Otherwise, it doesn't interest me, it's not a challenge any more. If there's some advantage to being a "star," or rather passing for a "star," it's being able to make projects that normally would never see the light of day . . . pictures that can only be done because you're interested in them, as was the case with *The Beguiled*, *Bronco Billy*, and *Honkytonk Man*. On the other hand, take the example of *Every Which Way but Loose*. No one wanted any part of it. The script had been refused forty-six times! Finally, I shot it and it made a fortune. What the studio lost on one film, it got back on another, and so forth. Today when you make a movie, you have to really want to make it. You can't think about the box office. I never think about it; I never did, even when I had some of my greatest hits. I am not arrogant enough to think that the public is going to rush to see any of my movies. Every time, I knock on wood, up to the last moment . . . because you never know.

Q: Your core audience would probably have recognized itself in *Honkytonk Man*, but that audience doesn't go to the movies to be faced with its daily problems.
A: Unless it is a case of pure fantasy, as in *Every Which Way but Loose*. But the story of a dying musician like Red Stovall in *Honkytonk Man* is not necessarily one that they want to see on the screen. But I do.

Q: Did a real-life singer inspire Red Stovall?
A: No, he's a collage: a mixture of Hank Williams, Red Foley, Bob Wills,

basically all of those country singers who drank hard, burned up their life on the road, and ended up by self-destructing.

Q: What are your own connections to country music?
A: I discovered it at the age of nineteen when I was working as a lumberjack in Oregon. At that time, I only liked jazz, particularly the West Coast jazz of Dave Brubeck and Gerry Mulligan. I was looking for girls and I landed in the town's only nightclub. Bob Wills and his band were playing there. Since I didn't know anybody and didn't know how to dance to this music, I spent hours listening to the band, while forgetting to try to pick up girls! After that, I started listening regularly to the small local country radio stations.

Q: On *Honkytonk Man*, did you draw from your childhood during the years of the Great Depression?
A: Yes, I was raised during those dark years. I had some contact with families like that during my wanderings from city to city, and I certainly met characters like Red Stovall. That probably helped me to re-create the atmosphere. But as you know, for me it was love at first sight for the book by Clancy Carlile, and although we pruned it a little, we remained very faithful to it.

Q: Since *Bronco Billy* and *Honkytonk Man*, you seem increasingly interested in family and community relationships.
A: You can only do so much with the lone hero. If you give him some family ties, you give him a new dimension. You build conflicts that enrich the story. In *Honkytonk Man* he has a family, but he is doomed to destroy himself. In *Tightrope* he seems to debase himself and drag his family with him. In *Pale Rider*, although he doesn't belong to the community, he gets close to two of its members unwittingly because they become attached to him.

Q: Isn't it the fact that you've become your own director that has allowed you to change your image like this?
A: That's right. It's allowed me to widen my register and control my career better. I recall a picture I made in Yugoslavia called *Kelly's Heroes*. It was a very fine anti-militaristic script; one that had some important things to say about war, about this propensity that man has to destroy himself. In the editing, the scenes that set the debate in philosophical terms were cut and they kept adding action scenes. When it was finished,

the picture had lost its soul. If action and reflection had been better balanced, it would have reached a much broader audience. I don't know if the studio exercised pressure on the director or if it was the director who lost his vision along the way, but I know that the picture would have been far superior if there hadn't been this attempt to satisfy action fans at any cost. And it would have been just as spectacular and attractive. It's not an accident that some action movies work and others don't. What makes the difference is the quality of the writing.

Q: *Honkytonk Man* is a picaresque journey through a forgotten American South. Was it familiar ground?
A: No, but I've had many opportunities to cross the country by car, observing little towns and storing these scenes in my memory. For *Bronco Billy* I criss-crossed Ontario, Oregon, Washington, and Idaho. In the first script the setting was in Oklahoma, but I made it in the Boise area of Idaho because you can capture there the "Mid-American" atmosphere that I was looking for. For *Honkytonk Man* I preferred central California to the flatness of Oklahoma, where the Dust Bowl had vanished anyway.

Q: Bruce Surtees' cinematography sometimes evokes the photographs of Walker Evans. During your research, did you consult photos and documents of the time?
A: Sure, I browsed through piles of books on the 1930s and the Great Depression. Photo albums of my own family also inspired me.

Q: Unfortunately, this kind of "Americana" seems to be vanishing from the screen. You are one of the few to remain faithful to that genre. Would you like to carry on with your explorations of the heartland?
A: Yes, I'd like to come back to it from time to time. Regularly, if I can! Today the only thing that Hollywood swears by are its space adventures, because that's what goes over well. For my part, I trust my instinct and I make the films that I believe in. If the public follows me, that's wonderful. If it doesn't, *c'est la vie*.

Q: Can one describe *Sudden Impact* as a black comedy?
A: Sure. There are a lot of comic elements in all of the *Dirty Harry* series, if only because Inspector Callahan's cynicism calls for a cynical type of humor.

Q: Some American critics blamed you for discrediting the judicial system, for advocating vigilantism and individual justice.

A: I can't help it if my sense of humor escapes some people. One of my favorite restaurants in Carmel is called the Hog's Breath Inn. When I asked the owner why he had chosen such an ugly name, he told me, "We want to make sure we only serve customers who have a sense of humor." A few months before his death, I had lunch with Hitchcock and afterwards we speculated together about the movies. Suddenly he concluded, "Don't ever forget that it's only a bloody movie!" He was sure as hell right about that. No movie can ever change the world or make it a more just place, even if it contains an important message. *Dirty Harry* touched a nerve because the country was up to its ears in bureaucratic inefficiency. But that character is a pure fiction. In today's society, no cop would be capable of assaulting the system while remaining so uncompromising. Even if some of them would like to have such power and if need be, go beyond the law, they just can't. After all, Harry Callahan never deliberately set out to go beyond the law; it was only under the pressure of time or when forced by the urgency of the situation. To come back to your question: I can't worry about these kinds of problems. I do the best I can. I can only hope that the audience will like the film and the critics will be more receptive to the positive than to the negative aspects.

Q: You were unpleasantly surprised by the accusations of racism brought against *Dirty Harry*.
A: When I hired blacks, I did it to give them work. Before filming the hold-up sequence in *Dirty Harry*, a scene that had been written for whites, I told Don Siegel, "I'm tired of always seeing the same stuntmen in this kind of role. What if we got some new faces?" A group of black stuntmen had just been formed and they were the ones I suggested. That they were all blacks was logical: there are as many black gangs as white or Asian gangs. It's absurd to conclude from it that only blacks commit crimes. Again, in *City Heat* we have changed all the casting and blacks have now taken two-thirds of the roles written for whites. That fits the real atmosphere of Kansas City, which was dominated by the jazz scene in the 1930s. Lord only knows what some critics are going to conclude from that!

Q: A number of your movies, *Sudden Impact* in particular, express the frustrations of today's America and the resurgence of populism.
A: Maybe I can be accused of being old-fashioned, of dreaming of an era when things were simpler, more obvious, and more honest. The power of bureaucracy is increasing as our planet is shrinking and the problems of society are getting more complicated. I'm afraid that individual independence is becoming an outmoded dream. Paperwork, administrative

red tape, committees, and subcommittees overwhelm us. It has reached such a point that in order to get elected, our politicians have to promise they'll keep their interference into citizens' lives to a minimum. That's the rhetoric that's dominated the recent presidential campaign. What Dirty Harry was saying is, "If you have to fill out fifteen copies of every report, the felon will have time to commit another crime before you've finished. There comes a time when you have to stop stalling." It's an extreme position, but that's where you get back to the irony: without it, the audience wouldn't go along. That's something I felt by instinct. For my part, I've succeeded in remaining pretty much independent, but to reach this stage I've had to fight. And I continue to fight every day.

Q: In your movies, irony is most often tied to something excessive, whether it's an improbable situation or the hero's extreme reactions.
A: *The Gauntlet* is a good example. I had seen on television the barrage of gunfire that followed the abduction of Patty Hearst by the Symbionese Liberation Army. It was a tremendous shoot-out, right in the middle of the city. Bullets flew in all directions and at least three buildings caught fire. I imagined what would occur in a city of middling importance like Las Vegas, where the police don't have anything to do but arrest a drunk from time to time. If it were suddenly announced that Public Enemy Number One had seized a bus and taken a police officer hostage, all the cops in town would want to be part of the action. It is most likely that their reaction would be excessive. Life offers you examples every day of the bizarre excesses you mention. The real is sometimes surreal. And anyway, as a filmmaker, excess is good dramatic material. What interests the public is the extraordinary, isn't it?

Q: *Tightrope* is based on the transference of guilt, a theme dear to Hitchcock. Was this what attracted you to Richard Tuggle's script?
A: What attracted me was that this cop has been abandoned by his wife, that he's got custody of the children, that he's intrigued by Genevieve Bujold, but doesn't want to get involved with her because he's got enough problems in his life. He may be more efficient than the hero of *The Gauntlet*, but he is not the type of man to attack the system head-on like Dirty Harry. He just wants to do his job well. But as crime follows crime and the crimes get closer and closer to him, you begin to wonder, "Could it be him? What is his connection to the criminal? Who is his alter ego?" And it does turn out that the criminal is also a police officer. The interaction of all these elements interested me.
Q: Why didn't you direct the picture yourself?

A: Richard Tuggle was anxious to direct it. He had written the script, which was excellent. He's the one who wrote *Escape from Alcatraz*. Why not let him direct it? I have enormous respect for anyone who can write a book or script. That's where the real work of creation takes place. The rest is in the interpretation or illustration.

Q: Have you ever written a first treatment and then given it to a professional screenwriter?
A: Not a complete treatment, but sometimes I may call a screenwriter and tell him, "Here's the idea. It's up to you to develop it." That was the case with *Pale Rider*. The writers developed the story, and then I added a few scenes that I wrote myself.

Q: It's to be hoped that *Pale Rider* will contribute to the resurrection of the genre, but isn't it a gamble to film a western today?
A: I don't know if the genre has really disappeared. There's a whole generation, the younger generation, that knows westerns only from seeing them on television. And I notice that audience ratings for *High Plains Drifter* and *The Outlaw Josey Wales* continue to be excellent. When someone asks me, "Why a western today?" I'm tempted to answer, "Why not? My last western went over very well." It may be that *The Outlaw Josey Wales* was the last western to have been a commercial success. Anyway, aren't the *Star Wars* movies westerns transposed into outer space?

Q: Beyond the western genre, are you interested in the West and its history?
A: In a personal capacity, of course, but in my pictures the approach has mainly been in the realm of mythology. *Pale Rider* is no exception; it's got numerous biblical references. However, since it's about the miners, I had to read a lot of works about the topic and the Gold Rush era. Again, we filmed it in Idaho, in the Sawtooth Mountains region. It's magnificent country, some of the most beautiful in the United States. As we did for *High Plains Drifter*, we built a whole town, from the ground up.

Q: Which of your films have given you the most satisfaction so far?
A: *The Outlaw Josey Wales, Bronco Billy*, and *Honkytonk Man* were the most satisfying because they were small films.

Q: Were they more personal too?
A: These films were more personal, better managed, and more independent because they were filmed in remote areas, far from Hollywood.

Q: What is the most exciting stage for you? Writing? Shooting? Editing?
A: Editing. It's the time when you're subject to the fewest constraints, because you are alone with your editor, putting together the pieces of the puzzle. While you are shooting you have to deal with some sixty or eighty people, who are bombarding you with questions; at every moment you have to find an appropriate answer. There is no chance to stall for time. It's exhausting and exciting, of course, because it's there that everything is being played out. You know that if the pieces aren't correctly shaped, you'll never be able to put them together. When I think about the number and the complexity of the elements that enter into play, I'm astounded that good movies exist.

Q: In the light of maturity and of the experience you've acquired as a filmmaker, how do you feel about your character's evolution?
A: I don't see my characters as one entity. Rather they are a series of variations. It's true that on screen, from film to film, it's the same face, the same physique, but with the coming of maturity, you change your perspective. This is especially true in the selection of subjects. It's probable now that I am choosing scripts that wouldn't have attracted me fifteen or twenty years ago, or that I wouldn't have had the audacity to make then. I can't imagine constantly redoing what used to work for me. Maturity has to be an incitement to progress, to develop, and, you hope, improve.

Q: In the course of your career, you've succeeded in altering your image profoundly. You challenge it again in almost every film. But isn't it difficult to live with this alter ego who sustains a whole mythology, who has been the subject of innumerable commentaries and analyses, and about whom books are now being written?
A: I know it's not about me. I know there is what I am as a person and what I am as an actor. And this image exists only in the mind or the eyes of the audience. I am very careful not to think about it. When I am editing a picture, I don't think about protecting or favoring myself. I think only about the character and his role in the story. Otherwise, everything would be off-center. And I suppose it is the same thing in life. When people write about me, I don't take it personally. If the article is positive, I tell myself, "Perfect. He understood what I was trying to do." If it's negative, I live with it by telling myself that it takes all kinds to make a world.

Q: But when you approach a new project, aren't you forced to take into account what your image was in the previous films?
A: You mean, how do I avoid repeating myself?

Q: Either repeating yourself or consciously embroidering variations on a pre-existing image. For example, Red Stovall, in *Honkytonk Man*, is a completely new character for you, whereas the policeman in *Tightrope* seems to have grown from some of your previous roles.
A: I don't think so. In the case of *Tightrope*, I was influenced neither by *Dirty Harry* nor by *The Gauntlet*. With that character, I started out again from square one. Even though some general character traits, such as my professional behavior, might appear similar. Of course, it is still me; I can only disguise myself up to a certain point. I can't appear all of a sudden as Quasimodo. But, internally, I approach every new character in a distinct way. That is true with the *Dirty Harry* series too. When I was preparing for one of the sequels, I forbade myself to watch the first one again. Even Dirty Harry has changed in fourteen years. He's changed as I have changed. I wouldn't want to reach the point where I am imitating myself. You and I know some filmmakers and actors who are reduced to that. I don't have this problem, but sometimes I wonder if the day will come and I'll tell myself, "Gee, I don't know what to do any more. Maybe I should go back to doing the things that worked so well for me back then?" That would be sad. When I started work on *Pale Rider*, for a minute I was tempted to see *Josey Wales* again and my first westerns. Then I told myself, "No, I can't do that. There isn't any connection. The only connection is that it is a western and there's a certain mythology associated with that genre. But I don't want to repeat myself, I don't want to be influenced by the past."

Q: The mythology that you play with in your pictures resonates with the core values of this country. As a result, they are sometimes treated as sociological phenomena. Does that make you uncomfortable at all?
A: I don't think about it . . . I would be afraid to think about it! I don't like people who take themselves too seriously and I especially wouldn't want to be categorized in that way. If I started analyzing the impact my pictures produce or what I represent in today's America, I would be paralyzed, incapable of functioning. It's not for me to dissect myself because I could never have the requisite objectivity.

Q: What is the best antidote against the spirit of seriousness? Black humor perhaps?
A: There is nothing like it!

Q: How do you see the future of Malpaso? Would you consider developing and producing projects in which you wouldn't be involved either as the director or as an actor?
A: It's a possibility. Maybe it's what I will do later, but right now I am anxious to keep Malpaso to its modest dimensions. I don't want to serve as a front man. I'm keen on putting my personal touch on everything I do. The reason for Malpaso was originally, "Whether I succeed or fail, I don't want to owe it to anyone but myself." It remains my motto.

Notes

1. Eastwood had done second unit work on Siegel films before *Dirty Harry*, but *Play Misty for Me* wrapped before shooting on *Dirty Harry* began. —Translator's note (KC).

Clint Eastwood:
The *Rolling Stone* Interview

Tim Cahill / 1985

Published in *Rolling Stone*, July 4, 1985, 18–23. Reprinted by permission.

Precisely two decades ago, a friend of mine insisted I go see a movie about the American West, a film made in Italy and shot partially in Spain. At the time, it was intellectually acceptable to be passionate about Italian films that limned the sick soul of Europe; the idea of an Italian western was oxymoronic—at best, like, oh, a German romantic comedy. What's more, in America the western as a genre seemed bankrupt, and going to see *A Fistful of Dollars*, which featured an international no-star cast headed by Clint Eastwood, some second-banana cowboy on an American TV series called *Rawhide*, promised to be entertaining in a manner the director, another unknown named Sergio Leone, probably never intended. My friend was a graduate student in philosophy, and she'd seen the movie three times because she thought it was "existential." The Clint Eastwood character was called the Man with No Name, and he went around rescuing people for no stated reason and outdrawing ugly, sweating bad guys who insulted his mule.

A lot of the violence was stylized, tongue-in-cheek comic-book mayhem, and you couldn't take it very seriously, though several critics did just that, describing the film as "simple, noisy, brutish." This sort of abusive critical reaction didn't keep audiences away, but it did rather dampen the enthusiasm of philosophy majors who had seen smatterings of Sartre in the Man with No Name.

Clint Eastwood starred in two more of the movies that came to be called spaghetti westerns, then he went back to Hollywood in 1967 to make *Hang 'Em High*, another popular success in spite of critical reactions like "emetic and interminable."

By the early seventies, an interest in Clint Eastwood movies among film buffs was considered a shameful and secret vice, like masturbation.

In 1971, Don Siegel directed Eastwood in the enormously popular *Dirty Harry*, a movie that sent some critics into fits of apoplectic name-calling. "Fascist" was one of the kinder descriptions.

That same year, Eastwood directed his first movie, *Play Misty for Me*. The studio had warned him against the project. Universal was reluctant to even pay him for a film in which he would play an easygoing, soft-spoken, jazz-loving disc jockey who inadvertently gets involved with a psychotic young woman. The movie opened to lukewarm but favorable reviews. Pretty good directorial debut, was the consensus, for some damn cowboy.

Eastwood went on to star in three Dirty Harry sequels, all of which minted money at the box office. He directed nine more films, including the classic western *The Outlaw Josey Wales* (1976). And though Eastwood could count on box-office success simply by whispering, "Dirty Harry," he often made choices that confounded his studios, critics and fans.

The 1978 film *Every Which Way but Loose*—a PG-rated comedy featuring an orangutan named Clyde—was another film the studio foresaw as an instant flop. The studio was partially right: nobody liked the film but the public. Clearly, Clint Eastwood knew his audience better than anyone else, and his box-office success has allowed him to direct what he calls his "small films." *Bronco Billy* (1980) features Eastwood as a none-too-bright Easterner who runs an anachronistic Wild West show. In the pivotal scene, Bronco Billy allows himself to be humiliated by a gun-toting sheriff rather than betray a friend. The message might be that loyalty supersedes macho on the list of desirable modern virtues, a concept some critics interpreted as "punning on points of identity." Maybe, the critics seemed to be saying, Clint Eastwood isn't actually Dirty Harry after all. Another small film, *Honkytonk Man* (1982), is a character study, set in the Depression, of a self-destructive country singer. *Tightrope* (1984), Eastwood's depiction of a troubled cop in New Orleans, was both a critical and popular success.

By the mid-eighties, critics were having a difficult time defining Eastwood. *Sudden Impact* (1983), the fourth Dirty Harry movie, got strangely mixed notices. "The picture is like a slightly psychotic version of an old Saturday-afternoon serial, with Harry sneering at the scum and cursing them before he shoots them with his king-size custom-made '.44 Auto Mag,'" scoffed one reviewer, while another felt that "many who have long dismissed Eastwood's movies as crude cartoons now suddenly understand that the violence has always been used with self-irony and moral intelligence."

The weight of opinion seems to be shifting toward the latter viewpoint. In an article in *Parade* magazine, Norman Mailer was adamant in his admiration: "Eastwood is an artist. . . . You can see the man in his work just as clearly as you see Hemingway in *A Farewell to Arms*. . . . Critics had been attacking him for years over how little he did onscreen, but Eastwood may have known something they did not." The *Los Angeles Times* noted that women in Eastwood's movies have always been strong, interesting as both heroes and villains, and that "Eastwood may be not only one of the best, but the most important and influential (because of the size of his audience) feminist filmmaker working in America today." The French film review *Cahiers du cinéma* noted the "self-parodying subtlety" in Eastwood's movies, while the London *Daily Mail* noted that Europe was discovering "hidden depths" in Dirty Harry. The *New York Times Magazine* ran a cover story on Eastwood the artist, appropriately titled "Clint Eastwood, Seriously."

It would be pleasantly ironic to report that this reassessment of Eastwood's career has come on the heels of declining popularity at the box office, but the man who formerly had No Name is, by some accounts, the most popular movie star in the world. Theater owners named him the top moneymaking star of 1984 and 1985, a distinction he also won in 1972 and 1973. Since 1955, his forty films have grossed more than $1.5 *billion*, a figure that rivals the gross national product of some nations (Malta, Mauritania, the Netherlands Antilles, Rwanda, Tonga, Togo, Chad, and Lesotho, among others). Moreover, a recent Roper poll found that Americans aged eighteen to twenty-four picked Clint Eastwood as their number-one hero. Ronald Reagan was a distant third (behind Eddie Murphy), which may account for the fact that the president of the United States has begun quoting from Clint Eastwood films when issuing challenges to Congress.

For all his renown, Clint Eastwood in person is affable, a gentle man who speaks in a whisper-soft voice. At six-four and 190 pounds, he is physically imposing, but there is none of the coiled-spring tension one senses in Dirty Harry. Of all the roles he has played, Eastwood in person seems most like the mild-mannered California jazz DJ he portrayed in *Play Misty for Me*, a man happily out of step with the times and secure in his private enthusiasms. He lives alone in Monterey, California, where he jogs, works out with weights, plans his next projects, and is sometimes seen in the company of actress Sondra Locke. He has two children by his former wife, Maggie: a daughter, Alison, fourteen, who appeared in *Tightrope*, and a son, Kyle, seventeen, who costarred in *Honkytonk Man*.

Eastwood is, as Norman Mailer noted, "a nice guy," a fifty-five-year-old man who has taken his chances and seems distantly amused by the sudden storm of critical acclaim after having weathered thirty years of dismissal and abuse.

This year, Eastwood was invited to the Cannes Film Festival to show his eleventh directorial effort, *Pale Rider*, a western in which he also stars. The movie was warmly received, and in the press conferences that followed, the questions sounded like something my philosophical friend might have asked twenty years ago:

One journalist wondered if, at the end of *Pale Rider*, Eastwood was really killing Sergio Leone, his artistic father.

The actor thought this one over—that is the kind of question you have to answer when people start taking you seriously—and said, finally, that he didn't think so: Leone and he were the same age.

Clint Eastwood understands that a good joke dies on the dissecting table, and like many of the characters he's portrayed on screen, he is often more interesting for the things he doesn't say than the things he does. Listen:

Q: You are, by some accounts, the world's most popular movie star. Do you sometimes wake up in the morning, look in the mirror and say, "Can that possibly be me?" I mean, does it surprise you?
A: If I thought about it enough, it might. Yeah, I guess so. I guess you'd look back and say, "How did a kid from Oakland get this far?" I'm sure other people do that to some degree. It's like waking up with a hooker—how the hell did I get here?

Q: Let's start with *A Fistful of Dollars*. How did that come about?
A: Well, at that time I'd done *Rawhide* for about five years. The agency called and asked if I was interested in doing a western in Italy and Spain. I said, "Not particularly." I was pretty westerned out on the series. They said, "Why don't you give the script a quick look?" Well, I was kind of curious, so I read it, and I recognized it right away as *Yojimbo*, a Kurosawa film I had liked a lot. When I'd seen it years before, I thought, "Hey, this film is really a western." Nobody in the States had the nerve to make it, though, and when I saw that someone somewhere did have the nerve, I thought, "Great."

Sergio [Leone] had only directed one other picture, but they told me he had a good sense of humor, and I liked the way he interpreted the *Yojimbo* script. And I had nothing to lose, because I had the series to go back to as soon as the hiatus was over. So I felt, "Why not?" I'd never been to Europe. That was reason enough to go.

Q: You've said that in the original script, the Man with No Name shot off his mouth more than his gun.
A: The script was very expository, yeah. It was an outrageous story, and I thought there should be much more mystery to the person. I kept telling Sergio, "In a real A picture, you let the audience think along with the movie; in a B picture, you explain everything." That was my way of selling my point. For instance, there was a scene where he decides to save the woman and the child. She says, "Why are you doing this?" In the script he just goes on forever. He talks about his mother, all kinds of subplots that come out of nowhere, and it goes on and on and on. I thought that was not essential, so I just rewrote the scene the night before we shot it.

Q: Okay, the woman asks, "Why are you doing this?" and he says . . .
A: "Because I knew someone like you once and there was nobody there to help."

Q: So you managed to express ten pages of dialogue in a single sentence.
A: We left it oblique and let the audience wonder: "Now wait a minute, what happened?" You try to let people reach into the story, find things in it, choice little items that they enjoy. It's like finding something you've worked and hunted for, and it's much more enjoyable than having some explanation slapped into your face like a wet fish.

Q: So you have a lot of faith in your audience.
A: You have to. You don't play down to people, you don't say, "I'd better make this a little simpler, a little more expository." For instance, in *Josey Wales*, when he rides off at the end of the picture, the editor I had wanted to superimpose the girl's face over him. He said, "We want the audience to know that he's going back to her." Well, we all know he's going back. The audience wills him back. If he rides off on the other side of town, the audience will say, "Well, he's gonna turn left." It's really looking down on an audience to tell them something they already know. Or tell them something they can draw in because it arises out of the story. I try to make that part of their job.

Q: To . . .
A: To think about it a little bit.

Q: You did two more of the Italian westerns with Leone: *For a Few Dollars More* and *The Good, the Bad and the Ugly*.
A: Yeah. The other two, the productions were glossier, more refined. The stories didn't mean a whole lot. They were just a lot of vignettes all shuffled together. I enjoyed them, they were fun to do. Escapism. And the American western at that point was in a dull period. But when Sergio approached me about being in some of the subsequent westerns, I thought it would be going too far. So I came back to Hollywood and did *Hang 'Em High*. Sergio was interested in expanding the size and scope of his films, and I was more interested in the people and the story line. I guess, selfishly, because I am an actor, I wanted to do something with more character study.

Q: You've described yourself as introverted. Do you think that's because you moved so much as a kid?
A: Maybe, yes. We moved around California a lot. We lived in Redding, Sacramento, Hayward. My parents were married around 1929, right at the beginning of the Depression. It was a tough period for everybody, and especially a young guy like my dad who was just starting out. In those days, people struggled for jobs. Sometimes jobs didn't pan out, or they couldn't afford to keep you. We drove around in an old Pontiac, or something like that, towing a one-wheel trailer. We weren't itinerant: it wasn't *The Grapes of Wrath*, but it wasn't uptown either.

It gives you a sort of conservative background, being raised in an era when everything was scarce. Once, I remember, we moved from Sacramento to Pacific Palisades because my father had gotten a gas-station attendant's job. It's still there, the station. It's at Highway 101 and Sunset Boulevard.

Q: Were you involved in any school activities?
A: Yeah. I played a little basketball. Some football in junior high. I didn't really get involved in team sports, because we moved so much. I did some competitive swimming, and one of the schools I went to had a great gymnastics program, so I diddled with that for a while. I wasn't particularly suited for it, because I was so tall, but I liked it.

I suppose one of the biggest things when I was a kid—I always liked jazz. A wide spectrum of jazz. Back in the forties and fifties I listened to

Brubeck and Mulligan. And I loved Ellington and Basie. I'd get books on everybody: Bix Beiderbecke, King Oliver, Buddy Bolden. I used to be very knowledgeable.

Then, up through the forties, I used to go to those Jazz at the Philharmonic things. One time, they had Coleman Hawkins, Lester Young, Charlie Parker, and a whole group of classic players. In fact, nowadays, when I talk to composers that are maybe ten years younger than I am, they're all jealous about that concert: "You saw those guys live!"

Q: You play some jazz piano yourself.
A: Yeah, when I was a kid, I played. Fooled around with some other instruments, but I was lazy. I didn't really go after it. I just started again in the last few years. I've been diddling around with composition. Five or six things. I used one as my daughter's theme in *Tightrope*, and I also did the theme for the young girl in *Pale Rider*.

I have some regrets that I didn't follow up on music, especially when I hear people who play decently. I played on one cut on the album for *City Heat*. After the session, Pete Jolly and Mike Lang and I were all talking about how we started out playing piano. We all started the exact same way, only those guys went on to really play. We began by playing blues: blues figures at parties. I was such a backward kid at that age, but I could sit down at a party and play the blues. And the gals would come around the piano, and all of a sudden you had a date.

Q: You had a country hit, "Barroom Buddies," a duet with Merle Haggard. When did you get interested in country music?
A: Well, I think you can say that Merle Haggard had a hit and sort of dragged me along. I was never terribly knowledgeable about country music. The first real good taste of it I got was when I was eighteen or nineteen, working in a pulp mill in Springfield, Oregon. It was always wet, really depressing. Wintertime. Dank. I really didn't know anyone, and someone told me to go out to this place where there was a lot of country music. I wasn't very interested, but this guy told me there were a lot of girls there. So I went. I saw Bob Wills and his Texas Playboys. Unlike most country bands, they had brass and reeds and they played country swing. They were good. It surprised me a little bit, how good they were. Also, there were a lot of girls there, which didn't surprise me at all. So I guess you could say that lust expanded my musical horizons.

Q: Why didn't you follow up on the music?

A: I was going to. I tried to enroll in Seattle University, where they had a good music program. I got my draft notice before I got in there, though, and ended up at Fort Ord [California]. And I guess I just failed away from music.

I served my two years and went down to L.A. City College, where I enrolled in business administration. In the service I had met some guys who were actors—Martin Milner, David Janssen—and when we got out, a cinematographer got me a screen test. I got an offer to go under contract with Universal, seventy-five bucks a week to start. They threw me out a year and half later. But it was a pretty good deal for a young guy. We had acting classes every day.

Q: Is that when you realized that being introverted could be an asset for an actor? That you could play on it?
A: I don't know if I played on it consciously. I know that for many years before I became known for the way I act now, I played characters that were not terribly talkative. Economical characters. Some books—even Stanislavsky's people—discuss the fact that sometimes less can be best. Sometimes you can tell more with economy than you can with excess gyration.

The *Rawhide* series was a great training ground. All of a sudden, everything you ever studied about being an actor you could put into play every day. It's one thing to work for a week in a Francis the Talking Mule picture—which was how it had been going for me—and another thing to be doing it all day for eight years.

It's like the story of the great classical trumpet player they found one day playing in a baseball orchestra at Wrigley Field. Somebody recognized him and said, "My God, Maestro, what is the greatest classical trumpet player in the world doing playing in a baseball band?" He said, "You must play every day."

In *Rawhide*, I got to play every day. It taught me how to pick up and run, how to make things up, wing things in there.

Q: The *New York Review of Books* recently ran an article about you that said, "What is most distinctive about Eastwood . . . is how effectively he struggles against absorption into mere genre, mere style, even while appearing, with his long-boned casualness and hypnotic presence, to be nothing but style." Do you want to comment on that?
A: Well, yeah, style. Take guys like Kirk Douglas and Burt Lancaster. They're terrific actors, but their style is more aggressive. Both of them

did some marvelous things and some films that weren't big hits but were great all the same: Douglas in *Lonely Are the Brave* and *Paths of Glory*; Lancaster in *Trapeze*. But their style was a little different than, say, Gary Cooper's or Henry Fonda's, because those guys were more laid-back, more introverted, and you were always leaning forward, wondering what they were thinking. With the Lancaster-Douglas school, there was never any doubt. Fonda or Cooper: you were never quite sure with them. They had a mysterioso quality.

Q: Which is something you strive for: that little taste of ambiguity.
A: Exactly.

Q: Let's go over a few of your films. *Dirty Harry*.
A: There was something there I felt some people missed. One critic said Dirty Harry shot the guy at the end with such glee that he enjoyed it. There was no glee in it at all, there was a sadness about it. Watch the film again and you'll see that.

Q: *Every Which Way but Loose*.
A: All of a sudden Norman Mailer comes out and says he likes this film, and because he's such a well-thought-of writer, people think, "Wait a second, maybe that wasn't such a bad movie after all." I thought it was kind of a hip script myself when I read it. Here's a guy pouring his heart out to an ape, and losing the girl. I like the correlation with some of my westerns, too. The guy purposely loses the big fight at the end because he doesn't want to go around being the fastest gun in the West.

Q: *Bronco Billy*.
A: It's about the American Dream, and Billy's dream that he fought so hard for. And it's all in the context of this outdated Wild West show that has absolutely no chance of being a hit. But it's sweet. It's pure.

Q: In the pivotal scene, Billy allows himself to be humiliated by the sheriff rather than allow his friend to be arrested. That played so against your established image: it must have been fun to do.
A: Really fun. It was suggested that Billy come back at the end and punch this guy out. That would have ruined the picture, the whole theme of loyalty. Billy doesn't approve of this kid being a deserter, and he doesn't know enough to intellectualize what his friend's feelings were about the war in Vietnam. He just knows he doesn't approve but he's going to stick

by his friend. Now if Billy had come back and kicked the crap out of the sheriff at the end, it would have wrecked all that.

There's no real excuse for being successful enough as an actor to do what you want and then selling out. You do it pure. You don't try to adapt it, make it commercial. It's not *Dirty Bronco Billy*.

Q: *Honkytonk Man*.
A: Red Stovall is based a bit on some self-destructive people I've known. He's wild and funny, but he's been a coward in his time. He won't face up to his ambitions. He's not that great a singer, but he writes some interesting things. When he gets his moment, he's already destroyed himself.

Q: And the studio suggested that it might be a good idea if Red didn't die in the end?
A: I resisted that.

Q: Your new one, *Pale Rider*.
A: It's a western. One of the earliest films in America was a western: *The Great Train Robbery*. If you consider film an art form, as some people do, then the western would be a truly American art form, much as jazz is. In the sixties, American westerns were stale, probably because the great directors—Anthony Mann, Raoul Walsh, John Ford—were no longer working a lot. Then the Italian western came along, and we did very well with those; they died of natural causes. Now I think it's time to analyze the classic western. You can still talk about sweat and hard work, about the spirit, about love for the land and ecology. And I think you can say all these things in the western, in the classic mythological form.

Q: You're not generally credited with having any sense of humor, yet certain of your films get big laughs in all the right places. The first half of *Honkytonk Man*, for instance, was very funny.
A: That's the way it was designed: a humorous story that becomes a tragedy. A lot of the humor is not in what you say but in how you react. Comedians are expert at that. Jackie Gleason in *The Honeymooners*: Alice zaps him, and his reaction—just the look on his face—cracks you up. Jack Benny could do that. Comedy isn't necessarily all dialogue. Think of Buster Keaton: the poker face and all this chaos going on all around him. Sometimes it's a question of timing, of the proper rhythm.

Q: Does it amuse you that the president is quoting from *Sudden Impact*?
A: Yeah, it was kind of amusing. I knew that "Make my day" would have a certain amount of impact in the film, but I didn't realize it would become a sort of "Play it again, Sam."

Q: I've read that you occasionally speak with Reagan on the phone.
A: Well, I don't know where that came from. I think some secretary or someone mentioned it. I've talked to him a couple of times, but they make it sound like I'm some great adviser.

Q: I want you to meet my secretary of state, Dirty Harry . . .
A: Yeah, right [*laughing*].

Q: You're not going to tell me what you talk about with the president?
A: I haven't really said that much. I was in Washington not too long ago, and I walked to the White House for lunch. We didn't discuss much of anything except the National Endowment for the Arts medal we were passing out. There were some former members of the NEA there, of which I was one. It was a small luncheon, a few laughs.

I mean, he doesn't ask me for advice. I could suggest some better places to go than that cemetery in Germany.

Q: And you're not going to run for political office.
A: That's something nobody has to worry about.

Q: You have a reputation for shooting your films quickly and bringing them in under budget. Do you think that has anything to do with having grown up in the Depression?
A: I would like to say it's just good business, but it may be that. It may be a background of not wanting to see waste.

Q: There's a rumor that people work quickly on your sets because you don't provide chairs.
A: That rumor derived from a comment I made. Someone asked why I liked shooting on location as opposed to in the studio. I said, "In the studio, everyone's looking around for a chair. On location, everyone's working." But there are chairs on the set and on location.

Q: You also have a reputation for bringing in young or underappreciated talent. *Thunderbolt and Lightfoot*, for instance, was Michael Cimino's first film. Some people might say that you do that because you get these folks cheap.

A: Nothing's cheap, and I don't think I'd cut off my nose to spite my face. I don't think I'd get somebody cheap just because I thought he was cheap. I think I'd want the film to be the best possible. Otherwise you're selling yourself short. An awful lot of directors are expensive, but you don't know how they got to be that way. Sometimes it's just a matter of salesmanship and agenting.

I haven't worked with a lot of big-name directors, but I came up during an era when they were all beginning to retire: I never worked with Hitchcock or Wyler or Stevens or Capra or Hawks or Walsh. I missed all that.

I suppose the most expensive director I've worked with is Don Siegel. I think I learned more about directing from him than from anybody else. He taught me to put myself on the line. He shoots lean, and he shoots what he wants. He knew when he had it, and he didn't need to cover his ass with a dozen different angles.

I learned that you have to trust your instincts. There's a moment when an actor has it, and he knows it. Behind the camera you can feel that moment even more clearly. And once you've got it, once you feel it, you can't second-guess yourself. If I would go around and ask everyone on the set how it looked, eventually someone would say, "Well, gee, I don't know, there was a fly six hundred feet back." Somebody's always going to find a flaw, and pretty soon that flaw gets magnified and you're all back to another take. Meanwhile, everyone's forgotten that there's a certain focus on things, and no one's going to see that fly, because you're using a 100-mm lens. But that's what you can do. You can talk yourself in or out of anything. You can find a million reasons why something didn't work. But if it feels right, and it looks right, it works.

Without sounding like a pseudointellectual dipshit, it's my responsibility to be true to myself. If it works for me, it's right. When I start choosing wrong, I'll step back and let someone else do it for me.

Q: The critics are beginning to say that you've made some pretty good choices.

A: Some of them. But it's luck. It's instinctive. It comes from the animal part of the brain: the instinctive, intuitive pact. The analytical brain can kill you as an artist. You want to stay in touch on a deeper level.

Q: Why do you think the critics have begun to reassess your career?
A: I think it just finally got to the point where people said, "Well, he does quite a few different things. Maybe it isn't all some cowboy or cop who happened to click." It's easy to dismiss those kinds of films unless you're consciously looking for the best in them. Then again, I've changed. I've done films, like *Bronco Billy*, that were unusual for me, unusual for anyone. At a Museum of Modern Art retrospective in New York, they liked *Bronco Billy* and worked back from there. The French worked back from *Honkytonk Man*, which was one of the best-reviewed English-language films of the year there. In Montreal, at the film festival there, they liked *Tightrope*. All those films accumulate, and after thirty years, people are beginning to look at a body of work.

Q: But how do you feel about it, this critical reassessment?
A: It's gratifying.

Eastwood on Eastwood

Christopher Frayling / ca. 1985

> Published as chapter 6 in Christopher Frayling, *Clint Eastwood* (London: Virgin, 1992), 61–67. Reprinted by permission.

Frayling: Could we talk about the origins of the "Eastwood style," in the Spaghetti Westerns of the mid-1960s? In retrospect, they changed both the look and the feel of the traditional Western.
Eastwood: Yeah, I think they changed the style, the approach to Westerns. They "operacized" them, if there's such a word. They made the violence and the shooting aspect a little more larger than life, and they had great music and new types of scores. I wasn't involved in the music, but we used the same composer, Ennio Morricone, in *Sister Sara* and I worked with him a bit there. . . . They were scores that hadn't been used in other Westerns. They just had a look and a style that was a little different at the time: I don't think the stories were any better, maybe they were less good. I don't think any of them was a classic story—like *The Searchers*, or something like that. They were more fragmented, episodic, following this central character through various little episodes.

Frayling: Someone once wrote that Leone's films are "operas in which the arias aren't sung, they are stared" [*laughter*]. But when you say "a look and a style," do you mean that their main contribution was a technical one?
Eastwood: Uh-huh. I think the technical effect is the biggest—the look and the sound. A film has to have a sound of its own, and the Italians—who don't record sound while they're shooting—are very conscious of this. Sergio Leone felt that sound was very important, that a film has to have its own sound as well as its own look. And I agree. . . . Leone'll get a very operatic score, a lot of trumpets, and then all of a sudden "ka-pow!" He'll shut it off and let the horses snort and all that sort of thing. It's

very effective. So, yes, I think you've hit on it when you say "technical"—that was the star—technical changes. The lighting was different, too. It wasn't flat lit. A little more . . . style.

Frayling: I've read somewhere that, when you were preparing for the role of The Man with No Name, just before you left the Universal Studios set on *Rawhide* for Rome and Almería, you bought the costume at a Santa Monica wardrobe store, and borrowed the leather gunbelt, pistol, and suede boots from *Rawhide*. Yet Sergio Leone has told me that the transformation of Rowdy Yates into The Man with No Name—the basic change of "look and style" from which everything else followed—was mostly *his* idea.

Eastwood *(eyes narrowing momentarily)*: He didn't accept that . . . ? Well—I guess I heard that too, and I heard stories where people would say that he would lay a rope down the line on the ground where I should walk—and all that stuff—and I thought "Funny, he's the only one who ever had to do that." But I guess it's normal for him—all of a sudden I go off back to America, and he does several films in the same vein and then drops out for a while, and he sees me going on to do other things and maybe that affected him. Who knows why a person says different things?

Frayling *(not feeling lucky, not pushing it)*: Whoever it was, the character's sense of visual style—the poncho in *Fistful of Dollars* (1964), the long-waisted coat in *The Good, the Bad and the Ugly* (1966)—was a world away from the fringed buckskins of Alan Ladd in *Shane*, or all those well-scrubbed army scouts in 1950s Westerns.

Eastwood *(visibly relaxing again)*: Yeah, that was accepted at the time—sixties—and yeah, that buckskin does look a little drugstoreish now. But we did similar things in *High Plains Drifter* and *Pale Rider*, where he's kind of a stylized character, with a little bit of a different look—the hats, the long coats, and various other things. But it was mostly the people who were *in* the clothes. Gian Maria Volonté had a good face, and all those Spanish, gypsy faces—that was just general . . . everything kind of tied together and made an interesting-looking film. You ask most people what the films were about and they can't tell you. But they tell you "the look" [*he mimes throwing the poncho over his shoulder*] and the "da-da-da-da-dum" [*he hums the opening bars of* The Good, the Bad and the Ugly *theme*], and the cigar and the gun and those little flash images that hit you, and we get back to "technical" again, technical changes. Maybe I had some contribution in there, and er, maybe not. . . . I remember we cut out quite a bit of dialogue together, on *Fistful*, before and during.

Frayling: I don't know if you recall, but in the Italian press of 1964 you were billed as "Western consultant" on *A Fistful of Dollars*.
Eastwood: Uh-huh? *(laughter, and quizzical look)*

Frayling: A lot of the technical lessons of the Italian films seem to me to have been carried over into your first Western as a director, *High Plains Drifter*: the sound effects, the heavy framing, the way in which the hero is presented . . .
Eastwood: Yeah. I don't really associate *High Plains Drifter* as closely with those films as maybe some do—other than the same actor and this mysterious drifting character who comes in, which is like the character in *A Fistful of Dollars*. But then that's sort of the classic Western—that's been done so many times before—with *Shane*, with William S. Hart, with . . . *[pause]* there's nothing really new under the sun there, it's just a question of styling. And it was the same actor playing it. Some elements that come with that character are going to come into other characters that I play, too, along the line. You adapt it to yourself, you know. . . . The *Fistful of Dollars* character, also—it was fun for me to do everything that was against the rules. For years in Hollywood there was a thing called the Hays Office, there were certain taboos that were put on the Western, even more so than other things. One was that you never could tie up a person shooting with a person being hit. You had to shoot separately, and then show the person fall—and that was always thought sort of stupid, but on television we always did it that way. . . . We did it that way on *Rawhide*—and everybody talked about it, and it was sort of a thing that hung over there. And then, you see, Sergio never knew that, and so he was tying it up and that was great—that's terrific, tie up the shots. You see the bullet go off, you see the gun fire, you see the guy fall, and it had never been done this way before. Those things seemed to me very bad for television. Where everybody was shooting sort of standard things, the typical television filming would be where the person is in the door CUT. CUT around to other person who says some lines. CUT walks up to him. Two head closeups. You never do see the two people together. So that was part of it.

Frayling: Turning to *The Outlaw Josey Wales* (1976, or twelve years after *Fistful*), which I think is one of your finest films as a director so far,

there's much less emphasis on "style," on the detached, comic-strip aspects of the Spaghetti Westerns, and much more on the kinds of things that might be on Americans' minds after the Vietnam war. It's about the rebuilding of a small community after the bloody dislocation of the American Civil War—but it could just as well be about post-Vietnam America. How conscious was that?
Eastwood: Right. It was inherent in the story, but I guess it made it attractive to me, but I didn't sit there and say, "Well, I'm doing this now because this parallels some situation in history, then and now, like Vietnam." But I think the dislocation could be the same after every war . . . *is* the same.

Frayling: In a way, *Josey Wales* puts the morality—the *American* morality—back into the character of "The Man with No Name." Josey is determined to get his revenge on the Kansas Redlegs— "I don't want nobody belonging to me," he says—yet he's constantly being deflected from his quest by various drifters who refuse to take his macho image seriously. Even the hound-dog he picks up along the way isn't taken in by the image. The punch line is that we should choose—whatever the odds against—"the word of life" rather than "the word of death." It's the gentle option, rather than the violent one . . .
Eastwood: Well, the thing that I liked about it was that it was a Western with a very good story and a central character, and the effects on this character and what life had done to this guy, and his search for something it would be easier to run away from—and by accident things always happen to him, which make him a better person. He starts out as a farmer, becomes a killer, and in the end, I think, becomes a farmer again—although the audience decides that. Because, like I said, the films that I did with Sergio, if they'd been done with less style, they would have been very poor shows because they weren't really good strong stories, and I like stories. It's not that we drifted apart, but I think we just became philosophically different.

I was drifting—naturally, being an actor—towards more personal, more real stories. And he wanted more production values as a director, so he was always going towards vaster and vaster scenes, with trains blowing up, and more Indians over the hill, or whatever—I'm just using examples, nothing specific . . . and I wanted more personal stories. He got into larger, epic pictures and I got into smaller pictures. In *Josey Wales*, there was a personal story that also had a large landscape to it, and that was ideal for me.

Frayling: It must be unique for an entire cinematic genre to depend on the fortunes of one individual, but, through the 1970s and 1980s, the future of the Western has to a large extent hinged on the box-office performance of your work. Why do you think that the Western virtually collapsed in the 1970s? Why, for example, did an Arthur Penn Western with Jack Nicholson and Marlon Brando—which must have seemed gilt-edged to those in the know—why did it go down so badly?
Eastwood: I don't blame all that on the Western as much as on the material . . . that Nicholson and Brando thing, *The Missouri Breaks*, for instance, was ridiculous. It wasn't a good script and they obviously felt so, too—why else would a guy dress up like his own grandmother? Brando obviously thought there's nothing here, I might as well enjoy myself. So he's going to go off and screw off somewhere. I think that if he'd truly believed it was a great piece of material and that he was going to contribute to something that might be a fine film, he might have thought otherwise. I like to think that, anyway.

Frayling: So what d'you think *your* particular contribution has been to the American Western of the 1970s and 1980s?
Eastwood: Well, the answer maybe is just what you said. Maybe that I was lucky enough to make a few of the most successful ones of that period. I don't have any great bolt of lightning from the sky about that one. I just feel the Western is part of the American heritage; the earliest American film, as you'll know, was *The Great Train Robbery*. Americans don't have many art forms that are truly American. Most of them come from Europe or wherever. Westerns and jazz are the only two I can think of which are American art forms. But *High Plains Drifter* was great fun because I liked the irony of it, I liked the irony of doing a stylized version of what happens if the sheriff in *High Noon* is killed, and symbolically comes back as some avenging angel or something—and I think that's far more hip than doing just a straight Western, the straight old conflicts we've all seen. *Josey Wales* just had a much stronger story as far as the personal, the individual was concerned, and a good character. *Bronco Billy* wasn't really a Western at all. . . . More Frank Capra than Western.

Pale Rider is kind of allegorical, more in the *High Plains Drifter* mode: like that, though he isn't a reincarnation or anything, but he does ride a pale horse like the four horsemen of the apocalypse, and he could maybe be one of those guys. It's a classic story of the big guys against the little guys, little guys versus big guys, the corporate mining which ends up in hydraulic mining, they just literally mow the mountains away, you know, the trees and everything . . . all that was outlawed in California some years ago, and they still do it in Montana and a few places. It was outlawed way back, even before ecological concerns were as prevalent as they are today. So we play on that in the film. It's kind of an ecological statement—the fact that this corporation is moving fast because they're afraid laws against it will come along. And so they rabble-rouse these other people and shoot 'em up—ruin their property—and a little girl prays for this figure that comes out of the mountains. He comes down, and there's a series of incidents, and he helps them . . . ! I like stories you can't guess the endings of. Most Westerns, you can guess the ending.

Frayling: So you think Westerns still have an audience, can still carry themes which are about today as well?
Eastwood: I think there's a market there, if somebody can make a good one—because in America, on television, Westerns do extremely well. Some of mine have been run many times—and, like the chairman of Warner Bros., Bob Daly said, he'll be selling *Josey Wales* for ten years. So if they do well on television, maybe that means there is a more adult audience. Maybe if these people could come out to the cinema, plus maybe find a group of people who haven't seen a Western recently . . . ! I mean if I was taking a poll—like those studios have to do, throwing the thing in hoppers and computers, which I wouldn't—I think it would come out positive. But I'm not sure . . .

Frayling: Certainly, country and western music, "new" and "old," has never been more popular—and Willie Nelson, and Kenny Rogers have both made Westerns (*Barbarosa, The Gambler*) on the strength of their success as singers. So maybe the way forward might be in modern Westerns. Urban cowboys. Electric horsemen . . .
Eastwood: Well, I think the Western *has* to be period. I don't think it can be modern. I don't think anybody's interested in a Western set today necessarily—or maybe they might be, depending on the film—I hate to say that definitely. Perhaps a picture about rodeo riding or something like that *might* help to excite somebody. Maybe. But I think a period Western is always that kind of escape—another time, times when things were more simplified . . .

Flight of Fancy

Nat Hentoff / 1988

> Published in *American Film*, September 1988, 24–31. Reprinted by permission of the author.

Clint Eastwood, I had heard, is somewhat of a jazz buff—otherwise, why would he take the director's seat for *Bird*, the film biography of jazz great Charlie "Bird" Parker? As it turns out, Eastwood is more than a buff, he's a downright enthusiast. When he talks about jazz, or Parker in particular, Eastwood's voice noticeably brightens. Like most moviegoers, I figured the off-screen Eastwood would be a taciturn man. But when he discusses his new film, there is nothing of the "star" about him. Jazz is a subject that opens him up. A pianist who used to play clubs in Oakland, California, Eastwood still writes music and has collaborated on the themes for many of his films including *Tightrope* and *Pale Rider*. Since listening to jazz is an integral part of Eastwood's life, *Bird* is a particularly personal film. For the moment, Eastwood has put aside the guns and car crashes in favor of a character study. He clearly wants *Bird* to be a portrait of that explosive musician and the sounds he made. Eastwood's pride in this project is not likely to be affected even if reaction to the film is tepid. He told me, that if *Bird* doesn't fly, another jazz film eventually will.

American Film: At what point did you decide to do a movie about jazz, and particularly about Charlie "Bird" Parker?
Clint Eastwood: I've done a lot of pictures with jazz scores, from *Play Misty for Me* to *The Enforcer*. But I had never done a picture about a jazz personality per se. Why Charlie Parker? When I was fifteen or sixteen, I'd seen him on two or three occasions, and I'd always been fascinated by him. There was something special about the way he played, a very confident sound. His presence was overwhelming. It was like Gary Cooper

or Clark Gable standing next to John Doe. There was a big magnetism there.

Another reason for doing the picture is that I'm fascinated by the forties and fifties. And I wanted the music to really be of that era. So often, when people do period films, they start deciding, "Well, we'll update this a little bit." And it loses its purity.

AF: So, in the movie *Bird*, you extracted Parker's solos from original recordings for the soundtrack?
Eastwood: Yeah, we used Bird's own recordings. No sound-alikes. On those original recordings, his solos are always up front, and it seems like everybody else kind of disappears. So we built around those solos by bringing in as many of the original sidemen as we could and then added equivalent players of today. From then and from now, we got Walter Davis, Barry Harris, Ray Brown, Jon Faddis, Ron Carter, and Red Rodney. Red knew Bird well.

AF: As you know, there are people who try to figure out where you are politically by the movies you do. *Dirty Harry* might indicate that you and Ed Meese could be members of the same law-and-order club. Yet films like *Bronco Billy* celebrate a gentler kind of independence. Is *Bird* going to further confuse your audience?
Eastwood: I don't know why anybody would want to look for political ramifications in any film. After all, if you love making pictures, if you like doing the whole spectrum, no particular picture has any bearing on what you feel in your own life.

I've always said, for instance, that Adolf Hitler must be a fascinating character to play in a movie. The role is probably an actor's dream. That doesn't mean the actor is a fascist.

I'm just a filmmaker. *Bird* does have roots in my own experience though. I was raised in Oakland, California, around this kind of music. A lot of it is out of the black experience, and I feel I know it as well as any white person around.

AF: You're one of the few director/producers with stature—both artistic and box-office—to try to make a serious film about jazz. Why has there been such avoidance of jazz in film and on television?
Eastwood: It's a crime, in a way. Hollywood has largely avoided treating the music and the players seriously because we're trendy here. We

think of culture in European terms—European music, European art. But when it comes to jazz—which is an innovation from the guts of American cities and is so revered around the world by really sophisticated audiences—we don't spend enough time on it. And most of the time, when we do make something about jazz, we go for the commercial angle.

AF: When you direct, you do something that reminds me of Duke Ellington—a distinctly noncommercial jazzman. He used to say that if he had to do more than two takes on a recording he'd worry, because, if it sounded perfect, it was dead. And you're known for preferring one take whenever it can work out that way.
Eastwood: Well, sometimes the imperfection of things is what makes them real. Many times, I've seen movies that are beautifully composed, beautifully laid out, but there's something dead there. And the deadness comes out of its having been overworked. The actors have been kind of beaten to death.

What I try to do—and it's just a matter of technique—is to get my performers in the mood before we ever start rehearsing. I'll say, "Would you like to rehearse one on film?" Because many times you do a rehearsal and you say, "Gee, that's beautiful. I wish we'd shot it."

So I tell everybody to just rehearse quietly, and I'll have the camera running. You get some marvelous little pieces because everybody's just doing it, they're not just sitting there thinking about acting in front of the camera. They're doing it for real.

AF: A character in the film that struck me as quite real was Chan Parker, probably the most important woman in Bird's life. Many of the women in your movies have been strong, whether in leading or supporting roles, and Chan is in that tradition. Has this approach to women's roles been conscious on your part?
Eastwood: No, I think I just gravitated toward that approach. Although it's true that the first film I directed was *Play Misty*, which had a compelling woman's role. It came right after *The Beguiled*. That film had seven major parts for women—Geraldine Page, Elizabeth Hartman, along with other wonderful actresses. But that was in the early days of feminism, and some feminists stood up at some functions saying, "Why are you oppressive to women?" I told them that I'd been reading all the time that there's not enough good roles for women. I was just trying to help out. It's ironic that a half decade later, people are calling me a feminist director.

Actually, my preferences for strong roles for women in my films stems from when I was a kid. I grew up on pictures in which the women always played very important roles. Barbara Stanwyck, Bette Davis. And Clark Gable's role in *It Happened One Night* was only good because he had Claudette Colbert's to play off of. Those movies are more true to life than many films now where you have the guys sort of motivating most of the stories and the women in secondary positions.

AF: You haven't tried to make this film in a commercial way. Nonetheless, could it be commercial?
Eastwood: I can't tell. If you judge the history of movies about jazz, they have not turned out to be very commercial. But I still wanted to make this, and I'm appreciative of Warner Bros. for allowing me to make it.

I told Warner Bros. that we weren't going to use a name actor, and they went along with me. Columbia had the script first, and they were talking about using Richard Pryor, which I think would have been wrong. He's done some wonderful things, but you'd see Richard Pryor, not Bird. People would be expecting a lot of gags. I wanted very good actors whom people could see as the characters.

AF: Was it much of a search to find the leads?
Eastwood: No. I'd always liked Forest Whitaker in other films. He'd been in smaller roles, but he'd stood out. He did a test on film that was also very good, so I said, "Let's go for it!" As for the role of Chan, I hadn't met her but, having talked to people about her and read about her, I saw the right look and the right quality in Diane Venora. She was the very first girl I looked at. I saw her on tape and she just jumped out as Chan. I said, "That's it!"

AF: The *Dirty Harry* series is popular with black audiences. Why do you think that is?
Eastwood: First, audiences, regardless of race or ethnic background, have the same feelings, the same frustrations. And blacks have just as much to worry about concerning crime as anybody else. Moreover, Harry is a loner out there, and blacks have the same feelings about the strengths of individuals, and the rights of individuals, as white people do.

Dirty Harry has a broad appeal because he's fighting the bureaucracy. He's trying to get things done. And it's hard to get things done. You're not only fighting the criminal element, you're also fighting the bureaucracy of society.

AF: In various ways, most of your pictures are like an extension of the Frank Capra films with Jimmy Stewart and Gary Cooper. The loner trying to fight the system. It's like an eternal theme.
Eastwood: It's the eternal theme of being different. Whether it's Mr. Deeds going to town and wanting to give money away so that people think he's a screwball, or Mr. Smith going to Washington and wanting to be different from what is perceived as a normal politician. Whatever the political philosophy involved, the basic point is that because a person is different doesn't mean he is necessarily wrong. And in the Capra films, the different person was always the one who was right.

AF: Is it fair to say that the basic theme—with variations—in your pictures is the Capra theme: the individual against the system? *Bird* would be part of that.
Eastwood: I guess that is the basic theme. Yeah. Nobody understood what I was doing at the beginning and some of them still don't understand me now. Some people, for instance, still cling to the idea that the *Dirty Harry* films are some kind of right-wing statement. You can look at those pictures that way if you're looking to pigeonhole somebody. But you can interpret them as other things too. If you want to take the time to think about it. You can certainly interpret Dirty Harry as an individual going against the system.

AF: What do you have planned, now that *Bird* is done?
Eastwood: I've got a few projects. Some of them are adventure films, some of them are different. Every once in a while, I like to do the unusual. A Bronco Billy kind of character. He is a favorite of mine. Because of the idealism. The guy is simply out of touch with the world as it is today. But he has a dream of the world he wants—traveling around with a little, broken-down, carnival/Western act, which is totally obsolete.

AF: You've said, "The more I branch out, the more audiences branch out with me, which I like." Have there been no exceptions?
Eastwood: They go with you to some degree, sometimes not wholeheartedly. But you hope they'll travel with you on some of your journeys and enjoy characters different than the more commercial ones you've done. But sometimes they don't go with you at all.

Certain parts of *Honkytonk Man*, for instance, were well received in France and other places, and some critics like it a lot. But the audiences didn't go with me. They don't like me to go on a self-destruct, and that was sort of a self-destruct movie. *The Beguiled* was also sort of total self-destruct, and the audience didn't enjoy that either. But I thought they were enjoyable films to do, and have no regrets about doing them.

AF: When you make a picture, do you have any sense of your audience?
Eastwood: No, I don't. I just see the project. I don't like to think in those terms. I don't see the audience. I make the film, and that's it. And they like it, or they don't. That's up to them. You're always hoping they're going to see in the story what you saw, but you have to make it, then let it go. You have to make it for yourself, otherwise you're not true to what you're doing. If you make it with an audience in mind or a reviewer in mind, you'll get fooled every time.

AF: T. S. Eliot said that you're likely to get fooled whatever you do, that once work is out there, people are going to interpret it in ways you never intended, and there's nothing you can do about it.
Eastwood: That's true. I've conducted cinema classes around the world, and people will sometimes put the wildest interpretations on something you've done. Whatever they say, I say, "That's right." It's their participation that I want. What counts is what gives them the best enjoyment.

AF: And has *Bird* given that enjoyment to you?
Eastwood: Yeah, jazz has been with me since I was a kid. I remember once going to work in Springfield, Oregon, when I was nineteen. I'd been used to living in the Bay Area where we had a lot of jazz. In Oregon, there is nothing but country music, except for one jazz program out of San Francisco late at night. Hell, just to hear a taste of it, I used to stay up late even though I had to get up early and go to work. I'd hear one or two numbers and I'd feel, wow, just fine.

That's what jazz does to you, and I hope people are going to feel that about *Bird*. Already, I've been getting some amazing reactions from musicians across the country. They come up—they're all young people, jazz people—and they say, "Thank you for doing a jazz movie, thank you for doing this story." Even though they don't know what the story is. That makes me feel just fine.

AF: As a director—and this is only the second film you've directed in which you didn't also appear—you seem to agree with jazz musicians who say that their playing is simply a matter of telling a story.
Eastwood: Exactly. Create a mood, then tell a story, and leave people

with some feeling, some thought about the persons in the picture, about that era, and maybe some understanding of what made people tick in that particular era. And with *Bird* hopefully they'll enjoy the music of that era—those who knew it at the time and those who didn't know it. And maybe those who didn't know it will go away realizing how much fun it was to make and to listen to that music.

Nowadays, a lot of people take jazz more seriously—as an American art form. But in Bird's days, they weren't thinking about that sort of thing. They just enjoyed playing what they wanted to play and they were happy coming up with new things. And they had a hot sound. You know, nobody's really shown how hot bebop could be. That's really what we tried to do in *Bird*. We tried to bring back how it really was.

Interview with Clint Eastwood

Michel Ciment / 1990

Published as "Entretien avec Clint Eastwood" in *Positif*, no. 351 (May 1990): 5–11. Reprinted by permission; translated from the French by KC.

Q: What was the origin of *White Hunter, Black Heart*?
A: A fellow by the name of Stanley Rubin, who I'd met a long time ago at the beginning of the fifties when he was a producer at Universal, was working for Ray Stark, and he asked me whether I'd be interested in reading a script that had been hanging around in Columbia's offices for quite a while along with some others. I think I read it in the plane coming back from France where I had shown *Bird* and the subject fascinated me. Then I read some later scripts that had been touched up, and finally the original book. It turned out that Columbia was going through a period of transition, being sold to Sony, and it was finally with Warners that I made the deal. Then I met Peter Viertel and found out the whole story of the novel, how he began to write it and the adventures of the pre-production period for *The African Queen*. It fascinated me, as obsessive behavior always does. Here was a personality that offered a real dichotomy. He could be full of charm and generosity, concerned with the down-and-out, and at the same time cruel to people in his entourage, if that was his mood. It was a very interesting character to explore.

Q: Did the script evolve once you had made the decision to film it?
A: I took the last script of Peter Viertel, Burt Kennedy, and James Bridges, cut out a few things and added a few, but in the main it was a work of adjustment. What I liked about this script is that it was faithful to the book, contrary to some previous versions, which had eliminated elements that in my opinion had to be preserved.

Q: Among the films you've directed, the ones that are about men of ac-

tion have a very tight narrative structure and a fast rhythm, while your films on artists—*Honkytonk Man, Bird,* or *White Hunter, Black Heart,* all about self-destructive characters—offer a suppler shape, a more relaxed tempo.
A: I don't sit down to try to make connections among the films I've directed. What I know, as I've said, is that I'm interested in obsessive behavior. The behavior of the *White Hunter* character is very different from that of the character in *Honkytonk Man,* who was a singer who hadn't known success, who even resisted it and was afraid of it. Bird, on the other hand, was very successful from a certain point of view but, from another, he was self-destructive. I don't think that Wilson's character, as he is portrayed in this picture, is completely self-destructive, but he's capable of being diverted from his goal. The irony is that he can still accomplish some very interesting things, while straying from his objective like that.

Q: Dozens of films have been made that evoke the world of Hollywood. Since you've now made one as well, what do you see as their limitations and in what sense do some of them seem to you to be faithful to the spirit of the place?
A: What guided me is not so much what I've seen in other pictures as what I've felt in my own professional life. I've often been the witness of conflicts between producers and directors. More than once I've heard the same arguments about budgets and watched people doing stupid things, although I never knew someone like Wilson, who's an amalgam of several people. I never knew Huston either, so I don't know what he was really like. According to testimonies of people who knew him, I suspect that Wilson is very close to him in many areas. I admire Huston's work a lot and I think he directed some marvelous films. Sometimes it's preferable not to know someone, in order to have more distance with regard to the topic you're dealing with. I spoke to numerous people who knew him: Peter Viertel, his daughter Anjelica, and so forth. When I began the movie he was already dead. If I had sat down with him and we had chatted together, maybe it would have given me some insights or, on the contrary, I might have listened to the reflections of a man talking about his past experiences, while I was more interested in the drama of the present moment.

Q: Did you do research in order to comprehend the character?
A: Yes. I screened some documentaries that had been made about him,

listened to several narrations that he did for films, and of course I had seen him as an actor on the screen.

Q: Did Peter Viertel tell you about the reasons that motivated him to write his novel?
A: He told me that during the filming Huston became hostile to Sam Spiegel, though he'd worked with him before. In his autobiography Huston says he was searching for a period of three weeks he could use to go on safari while he was in Africa. That's what gave Peter Viertel the impetus to write his novel. He was in the presence of someone, surrounded by all his technical crew, who was supposed to be scouting locations and getting ready to direct a film and who left in search of elephants to kill! What happens when this tragedy takes place and how does it affect a certain group of people?

Q: You avoided two dangers in portraying Huston: on the one hand, not to be capable of suggesting his presence, and on the other, to attempt an imitation.
A: The main trap would definitely have been to do a sort of imitation like the kind you see in nightclubs. What I tried to do was to think like him, to seize on the very particular development that was his, sometimes a little condescending but deliberately so. He had a way all his own of asking people to listen to him. I wanted to recreate this kind of attitude. Being tall myself, pretty much Huston's height, observing his behavior and his diction in the movies, striving to reconstruct his turns of thought, after that things came very naturally. I wanted to seize the interior feeling, the philosophy, to share the same attitude with respect to the world. I didn't really try to imitate his gestures, though I often acted with a cigarette in my hand because he was a chain smoker. But also, because the character is called John Wilson, there is a fictional side, and I didn't want the spectator to be overwhelmed by the resemblances.

Q: The character is close to Huston, apart from the fact that the latter didn't film documentaries in London during the war, but in the Pacific and in Italy.
A: When I was drafted into the army, at the time, in fact, when Huston was shooting *The African Queen*, one of my auxiliary jobs, besides swimming instructor, was to project training films for the soldiers. I kept showing *The Battle of San Pietro*, one of my favorites, which I must have seen around fifty times during my two years in the service! To have lis-

tened to the commentary spoken by Huston in this film very early in my life made me familiar with his voice.

Q: Did you think about another actor to play the role?
A: No. I liked the role and as soon as I read the script I immediately thought of playing it. It was afterwards that I considered directing it.

Q: Obviously you're attracted by artists—folk singers, jazz musicians, film directors—and by the relationships between art and life.
A: Whenever you want to film a story, it's always interesting to grapple with the unusual, and Huston was a thoroughly unusual personality, the same as Charlie Parker.

Q: The film isn't about the making of a film—that's also unusual. Even the characters of Humphrey Bogart and Katharine Hepburn are seen as silhouettes in the background.
A: Because that isn't the story I want to tell. People have already seen *The African Queen*. *White Hunter, Black Heart* is another movie. It tells how someone came to film *The African Queen* and how this character becomes obsessed by things that don't have anything to do with filmmaking and nevertheless succeeds in making his movie. It's like someone who takes a fall and yet lands on his feet.

Q: Outside of the two scenes on racism you share the points of view of all your characters by turns. You give each his chance, like in the conversation about simplicity in art.
A: Absolutely. The screenwriter in the film is playing a little bit the role of a conscience, he has his own philosophy and sticks to it even though the director, Wilson, sweeps everyone away in his wake inasmuch as he's the commander-in-chief of the project. That's what I liked about this story, that it didn't confine itself to one character expressing his ideas. Everyone has his reasons. Paul Landers—inspired by Sam Spiegel—says some true things also. He's not the "bad guy." He has his own responsibilities. The movie and the novel are about the interaction of several individual philosophies. The only "bad guy" in the story is Wilson's obsession. What attracted me to this story is not only the dramatic aspect but also the exchange of ideas. I *also* believe in simplicity in art, but I believe just as much that there aren't any rules.

Q: Do you think that artists, as they grow older, tend towards simplicity?

Are you sensible of a similar evolution in your work since *Play Misty for Me* and *High Plains Drifter*?
A: It all depends on the project. But I do think that when an artist feels more confident in his capacities and when he has more experience, it's easier for him to be simple. When you've asserted yourself, people know your work better and you can draw some simpler lines instead of putting down blotches here and there. A lot of young directors who come from television believe that they have to make their presence felt onscreen, that they need to constantly move the camera. Being an actor frees me from having to impose my presence as a director, so that the public can remain inside the story without being distracted by the "interesting" angles of the man behind the camera.

Q: There is also a discussion on art in relation to the audience where Wilson claims that one must not think about the spectators whereas Peter opposes movies that have unhappy endings.
A: Again I consider that they both have very solid viewpoints. Wilson is at a stage of his life as an artist where he believes he must be completely honest with regard to the subject he's dealing with and to know whether or not people will want to see his film is not his department. I agree with this position. If, as a filmmaker, you believe that a car has to go through a shop window because the public will like it, you're going to make a movie that won't have a lot of substance. Once you believe in a project, it's necessary to go ahead, and with luck the public will follow you. A lot of people advised me not to make *White Hunter, Black Heart* because it didn't correspond to marketing studies on public tastes, and, although I didn't use the same terms as Wilson, I told them that you couldn't worry about the supposed desires of audiences. I'm like a guide: I lead the tour, and if people don't like it they can leave along the way. In the movies, spectators always have the possibility of walking out. That leaves the final decision on what they want to watch to them! I've felt that since the time of *The Beguiled*. Albert Maltz had written a script with a happy ending: the hero who lost his leg went off into the sunset with the girl. Don Siegel and I thought that the conclusion of the novel had much more strength as an anti-war statement. We adopted John Wilson's point of view back then: we decided to go ahead and to be faithful to our convictions.

On the other hand I can understand the screenwriter in our movie when he says that there are enough misfortunes in the world and that the project they're working on gives them the opportunity to bring a little happiness. And in fact on this particular film, *The African Queen*, that's what happened. But it was strictly due to the Hays Office of the time. The conclusion of the script was pessimistic, as Huston had wanted it.

Q: There's one strong idea in the book: the one that life (here the elephant hunt), for an artist, can take precedence over his art. It was typical of Huston, the opposite of Hitchcock for whom the cinema was everything.
A: It's another aspect of the character that pleased me: he was interested in other things besides his art. He liked women, gambling, living the high life, traveling. He could have a life parallel to his work. I could identify with this type of behavior. But, because of this very fact, he became attracted more and more by other things, so that what interested him in life moved him away from his art to the point that he nearly lived a tragedy. And the tragedy brings him back to reality.

If you study Huston's life, you realize that at the age of nineteen he thought he didn't have long to live because of a heart defect a doctor had notified him of as a result of a misdiagnosis. It drove him to elaborate a personal philosophy according to which he would profit from life to the maximum. He didn't take care of himself—he was a confirmed smoker, a heavy drinker—, and yet he lived to be more than eighty. Paul Newman spoke to me about him when we were acting at the same time, each in a different movie, in Tucson, Arizona. He was starring in *The Life and Times of Judge Roy Bean* and I was doing *Joe Kidd* with John Sturges. Huston drank martinis and smoked cigars all night long, slept from one o'clock to four o'clock in the morning because he was an insomniac, did everything he shouldn't do to live to be old, and yet he died at a very great age! It was the same thing with John Wayne, who was first of all the opposite of a health fanatic.

Q: The style of your last two films is very bound to their topic. *Bird* was an extremely free conception like a jazz improvisation. *White Hunter, Black Heart*, on the contrary, has a linear narration like, precisely, a movie by Huston or Hawks, the odyssey of a man who, at the end, finds himself.
A: I've always thought that every film imposes its own life, its own rhythm. I suppose that also had to be the case for Huston because he shot some very different kinds of movies. Hawks, too, could direct *Red River* on the one hand and *His Girl Friday* on the other with almost opposite rhythms and points of view. My philosophy of filmmaking always

seemed to me to be similar. Every film takes control of its director, not necessarily intellectually and sometimes even on a purely emotional level. You find yourself directing and doing the editing in a way that's maybe different from everything you've done up to that day. But maybe there are directors who make all their films the same way . . .

Q: You have, of course, added quite a lot of elements to the script: the habit, for example, that John Wilson has of sketching while he speaks to people.
A: While I was discussing Huston's particular characteristics with Peter Viertel he disclosed to me that he was a very good draftsman and that he liked to sketch as a pastime. I thought I could use this detail and that it would be interesting to see him represent the woman as Hitler. It's the kind of idea that occurs to you during the filming.

Q: How did you conceive the color scheme of the movie with Jack Green?
A: Africa and its skies have a very particular look. England too. I don't recall precisely what concept we elaborated for the cinematography, except that I wanted to maintain a certain rhythm in the film and to oppose England to Africa, although this isn't a big African adventure picture but a very personal story that takes place in Africa. But Africa has skies like Montana and I didn't want to overlook this dimension. I wanted to achieve a happy marriage between the intimate story and the dimension of the landscape. The cinematography would not be dark like in a nocturnal movie such as *Bird* but on the contrary rather luminous.

Q: For the opening of the film you create a very dynamic movement by means of camera movements and the editing, which sweeps the spectator off toward Wilson's house. Was it planned like that in the script?
A: Yes, and the scenes were filmed consequently to create this kind of impetus. I wanted to enter very quickly in the film and give the public a foretaste of the characters without wanting to explain too much: this is how they are, this is what they do, here's an idea of their philosophy and let's pass on to what comes next . . .

Q: How did you find Jeff Fahey, who plays Peter?
A: He's an actor I had considered two or three years ago for another picture, but he wasn't free at the time. I regarded him as a very talented young actor. Then I realized he would be great for *White Hunter, Black Heart*.

Q: Playing a part yourself and directing must change your relationship with the other actors?
A: It's definitely difficult but, on the other hand, I've done it so often that I know I'm capable of it. Once I'm in the scene myself, I play it with all possible concentration. It's true that during rehearsals I'm maybe only 50 percent in what I'm doing, the rest of my attention is devoted to setting up the shot. The first time I gave myself up to this kind of exercise in 1970 for *Play Misty for Me*, it seemed a little schizophrenic to me, but after the first two or three days of filming I got used to it. As for the other actors, I can devote more time to them because I know my own character very well, since I've already worked a lot on the script and thought about the direction. If you really care about the project as a whole, it shows, and the whole crew will be very aware of it. On the other hand, if you're only interested in your own character, everyone will realize that too . . .

Q: The movie has for a theme a metaphysical quest like *Moby Dick*, which Huston would shoot some years after *The African Queen*.
A: That's a reflection of Huston's personality. He had such varied interests that they could conflict with his practice of filmmaking. In certain pictures he made, you can see the part he liked best. For example in *Reflections in a Golden Eye* there's a sequence with a horse in the woods and you are aware that Huston very definitely liked filming that. On the other hand, in other sequences, you don't find his soul as much. From this point of view he was impulsive. In his autobiography he speaks of his obsession with elephants and it may be that Peter Viertel felt a certain emotion in the face of their extermination. This was probably not his main preoccupation in 1953 but in my view it's become an important topic for our time. At any rate for me. And it's probably one of the subtexts that attracted me to this project. This animal, the elephant, is a tie between the prehistoric era and today.

Q: Isn't there a contradiction between his very violent attack on the anti-Semitic woman and his tirade directed at Paul, the producer, whom he calls a Balkan rug peddler and to whom he declares: "It's way too difficult a subject for your small little brain to grasp . . . Why, I'd have to explain to you the sound of the wind and the smell of the woods. I'd have to create you all over again, and stamp out all these years you spent on the dirty pavement in cramped shoes." Apparently for him, the Jew cannot understand the WASP ethic of the Hawkses and the Hemingways.
A: I don't think that by calling him a Balkan rug peddler he was necessar-

ily referring to the fact that he was Jewish. He's alluding to the attitude of an individual who was a hustler during the greatest part of his life. It's one of the interesting aspects of the script. On the one hand John Wilson admits that he was also a hustler, and probably also in cramped shoes, and on the other he's going to persecute Paul for similar behavior. I think he's cruel in general with respect to Paul Landers, judging that he lacks sensitivity, and it doesn't make any difference whether he's Jewish or not. With regard to the irony of the scene with the anti-Semitic Englishwoman, Peter Viertel told me that he didn't have to write it: it actually took place at the time. Viertel witnessed the conversation between Huston and this woman and it piqued his curiosity to the point that he immediately went up to his room and noted the exchange word for word.

Q: His attitude with respect to blacks is much more coherent than towards Paul. He fights to defend the honor of a black, he loves Kivu and feels guilty for his death.
A: With Wilson—like with Huston—there was a very strong feeling for the victims of society; he felt drawn to them. On the other hand he could appear very brutal towards people who worked closely with him. During the filming of *The African Queen* there really was an antagonism between him and Spiegel. I've witnessed this in my own life, I've seen directors who would oppose producers simply because they were in front of them. Don Siegel is a very good example of this type of behavior. Don completely lacked respect for producers, it was part of his character. When we were filming *Dirty Harry* I told him, "Don, this time you're producer and director at once. You won't have anyone to hate on the set anymore!" He would always say, "I don't know what a producer does." It's true that some producers don't do anything, but others are great workers. Sam Spiegel was one of them and he produced some remarkable movies. For a reason I'm unaware of there was a conflict between Huston and him on *The African Queen.*

Q: The script of *The African Queen* is by James Agee. What was Peter Viertel's involvement?
A: He was hired to rewrite certain scenes and adjust the script in the direction Huston wanted. But in fact he was more of a buddy. As Wilson says: "Don't worry about the script. We're going to Africa to have a good time!" He took his pal along with him to do some retouching and go hunting.

Q: Women are especially badly treated in the movie, from the secretary to the mistress with her little dog and of course, the anti-Semitic woman.
A: The picture is less flattering towards the character of Wilson and the way he treats them than with respect to women in general! He's cruel to a secretary who is very efficient! Once again, it's because he feels close to her.

Q: Do you consider it easier to film action scenes than confrontations between characters?
A: To a certain extent, yes. For example it was difficult to film the sequence where they go downriver on a boat because there were crocodiles in the water and we needed helicopters to shoot it. Technically that posed problems, but you can solve them if you're prepared to take the time. But when you have two people in a room you have to bring out all the constituent elements of the scene, otherwise you won't manage to hold the attention of the audience. The sequence can crumble because of bad performances by the actors or an inadequate rhythm and then you will lose the public more easily than in an action scene.

Q: Wilson declares that Africa revealed to him aspects of his personality. What were your own reactions on encountering this continent?
A: Before shooting this picture I had never been to Africa, and I must say I adored it. There's something special about feeling so far from home, and even with today's means of communication, it's still very far. But when you think that Huston and his team had to travel to locations in a DC3, that must have been a real expedition! I liked the Africans a lot, particularly those of Zimbabwe. The landscape has a particular tranquility and it makes you think about the world in different terms. We filmed on Lake Kariba, then at Tiger Bay, and at last in Hwange, where we shot the elephant hunt. Then we went back to Victoria Falls. We filmed for seven weeks in Africa and two and half in London.

Q: The music is very unobtrusive.
A: I didn't want a typical African score, and I didn't want the music to take over the picture. When I was filming the soccer game, the extras were so great that they got carried away and began to sing and dance. I decided to keep on shooting. After editing this sequence I thought it would be nice to repeat it at the end. I asked Lennie Niehaus for a very sparse score. He had the idea of contacting Emil Richards, who's an expert in percussion instruments and a jazz drummer. His passion is collecting

percussion instruments from all over the world. He brought us into a big room full of thousands of drums and we spent the whole night there gathering all the audio materials we needed for the score. The only other instrument we used is an alto flute for certain sequences, and that's all. Lennie Niehaus was the arranger for Jerry Fielding, who I'd worked with, and after Jerry's death I was looking for someone who would be creative in the same direction. In the case of *Bird* it was more complicated than for *White Hunter, Black Heart*, where we were only looking for different sounds. For *Bird* I asked Charles McPherson to follow the filming. I asked him to use the musical themes that corresponded to the states of Parker's soul and to play them as if they were in his head.

Q: The editing on the other hand is quite complex.
A: I have a concept and I see the film edited in my mind. Sometimes a sequence is longer than you think it needs to be. For example the airplane scenes in this picture. Generally I also have an idea about the editing when I begin to film a sequence, so that I know the material I need. When the picture is finished, I don't sit down at the editing table for an eternity. I assemble the elements as I'd conceived it at the beginning, I give my chief editor some ideas and he does the editing. If, for any reason, it doesn't look like what you wanted, you retouch it, you make adjustments. Sometimes everything falls into place and it's marvelous.

Q: The film itself looks like a sketchbook like the one Wilson carries with him. It's a series of drawings whose strokes are not heavily drawn.
A: I don't shy away from dramatic pronouncements, but for this film in particular it seemed to me that it was rather a fragment of someone's life. He had a life before this, he'll have a life after it, but he's going through an experience at this moment that will influence the rest of his existence. I have a project for this spring that will be full of action. It's another cop picture, very different from this one. It has its own character and if it's done well it can turn out to be something good. It's an original script titled *The Rookie*. Charlie Sheen will play the rookie and I'll play the mature cop *(laughs)*.

Q: What is your debt to Don Siegel, who was in a way your mentor and whom you were able to observe at work when you acted in his films?
A: I've been asked that before and I can never give a satisfactory answer. I know that he had an influence on me, but I can't say precisely what, except that he had a personality close to that of his predecessors Walsh,

Ford, Hawks, or Wellman (for whom, incidentally, I played a small role), a personality like you don't find anymore today in the world of film. They were men who were direct in many ways. Don had a lot of audacity and the reason we got along so well is that we encouraged each other to prove our daring, like with *The Beguiled*, for example. I used my influence on the studio to go ahead with it and to be as faithful to the book as we were able to.

Q: Did you meet with difficulties in getting *White Hunter, Black Heart* produced?
A: I think that Warners really liked the material and the script but that they probably would have been happier if I had come up with another action picture. And although *Bird* was not a success comparable to *Roger Rabbit*, Warners realized, because of the very good reactions the picture got in a lot of places, that they could be proud of it. It's another aspect of filmmaking. I've always tried to convince the studio that it's nice to make movies that rake in a lot of money and make the shareholders happy, but that it's also possible to be proud in retrospect to have produced some pictures. There are many pictures produced by studios in the past that were probably not commercial successes, but they're happy today to have them carry their logo.

Interview with Clint Eastwood

Thierry Jousse and Camille Nevers / 1992

Published as "Entretien avec Clint Eastwood" in *Cahiers du cinéma*, no. 460 (October 1992): 67–71. Reprinted by permission; translated from the French by KC.

After the vision of *Unforgiven*, it seemed to us to be indispensable to meet with Clint Eastwood. We did so at the end of this past August, in the course of an intensive publicity tour. Reserved, humorous, perceptive: Clint Eastwood, the man as he is.

Q: *Unforgiven* is a Western relatively different from the ones you have directed or acted in before. Why the desire to take up this genre again, and what would you say is the difference between this one and the others?
A: I couldn't tell you exactly why I wanted to make a Western again, because I didn't have any reason to make one or not to make one; it wasn't a decision that came out of a particular trend, there wasn't any prior reason in fact, and that's what made the project all the more exciting to me: I prefer to do things without giving myself a starting direction. So why a Western? That seemed to be the only possible genre the story was calling for, because in fact everything grew out of the story. In any case, I've never thought of doing anything because it's *in fashion*, on the contrary I've always felt a need to go against it. And anyway, I probably feel a little guilty of always having tried to go against success like that, against the fashion.

As for what makes this Western different from the others, it seems to me that the film deals with violence and its consequences a lot more than those I've done before. In the past, there were a lot of people killed gratuitously in my pictures, and what I liked about this story was that people aren't killed, and acts of violence aren't perpetrated, without there being certain consequences. That's a problem I thought it was important to talk about today, it takes on proportions it didn't have in the past, even if it's always been present through the ages.

Q: *Unforgiven* is dedicated to Sergio Leone and to Don Siegel. What relationship does your film have with their cinema?
A: In my mind, the film doesn't have much to do with Sergio and Don. But it's equally true that we never know to what extent the things of our life, the people we've worked with or haven't worked with, will come to play a role in what we do—whether it's John Ford, for instance, or others. They're two people I'd worked with at important moments in my life, and both of them, ironically, died in the course of the last couple of years; that's why I wanted to pay homage to those two men who had influenced me so much, whether they had anything to do with the film or not. I like to think they would have liked the story. Maybe not, but I think Don would have liked it a lot.

Q: Did you change the screenplay, for instance regarding the theme of violence?
A: The theme of violence was already present in the screenplay, as well as its repercussions on the characters, whether they're the victims or the perpetrators. This theme is interesting in a Western because Western stories have always been built around violent behavior, a frontier of violence in man. And this one called certain things into question, notably concerning the theme of justice. You could think that if the Little Bill character [*Gene Hackman*] had granted justice to those women in the beginning, that would have changed the whole story. And his lack of concern in the face of an act of violence, or even his indifference to it, actually sets the story in motion—straight towards his own death.

Q: Is there a connection between the political situation in the United States today and your film?
A: I think you could make some comparisons, yes. But that wasn't the original intention. Deep down, it's a matter of eternal concerns, not just those of a given era, but considering the present situation in the United States, it seemed to me this was the right time to make this picture. Even though the screenplay of *Unforgiven* was written a long time ago, I was quite influenced at the time of making the picture by a number of recent events.

Q: Such as the Gulf War, for instance?

A: No, I wasn't thinking any more of the Gulf War than of other international conflicts, but rather of domestic conflicts America is prey to at present.

Q: You were directly engaged in American politics when you became mayor of Carmel...
A: Yes. I was mayor of Carmel, but only for two years. And during those two years I even made two films, *Bird* and *Heartbreak Ridge*... I've been a Republican because I chose that party at the time of my military service at the beginning of the fifties, and I voted for Eisenhower, but I have a tendency to consider myself more of a "free thinker." My political choices don't really fit in with any of the camps, and actually I feel myself to be something of a libertarian, in the sense that I think you have to let people live in peace, respect individual freedoms.

Q: Do you think it would be possible to reconstruct your personal trajectory through all your films, which all to a certain extent tell a human story, your story?
A: Well, I'd rather say that from one point of view there's a little bit of me in all my characters, and from another point of view there's nothing at all of me in all the characters I've had to interpret. After all, I don't have to be in agreement with any of the characters I've played. Some of them absolutely don't correspond to my philosophy, others undoubtedly do more. I've played a few good characters that were "losers," like the fellow in *Honkytonk Man* for instance, men who self-destruct. But I chose to play them because I know a lot of people who are like them, and I'm somewhat fascinated by them. So, even though I don't resemble them deep down, I've seen so many of those men given up to self-destruction, who didn't make use of their talent— when they had a talent... I don't know. Some of my pictures, more than others, get a message across that I agree with. And finally, I always see an implicit message there that corresponds to what I am.

Q: Is it true that *Unforgiven* will be the last of your films where you will also appear as an actor, and that in the future you will only act for other directors?
A: I began to direct my own films in 1970. At that time, the only means I had to be able to direct was to act in the films... It was a practical question at the time. Afterwards, I grew to like it. There was one of my pictures, the second or third, that I didn't act in [*Editors' note: his third film,*

Breezy, *with William Holden, which was a financial disaster . . .]*. Then I continued doing both things when I was especially involved with a project. But in the future I don't think I'll do it so continually. It's a lot of work to act in a film you're directing. So from now on, I think it will be easier for me to let someone else have the job of directing when I'm acting, or of acting when I'm directing.

Q: You're a producer too . . .
A: Yes. But it's easier to be an actor and a producer, than an actor and a director.

Q: Do you differentiate between films like *Pink Cadillac* and *The Rookie* on the one hand, and films like *Bird, White Hunter, Black Heart,* and *Unforgiven* on the other hand, or in your opinion do they all come from the same development?
A: I consider them all to be different, because none of them is really connected to the others, it seems to me . . . There could be similarities between some of the characters, in the problems they try to confront, but I don't think there's a real relationship. And if there had been one, I probably wouldn't have done it in such a repetitive way.

Q: Do you consider the films in the first group to be commercial films, and the others to be less accessible films?
A: I don't make my films with regard to the commercial aspect. In that respect I'm entirely in agreement with the phrase of John Wilson in *White Hunter, Black Heart*: *"I won't let eight million popcorn eaters pull me this way and that."* . . . If you're constantly thinking about what the audience's reaction is going to be, you stop thinking in terms of how the film should look, because the film will end up by being made around preconceived notions, on a hypothetical expectation of what the audience will do. It's impossible to tell a story with ideas like that. And most of the time your work will be degraded by the contact with this kind of compromise. The essential thing is to stick to what you want to say, to the impressions you want to express in a picture. Then afterwards, it's up to the audience to accept it or not. Having had both sorts of experiences, it finally seems to me that all you can do is resign yourself to fate. The audience seems to know what it wants to see and what it doesn't want to see, it seems to sense whether such and such a picture will agree with them or not.

Q: For years your production company, Malpaso, has collaborated with

Warners, which is distributing your latest film. Are you completely independent?
A: Yes, I am independent. Warners has distributed most of my films and shared in their financing. But I work in complete freedom. The people at Warners have been very supportive for more personal projects, like *Bird*, without forcing a commercial obligation onto it that would have changed the nature of the film. It wasn't *Batman Returns* . . . And I think in the long run they thought the film was good. Not every picture can be a great financial success. But you have to try, or else production companies wouldn't be able to take the liberty of working with proper means. Of course, it's not always the best pictures that are the most successful. Sometimes you get lucky, the film hits home, and people are knocking each other over to see it. It's like a "home run," to use a baseball term . . .

Q: You've worked with two cinematographers in particular, Bruce Surtees and Jack Green, and you seem to attach great importance to the lighting in your films. As time goes by this lighting gets darker and darker. Why?
A: Jack Green was camera operator on *Tightrope*, and he replaced Bruce Surtees as cinematographer when Bruce fell ill. He did a good job, and I decided to give him a chance by continuing with him. There are some of my films that I conceive more as brightly lit films, and so you have the lighting I asked Jack for in *White Hunter, Black Heart*, which isn't a particularly dark film. *Unforgiven* is quite simply a "stormy" film . . . What you have to remember is that it takes place at a time when people didn't have much to use for lighting, and the only artificial light came from oil lamps. So if in shooting a night scene we had decided to flood the action with light, people would have done right to ask us where all that light was coming from . . .

Q: In several respects, *Unforgiven* reminds me of *My Darling Clementine* by John Ford, a film that already had this very dark lighting scheme, and your acting is not without a connection to Henry Fonda's. Have you seen this film?
A: Yes, and even if I'm not sure that *Unforgiven* is much like *My Darling Clementine*, I know what you're trying to say. Ford's picture has a number of nocturnal scenes, all right. Maybe I was unconsciously motivated by an idea close to Ford's. I tried to light my film—or rather I asked Jack Green to light it—like a black and white film. The costumes and the scenery were likewise conceived as a function of this particular lighting scheme, like one in black and white.

Q: It seems you like to remain loyal to the people you've worked with, like Bruce Surtees, then Jack Green, who turn up in the credits for most of your films, or Joel Cox, your editor since *Sudden Impact*. Is this a desire to have a "film family," with people you can trust in completely?

A: Some of the people I've worked with have seemed trustworthy to me, sure. Of course, it's certainly easier, when you're working with someone, to be able to communicate, to be able to explain to him in a few words how you see things. And that's possible for me with the people you mentioned. I don't have any trouble making Jack Green understand how I envision a scene and how it ought to be lighted. So if I were to find myself with a new cinematographer for every picture, someone I didn't know, I'd have to start all over again. It's the same with Joel Cox, my editor, I can call him up on the phone because I know he'll understand very quickly and very accurately what I expect from the editing of a scene.

Q: Your films appear to be very detached from all that is going on in American cinema at present, and to only depend on yourself. Do you have the feeling that you're playing the "lone rider" in the cinema as you conceive it?

A: In the American cinema I've always felt I was a little bit "somewhere else" *(Laughs)* . . . There certainly has to be room for a great variety of movies in any country. But it's true that in America today, everything is subject to the sway of statistics and information science to such a degree, in the form of data that tell you who is going to see what, where and when, that people impose it on you to make a certain type of picture under the pretext that the age of the audience is exclusively between sixteen and twenty-one . . . I would especially hate to have to work that way, it would seem incredible to me to have to make a picture entirely for people between sixteen and twenty-one. With a little luck, a sixteen-year-old could like my film, in the same way a person of forty or more could. Why force adults to stay home by insisting on producing only films that aren't meant for them? I recall the last time I was in France, the *Cahiers du cinéma*, I think, asked me why the United States was no longer producing anything but children's pictures . . . And it's a question that bothers me: why must important themes be treated on an infantile level? If it's really difficult to get people to leave home to go to the movies, you have to want to take up the challenge. Instead of which, the types of pictures that get made are more and more limited.

Q: Then what do you think of Hollywood today and those who reproach it for its violence?

A: I suppose there's room for what they call program pictures, the films that draw crowds with action, according to a certain mentality that says that if there's not an action scene every five minutes, the picture will seem boring and the audience will get up and leave. . . . But I'd rather think—maybe I'm wrong—that audiences are more intelligent than people believe, and that it's enough to tell them a good story for them to want to keep their seats, to see how a character is going to evolve, how a story is going to take place, instead of saying, "I'm going to keep my seat because in five seconds an armored car is going to crash into the wall". . .

Q: Do you attach importance to your recognition as an *auteur* in Europe?
A: Yes, very much. This time, the U.S. has been very appreciative of *Unforgiven*, and they've begun to recognize that I might be a director. But it all started here, a number of years ago. Actually, the Europeans encouraged me much more from my first film as director, *Play Misty for Me*, than the Americans, who had a hard time convincing themselves I could be a director because they already had a hard time recognizing me as an actor. They were asking, "Why is he doing that? Who does this guy think he is?," that sort of thing. The Europeans, on the other hand, supported me a lot in the beginning and tried to find some value in what I was doing. But that's an historical process, it's far from concerning only me; quite a few other directors have had this sort of reaction in the past. Especially here in France, there are those you call "cinéphiles"—is that the word?—who are interested in movies not only as an entertaining spectacle to eat popcorn by. Now the rest of the world is beginning to come to an agreement around this way of thinking. The coming of film schools in the universities and other places causes people to begin to think of film in terms of artistic merit. France was a pioneer, with the creation of cinémathèques, for instance, but I believe that today this influence is felt all over.

One of my favorite pictures is a film by William Wellman from the forties, *The Oxbow Incident* [1943]. I worked with him once, I had a small role in one of his pictures, not one of his best [*editors' note:* Lafayette Escadrille, *which Wellman directed in 1958*]. And I asked him quite a few questions about *The Oxbow Incident*, which I thought was a great film. He told me that at the time, the wife of one of the studio bosses had hated the film at its first screening—she thought it was the worst crap a studio had ever financed—and then the producers had more or less gotten rid of it by distributing it as a B film. But when it was released in France, the critics were very appreciative of the film, they emphasized the value of its point of view, of what it had to say about capital punishment, about mob violence, about justice: Wellman's picture had a right to excellent reviews. Then it came back to New York by way of France, and the Americans began to see its qualities too, but it was already too late, the film was at the end of its run and was taken out of distribution. It was a terrible fiasco—and totally unmerited. Today, people see it again with a different eye, and, I hope, in the U.S. as well as elsewhere . . .

Q: Can you explain to us the choice of the title *Unforgiven*, which has no equivalent in the French language. Moreover, there is already a film by John Huston that bears the same title.
A: Yes, I think I was given to understand that there is no French translation for "*Unforgiven*," and that the film is being called "*Eem . . . Impitoyable*," that's it. Huston did make a picture by the same title, in the fifties I think [*editors' note:* The Unforgiven, *1960*]. Well, it's a good title, it seemed to me to suit the film perfectly, and since I think the film by Huston isn't one of his best, like *The Treasure of the Sierra Madre* or other classics, I didn't see anything wrong in using it for mine.

Q: What do you concentrate on above all at the moment of beginning a film?
A: I try to concentrate above all on the story, because it's there that it's all tied up, it's the "kernel," so to speak. Then I try to see how the image can best agree with the story, what form I want the story to appear in, with what emotions, what sonorities. In *Unforgiven*, there is this storm that becomes almost a character itself, a determining factor: the three protagonists, as they approach, seem to be bringing the storm along with them. This sort of thing isn't written in the screenplay, it gets inserted later on. But the basis of the drama, the question of justice and violence, all that was already present in the screenplay.

Q: In your films, art is frequently connected to destruction and self-destruction, as in *Bird*, *Honkytonk Man*, and *White Hunter, Black Heart* . . . Is this a subject that fascinates you?
A: *Bird* and *White Hunter, Black Heart* are in fact two pictures that deal with this subject, like *Honkytonk Man* with its character who has a real talent and "kills himself" before this talent has really had time to express itself. I find it hard to explain what fascinates me about this subject, they're things you so often encounter in real life, probably that's what attracts me to it. Take Charlie Parker, for example, it's such a great loss, such a waste when someone very creative, gifted, the bearer of new

ideas, self-destructs as he did. No one can ever properly understand how a person could have so much talent, so much enjoyment in playing, and at the same time set in motion his own destruction. That remains a mystery, and undoubtedly I've always been fascinated by mysteries.

Q: Several months ago, we interviewed Jodie Foster for her first film as director, and according to her actors probably possess more aptitude for directing a film, because they succeed in functioning naturally at the emotional and intellectual level at the same time. What do you think of that idea?
A: There are indeed quite a few precedents, actors who directed their own films. You can go back to William S. Hart or Charlie Chaplin, Welles, and so on. Directing seems to be a natural extension of the actor's performance. When you find yourself involved in a story in front of the camera, you're not so far from being able to find yourself behind the same camera. If you've come from editing, or from screenwriting, the gap is greater, because you're used to working alone and you haven't had any experience with a film crew. And then an actor undoubtedly has a greater understanding of the language of filmmaking, its difficulties, its insecurity, things that are inherent in the production of a film. But at the same time, I can't say that there's a rule. It's an individual question. An actor might have the aptitude I'm describing for directing a film, but that depends heavily on the capabilities of each one. There are editors and cinematographers who also make wonderful directors . . .

Q: What do you think of the behavior of Little Bill Daggett (Gene Hackman) in your film? Do you consider him to be a sort of dictator?
A: I think he's a good sort, at least in appearance. He has a certain charm . . . I believe he thinks he's doing the right thing, just a man who's doing his job. He probably has a violent past, the same as William Munny, my character, but he hides it behind a rational appearance. He's the representative of the law, and so he's on the side of the Good . . . But he isn't prey to guilty feelings like Munny with regard to his past deeds. He's deeply convinced he's doing right with his decision to have total gun control, and he believes that the acts of violence he commits for the sake of setting an example are a lesson that will discourage everyone else from coming to town to make trouble. He's a sadist at heart, and whether this sadism is innate or whether he's developed it in the course of the acts he's committed all his life is something that can't be known. But in encouraging violence as he does, violence giving rise to violence, it's also

his responsibility that comes into play. Deep down, he considers himself to be a worthy human being, he's building a house so he can sit on the porch and watch the sunset, he'd like to live a good life, a quiet life . . . But he has no way of stopping the wheel of destiny.

Q: With *Unforgiven*, did you intend to tell the truth about what the West was like, or is it a fable?
A: I think it's more of a fable, but a fable that would demythify the West, in a certain way, by appealing to other elements than the classical Western. As, for example, the fact that it's not so easy to do things, that people's aim isn't so precise, that guns don't always work every time they're fired the way they're supposed to. I don't know if that's the truth about the West, but the film probably does approach it. Oddly, it contains two stories that coexist in parallel, the one of the journalist who wants to print the legend of the West, and the one that runs through the film and contradicts it completely. The meeting of these two stories was what I liked about the script. Everyone changes in the course of the story, everyone starts out from one place and finishes somewhere else, just as in real life we learn something every day that transforms our way of looking at things. All these characters are taught a lesson in a tragic way, at least for most of them. And from the tragedy everybody can learn something.

Q: Do you think you have related the story of a vengeance?
A: I don't know that it's a question of vengeance, even if there is a connection to vengeance in the film, because of Morgan Freeman's character who gets killed. You could see the triumph of vengeance there, but, deep down, no one wins anything at all in this story; everyone suffers some sort of a loss, whether it's a part of themselves or . . . their life. And that's what happens when people indulge in violence in order to obtain justice.

Q: A last ritual question: What are your next projects?
A: I'm getting ready to make a picture in which I'll just be an actor, and where I won't have a hand in the production this time: I'll be a humble employee. This film will be directed by Wolfgang Petersen, produced by Castle Rock-Columbia, and John Malkovich and Rene Russo, among others, will be in the cast, which isn't complete yet. As director, I'm working on a project I may do next year. But it's only at the planning stage at present . . . On the other hand, I'm planning to do this other part as an actor and only as an actor, for the first time in quite a while, and it has a

good chance of being well received, I think, I hope. In any case, this time I'm letting someone else have all the responsibilities and the headaches *(Laughs)* . . .

Any Which Way He Can

Peter Biskind / 1993

> Published in *Premiere*, April 1993, 52–60. Reprinted by permission of the author.

You're Clint Eastwood, huge box-office star and iconic leading man. In four decades, you haven't won an Oscar. So you try directing a great movie—and not giving a damn.

It is 6 P.M. on a Saturday night in Alberta, Canada, on the set of *Unforgiven*. Clint Eastwood likes to shoot westerns in the autumn, so the production descended on the town of Longview just as the leaves were beginning to turn. But now it's four weeks later. The trees are bare, and the production is bumping up against winter.

The cast and crew are expecting to break for their day off, Sunday. But there's a storm coming in. The weather service in Calgary says it's supposed to snow twelve inches on Monday, with freezing weather the rest of the week—meaning the snow won't melt.

They still have half a day's shooting in the town. Then, on Monday and Tuesday, they're scheduled to do a pivotal exterior scene, the one under the pine tree where the whore rides in, tells Eastwood's character, William Munny, that Little Bill Daggett has beaten his partner Ned to death, and Munny takes his first, long pull from the bottle of whiskey that will send him on a rampage of killing. There are eight and a half pages of dialogue. Eastwood wants to see the town in the distance—with no snow on the ground.

Executive producer David Valdes comes up with a nutty idea: shoot into the wee hours of Sunday morning; wrap at 2 A.M.; go back to the hotel, an hour away; let the crew grab four hours of sleep; on Sunday, go up to the hill, without breaking for meals, and do the Monday and Tuesday sequence till the sun goes down; then film the scene where Munny emerges from the bar in the rain, through the night into Monday morning. Had Valdes called the studio, they would have gone ballistic—Eastwood and Co. were about to break every rule in the book: double time for working the crew on Sunday and a hailstorm of penalties for not feeding the crew when they're supposed to be fed. The weather report has been wrong before. Valdes is not going to be a popular guy in Longview (or in Burbank, for that matter) if the storm passes a little to the east or a little to the west of them. But the alternative is to risk having to shoot the scene in California later, which would cost hundreds of thousands of dollars more and forfeit the tie-in to the town.

They complete the eight and a half pages on Sunday and continue on into the night, twenty-one hours straight. It's so cold, the water from the rain machines is freezing, making for a treacherous purchase on the muddy ground. The horses are slipping and sliding all over the ice, and the people aren't doing too well either. It's so cold, Eastwood's teeth are chattering. At about 2 A.M., pissed-off crew members are demanding pizza. "We're in Bumfuck, Alberta," Valdes screams back, "and there's no Domino's around the corner."

At 5:30 or so Monday morning, Jack Green, the cinematographer, turns to Eastwood and tells him there's time for only one more shot before dawn. Fifteen minutes later, they're finished. The first snowflakes begin to fall—and don't stop until the following evening. A foot of snow arrives on schedule. Winter in Alberta has begun.

Clint Eastwood hasn't been to the Oscars since 1973, when he was asked to present the Best Picture award and ended up subbing for host Charlton Heston, who was stuck on the freeway. "Howard Koch said, 'Here's the script,'" recalls Eastwood. "It was a parody of Moses, *The Ten Commandments*, thou shalt not be this and that, all relating to movies. Bad material, even for Moses. I said, 'You gotta be kidding. Never invite me again.' 'Will you come back if you're nominated?' 'Yeah, I'll do that.' Koch says, 'Then I don't have to worry.'"

Well, Eastwood might have come back with *The Outlaw Josey Wales*, and most certainly with *Bird*, but as it turned out, he stayed away for nineteen years. In the twentieth year, the Man With No Name finally rode into town with a clutch of nominations for *Unforgiven* in his saddlebag: Best Picture, Best Director, Best Supporting Actor, Best Original Screenplay. Not bad for a guy who used to be dismissed as a cowboy, one of whose films was derided by Rex Reed as a "demented exercise in Hollywood hackery."

It's been a long and twisted trail from *A Fistful of Dollars*, the first spaghetti western Eastwood did for Sergio Leone, in 1964, when Lyndon Johnson occupied the White House, to the Dorothy Chandler Pavilion in this, the spring of the Clinton presidency—thirty-nine pictures, with another, *In the Line of Fire*, in the can and scheduled for a summer release, and still another, *A Perfect World*, which he directs and costars in with Kevin Costner, set to begin shortly. Sixteen of them he directed himself. Eastwood, always philosophical about the Oscars, once said, "I figure that by the time I'm really old, somebody at the Academy Awards will get the bright idea to give me some sort of plaque. I'll be so old, they'll have to carry me up there.... 'Thank you all for this honorary award' and SPLAT. Good-bye, Dirty Harry."

Standing around the Westin Bonaventure hotel, in downtown Los Angeles, watching director Wolfgang Petersen shoot inserts for *Line of Fire*, Eastwood is uncomfortable talking about his Oscar prospects. *Unforgiven* is the frontrunner, after grabbing a slew of critics' awards, and it makes him nervous. Or maybe it's the inserts, pickups, bits of business, whatever, that make him impatient. He is legendary for working quickly, coming in ahead of schedule and under budget. It's a matter of pride to him—more, a way of life. Recalls Frank Wells, who was president of Warner Bros. during the seventies, "His favorite time was the last day of a picture. He would call me, and I would guess how much under budget he was." Eastwood is fond of saying things like, "The more time you have to think things through, the more you have to screw it up."

In the Line of Fire boasts a very good script, by Jeff Maguire, a bit along the lines of *Tightrope*, or even *Unforgiven*—films in which the character Eastwood plays is less a superhero than an ordinary guy with a Past, a guy who's been damaged by life, a guy who has to live with something he'd rather forget. Here he's an aging Secret Service agent who is convinced he let John F. Kennedy die, those many years ago in Dealey Plaza, by not moving fast enough, perhaps paralyzed by a flaw in his character. It is a story of Conradian dimensions—whether the execution matches the ambition remains to be seen. Like *A Perfect World*, *Line of Fire* represents a more commercial, less personal choice for him than *Unforgiven*.

Eastwood, who had director approval, selected Petersen, best known for *Das Boot*. People in advanced stages of megastardom often hire flunkies for the express purpose of second-guessing them and making their lives miserable. But Eastwood, it is said, does not operate that way. When he decides his employees can perform the jobs they've been hired for, he leaves them alone, relies on their judgment, and if they come through, he hires them again—and again. Glenn Wright, his costume designer, has been with him since the *Rawhide* days. Eddie Aiona has been his prop master for some twenty-five years. Joel Cox, his editor, started working for him eighteen years ago. Valdes began as a second assistant director thirteen years ago,

Listening to the people who work for him saves Eastwood enormous amounts of time. He doesn't audition actors; he looks at tapes supplied by his casting director. When Valdes or the production designer chooses a location, he often won't see it until the day before the shooting begins. The look-of-show meeting is usually over in ten minutes because he can count on cinematographer Jack Green (twenty-two years) to react to a script the way he does. Eastwood lets Cox put the first cut together himself, from rushes of Cox's selection. Five to six weeks after the film wraps, the editing is finished.

Eastwood's people have a refreshingly casual approach to making movies. "It's fun," says Valdes, "and everyone realizes we're not curing brain cancer." Cinematographer Bruce Surtees, who worked on a number of Eastwood's pictures, once said, "There's no trick to lighting. You turn on a light, and if it looks good, you use it. If it doesn't, you turn it off and put it some other place."

No one sits around waiting for the sun to go in or out of the clouds on an Eastwood set. His luck with weather is a legend in the business. If he needs snow in the Mojave Desert in July, it will snow. But it's not all luck. He moves so fast, he doesn't have to worry about matching one part of a scene with another. "Once you get that kind of velocity, suddenly weather doesn't matter," says gaffer Tom Stern, the baby of the group, who's been with Eastwood for a mere eight years. "Instead of calling it adversity, you call it serendipity."

Eastwood hates overlighting, which he associates with television, especially in his thrillers. He prefers a noir-ish, chiaroscuro effect. Pauline Kael once wrote, apropos of *Bird*, "The picture looks as if [Eastwood] hasn't paid his Con Edison bill." On *Firefox*, which is a bit on the murky side, there is a shot that is so dark, only Eastwood's elbow is visible. The cameraman wanted to do another take. Eastwood said, "Am I in the frame?" "Yeah." "Can you hear my voice?" "Yeah." "They know who I am. Let's print it and move on."

In an industry where first takes are virtually always rehearsals and actors don't get serious until the fourth or fifth, where it is not unheard-of to shoot thirty, forty, fifty takes of the same scene, Eastwood is famous for shooting rehearsals—and not just rehearsals, but first rehearsals. He walks the stand-ins through the scenes, to get a rough sense of blocking, light placement, and so on. Then, says Green, he brings in the actors. "They're working with the words for the first time, and we're rolling.

They have to paraphrase or deal with props in a naturally awkward way. If they do hit the light, we're lucky; if they stay in the frame, we're really grateful." On the other hand, says Jeff Fahey, who played the writer in *White Hunter, Black Heart*, "he'll never walk away from something until he has what he wants."

Usually Eastwood will do no more than three to five takes, and print two. On *Bronco Billy*, Scatman Crothers had just come off *The Shining*, where Stanley Kubrick had put him through something like fifty takes on one scene, and he was almost paralyzed with fear. Eastwood did one take and printed it; Crothers nearly burst into tears.

Eastwood's method works. It lends his pictures a fresh, improvisatory, realistic flavor. The extraordinary first scene of *Unforgiven*, in the whorehouse when the woman is cut, is a first rehearsal. It has the impact of real violence; it's over in an instant, and we're not really sure what has happened. We feel like voyeurs, as if we walked down the hall, passed an open door, looked in, and saw something unspeakable.

Eastwood has never believed, as Sam Peckinpah did, in drawing out violence, aestheticizing it, and indeed, these two masters of the western never worked together. "One time I was talking to a class at USC and somebody said, 'How come you never worked with Peckinpah?'" recalls Eastwood. "I said, 'Well, he's never asked me.' And all of a sudden some guy got up in the back and said, 'I'm asking you now!' I look up and it's Peckinpah sitting in the class. He was so wild; he'd go off and live in whorehouses. Some of those guys were amazing—John Huston, staying up to all hours doing whiskey and then directing the next day. I can't do that. I always have to train up, run, like it's an event."

The Bonaventure, where the endangered president makes a campaign stop, has a cold, inhospitable lobby consisting of a cavernous atrium punctuated by concrete columns. Someone has spent a good deal of money to create a series of small concrete pools filled with stagnant-looking water covered with a dull gray film. One finds oneself looking in vain for floating condoms. Watching Petersen do take after take of his insert, it's clear what Eastwood is thinking, but he would never say anything. Nor will Petersen, a short, lively man with shaggy blond hair and an engaging smile, admit to being intimidated by his star, who could get an Oscar for directing. And maybe he isn't. "Clint knows if I'm directing the film, to let me alone," says Petersen. "He's not a guy to step up and say, 'Shoot it this way.' Still, sometimes, when I say, 'Clint, this was great, but please, let's do it again,' he says, 'If it's great, why do it again?'"

Despite the fact that *Dirty Harry* was made more than twenty years ago, Eastwood is constantly beset by fans asking him to make their day. Once a cop lurked about the Eastwood-owned Hog's Breath Inn in Carmel, California, for a week, waiting for the actor. Eastwood finally showed up; the guy entered and in one sudden sweeping movement pulled an enormous .357 magnum from the small of his back. The customers hit the floor. But he only wanted Eastwood's autograph on the barrel—he'd brought along his etching tool. Eastwood signed it, thought for a moment, and said, "Don't go leaving this around anywhere," like the guy might do a liquor store and drop the gun on the floor.

Now a large, buxom woman pushes her way through the crowd of onlookers and tourists surrounding Eastwood on the *Line of Fire* shoot. She is yelling "Clint, Clint, let me at 'im." She heaves up in front of him and bellows, "East Clintwood! I got all your records!"

Eastwood was born on May 31, 1930, in San Francisco, right in time for the Depression. His father scratched out a living at odd jobs before ending up in Oakland at Bethlehem Steel. After high school, Eastwood traveled around, mostly in the Northwest, working at Boeing, Bethlehem, fighting fires for the Forest Service, hauling lumber at a Weyerhaeuser pulp mill, baling hay, and so on. He once described himself as a "bum and a drifter," but he later attributed his sure feel for the blue-collar audience to these experiences.

After a stint at Fort Ord as a lifeguard during the Korean War, he went down to Los Angeles to find work as an actor. Every day, he said, was like getting slapped in the face with a wet towel.

In 1954, he got a job driving a truck around the Universal Studios lot and eventually hired on as a contract player for seventy-five dollars a week, acting in a couple of cheapies that later became shlock classics, *Tarantula* and *Revenge of the Creature* (from the Black Lagoon). Eventually, Universal let him go (because his Adam's apple was too big, his buddy Burt Reynolds once joked).

For two years, he scrambled, digging swimming pools, pumping gas. Then, in 1958, through a chance encounter, he got the part of Rowdy Yates, the sidekick of Eric Fleming's Gil Favor in *Rawhide*, a TV western that ran on CBS for seven years. In 1965, Fleming left the show (a year later, he was killed by a crocodile while on location in South America, according to director Ted Post), and Eastwood had the series to himself.

In 1964, his agent asked him if he was interested in starring in a western to be shot in Spain by an Italian named Sergio Leone. "I had questions, normal questions, like who is Sergio Leone? It wasn't like Fellini was offering to do it." For $15,000, he agreed to go over to Spain during his hiatus from *Rawhide*. He even brought his own cigars, which he found at a tobacco shop in Beverly Hills. "They were about that long," says Eastwood, placing his hands about a foot apart. "I said, 'I'll chop 'em in threes.' Boy, they tasted ugly. Put you right in the mood for killing."

"Leone knew 'good-bye,' and I knew '*arrivederci*,'" says Eastwood, and they communicated through gestures and intermediaries. The script was wordy, and Eastwood cut out dialogue by the mouthful. "Whenever I had a problem, I'd use my street psychology, Psych 1-A. I'd just say, 'Well, Sergio, in a B western, you'd have to explain. But in an A western, you just let the audience fill in the holes.' He'd say, 'Okay.'"

Eastwood did two sequels to *A Fistful of Dollars*. When the first of his spaghetti westerns arrived in America, in 1967, the critical reaction was mixed. The films were acclaimed—and disdained—for their hip, surreal cynicism.

The trilogy established the formula for the Eastwood western: the Man With No Name squinting in the fierce midday sun, laconic, cool, and laid-back but remorseless and vengeful at the same time, coming from nowhere, going nowhere, without a past, without a future. He was the antithesis of the liberal Freudian western hero of the fifties—Paul Newman's Billy the Kid, say, in Arthur Penn's *The Left-Handed Gun*. "I was the king of cool," says Eastwood.

The western was *the* American genre, as critic J. Hoberman has said, the one in which America stared itself in the face and asked the big questions: What is good? What is bad? What is law? What is order? Eastwood's westerns were no exception. The pasta pictures were the cultural Muzak for the post-Kennedy era; the Man With No Name became the big-screen version of J.F.K., who forced Khrushchev to back down over the Berlin Wall and the Cuban Missile Crisis, launched the Bay of Pigs, and cultivated the Green Berets. Along with the James Bond pictures, Eastwood's films ushered in a new era of cinematic violence. Some fifty people are killed in *A Fistful of Dollars*. The line between the hero and the heavy was becoming blurred. With the war in Vietnam heating up, there was no time for niceties.

"In *Josey Wales*, my editor said, 'Boy, you shot him in the back,'" recalls Eastwood. "I said, 'Yeah, you do what you have to do to get the job done.' I think the era of standing there going 'You draw first' is over. You don't have much of a chance if you wait for the other guy to draw. You have to try for realism. So, yeah, I used to shoot them in the back all the time."

Eastwood and Leone changed film history together, but they barely knew each other. After *The Good, the Bad and the Ugly*, Leone wanted Eastwood to do *Once Upon a Time in the West*, but Eastwood had had enough. "I went home, and I didn't see him for a lot of years. I think he was resentful—I had started becoming successful. And he didn't do a lot of movies. Many years later, when I went over to Italy for *Bird*, he called. We went out together one evening and got along better than in all the times we had worked together. I left, and he died. It was almost like he had called up to say good-bye."

Eastwood's first American western, *Hang 'Em High*, in 1968, for United Artists, was in the spaghetti mode. His next picture, *Coogan's Bluff*, began a lengthy collaboration and friendship with director Don Siegel. "When we met, it was a very sort of surly relationship," says Eastwood. "'I don't like your suggestion for this.' 'I don't like yours.' Finally, we just zeroed in, started agreeing on a few things, and then we became fast friends."

Eastwood had always wanted to direct, and he picked a small story, *Play Misty for Me*, to start with. The studio, Universal, preferred he stick to his six-guns. This was a sort of proto–*Fatal Attraction*, in which a disk jockey gets involved with a psychotic woman. Eastwood prepared well, perhaps too well. The night before the shoot began, "I was lying in bed, going over the shots in my mind. I had them all planned out. I turned out the light, thought, 'I got this now.' All of a sudden, I went, 'Jesus! I got to be in this thing!' I turned on the light and started approaching the scenes all over again from the actor's point of view. Needless to say, I didn't get much sleep." The critics were not nice, Eastwood recalls. "They said, 'We're not ready for him as an actor, much less a director.'"

Misty was a modest hit. And then came *Dirty Harry*. The tenor of the film was evident from a tag line that was never used: "Dirty Harry and the Homicidal Maniac. Harry's the one with the badge." But the critics were not amused. In the highly polarized political climate of 1971, many people felt that *Dirty Harry* said it was okay for cops to trample civil liberties in the pursuit of crooks. Plus, the Scorpio Killer wears a peace sign, as if Siegel and Eastwood were turning a whole generation of kids who fought for social justice and an end to the war in Vietnam into a bunch of Charles Mansons. Kael was particularly vocal. She wrote that Dirty Harry is a man who "stands for vigilante justice" and termed the picture "fascist." Eastwood answered his critics by insisting it was just a defense of victims' rights. "The general public isn't worried about the rights of the killer; they're just saying get him off the streets." So far as the peace sign went, "that was a thing where the actor wanted to do it and everybody just thought, 'Well, that's irony. A lot of people hide behind the guise of being peaceful, and they'll be the first ones out there advocating violence.'"

After *Dirty Harry*, Eastwood was given considerable freedom at Warner's. "The guy had a story sense about his own persona that nobody else had," recalls Wells, who is now president of the Walt Disney Company. "You'd make the deal and not see him again until the preview—of an under-budget movie. We always did what he wanted to do." Except in the case of *Dirty Harry*. Eastwood did not want to do a sequel, but the studio was implacable. Ironically, *Magnum Force* was based on an idea spawned by the febrile brain of wild man John Milius. Eastwood considered it a liberal riposte to *Dirty Harry*. "It showed that just because these guys were killing people who deserved to be killed doesn't mean that's the way society should go about it."

"Eastwood was typed early on as a guy who could do only one thing—Harry—over and over, and he was the only guy in the mix who thought, 'I can do better than that,'" says Dennis Shryack, who co-wrote *The Gauntlet* and *Pale Rider*.

In real life, Eastwood was far different from the character he became identified with. He did collect guns, but he didn't care much for hunting. It's said he once stopped his daughter from stepping on a cockroach. "I don't like killing," he says. "It's one thing to fantasize about it in a movie, but I never saw the sport in removing a life from the planet."

In 1976, he directed himself in *The Outlaw Josey Wales*, another tale of revenge and his best western up to that time. Even though critics constantly compared him to John Wayne, Eastwood—and the Duke—knew different. Wayne wrote him a letter after he saw *High Plains Drifter* (1973). "He said, 'That isn't what the West was all about. That isn't the American people who settled this country,'" Eastwood later recalled. Eastwood's westerns were more akin to Elizabethan revenge tragedy than to John Ford. "I was never John Wayne's heir," he once said.

Ford believed deeply in the civilizing impact of society, the transformation of the jungle into the garden. In Ford's dusty towns, there is always a church or a school going up, the frame building standing starkly against the raw landscape. Eastwood's westerns are about darkness and pain, and even when the evil has been avenged, the wounds rarely heal. In *Unforgiven*, there is a house going up, built by Little Bill Daggett, Gene Hackman's sadistic sheriff. At the end, with Munny's weapon aimed at his head, Daggett says: "I don't deserve this . . . to die this way. I was building a house." Munny replies, "Deserve's got nothin' to do with it," and pulls the trigger. Ford westerns are about deserving, and this scene would never have happened.

Until 1976, aside from the Dirty Harry movies, Eastwood for the most part worked for Universal. But he had long been dissatisfied with the way the studio was marketing his movies. The Universal tour was the last straw. "I had a really nice bungalow, a very comfortable place to work," he recalls. "But I'd walk out of my office and the bus would be sitting there with people yelling. So finally I called Frank Wells [at Warner's] and said, 'I'll move over there if you've got a space for me, but if you ever have a tour, I'm leaving.' He said, 'We're not in the tour business.'"

Moreover, Eastwood had an itch. His career has always gone against the grain. He was making genre movies in an era when the most interesting work was devoted to subverting genres, particularly the western, which more or less died under him. He was riding tall in the saddle in an age of antiheroes; he was the laconic star for Nixon's silent majority. If *Dirty Harry* was a decade ahead of itself, when the Reagan-era zeitgeist caught up with him, in 1980, Eastwood had already moved along. While George Lucas and Steven Spielberg were busy reinventing the old formulas that Penn, Scorsese, Altman, and others had buried, one thought, for good, Eastwood started tinkering with his image, journeying into the shadows of his own persona.

He told writers Shryack and Michael Butler that he regarded their script *The Gauntlet*, in which he plays a feckless cop, as a bridge to a new kind of character. In 1980, the beginning of the Reagan era, he further cut the ground out from under himself in the self-mocking *Bronco Billy*, where cowboy Billy is a purveyor of illusions. While Reagan was using the symbols of the West to promote the illusion of a heroic America that no longer existed, Eastwood was increasingly obsessed by the limitations of the human condition. "Exploring the dark side sort of came about when I started doing things like *Bronco Billy*," he says. "I've played winners, I've played losers who were winners, guys who are cool, but I like reality, and in reality, it's not all like that. There's sort of that frailty in mankind that's very interesting to explore. Heroics are so few and far between."

When *The Gauntlet* didn't do as well as hoped, Warner's became concerned that Eastwood was making the wrong choices. He always had a streak of Burt Reynolds redneck humor about him, and when he wanted to play opposite an orangutan in *Every Which Way but Loose*, Warner's did some market research that indicated a negative reaction to the title, to the orangutan, and even to the idea of Dirty Harry in a comedy. But Eastwood doesn't have much truck with market research and went ahead anyway. It cost about $8 million and grossed about $85 million (about $150 million in today's dollars), making it his biggest film. Even *Bronco Billy* grossed $33 million.

Finally, the East Coast establishment climbed aboard. In 1980, the Museum of Modern Art in New York gave him a retrospective. Two years later, Robert Mazzocco wrote a widely read appreciation in the *New York Review of Books*, calling Eastwood "the supply-side star." The essay registered his anointment by Upper West Side "neos"—both liberals and conservatives. Then, in 1985, the French, who had always lauded Hollywood directors without honor in their own country, gave Eastwood a retrospective at the Cinémathèque, as well as a Chevalier des Arts et Lettres decoration.

Mazzocco was right. Eastwood had indeed benefited from the Reagan-era cultural shift. But liberals applauded him, too, falling all over themselves to find the bleeding heart behind the "fascist" veneer. His acting, previously "stiff," became "spare and stylized." *Honkytonk Man* was compared with *The Grapes of Wrath*. The *Los Angeles Times*, doubtless with *Sudden Impact* in mind, called him "the most important and influential . . . feminist filmmaker working in America today."

But just as Eastwood was never a fascist, his new liberal threads did not quite fit him either. In the early years of the Reagan administration, he gave a reported $30,000 to a former lieutenant colonel in the Special Forces named James "Bo" Gritz to launch an "incursion" into Laos, and then agreed to act as Gritz's liaison with Reagan.

"I said, 'If there's a possibility of saving just one person, I would certainly spend any amount of time and effort necessary,'" recalls Eastwood. "But it wasn't *The Dirty Dozen*—I think they ended up spending most of the dough hanging around Bangkok. They brought back a bunch of bones—some of them weren't even human. Remains weren't worth risking lives for." (Gritz denies dribbling the money away in Bangkok and insists that the remains were human.)

A registered Republican for most of his life, Eastwood criticized Reagan for visiting a military cemetery in Bitburg, Germany, where SS troops were buried. He ran for mayor of Carmel in 1986 and won—but spent $25,000 to land a job that paid $2,400 a year. Although Eastwood feels his two-year term was plenty, his editor, Joel Cox, says, "I think it was the best thing that ever happened to Clint. He's always been a loner. It sort of opened his personality a little bit."

Eastwood rejected George Bush's request for help in the last election. "I think what the ultra-right wing conservatives did to the Republicans is really self-destructive, absolutely stupid." He voted for Ross Perot. "Perot was kind of out there, with dirty tricks and all. But in the final analysis, he's the only one I believe. I would have loved to have seen four years of the little guy from Texas rolling his eyes, screaming and yelling, 'Time to bite the bullet.'"

In the last ten years or so, Eastwood has chosen more personal, character-driven projects: *Honkytonk Man*; *Bird*; *White Hunter, Black Heart*; and *Unforgiven*. He gets away with it because he is so financially responsible. Asking Warner president Terry Semel about Eastwood is like asking a kid about Santa Claus on Christmas morning: "Clint is the best producer I've ever worked with. He is more careful with our money than he is with his own." Warner's is not going to lose much on an Eastwood picture, no matter what it's about. Says Valdes, "I think if Clint Eastwood wants to make a cooking show, he will call [Warner chairman] Bob Daly or Terry Semel, and we'll be doing a cooking show." *Bird* is a period drama about a black jazz musician—an alcoholic, a smack addict, and a wife beater—who dies at the end. But Eastwood knew he could bring it in under $10 million, including his fee, at a time when an average picture cost $18 million. And he did.

At the same time, Warner's counted on him to deliver commercial product. The problem was that *Heartbreak Ridge*, *The Dead Pool*, *Pink Cadillac*, and *The Rookie* were not that commercial. For the first time, Eastwood's career looked as if it might be in trouble. Then came *Unforgiven*—not, on the face of it, much more of a box-office draw than *Bird*, a risky project for someone who hadn't had a real hit in nearly ten years. But as with *Bird*, he kept the costs down. He brought it in in fifty-two days for $14.4 million, excluding his fee. With some exceptions, Eastwood always had trouble getting marquee names for his movies; they were seen as *his* movies. "You'd start talking about Meryl Streep and end up with Patty Clarkson," says Marco Barla, Eastwood's project coordinator. Hackman didn't want to do *Unforgiven*. "The violence of the characters I portrayed had begun to wear on me," he says. But Eastwood convinced him that the film made a statement *about* violence. "He was very explicit about his desire to demythologize violence," adds Hackman. Later, Hackman quipped, "I'm really glad Clint convinced me this was not a Clint Eastwood film."

"When *Unforgiven* came out and started doing business, I was shocked," says Eastwood. "Because I never try and romance the audience. You've got to forget that there's somebody out there eating popcorn and Milk Duds. I figured that if people want to see it, they'll see it. If they don't, screw it." Eastwood, sitting in his trailer between takes on *Line of Fire*, is dressed in a conservative gray Secret Service suit, scuffed and ripped in places from his exertions in the name of national security. He looks tired. There is a half-pint container of milk on the table. "Better get rid of that," he says softly to Frances Fisher, whom he has been seeing for some time and refers to as "Bad Fran." "Else you'll be *Big* Bad Fran."

Eastwood has said he doesn't know if *Unforgiven*, which has now grossed more than $100 million worldwide, will be his last western, but it should be. He's come full circle. *Unforgiven* is *Dirty Harry* turned on its head. After two decades, Harry, still above the law, has become the sadistic sheriff, Hackman's Daggett, while Scorpio has evolved into Munny, the killer now reformed. By killing Daggett, Eastwood purges the identity that has imprisoned him throughout his career.

Richard Schickel once said that Eastwood is a man who works in the American vernacular, an artisan whose art emerges from the craft. As Barla puts it, he is like a body-and-fender man who's been beating out dents for thirty years and then builds his own car. Everybody oohs and aahs, and it goes in a museum. Eastwood, of course, will never make any extravagant claims about his own work. "I sort of just do my thing and make films, and the body of work just sort of adds up year after year," he has said. "Eventually you do something someone thinks is okay."

More than okay, and the beauty of it is, he's still working. *In the Line of Fire* is not *Unforgiven*. But neither is it *Dirty Harry*. Yet the executives at Columbia Pictures just can't get *Dirty Harry* out of their minds.

Line of Fire's killer (played by John Malkovich) has been taunting Eastwood's character, Frank Horrigan, insisting that history is about to repeat itself. There's a scene in which Horrigan stands by Kennedy's grave, staring at the flame, and mutters to himself, "It's not going to happen."

When the execs heard that, a light went on: if he spits out "It's not gonna happen," it could resonate like "Make my day." They could use it in the trailer.

They ask the screenwriter, Jeff Maguire, to add the line during the climactic fight between Eastwood and his doppelgänger. There's no way to do it, unless Maguire makes the killer—a clever fellow, and by no means a cardboard villain given to thundering imprecations—shout something like, "I'm gonna kill you," or "You're a dead man." Maguire doesn't want to do it. But he's only the writer, and, worse, this is his first script. So it's up to Eastwood to draw a line in the sand, tell Columbia, "It's not gonna happen." But it's not his picture.

Under pressure, Maguire rewrites the dialogue. Malkovich looks at the new pages and says, "Why would I say that?" One day, while they're shooting the fight, Eastwood says, "Let's do it." They shoot the scene. Malkovich threatens; Eastwood fixes him with that cold stare and retorts, "It's not gonna happen." But he doesn't pause for effect. He says it quickly, swallows the words. They are nearly inaudible (they ended up reshooting the line so it can be used in the trailer). But no one can say Eastwood is hard to work with, or throws his weight around, or is on a star trip, or acts like Dirty Harry. He doesn't. He's not.

America on the Brink of the Void

Henri Béhar / 1993

Published as "L'Amérique au bord du vide" in *Le Monde*, December 16, 1993. Reprinted by permission; translated from the French by KC.

In *A Perfect World* the chief players are a child and his kidnapper (Kevin Costner) on the run. If the film describes an intimate, complex relationship, which allows Clint Eastwood to reflect on the relations between a father and a son, it brings to the screen one of the wounds of American society—and certainly also of ours: the irruption of violence. Furthermore, the film is the occasion for a confrontation between two moralities, two purely American types of hero, two generations of actors. All of this is high stakes, as Clint Eastwood explains here.

Q: After *Unforgiven* and the Oscars, was it difficult to approach a new project?
A: Wait, let me think back . . . That's a long time ago already.

Q: A long time, barely a year?
A: *(He laughs.)* Let's see . . . *In the Line of Fire* lasted until the Oscars . . . Yes, *A Perfect World* was already underway.

Q: The theme of fatherhood, of the absence of the father . . .
A: . . . was very clearly developed in the original script, which the film stayed close to.

Q: You seem to consider the default of the father, a poor understanding of the notions of "machismo" and virility to be responsible for many social problems . . .
A: There's been a lot written about that, it's a major preoccupation of contemporary society, especially in the United States.

Q: However, *A Perfect World* takes place at the end of 1963, just before the arrival in Dallas of President Kennedy, whose bodyguard you were in *In the Line of Fire*.
A: This "Kennedy connection" was already in John Lee Hancock's script. I didn't discuss it with him, but it's always seemed interesting to me to deal with the present day in the context of the past. *Unforgiven* took place in 1880, but it dealt with armed violence, a problem that couldn't be more contemporary. *A Perfect World* takes place at one precise moment of one precise year, just on the brink of a great turning towards the void that will take hold of America.

Q: This casts a tragic shadow on the whole of the film . . .
A: Yes. You don't really know where this element has its place in the picture, or if there is a place for it directly. But you feel it like an echo of Red's disenchantment and his rebellion with regard to the political system. I thought it was good to situate this film at this particular time, which was a bit strange and as though in a state of suspense.

Q: The action of *A Perfect World* takes place around the time of Halloween also . . .
A: Halloween is a holiday when kids disguise themselves as monsters or witches. That gave me a chance, in the middle of this chase, to play with the Casper the Ghost costume, which the boy is wearing for the first time in his life.

Q: . . . thus maintaining a constant presence of death . . .
A: Skeletons, masks, yes . . .

Q: . . . in a film that's sunny for nearly all of its length.
A: Exactly.

Q: The scenes between Kevin Costner and the child, almost always in a moving car, have something very free, nearly anarchic. Your scenes most often immobilize you inside the metallic trailer that serves as your headquarters.
A: That was entirely deliberate. Butch is in search of freedom—even though he doesn't have any illusions about his "new frontier," Alaska. He only knows it from a postcard sent long ago by a father who probably doesn't exist and who, if he exists, doesn't have anything to do with him. Then there's Red in his steel shell, who maybe, at an earlier point in

time, could have helped Butch, but he's messed up a number of things in his own life. Among which, specifically, is fatherhood. The two characters have their attractions, but also their limitations.

Q: There's no winner in the moral fight.
A: No. Unless, maybe, it's the child—at least the hope that, in spite of his emotional injuries, he'll profit from the adventure, and will be able to grow up, to mature, to age gracefully.

Q: Was it you who approached Costner or the other way around?
A: We were the ones who approached him.

Q: He presented a double danger, however: He could play on the sentimental string, as he did in *Field of Dreams*, and he could utilize his incontestable charisma to make Butch a hero.
A: I rarely indulge in sentimentality, and Butch couldn't be completely a hero. I tried to preserve a certain toughness in Kevin. I didn't want him to have a "paternal" attitude towards the kid. Butch doesn't know anything about children, he's spent too much time in prison . . . I wanted him to treat the kid the way he would treat any guy. Kevin isn't used to playing this interior toughness, inasmuch as he's very close to his own children. But he's a determined worker, it was enough to put him back on track from time to time.

Q: Consequentially, you brought his character closer to those which Bogart, Cagney, Mitchum, or Gary Cooper played in the forties.
A: Yes. Actors of that generation weren't afraid to approach this type of role. Those of the present generation have . . . a certain image of themselves.

Q: Encouraged by the manner in which Hollywood functions today?
A: Yes.

Q: Pampered by an industry at his feet, would Costner therefore generally play it safe?
A: I can't answer for him. But if in certain films he's played it safe like in his first big role, he didn't do it here. Butch isn't a "man who liked children and dogs," a romantic hero you can take cover behind. Think more of Bogart in *High Sierra* or *The Treasure of the Sierra Madre*; those weren't conventional films or conventional protagonists . . . But these types of

roles let people construct a career that would have duration . . . In the same way, women in the films of the forties were much more interesting than those of the fifties, sixties, seventies, and eighties. And this is the direction in which we worked on the character of Laura Dern. I wanted her to actively participate in the investigation, I didn't want her to be a jellyfish, or a decorative element, or the gal on the job who adds to the mistakes or gets into situations that only men will be able to get her out of. I wanted her to have a point of view, opinions, a more open conflict with me, and above all not a love story.

Q: Did you ever consider playing Butch?
A: The character could be any age but it seemed that a man of sixty who goes off in search of an eighty-year-old father would be ridiculous. I thought it was better if Butch were about thirty.

Q: So name five—or even three—Hollywood actresses in your age group . . .
A: *(He laughs.)* I see what you're getting at . . .

Q: . . . who are capable of carrying a film on their own account, or at least of sharing it with you.
A: If the script permits it, I'd be the first one to celebrate.

Q: Speaking of Simone Signoret in *Madame Rosa*, a producer once quipped: "She's lucky to be European. Here, as soon as she got her first wrinkle, she'd have been relegated to playing grandmothers on daytime soaps."
A: It's appalling, distressing, idiotic, but unfortunately it's not untrue. In Europe, you keep actresses of the range of Jeanne Moreau or Sophia Loren on top. In the United States, no matter how hard I think, I don't see any. Sometimes an actress of eighty might get a great part, like Jessica Tandy and Miss Daisy, but there aren't any decent parts being written for women of fifty any more. Maybe that's why people like Jane Fonda, if they don't exactly take early retirement, at least stay away from things . . .

Q: Or else they have recourse to cosmetic surgery.
A: They're almost forced to by the fashion industry, where everyone's got to be eighteen years old, where anyone older than thirty is finished, terminated, the horse kicked out of the barn, if I can put it like that. Moreover, this isn't a question of sex: it applies to men as well, if not as

much as to women. The system pushes you to be something you're not and if you give up, you destroy yourself. Unless you completely shut your eyes. For me, a woman who is maturing and aging gracefully is sexier, and more exciting, than one who's determined to want to look twenty years old.

Q: Both *Unforgiven* and *A Perfect World* strip violence bare of all its allure.
A: Violence is never beautiful.

Q: The release of *Unforgiven* in the United States coincided with the controversy surrounding *Cop Killer* and the split-up between Ice-T and Time Warner. Similarly, at the time of *A Perfect World*'s release, we witnessed the staging of a general accusation against the film industry, television, and the media, the attack coming from both the Attorney General, Janet Reno, and from President Clinton, scarcely two weeks ago.
A: Actually, I'm beginning to be annoyed by politicians who suddenly start blaming television, the movies, and so forth. You can call TV too violent, or movies too violent. You could just simply blame bad television and bad movies. But when a politician gets involved in this kind of diatribe, I never know whether he's doing it to serve his country or to serve himself. When you're looking for scapegoats, the movie and television industry make a choice target: they never fight back. Television puts up its umbrella and Hollywood beats its breast . . . Janet Reno is probably trying to get herself forgiven for the enormous fiasco of Waco, which was the most violent thing I've seen on television lately! And I don't know very many TV programs that display as much violence as the television newscasts.

Recently, a man was arrested in Northern California for kidnapping and afterwards murdering a young girl. As it turned out, he had already been convicted on two occasions for the same offense! The state of Washington is considering passing a law according to which the third conviction for a major crime will condemn you to life imprisonment without possibility of parole. But how many people will have to die before this third conviction? All the values in this country have changed so much.

I was raised with the idea that crime doesn't pay. But the legal system has become unbelievably devious, and the average conviction for murder today is five and a half years in actual fact . . .

Q: During a recent debate on violence in which the filmmaker Steven Soderbergh took part, some eloquent numbers were advanced: every

year, in France, in Italy, in Germany, fewer than about fifty people are killed by automatic or semiautomatic combat weapons. In the United States: more than ten thousand!
A: Yes.

Q: For Soderbergh, the reason was simple: these weapons are forbidden in Europe. The recent adoption of the Brady Bill, the law to which the name of James Brady is attached, Ronald Reagan's press secretary at the time of the assassination attempt by John Hinckley—does it appear to you to be a first step in the right direction?
A: I was always a backer of this bill.

It establishes a federally mandated waiting period of five days between the application for the purchase of a handgun and its transfer to the purchaser. In California, however, the waiting period is already fifteen days. On the other hand, almost all Swiss families with a family member in the national guard have assault weapons at home. Simply put, Swiss society doesn't encourage people to use them. Could that be because, in our society, the guilty pass through the system so quickly that nothing is taken seriously any more?

Q: There are several kinds of violence in your film: the brutal kind, to which Costner's character yields during a crucial scene is a reaction to the grandfather . . .
A: . . . who slaps his grandson almost by routine, as if it were normal that a kid is something to slap, yes.

Q: There is another, subtler, violence: the one exercised on the small boy by his mother who, as a Jehovah's Witness, forbids him to wear a disguise like the other children . . .
A: It wasn't my intention to attack the Jehovah's Witnesses. It's a fact that they don't celebrate Halloween or Christmas, but you could find plenty of children among them who don't suffer for that. Every religion has its commandments and its constraints—but beyond that, the family group, society, has always played with the punishment that consists of saying: "No, you can't go play with your buddies, you're grounded, you've done something very bad . . ."

Q: Aren't you soon to be directed by Steven Spielberg in *The Bridges of Madison County* . . . ?
A: Spielberg and I have known each other for a long time, I had directed

an episode of *Amazing Stories*, with Harvey Keitel, for him. We spoke very briefly about this project but decided to take up the discussion again after the release of our respective films. Mine is out now and his, *Schindler's List*, will be coming out in the United States next week.

Q: Don't you also have the intention of shooting a film on golf, in which would you direct Sean Connery . . . ?
A: After doing *Unforgiven, In the Line of Fire,* and *A Perfect World* practically back to back, I intend above all to take a vacation with my family!

Q & A with a Western Icon

Jerry Roberts / 1995

Published in *Daily Variety*, March 27, 1995. Reprinted by permission.

After helming nearly twenty films and starring in dozens more, Eastwood's work as a director and actor has reaped box-office bonanzas and yielded awards all over the world, including an Oscar for his direction of 1992's Best Picture, *Unforgiven*. But he's also got an Oscar on his mantle for producing the esteemed Western pic, and his new Oscar courtesy of receiving the Irving G. Thalberg Memorial Award is for almost thirty years of producing achievements. "The Man With No Name" has been wearing *three* hats since his Malpaso Productions outfit kicked off with *Hang 'Em High* in 1968.

This exclusive interview with Eastwood was conducted for *Daily Variety* by film critic Jerry Roberts.

Daily Variety: The Irving G. Thalberg Award is rarely presented to producers who remain contemporary figures. And it has never been given to someone who is known primarily as an actor. Were you surprised when you were selected?

Clint Eastwood: Yes, I was surprised. But I formed Malpaso Productions in the mid-1960s, so for thirty years I've been directly involved in the total process of making the movies I've done. If you want to say I'm a contemporary figure, I'm what you would call a longtime contemporary. It's one of those deals where I just outlived everybody. I started in the Italian Westerns in 1963 and '64 and came back here and formed Malpaso for *Hang 'Em High*. I didn't take a producing credit then, but started to later on. We worked mostly for Universal first, and after *Dirty Harry*, for Warner Bros. We gradually moved the company over and settled with Warners in 1976.

DV: Why did you leave Universal?
CE: Universal eventually got more into the tour business than the picture business. You couldn't go outside your office without some tour going by. And Warner Bros. had a bigger lot, more resources and their promotions department was pretty good. The first picture we did at Warner Bros. was *The Outlaw Josey Wales*. With the exception of a film for Paramount (*Escape from Alcatraz*) and one for Columbia (*In the Line of Fire*), we've done everything for a Warner Bros. release. We're not exclusive with them. It's sort of a handshake deal. If somebody else has a great job they want me for—like *In the Line of Fire* for Castle Rock—then I'll go do that.

DV: The definition of the title of producer depends on who you talk to. What is your own definition of that job as you perform it?
CE: Producers get the least amount of attention and gratification on a film. They're not as hands-on as the director and the actors. But by and large they finance and envision the project. The producer is the person who puts together the elements and then lets the director run with the ball.

DV: How has the profession of producing changed over the years?
CE: In the old days, producers were knowledgeable on all aspects of filmmaking, plus they were the presidents of the company. In the late sixties and seventies, many producers merely packaged the deal and then walked away from it.

In the old days, the Hal Wallis kind of producers were a little more hands-on. They knew lighting. They knew when the director was b.s.-ing them. They relied on the unit manager to do the auditing, but they had their eyes on the overall project.

How I fit into it—I'm fairly good at watching things. If you're responsible and have figured out your needs, there's no reason to be over budget or have late miscalculations. You hire good people and they're going to make you look good. It's like riding a horse. It can make you look noble and elegant up on it or it can make you look like a bum.

A producer has to be a salesman for the project. He has to raise enthusiasm to finance it. You have to sell it to actors if you want a name cast. You have to sell the different elements to a director. It's a difficult process, but if you have a track record, if the studio has shared in your good luck in the past, it will put its faith in you again. If you have had a hit picture recently, that helps.

DV: Money management, enthusiasm, persuasiveness, and packaging seem, then, to be the major tasks of the job.
CE: Producing is also something that you don't go to school for. You can go to cinema schools and learn cinematography and editing. You can't teach someone how to be a good producer. It's more of an apprenticeship. David Valdes is a good example, a terrific producer. He came up through the ranks with me. He was an assistant director, a unit manager, then after some pictures in those capacities a producer.

DV: You have said that you learned aspects of directing from Sergio Leone and Don Siegel. Can you recall anyone who influenced your producing style?
CE: I've worked with some really good producers and I've also worked with some who were just deal packagers. But I looked up to Hal Wallis, who was a very intelligent and savvy producer. He seemed to know how to pull together the whole team. He seemed to know every aspect. I never worked with him on a film. I never worked with Billy Wilder, either, but I've admired him from afar.

DV: Some of the more independent directors have always had aversions to producers.
CE: Don Siegel used to say, "The trouble with producers is that they don't know what they do." He set up an antagonistic scheme between him and the producer, as if the producer was the big, bad tax man in the sky or something. So on a couple of projects I said to him, "This time you be the producer and the director and you'll have nobody to hate."

DV: It's probably not coincidental that one of the most notorious vilifiers of producers among directors was Sam Peckinpah, who worked for Siegel.
CE: Those were the last of the cantankerous guys, the guys in the tradition of Ford and Raoul Walsh.

My way of going about things is a little quieter than the way those guys did. I came out of the acting end of the business, which is an odd way to get into producing. Most actors think of producing as headaches. But I was interested in what went on around me, and I found that the more I knew about what other people did on a film, the more understanding I had, the better I liked it.

DV: What gives you the biggest joy in the process of producing?

CE: You read a script you like and say, "OK, I have nothing but a bunch of pages"—but it's the nucleus. It's the most important element. To me the most important thing is the blueprint. Then you organize your team: Who's the director for this? Who do I cast? Who does the production design, the cinematography, the sound? All those components are allied in making the movie and I like matching them to the project.

DV: You seem to choose to work with the same people. Jack N. Green, for instance, is your regular cinematographer.
CE: I've promoted a few people up through the ranks. You're always confident when you have people who are good and who know your shorthand. Because there's understanding there, a shared history. These people understand completely—sometimes without any words at all—what you want.

DV: How much did your TV experiences on *Rawhide* aid in your development as a producer?
CE: *Rawhide* was a good training ground for me. Over seven years I gradually learned how different directors direct, lighting techniques, other aspects. I subconsciously absorbed things and then started paying attention. We had different producers on the show over the years. I tried to emulate the things they did well and discard the methods that didn't work.

DV: Several of your associates mentioned that being a child of the Depression in Northern California had something to do with your fiscal responsibility as a producer.
CE: My parents and other people of that particular period had it rough. Some of them were not getting by so well. My father was very conscious of that. It was a struggle and there weren't many jobs. He said, "Nothing ever comes from nothing," and "If you get a buck save it." You finished everything on your plate and we never thought in terms of waste. This gives you respect for financing.

If somebody asks you to be in charge of the funds, you have to have a certain respect for them and for the funds. At Warner Bros. (cochairmen and CEOs) Terry Semel and Bob Daly don't want to look at a film if I haven't finished it. I say to them, "You're financing this thing. You should be able to look at it any time you want."

There's a famous story about Jack Warner. One day he walked onto a big, expensive set on a sound stage and looked up at the ceiling and there are these painters up there painting the ceiling. He said, "What are those guys doing?" Someone told him they were painting the ceiling. "Well," he said, "it better be in the picture."

DV: There's a running joke about "Malpaso weather"—that your productions have been blessed with getting the shots and getting out in time before a blizzard hits. Also sudden snowfalls necessitated changing locations on a few pictures—*Pink Cadillac* and *Pale Rider* among them. You used an unexpected dusting of snow for effect in *Unforgiven*.
CE: You occasionally have to think fast on your feet. If a hurricane hits, what do you do? You drop back on fourth down and punt. You do the best you humanly can to bring things in control for the least amount of money. I've been lucky a few times.

DV: One thing that crops up in conversations with your associates at Malpaso is that your sets are by and large fairly quiet.
CE: You're there to do the job and a good comfort zone is part of that. There was a good comfort zone on *Unforgiven*. It was a pleasure to go to work every day. The same thing was there on *The Bridges of Madison County*. It was very nice and enjoyable. Whether that translates into the final film, we'll have to wait and see.

"Truth, Like Art, Is in the Eyes of the Beholder": *Midnight in the Garden of Good and Evil* and *The Bridges of Madison County*

Michael Henry Wilson / 1998

Published as "Clint Eastwood: 'Personne ne me demande plus de porter un sombrero, Dieu merci!'" by Michael Henry in *Positif*, no. 445 (March 1998): 19–23; in English in Michael Henry Wilson, *Eastwood on Eastwood* (Paris: Cahiers du cinéma, 2010), 130–41. Reprinted by permission of the author. Interview conducted on January 21, 1998.

Q: Many American critics questioned your choice of a material as ambiguous, ironic, polyphonic as *Midnight in the Garden of Good and Evil*.
A: What amuses me is the state of confusion this country's critics are in. They keep complaining that we are not making character-driven films like in the 1930s and '40s, but on the other hand they rave about action-driven movies that are devoid of any complexity. I think the influence of television has transformed the way movies are perceived. There is a whole generation, the MTV generation, which wants things to keep rolling all the time. You never linger; you never revisit anything. *Midnight in the Garden of Good and Evil* is not the only film to have suffered from this syndrome this year; we could mention several other examples. Whatever the case may be, I can't worry about it. I filmed the story that I wanted to film; it's as simple as that. That desire is what guided me. When I undertook the film, I knew it wouldn't be for all tastes; some would love it, others would hate it, and there would be few reactions in between.

Q: John Berendt's book was not a piece of fiction, but an anthropological essay disguised as a diary. What intrigued you initially in the material?
A: John Lee Hancock, the screenwriter of *A Perfect World*, talked to me about it two years ago. The title itself sounded interesting, and also the fact that it took place in Savannah. I forgot about it, and then last year he called me back because he wanted to submit the script he had been working on for a long time. The book was reputed to be unadaptable, but he thought he had found a solution. He also told me that the studio would end up discarding him because they preferred to treat the piece as an outright comedy. As I didn't know the book, I read the screenplay without any preconceived notion and I liked it. It prompted me to read the book, so I was able to appreciate all the difficulties that John had to overcome. Personally, I wouldn't have known where to start! I then called Terry Semel, the Warner Bros. honcho, to tell him that it was a good script and that I wanted to direct it if nobody else had shown interest in the project. Semel told me that they didn't quite know in which direction to go with it. I told him it could be an interesting character study because it involved an ensemble of odd people. Soon after, on my way back from New York City, I stopped over in Savannah. I looked around, met some of the participants, got a feel for the city, and sort of conducted my own inquiry. When I came back, I said, "OK, I'm ready to start."

Q: Didn't your involvement trigger a revision or restructuring of the screenplay?
A: There was some rewriting. I asked John to reintegrate some scenes from the book that he had deleted. One of them was the episode when Jim Williams [Kevin Spacey] is in jail and tells the narrator a second scenario of the killing. That was one of my favorite scenes in the book, the idea that an incident can be told from several points of view, like in *Rashomon*. We either added or subtracted scenes. We agonized, for instance, about the bridge club for married ladies. Rather than eliminate it altogether, we kept a shortened version. We could have easily dropped the black cotillion ball, but for me, such details, the way they compose an atmosphere, are what makes the film more than a straight court drama. I like court dramas, but I didn't feel it should be the whole movie.

Q: Were some episodes shot and then deleted in the editing?
A: Yes, and I miss some of them. I had enough material to do a three-and-three-quarter- or even a five-hour film. I had to suppress some good,

very good scenes because we needed to preserve a certain rhythm. The relationship between the writer, Kelso [John Cusack], and the singer, Mandy [Alison Eastwood], was more developed, and so was the one between Mandy and her pianist friend Joe. Mandy was already a composite in the book, but John Hancock went even further by giving her some attributes of Nancy, Joe's partner, as well as of his first wife. He also made her younger to insinuate the sort of romance and charm that the town and its inhabitants exude. Minerva? She's a composite too. Several voodoo priestesses were the inspiration for the original novel, but the main one in the film, the one Jim Williams consulted, was based on a character that Hancock actually met. She lives seventy-five miles from Savannah and refuses to talk about anything. She is one of the rare participants who didn't try to capitalize on the success of the book.

Q: Did you ever consider calling on the author, John Berendt, to adapt his book?
A: He didn't want to. He was approached, I don't remember when. He was convinced it couldn't be adapted. It was never conceived as a film, and he didn't see how it could become one. After seeing the finished picture, Berendt was very complimentary about both the screenplay and the direction. As I see it, one of the most inspired decisions was to collapse into one the four trials from the book. John Hancock managed to distil the essence of the whole affair in one trial, whereas in reality, hung juries were unable to pronounce a judgment and it took years.

Q: More than the book, the film focuses on the ambiguity of the main character, Jim Williams. His cunning recalls the infamous Claus von Bülow.
A: That's what was on our minds. That idea was more diffuse in the book, which is filled with anecdotes and digressions. We had to accentuate the dramatic points, whereas the book is all atmosphere. I wanted Jim Williams to be more alive, more present; the same held true for the journalist. In the book, you don't learn much about him. His is the voice of a detached observer. In the script, he became John Kelso, a vivid character who has more interactions with Williams, almost becomes his friend and is all the more disappointed when he is lied to. Kelso is the outsider with whom the audience can identify, as he enters into this world. John Cusack's performance has been underrated. It may be less flamboyant than Kevin Spacey's, but it is with him and thanks to him that you take this journey.

Q: You managed to unearth a familiar theme: Kelso is a stranger who lands in a corruption-infested town and arbitrates the power plays between various clans. *Midnight in the Garden of Good and Evil* can be seen as a quirky, laid-back variation on the premise of so many of your westerns.
A: The difference is that this stranger doesn't really get into a conflict with the inhabitants of a sinful city, but harbors questions in his mind because the people with whom he interacts are so ambiguous. It is also about tolerance . . . tolerating other lifestyles, learning to be less judgmental. It's an important aspect of the film, but surprisingly it was hardly mentioned by the reviewers.

Q: This is a world where everything turns out to be relative. You have Kevin Spacey state, "Truth, like art, is in the eyes of the beholder."
A: We'll never know the truth, and I like that ambiguity. Williams tells us two different scenarios [for the crime] with the same conviction. It leaves Kelso in a quandary, but life is like that. One of the detectives who conducted the initial investigation told me that he didn't believe either scenario to be true. When the police were called, an hour or so after the murder of his lover, Williams was waiting for them with his attorney. According to them, the boy must have stubbed out his cigarette on Williams's antique desk, and an enraged Williams must have taken out one of his old Lugers, fired, then quietly dressed the place so that it would look like self-defense. You are free to choose your own version of the crime.

Q: Kevin Spacey's character is portrayed ambiguously as a sophisticated gentleman, who is probably guilty of a criminal plot. His elegance is reminiscent of Otto Preminger's heroes, especially the dandy portrayed by Clifton Webb in *Laura*. As in *Laura*, the grandfather clock serves as a dramatic and symbolic device at a crucial moment in the story.
A: In Savannah you hear a thousand different stories about Jim Williams, but even those who interacted with him and attended his parties concur with others in describing him as a mysterious character. Those who liked him were fascinated by this mystery; those who disliked him viewed him as a dangerous pervert. He was an enterprising guy who was clever, watchful, and very observant. Berendt suggests that very well when he compares Williams's eyes to the tinted windows of a limousine; he can see you from inside, but you can't see him when looking from the outside. He remains impenetrable. You don't know what his smile might hide.

Q: In the book, Jim Williams's death is told in a single paragraph. In the film, it comes as a form of poetic justice. You conceived a very elaborate sequence that forces us to reinterpret the series of events.
A: It's like a third version of the murder. Williams's machinations come back to haunt and crush him.

Q: Kevin Spacey's portrayal is brilliant. Did you discuss his role with him?
A: Yes, at the beginning of the project. But we didn't rehearse anything. He doesn't like to rehearse; he'd rather jump in. John Cusack felt the same way. However, all the actors did in-depth research. Kevin met Williams's family and friends; he befriended his sister Dorothy. Jack Thompson, who is Australian, spent a lot of time in the company of Sonny Seiler to capture his Southern accent, his style as a lawyer, and also to have his take about the case. Cusack had extensive talks with Berendt. They all formed their own ideas of what happened that evening in Jim Williams's house, just as the inhabitants of Savannah did in real life.

Q: Savannah was bound to lure you with its lingering memories of Johnny Mercer.
A: Let's say it was one of its added charms. His great-grandfather built the Mercer House on Monterey Square. But though Mercer was Savannah's favorite son, he never lived in this house and has no connections to our story. Except that Joe and Mandy are blues musicians and that gave me an opportunity to play Mercer's tunes throughout the film!

Q: John Berendt describes Savannah as a vestige of the old South, "as remote as Pitcairn Island."
A: It's a little-known world, off the aerial grid. There are no direct flights from New York or Los Angeles. Even the citizens of Atlanta view Savannah as alien to Georgia. Already at the time of the Civil War, Savannah had its own agenda. When the Union troops approached, the city's fathers quickly opened negotiations and dissuaded them from burning the town down by bringing them bourbon and throwing beautiful receptions. Thus Savannah was spared. General Sherman was even able to telegraph Lincoln, "I offer you the jewel of the South as my Christmas present." Since then, it has somewhat resisted changes and the waves of immigrants. That is particularly true of the old city, which was built around twenty-one plazas designed by James Oglethorpe on the model of Roman military camps. Some of its churches and synagogues are

among the oldest in the country. Jim Williams was passionate about restoration. His popularity came from that. He did it his own way. When he wanted to restore an old building, the Pink House, to open a bar-restaurant and the city council opposed the project, he threatened to replace it with a parking structure and the next day positioned a crew of wreckers ready to bring it all down. He immediately won his case! To some extent, it is a liberal city that tolerates different lifestyles, but it is also a small provincial town where jealousies and gossip run rampant. Rumors are the inhabitants' favorite pastime. It's unbelievable, for instance, the tales they spread out, and the scenarios they built, about our movie production even before I showed up.

Q: Throughout the film you take time to observe and appreciate the rituals of that micro-society. We are looking at a tribe threatened with extinction.
A: Today, most of the time, movies are content with shorthand. Maybe audiences are more impatient, or maybe it's the filmmakers, I don't know. Sometimes, I'd say I was making this film strictly for the people who are interested in detail. The others, the MTV generation, will doze off at times or be bored throughout. What you call "rituals" is precisely what I was interested in and wanted to spend time on.

Q: Some have complained that you gave too much room to the transsexual, The Lady Chablis.
A: She was a colorful character, in life as well as on screen. Her outrageousness was part of the overall atmosphere of Savannah. Furthermore, I love characters that may have nothing to do with the final outcome but are still part of the story. The Lady Chablis forces John Kelso to see things a little differently. It's again the tolerance factor. I like very much how their relationship evolves. They are like the Cary Grant and Rosalind Russell of the 1990s!

Q: For some time you have been more and more attracted to stories that rely on the development of a character, or even several characters like in *Midnight* . . .
A: The action-packed movie was fun when I started, let's say when I was in my twenties or thirties. Sometimes, the material had a good story; sometimes, it had great action, lots of movement and color. But at some point in your life, that's enough. You look for character studies instead, even if it's less commercial. When I was making *Unforgiven* I thought it

was going to be unsuccessful. It wasn't a shoot 'em up like *The Wild Bunch* or the Sergio Leone westerns. It departed from the tradition I was part of. Gunplay was sad. You saw kids being killed for nothing. I thought the picture would be rejected for all those reasons.

Q: In the meantime you surprised everybody by gambling on a "woman's picture" like *The Bridges of Madison County*. Was this another attempt at renewal?
A: What can I say? Some forty years later, people are still trying to pigeonhole you. When I did the *Rawhide* series I was identified with the TV western; when I did the Leones, with the offbeat European western; when I did *Dirty Harry*, with the urban cop drama. Later, when I tried to undertake an oddball project like *Every Which Way but Loose*, I remember warnings and even virulent opposition: "There's no shooting. It's not your kind of subject. You're going to antagonize your fans." But what is "my kind of subject"? I don't know. I tell different kinds of stories; that's all. When I grew up, I liked all kinds, from *The Grapes of Wrath* to *Sitting Pretty*. Why should I still be making the same pictures that I started out with? Why should Dustin Hoffman have to play *The Graduate* for the rest of his life? I don't know if this is specific to America. But in the case of *Midnight in the Garden of Good and Evil*, no one else wanted to do it. The same thing happened with *Bird*; the script sat around for years. Nobody wanted to do *Unforgiven*. You may think that I was the least likely director for these three projects, but in fact I was the only one to find them appealing!

Q: The rural Iowa of *The Bridges of Madison County* is at polar opposites from the urban and slightly decadent microcosm of *Midnight in the Garden of Good and Evil*. But aren't there similarities between the two pictures, both adapted from bestsellers?
A: Both pictures were very pleasant experiences. Thank God nobody was asking me to wear a sombrero in them! I have to say that John Berendt's book was much more intelligent, better written, than that of Robert James Waller, whose prose tended to be a little too flowery. But I was taken by the brilliant simplicity of the theme. There was no soap opera, no incurable disease, no *deus ex machina* like in *Magnificent Obsession* [directed by Douglas Sirk], only the encounter of two outsiders, one a globetrotting photographer, the other a frustrated housewife. They discover that their life is not over, that it can still bring them feelings that

they didn't think they could ever experience again. The story had a sort of magic; it didn't resemble anything that was done then in film or literature.

Q: You refocused the novel. It isn't any more the story of "the last cowboy" that Waller had set out to write.
A: The novel was written from the man's perspective, that of Robert Kincaid. We preferred to tell the story through the woman's point of view, Francesca's. And we simplified considerably the protagonists and their aspirations.

Q: You were the one who chose Meryl Streep as your acting partner.
A: She's like Gene Hackman and Morgan Freeman. She's always ready and gives you everything you might expect from her. She wasn't crazy about the book, where the woman wasn't in the foreground, but she liked the screenplay [by Richard LaGravenese] for its truthful depiction of behaviors and emotions.

Q: In *Midnight in the Garden of Good and Evil*, emotions are contained or hidden under beguiling appearances. In *The Bridges of Madison County*, they come flowing to the surface. We even see the hero shed tears.
A: Jim Williams is not the kind of man who betrays his emotions. He has to retain a certain mystery. On the contrary, there's no mystery to Kincaid, who is very open and who, in spite of his sometimes flippant ways, gets pulled in deeply. It's a romantic love story. It starts out innocently enough. They appreciate each other, until they become friends and later lovers, at which point they are obsessed with each other. You never question their sincerity.

Q: Did you see aspects of yourself in the character of the photographer?
A: Maybe. A long time ago, I used to travel around like Kincaid in a pickup truck. In my early days as a director, on *High Plains Drifter* for instance, I would do that to scout locations. I'd get in a pickup truck by myself, drive up to the Sierras, come upon a location I'd like and make some arrangements to use it later for the production. So in that sense I was like him. I didn't run across any Italian housewives, but I could have. I will admit that there's certainly a bit of myself in Kincaid, whereas I don't identify with any of the characters in *Midnight* . . . even though I found them all interesting.

Q: Despite its strong sensual dimension, you approach this brief encounter with a restraint that has become rare in film.
A: I wanted to tell the story without the explicit sexuality that is *de rigueur* today, more like they used to do. The housewife commits adultery, and you sympathize with her, but at the same time she has doubts, anxieties, like anyone caught in that situation. Francesca and Kincaid are both misfits. They are not "liberated" types who are looking for a good time. As their relationship evolves, they realize they were missing something. For them, it's a unique experience. They have never known anything like it, and will probably never know it again.

Q: Steven Spielberg, when he was considering directing the film himself, couldn't think of anybody but you to embody Kincaid.
A: That's true. But after *Schindler's List*, he wanted to relax for a year, so I inherited the film. I confess that I liked the character. I liked his independence, his integrity. He's someone who has a passion for what he does, but nevertheless is far from irresponsible. He is self-contained. Plus he has the good fortune to devote himself to a creative activity.

Q: Men of action tend to disappear from your films in favor of artists, musicians, writers, or show-biz personalities. Before the Kincaid of *The Bridges of Madison County* there was the Red Stovall of *Honkytonk Man*, the Charlie Parker of *Bird*, the film director of *White Hunter, Black Heart*. In *Midnight in the Garden of Good and Evil*, Jim Williams collects and restores art objects. In *Absolute Power*, Luther devotes himself to painting. These characters all cultivate an artistic passion that sets them apart.
A: You can add *In the Line of Fire*, where the hero is a music lover even though he's part of the Secret Service. And that's not all! In my next picture, *True Crime*, which is adapted from a book by Andrew Klavan, I portray a writer/reporter who is covering criminal investigations and has lots of bad habits. At one time, he was demoted because he let out a guy he thought was innocent but turned out to be guilty. A similar situation presents itself and his past comes back to haunt him.

Q: Can artists be viewed as the last individualists?
A: Sometimes, maybe. Yes, if you are talking about an artist like John Steinbeck. He always wrote about the individual and the individual's struggle. His were fascinating stories. Some great movies have been made out of them, such as *The Grapes of Wrath* and *Of Mice and Men*, the first

version. They were stories that lent themselves to making good films because they were about the common man, about individuals fighting for their survival.

Q: Rather than using country music, you featured jazz in *The Bridges of Madison County*. Didn't you even invent from scratch the scene at the Blue Note?
A: In the novel, they would meet in the restaurants of Des Moines, but it seemed to me very unlikely that an illicit couple would show up so openly. As Waller's Kincaid played the guitar and was a fan of bluegrass, I thought, "Why couldn't they go out to a small jazz club, to a roadhouse frequented by blacks, where no one would recognize them? They would probably be the only white couple. And they would have that music in common." Given that background, I used recordings by underrated or forgotten jazzmen such as singers Johnny Hartman and Irene Kral. Why Hartman rather than Sinatra, Nat King Cole, or Tony Bennett? Because you don't hear Hartman every day. Also his ballads are connected to memories from my youth. I heard him sing in San Francisco with Dizzy Gillespie's band. I also remember a dancing party with a girlfriend, where I was wearing a white tuxedo jacket and we were both under the spell of Hartman's unique voice.

Q: Like *Midnight in the Garden of Good and Evil*, *The Bridges of Madison County* has the feel of a novel. Its emotional orchestration implies a slow modulation. That slowness is essential to give the characters time to change and mature.
A: These are films that don't work if you don't tell the story in real time. If you sped up the tempo on a film like *The Bridges of Madison County* you would be left with a skeleton. You would lose the inner conflict of the married woman, her hesitations, her contradictory yearnings, and there would be nothing left of what had interested me initially as an actor and a director. Those characters have to grow. Otherwise, you wouldn't care when they part. This brief encounter may be banal, it could happen to anybody, but I wanted the audience to root for them, identify with them, and see parallels in their own lives. It's harder to achieve because people who are looking for a fast pace always resent such slowness. These films are the most difficult to pull off.

A Conversation with Clint Eastwood about *Mystic River*

Charlie Rose / 2003

From *The Charlie Rose Show*, October 8, 2003. Reprinted by permission.

Charlie Rose: If the mark of a great director is getting amazing performances from his actors, Clint Eastwood has reached that point. He himself has said, "This is as good as I can do." *Mystic River* opened the forty-first New York Film Festival on October 3. I'm pleased to have Clint Eastwood on this program for his first solo interview. Welcome.
Clint Eastwood: Thank you.

Rose: When you read this book, did you immediately say, "I've got to have this? I've got to make this? This is the movie I've been waiting for?"
Eastwood: Yes. Yeah, I read it as a synopsis in a newspaper, in a column, and I—I knew of Dennis Lehane, and I was curious about it so I read the synopsis, and I said I've got to have this, I think I can make an interesting movie out of this. It was a little bird in the back of the brain, and when I read the novel, then I was more convinced that I could be—it could be an interesting movie.

Rose: What was it about it? The story? The characters?
Eastwood: It was a complex story. And I've done a few complex stories before. But it was—the fact that it was an unraveling of a mystery that goes back several generations, and when you start out, you start out with young guys as eleven-year-old kids on the street playing street hockey, and then this incident happens, this abduction happens to one of them, and then years later they are reunited through a tragic event, and so in the reuniting they see all the various things. You see what their lives

have been like, and what that abduction that happened thirty years ago, what effect it still has on everyone.

Rose: Child abuse though, and the victimization of children, has always been something that has interested you, because you know the consequences for them?
Eastwood: I think that was one of the intriguing parts, the stealing of someone's life—the stealing of innocence. I think it's the most deplorable crime that I can think of. I think it's a capital crime. If there is a capital crime that would certainly be the epitome.

Rose: The innocence of the—
Eastwood: Yeah, just to take someone's life away from them, take their youth away from them. I think that that character played by Tim Robbins—I think Tim captured that beautifully in the film, that you can see all over him and—in every scene, how he has been robbed of his youth and his innocence: the chance to grow up and to learn things in its normal stride. Very interesting subject matter, and to have this picture unravel, this story unravel along with it and one of the three fellows is now a police officer, played by Kevin Bacon. And he and his associate, Lawrence Fishburne, have to unravel this while Sean Penn's character, Jimmy, is in a bereaved situation. You have a family grieving on one side, and you have this trying to solve this mystery on the other, working simultaneously together.

Rose: There are those who want to say Clint is in a sense, because of his exploration of violence in a whole series of films, is almost commenting on his earlier work and that this is an evolution. Do you buy that? Is that part of your own—
Eastwood: I guess that's an interpretation that somebody could have, somebody may have had, but I don't think so. I think my earlier work was a different person. I was a younger person. Young guy with a brass ring, things were going rather well for me in the motion picture business as an actor. I did what came along. Some of it was a lot of fun at the time. Would it be fun today if I was doing it? No, probably not. Because I have matured, I have different thoughts about things. Different philosophies, as I think everybody should.

Rose: If you are not growing and evolving—if you are not moving forward you are standing still.

Eastwood: If you're not going upward, you are going downward or stagnant. I don't intend to be stagnant. And that is—I think it's helped me in the long run because over the years, I've reached out and tried other things, some of them successfully and some of them maybe not so. But I have at least tried them in order to branch out. I could have been very comfortable saying I'm an action star, I've got a lot of things, and if people want me to shoot, then—

Rose: I'll give them what they want.
Eastwood: I gotta fire six shots or only five, and that kind of business. But that was then and now is now. I can't get as intellectual maybe as somebody who is in a more objective position. I'm just doing things as I—you know the ramifications of *Dirty Harry*—to me, Don Siegel and I thought it was a good detective story and not much else.

Rose: What about *Unforgiven*, though?
Eastwood: Well, *Unforgiven* was a screenplay that I bought ten years earlier, maybe even earlier than that, maybe ten, eleven years. As I read it at the time, I liked it very much and I always felt I needed to mature into it.

Rose: I always wondered why you waited ten years to do it. It was not right for you at the time you bought it?
Eastwood: I could have done it then. But it was to me—it was something I knew I could do at a later time. I felt it would be better for me to do at a later time. So that's why I held on to it. One day out of a whim in the early nineties, I just said, OK, it's time to bring this out. I took it out, I reread it and got stoked up and started in.

Rose: Do you think it's the best movie you have ever made?
Eastwood: I don't know what the best movie I ever made is. I just make them. It's for somebody else to judge them. I am happy with the current one.

Rose: You've got to be happy, people are saying that this ranks right up there with *Unforgiven*.
Eastwood: Well, I hope it does. When I look at the film, I think this is what I intended to do. It came out the way I intended. Now, whether it's good, bad, or indifferent, it's got to be the eyes of the beholder out there. This child has now gone out into the world to be judged on its own merits.

Rose: Tell me about the casting of Sean Penn, whose performance has been praised one side up and down the other, as have other actors in this. Sean's performance is just extraordinary.
Eastwood: Well, Sean is the first actor I cast in the film.

Rose: Why did you want him?
Eastwood: I just felt it's very, very hard to find. These people have all got to be in their early forties, mid-forties. So I needed actors in that range. But Sean has an edge to him. I was a particular fan of *Sweet and Lowdown* and several other performances he had done. I think everybody rates Sean—I'm fond of saying everybody rates Sean very highly and I think he is better than he is rated. But he is—he's terrific. And what's even better for me was that when he came on this, he's extremely easy to work with and very professional and ready to go.

Rose: Well, that's what they say about you.
Eastwood: Well, maybe so, and I hope maybe I had some influence on it.

Rose: You are not a guy that does twenty takes, you are a guy that does three or four takes.
Eastwood: Well, I'm a ready to go person, and I'm trying for things right away. And all of these actors got with that spirit, and I had worked with two ladies—Laura Linney and Marcia Gay Harden are terrific ladies that I have had the pleasure of working with, and it gave us a chance to reunite with them, and they're great roles. I hadn't worked with the guys, but I ran into Kevin Bacon some years ago in Deauville, and he said, "God I would love to work with you." I said, "Well, I'd like to work with you," and it was one of those kinds of things. So all of a sudden you go back and, "Hey, I remember that we talked about that." And he's a terrific actor, and Tim—I have always thought he was great and did some great things—he's a fine director. These guys have all directed films, by the way, and all very well. So it was a great experience. They loved the material. They loved the book, the script, and they were ready to go.

Rose: So you got a great script, you got a great story, you got great actors. What did you do?
Eastwood: Nothing. *(Laughter)* I just showed up—when you have all that, the casting—a lot of people—I have heard other directors say this, too. I've heard them say that if you have a really good story and you cast

it, you are 90 percent there, and there's something to that. Of course there's a lot of detail and a lot of things to be done, but to downplay the importance is fine because you *are* there. You are on the road. You've got a thing and it's for to you screw up. And that's the way I felt about this and the way I felt about *Unforgiven* and the way I've felt about a lot of shows. I've got the cast I want, I've got the story I want, now it's just for me to drop the ball.

Rose: This is the best ensemble you have had since *Unforgiven*.
Eastwood: Well, I think it's one of the best ensembles I've had, period. It's as good as any I've had, yeah.

Rose: There's no—in *Unforgiven* there was Clint Eastwood as an actor. In *Mystic River* there's no—
Eastwood: We didn't have that problem here. *(Laughter)* No, *Unforgiven* was a really nice role for me, too. That had another satisfaction but in this one, it was easier, because I didn't have to be in it.

Rose: Easier?
Eastwood: Yeah. Now, *Unforgiven*, in constructing that film, there were a lot of sequences I wasn't in, so it did give me a breather here and there. But in this one it's nice to be behind the camera.

Rose: Someone wrote about the film—because a lot of people saw it when it was screened, I guess, at the Cannes Film Festival—they talked about, there is a restraint here. You had such powerful performances that you—it almost has an element of restraint, on your part. The directing is very straightforward, because the performances are so powerful.
Eastwood: It's a philosophy of mine that you don't intrude.

Rose: Intrude was a word they used.
Eastwood: You do not—if I started intruding and getting fancy and trying to dazzle people with whatever tricks I may or may not have as a director, all of a sudden, I'm tampering with something. To me—I guess coming from the acting side of the business or art form or whatever you want to call it, I revere the performances. I want to see this ensemble at their best. I do a lot of things but I don't want people to see—to visualize a camera and a camera operator and a guy with a focus thing and another person there at the back. I don't want people to visualize that in the movements around in the picture. So I keep everything as quiet

and subtle as I can, at the same time punctuating the points you need to punctuate.

Rose: Does your biggest impact come in the editing room, then?
Eastwood: Well, the biggest impact comes in structuring—getting all the pieces. Once you have all the pieces, one of the more enjoyable parts of directing a film is the editing room, because at that point you no longer have a crew, a large crew, large expenses and people and actors and trailers—and you just get up in the morning, you go to a room, with an editor and maybe an assistant editor, and you sit there and you start running down through sequences.

Rose: You start putting all the things together. You've got all the elements there.
Eastwood: Exactly.

Rose: You have never wanted to write?
Eastwood: Well, I've written a lot. I've written sequences and rewritten scripts, but I have never had that knack.

Rose: It's a knack, it's not—you never felt you had the skill. Or the knack, what does that mean?
Eastwood: Well, it's a knack. It's a very interesting process, if somebody can just sit there and think up a story. You think of a story, a complicated story like this one, starting with the book, to write all that out. It takes a lot of thinking and it takes a vivid imagination. And then the screenwriter, the same thing. If you are starting the screenplay from scratch—if you're adapting, of course you're adapting other material. But if you're starting from scratch, to just come up with a screenplay, you always go, wow—and if you look at enough bad ones, and I have over the years, and back in television, where people are just kind of hacking them out—you really appreciate the good ones when they come along, because you appreciate the effort and the talent that goes into it. So what the director becomes, and the actors too, are interpretive, interpretive people, interpretive artists, whatever you want to call them.

Rose: Was it difficult to get this made? When you took it to Warner Bros. and said this is what I want to do, they've always had an attitude, whatever Clint wants to do, we want to back him because he's been good for us.

Eastwood: Well, that's most of the time. On one or two occasions—years ago I took—this is when Frank and John Calley—

Rose: Frank Wells and John Calley were there—

Eastwood: I took it to Frank—Lenny Hirshan took a script that I liked called *Thunderbolt and Lightfoot* to them. And they said no, we don't want to do it at this price and all that, and so—about twenty minutes later we had a deal with United Artists, so we went over there and did it. The picture was successful, and so Warners was a little chagrined at that point. However, they have been always very good about leaving me alone. I sort of act as an independent production there. They liked this script, but they knew it was unrelenting and it had—it wasn't—after all this is the studio that's releasing *The Lord of the Rings* and *Harry Potter* and the *Matrix* movies and all these movies with what they call high concept things and lots of action, tons—and all of a sudden here a guy comes along and says, I got this thing about an abducted guy, and you know, these guys meet later on—

Rose: And there's child abuse, and there's a revenge and it's very dark—

Eastwood: Yeah, it's very, very dark and at the end this happens and that happens. And they're sitting there going, yeah, excite me some more. *(Laughter)* I couldn't excite them any less, probably. But anyway, Alan Horn said, "We'll do it, but only at a certain price."

Rose: The price was $25 million, it's said, which is cheap for a film today.

Eastwood: Yeah, well, actually, he would have gone higher than that, a little higher than that, but we had—again, I'm back to where I was thirty-three years ago. I was in fact saying, well, you take the Screen Directors Guild minimum and just go ahead.

Rose: You took the Directors Guild minimum yourself, and the actors worked probably at minimum—

Eastwood: No, they didn't actually, the actors, they came in a little bit better, because you can't get actors—you can't do that, but I can do that, because it's a project—I'm the salesman of the project as well. But you have to pay the actors, and Sean and Tim and Kevin and Lawrence and Marcia Gay and Laura, they all deserve—I would never try to slight the actors. I would love to give them double, but that doesn't always work so well, so there you go.

Rose: Donald Sutherland, you remember the story he told at the Kennedy Honors? Donald Sutherland comes up to introduce a film about you, and he said, "You know, every actor wants to get a call from Clint saying I want to you be in my movie." So Sutherland says, you call and you say, "I want you in my movie and the pay is $100,000," and the first thing the actor does is say, who do I send the check to? *(Laughter)*
Eastwood: Yeah, he said, "Give me a few days to raise the money," right. That was something. *(Laughter)* Don loves that joke.

Rose: I do, too.
Eastwood: It's sort of a typical actor's joke, they're so desperate to work.

Rose: "I'll pay you." Was there much playing with the script or pretty much what was on the page got to the screen?
Eastwood: Once the script was completed?

Rose: Yeah.
Eastwood: Pretty much stayed with it. I always stay in a state of flexibility and I figure a script is a blueprint, but it's not a blueprint you have to stay with exactly. If something comes up that looks better or kind of enhances the sequence I'll go ahead and do it. So I sort of wing along that way. But this material was so good we weren't doing a lot of repairs and the actors kind of—everybody kind of liked it the way it was, and there we were. Sometimes I have done it with outright improvisations—I still do that, and we've done some here.

Rose: Two things that are extraordinary about this as you go through it. There are lots of things. But in the beginning is the scene with the kids, and that's the first thing you see, and I'm told that it had a powerful meaning for you to see this opening scene. Number one. I don't know if it's true or not. The other thing is at the end you have in a narration summing up, some sense of really tying up this story. And a realization of how it's come to be. You see it both in the parade, you know, the characters, the relationship between them, it really has come full circle from where it began. The recognition by all of them of what's happened, what it means, and that life goes on.
Eastwood: Yeah, well, we revisit every single character and what the impact of the story has had on them. And Marcia Gay of course is feeling one thing, and Kevin Bacon's character is feeling another, and there's

somewhat of a hope in some of the characters, and somewhat of a terrible loss, heart-wrenching loss in other characters and one has been given—has found his Lady Macbeth to give him complete strength and start him off on a new life and cover his guilt.

[Charlie Rose shows a scene with Tim Robbins and Sean Penn]

Rose: Let me talk about Tim Robbins here, because with Sean, he has in both his—other roles we've seen him in, he plays strong characters. Tim has done that, too, and strong characters who have a certain moral code. Here you see Tim—in your own words he has transformed himself.
Eastwood: He has, and people have asked what did we do to him to transform him, has he got some trick of makeup or what have you. But he didn't. Tim just put himself in that state, and he felt that he understood how this person would be. Someone who has had that kind of incident inflicted on him at a young age and the baggage he has to carry.

Rose: He was a victim of pedophiles, and in the opening scene you see him taken away. He shows that—in the way he holds his shoulders, in the way he looks down—he's haunted by that experience.
Eastwood: Exactly. It's all up to him. I think he's absolutely brilliant in this particular thing. And I mentioned to you earlier, the casting—it would have been easy to take a smaller person who looked more vulnerable, but Tim's a big man. He's six foot five and he's a—but in a way it became even better, because he's a kid who, though his life was robbed, he did have some elements—he went on to be shortstop in high school baseball, and what have you. So he had somewhat of a life, but still he is carrying this burden all the time. And here he is now a father with a young boy of his own, but he isn't the man he should have been.

Rose: When you have had this experience that you have had, are you always drawing on things you have done before? I mean somehow, scenes, in the same way that they always have certain classic elements, vengeance, and jealousy and love, and you have expressed those in different ways. Are you thinking about other movies, movies you have seen, you know, as you construct?
Eastwood: No, not really, at least not consciously. Everyone is a product of what they have viewed in their life. I grew up watching movies in an era when there wasn't any television, there wasn't anything else to listen to in the home—

Rose: So you were shaped by John Ford and Sturges and Howard Hawks.
Eastwood: Absolutely. Absolutely, those were the guys, plus a ton of other people we don't know the names of, who made all the B movies that went on. Sure you're shaped by things you've seen that were good. You said, Gee, I like that, or I like the way this was done. But I didn't really think of any particular movie. I just think in terms of what I wanted to accomplish in every scene.

Rose: The idea of shooting and getting it ready, the fact that you are famous for, in a sense, simplicity, and for getting it done—is that because you believe that actors ought to be able to perform it and ought to be able to do it, and that shooting twenty takes and twenty-five takes almost says something about the insecurity of a director or the insecurity of an actor?
Eastwood: Sometimes it is. Yeah, sometimes the insecurity of the actor, or the director, or both. I like to feel—to me what the audience must feel, and what I like to feel as the first audience to see the performance, is that this is happening for the first time. I'm hearing these words for the very first time. And that's what you want to project to the audience. And if an audience can come out of a movie and think, "Boy, that was just so *real*. Because those words must have been said for the first time." So I try to make them happen the first time. Now, it doesn't always happen that way. Sometimes it's more difficult. Sometimes you have coverage on the thing. The scene you just showed with Sean and Tim and on the porch. Sean had a very, very difficult scene there, so what I did is, I set it up and did all the shots up to it. I introduced Tim on the porch, and he's lighting the—And he looks around, and there he is, and I took him out and brought it across from the backside and then I worked—I got set on Sean for where the shot was going to move as the sequence progressed, and then we rolled it. There's no running or anything. I didn't want to burn him out. Because I know it's very difficult if somebody starts going eight or ten or twelve takes and the guy is just dry as a bone. And I don't mean just eye moisture, I mean mentally wrung out. It's very tough stuff anyway. And every father who's watching this is going to be squirming in their seat at this kind of scene, and feeling—and mother, too, for that matter. They are all going to feel for him there. But I just wanted to give him the opportunity to say it for the very first time. And then I did it—very little coverage, and I came around, and then Tim was very cooperative, being a sport and doing his part last, because he was more reacting than Sean was.

Rose: I suspect that that is because you are an actor. You understood that, and that would influence your knowledge of that.

Eastwood: Well, yeah, it is. Because I direct in the way I would like to be directed. And so I like to come in to a set and I like to bring what I can bring, and if that's bad, or there's something wrong with it, or the director has an added interpretation or something, some other innuendo that I can add to it, then so be it, but I like to at least come in with what I've got first. I don't want somebody to come in and say you place your hands here, and please say the line like this, and they tell you how to read the line. I worked for a director years ago who was a wonderful director— *(Laughter)*

Rose: I would have loved to have been there.

Eastwood: —Vittorio De Sica. And he gave you line readings, he'd say, "Look me, look me," and then he'd come in and he'd walk you in and he'd do the thing, and I'd always laugh because he was a rather jovial guy, and a little on the heavyset side, and he'd dance around and do the kind of thing—So I'd go, "Okay." And I didn't object to it. Now, if it had been an American director I probably would have said, "Hey, knock it off. Let me just come in, I'll come in and show you what I can do." But he was so charming doing it that it was great fun. But normally, I like to see the baggage, I like to see what the bag of tricks is, and then unravel it. And then it's up to me to set a nice atmosphere in which everyone can work, which is calm and the least amount of adrenalin is expelled before the scene goes, and save it *for* the scene and not save it in all kinds of nervous gestures and screwing around on my part.

Mystic River: Eastwood, without Anger or Forgiveness

Samuel Blumenfeld / 2003

Published as "*Mystic River*: Eastwood, sans colère ni pardon" in *Le Monde*, October 15, 2003. Reprinted by permission; translated from the French by KC.

Samuel Blumenfeld: *Mystic River* comes out just before *The Matrix Revolutions*, another Warner Bros. production with an enormous budget. What does Warners think about your film?
Clint Eastwood: I'm not especially interested in coming in first at the box office. I'm counting on word of mouth. On the set of *Mystic River*, I often joked that my greatest ally was *Matrix*. Warner Bros. was producing the last two parts of the trilogy and had forgotten my picture. They left me alone. It was a low-budget film for them.

SB: *Mystic River* is very close to the series of social films that Warners produced in the 1930s. Warners should be especially proud of you . . .
CE: I made *Mystic River* with respect for tradition. But I doubt that most Warner Bros. employees know the history of their company. Iconic Warner Bros. actors, particularly James Cagney and Humphrey Bogart, have influenced me greatly. They were not afraid to get involved in projects outside of the norm. Bogart's haircut in *The Treasure of the Sierra Madre* is amazing—his hair goes flying in all directions. There was nothing glamorous about him. Cagney could commit the worst horrors onscreen. He seemed to be ready for anything, and laughed at what the public thought.

SB: What was it that attracted your attention in the novel by Dennis Lehane?
CE: The mixture of genres. You don't know if it's a mystery or a drama.

There are two parallel stories that eventually merge, and the complexity of the narrative structure really excited me. I suggested to Brian Helgeland, who I'd worked with before, that he should adapt the novel. He's originally from Boston, where the novel takes place, and that was crucial to me.

SB: The city is a major player in many of your films . . .
CE: A city is a character. Otherwise, I could have shot *Mystic River* the old way, as Warner Bros. suggested, in a studio in Toronto, where production costs are lower. But that made no sense. Before shooting started, Tim Robbins, Sean Penn, and Kevin Bacon scattered all over Boston, soaking up the city's atmosphere. I had them meet Dennis Lehane. Kevin Bacon spent time with the local police.

SB: The way in which Boston emerges here, divided by a river, brings us back to *The Night of the Hunter,* back to an ancestral curse laid on the characters' heads.
CE: Many people in Boston don't know that there is a Mystic River. Real Bostonians know it, there's an entire neighborhood around it called Mystic. The name has weight and symbolism, as I was aware. There was a reason to go prowling around there.

SB: As the story progresses, the lighting of the film becomes darker and darker.
CE: The idea was to achieve desaturated colors. It took a ridiculous amount of time in the lab, much more than usual. I remember a screening where I said that the color scheme of my film wasn't supposed to look like Dorothy and Toto in *The Wizard of Oz.* I wanted cold colors, no warmth at all.

SB: Cinema is often interested in the figure of the sadist or the killer. Since *Sudden Impact,* your films have ceaselessly investigated the theme of the traumatized child.
CE: The loss of innocence obsesses me. In *Mystic River,* the rapists and the murderers aren't important. On the other hand, Tim Robbins has an obvious vulnerability that interests me more than anything else. It also has dramatic resonance in the film. In the final parade sequence, on Columbus Day, we understand that this trauma won't end with Tim Robbins. His son will never know why his father disappeared. His mother

doesn't understand anything about what's happened, to her husband or her son.

SB: During that scene, what's the significance of the gesture of the police inspector played by Kevin Bacon, when he points his finger like a gun? It's a very strong image.
CE: And very ambiguous. I tried to frame it in a way that would leave its meaning open. It's understandable that he feels guilty regarding the wife of the Tim Robbins character. He couldn't solve the mystery in time. But by the same token, his gesture can be interpreted as a warning to Sean Penn, meaning it's possible that he's going to enforce the law at any moment, or as an acquiescence in the code of silence and solidarity that goes back to their childhood. I also wanted to restore another dimension. Sean Penn, whose daughter has been murdered, bears his grief all through the film. He's as much marked by injustice as all the other characters.

SB: Kevin Bacon's body language recalls yours in *Dirty Harry*. Was it your idea to suggest this allusion?
CE: It was his. He asked me if it would bother me if he wore Dirty Harry's shades. That was fine with me, because his performance had a certain subtlety. If I had been forty-five, I might have played the role of the detective myself.

SB: Tim Robbins and Sean Penn are directors themselves. Did that make your job easier?
CE: That's something I very much appreciate. An actor with experience in directing is much more aware of the responsibilities faced by a director. He always comes on time. He's capable of seeing the film as a whole. Here, that was essential, because it's an ensemble film, where the actors had to precisely adjust their performances with regard to other cast members.

SB: What are your thoughts about Arnold Schwarzenegger's election as governor of California?
CE: Politicians have to make unpopular decisions. Schwarzenegger is going to figure out the nature of his job. I wish him luck, he'll need it— it's going to be difficult for him.

SB: You were mayor of Carmel, California, for a brief period. Why didn't you continue your political career?

CE: I knew that I was elected for two years, and I had no wish to run again. I was able to shoot two films during my term without failing in my duty as mayor. Everyone imagined I was going to run for the White House, especially with a former actor, Ronald Reagan, in power. But I love the movies too much for that.

Staying Power

Amy Taubin / 2005

Published in *Film Comment* 41, no. 1 (January/February 2005): 26–33; expanded as "online exclusive," ⟨http://www.filmlinc.com/film-comment/article/online-exclusive-clint-eastwood-interview⟩. Reprinted by permission of the author.

Age has clenched Clint Eastwood's face tight as a fist, but he has never been more tender, vulnerable, and heartbroken than in *Million Dollar Baby*. It's not surprising that the camera still loves Eastwood's visage, finding unchanging beauty in the skull beneath the skin. His facial bones, if anything, appear more finely chiseled than in his youth. But the muscles that hold the thinned skin have contracted, pulling brow and eyes down and inward, so that the signature squint is deeper and less yielding, even to laughter. Eastwood never had one of those expressive, easy-to-read faces. He made a virtue of his guardedness, subtly adjusting a personal character trait to fit dozens of different fictional characters and stories. As both director and actor, he has applied a single style—stripped-down realism—to an enormous range of genres: westerns, cop thrillers, biopics, screwball comedies, psychodramas, even a three-handkerchief romance. At first, he tinkered with their formulas; then he turned them upside down.

Loss, regret, and the things one does and doesn't learn from experience are the themes of the late Eastwood films, among which *Million Dollar Baby* is one of the greatest. *Unforgiven* may be more magisterial, but *Million Dollar Baby* is the tougher work of art in the sense that it's easier to fuel a film with anger and the desire for revenge, as *Unforgiven* is, than with a grief that can never be assuaged. *Million Dollar Baby* starts out bittersweet—it could be a thirties studio picture about a broken-down boxing trainer who gets a second chance when he takes a hungry young fighter under his wing—but it ends up akin to *King Lear*. And much of the emotional power of the film comes from Eastwood's performance. In the past, Eastwood the director has treated Eastwood the actor perhaps too much as a functionary. Since a large percentage of the world's population enjoys seeing him onscreen, it hasn't been such a bad strategy. But here, for the first time, he gives himself the kind of liberty that he has, so generously, given other actors: to explore the character in the moment as the camera rolls.

Eastwood plays Frankie Dunn, a physical and emotional wreck of a man who has spent a lifetime in the fight game and now owns a rundown gym and occasionally manages a boxer. Frankie's body barely cooperates anymore, but what has really dragged him down is his estrangement from his daughter (Eastwood leaves it for us to imagine what terrible thing happened between them) and also that one of his fighters was badly injured in the ring. That fighter, Scrap (Morgan Freeman), is now Frankie's sole employee and his only friend. Scrap encourages Frankie to work with Maggie Fitzgerald (Hilary Swank), who's trying to rise above her own family horror show and believes that a boxing career could be her way out of grinding poverty. Frankie wants no part of this venture, but Maggie's persistence, courage, and passion for the fight game prove persuasive.

"Always protect yourself" is the basic boxing lesson Frankie tries to drum into Maggie's head. But Frankie has a problem figuring out when protectiveness—of oneself and the people one is committed to—closes off the possibility of living fully. More than a film about boxing, *Million Dollar Baby* is about the relationship between parents and children, specifically between fathers and daughters. Maggie gives Frankie a second chance at parenting, and Maggie knows, just as we in the audience know, that Frankie is the best father any daughter could wish for. The heartbreaking thing is that Frankie, almost assuredly, will never feel that way about himself.

This is the most musical of Eastwood's films in that so much meaning and feeling is carried by shifts of tempo and tonality. The shifts that happen within the dialogue scenes are extremely delicate—the three leading actors play off one another with the subtlety and spontaneity of jazz musicians. The fight scenes, however, are explosive and brutal. Shot with two cameras, and virtually unchoreographed, they have a rawness that makes them scary to watch, especially since it's clear that Swank is doing all her own fighting. Swank is terrifically game and courageous, both in and out of the ring. Her eager, bright spirit is a great foil for Eastwood, and together, they create a complicated map of loyalty, trust, and love.

Q: Your voice on the phone is much younger than it is in the movie. Actually it's different from any of your movie voices.
A: It depends on what character I'm being this week, but it's usually just the same old me.

Q: This is one of your strongest films and one of the most painful as well. It seems to be in part about disappointment and not realizing that, in the scheme of things, you've done okay, the best you can. I'm kind of at cross-purposes because I don't want to tip off people to the end of the movie, but the end is important. What do you want people to be left with at the end?
A: It's probably as tough to answer as doing the film to begin with, or getting someone to finance the film. It's another one of those projects, of which I've done two now, where I have to do a little arm-twisting to even get made. But by the same token, there's something about the disappointments in life and the lack of spiritual feelings that this man has, and this young girl who becomes his surrogate daughter. There's something about her struggle to be something, to get to the top, which is very much like Hilary Swank herself. She came out of very poor beginnings and wanted to be an actress, so she understood this girl completely. It's the least obvious thing—to want to be a female boxer to gain some place in the world. Morgan's character of Scrap had that dream before. It didn't happen for Scrap, but he reaches down to people, even the young retarded boy who obviously doesn't have any talent in the boxing area. So there's Scrap's sympathy for people and there's Frankie's disappointment about his daughter and family and consequently not wanting to make lasting relationships with anyone, but finding rejuvenation with this girl. And then, of course, when the tragedy happens, it becomes the toughest fight he'll ever go through, that anyone could go through. And where it leads—there's no answer to it. Nobody knows what they'd do in that situation. There's no way to predispose that. You could say, does that mean you believe in euthanasia? Not necessarily. But who knows? It's a supposition unless you've been put in that position. It was a demanding picture to make—these people living on the periphery of society, at least as we know it and as most of the people who are going to view the movie know it. There it is—that's all I know about it.

Q: How do you go about finding that character—Frankie? You don't live on the periphery and as you said, you've never had to make the kind of choice that he eventually has to make. How do you do that as an actor?

Do you have the sense that you're reaching into yourself? I knew immediately how Hilary Swank had found her character—that the physical life of that girl who wanted to box had taken possession of her. It wasn't that she was thinking it, but more like the physical being of the character took possession of her. When that happens it's a great gift for an actor. You just have to clear out and let it take over. But what you're doing is different because the guy has buried his impulses and desires so deep. He's refused so much. Are you able to talk about the process you used as an actor?

A: The process is the one you use all the time. It's just that the obstacles and the objectives are different each time. It didn't take much to imagine how this person would feel. I think just the human imagination—you can put yourself in the place of most everything. At my age, I've seen enough of high points and low points that I have enough to draw from for this [role] and ten more like it. But when I saw the script, I thought I'd like to direct this film, and then, I thought, I'd better play Frankie. Most decisions for me are not done on an intellectual level. I just kind of grab it. I knew Morgan would have no problem at his end. Hilary, I didn't know but I've admired her work, even in things that weren't as flashy as *Boys Don't Cry*. She brings a certain personality and realness. I knew she would be ready for this, if she was willing to put out the work to be that athlete. And she was. She's a very determined person. She worked incessantly, training four hours a day for four months and we got her very muscular and about eighteen pounds heavier. She became that person. We all became the people that we were.

Q: On your sets, do people go around in character? Do you?
A: For me, because I've directed myself so often, I go back and forth. I always carry a certain amount of it, but I can live and think about other things. The character is sort of seated in your mind before you do the picture. It's like doing a play. You have it in your mind but you can have a life and go to dinner and then pull yourself into it. The only difference in movies is that you're doing it a hundred times a day. It's a technique that you develop over the years. Some people find it very difficult, others find it not easy but less difficult.

Q: Do you like to act?
A: You know, I do. I've threatened to quit, but maybe that's a defense mechanism, because there aren't enough good roles at my age. That's probably true, and if it is, I'll stay behind the camera. The reason I started

directing thirty-seven years ago was I thought someday I or the audience would probably look at the screen and say, "That's enough of that." I had a great experience directing the last film [*Mystic River*] without being in it. I'm always amazed looking at other actors when they're conquering the difficulties of different sequences. But this one, I thought Frankie Dunn is interesting, and I'll be able to do it as well as the next guy.

Q: Watching you in different roles over the past ten or fifteen years, you see those characters in the context of your whole screen history, which has been from the beginning so much about your powerful physical presence. And I think it's been extraordinarily moving and important to see the effect of age on the Eastwood icon. It makes a film like *Blood Work* so much more than just a thriller. If you had started out as an older character actor that wouldn't be the case. It's kind of like the auteur theory applied, not just to you as director but to you as an actor, and each role is part of one body of work. Do you think about that? I think it must take enormous courage to keep putting yourself up when you know everyone is making the comparison to the iconic image they carry in their minds.
A: Either stupidity or courage. No, I just don't think about it. I guess I've been enough of a realist, so this is who I am at this point in life. I've always felt people must progress. If there's any advantage to age, it's knowledge and experience, and until the day that some sort of presenility sets in, I figure I'll just go ahead and explore that. But if you're not willing to accept your age, you can't do that. You just sit there and say, Well, forty years ago, I was this guy who came running in and I wielded this gun. Not that I couldn't now to some degree do that [*laughs*] but it just isn't right. It seems right to play what's in my zone now. I made fun of aging in *In the Line of Fire*, but now is the time to say this is what you are and what you're going to be. I could dye my hair and say I'm thirty-five again. But I'm not, so I don't do that. Take advantage of the great opportunity that is there to play a person like Frankie with street-style wisdom.

Q: But when I listen to you now on the phone, you don't sound nearly as old as Frankie, and I suspect you also move more easily than he did. How much character work did you do to create him?
A: Naturally, I take on the voice for what I feel the guy is like, and it takes you over completely. When I started out, we used to sit around and talk about performances and intellectualize. But at some point, you realize that you have to play on an organic level. And once you get past the ner-

vousness about technique, and past the fact that you have to say lines that were written for the character, you realize you have to bring it from within. It's an organic art form. Not that that means actors aren't intelligent. That isn't the case at all. But you have to be willing to work from within to give an effective performance. Yes, I'm playing an older guy. Your voice becomes different, your movement is different. And the physical part then changes as the story unfolds. As he becomes more beaten down by the obstacles he has to face and the decisions he has to make, he becomes a whole different figure almost. Just, for example, in that little sequence where the nurse says, "We had to sedate her," it's this pathetic situation and you don't have to say anything, it's just there within your being, and hopefully, if it's really there, it translates to the audience.

Q: When you say that, it's you the actor talking, but how do you negotiate that with you the director, who's probably wondering if what you, the actor, is doing is enough for the scene? How do you keep yourself from looking at the scene from the outside, when you're performing in it?
A: That's the thing that is most difficult. How do you look at and have a discussion with another actor as the character, without critiquing what they're doing as the director: Why is she doing that with her mouth? What's this expression? You have to get in there with intensity, and you have to be there with the program. Otherwise you get this glaze-over effect and you would never be able to reach as deep within as you have to for a difficult sequence. But every scene is different. Sometimes it's all right to come in and be preoccupied like in life. And in other scenes you have to push yourself down to the very bottom and be there in the situation with the other actors, and you can't think about what the camera's doing. But you learn that from years of experience. When I started directing, I had to be in the picture to get it made. And then I kept doing it because the people I wanted weren't available or had passed away. Circumstances just led to this body of work, and here I am in my seventies, going, Well, I'm still here, still cooking. I still have ideas and things I want to explore. And maybe I should be thankful for that.

Q: In this film, the actors play so beautifully off one another. The timing and the sense of spontaneity and being in the moment and of people really talking to each other is wonderful.
A: Thank you. Everyone directs movies differently, but the way I get that is just by doing it. Certain scenes I'll rehearse if there are technical dif-

ficulties of lighting and camera. Fortunately I have a camera crew that's very well oiled, so they pretty much know where I'm headed, without much explanation. And then, when we get to the point where I'm doing it, no one asks questions when I'm trying to get into the part. The objective is to make everything sound like the first time it's said, so the only thing I can do is try to pick it up the very first time it is said. So a lot of times I'll do it that way. I know some people don't like to do that. And if it doesn't come out perfect the first time, you have to go onward and upward with it. But you'd be surprised with good performers how interesting something can be the first time they try it. And sometimes the rhythm or the timing isn't right, so you say let's do it again with a little more tempo, or let's not make a moment out of something that shouldn't be a moment, or let's make a moment out of something that should be a moment. I think that's what keeps me doing it at this stage in life. It's that every sequence has its own little challenges. And there are no rules. The rule is whatever it takes. There is no style for every scene. It's whatever it takes to get there. You have to understand the people. You have to set an atmosphere and a tone where everyone can feel extremely relaxed and there's no tension to obstruct what you're trying to do. And it's amazing what good things will come out of it.

Q: How much do you think of acting in relation to playing music? It struck me when you were talking about tempos. You are a musician. This is really two questions at once. I also wondered why it took you so long to write an entire score yourself. You've only done it for the last two films.
A: I've written themes for *Unforgiven* and further back for *Tightrope* and *Bridges of Madison County*. Yeah, I've also thought of the tempo of a scene, whether I was writing the score or not, and if I had a musician coming in to score the picture, I'd always get somebody who felt the tempo of the movie when I showed it to him. Or if I was getting someone before I shot the movie, I'd tell them what I thought the tempo would be like. I do a theme based on what the mood of the picture calls for. I don't do it because I want another job, but sometimes you feel you can do it better than you can explain it.

For instance, with *Mystic River*, I just sat down and started playing a triad, because I was thinking of the three guys, and then I started building chords around it, and I thought, Yeah, it could be something simple like that. I wrote a theme and a little bridge to it. And with this one, I was playing this Floyd Cramer-esque blues and I thought if I could give this a little rural twist, it might be an interesting theme, and then I wanted the bridge to it to be a little more melodic maybe, more like it's coming from somewhere else, representing her and everything about her. So they just come together like that. I did it all in pieces. I edit here in Carmel, and I knew this jazz guitarist so I went over to his studio and I played him the theme. He learned it on the guitar, and then we sat down and played it through about four times at different tempos and one time strumming chords and another time picking and one time in tempo and then free of tempo, and I walked away with it. He thought it was just mock up, but I thought I'm going to use that. Then I went to another friend across town who has a nice computer setup, and he mocked up some synthesized strings and oboes and what have you—a very simple score of the same theme. And then later I had Lennie Niehaus write some violin, cello, bass, and oboe parts and do it real. I don't mind synthesized music to some degree, but nothing replaces the real deal.

So I just pieced it together that way. And I could use the mock-up thing as I was cutting the film. Joel Cox and I would put these pieces in and try them. And when we got to where we wanted it, we put in the real music, and we got it the first time and never had to go back and do it again. It's kind of an odd way of doing things, but it's the only way I know how—the odd way.

Q: What I liked about it was that in very subtle ways, it affected the meaning. Like at the end when Frankie walks down the corridor and out the door. It just gave you a glimmer that although this guy might never know he did the right thing, somehow the cosmos knows he did the right thing. That's just the sound of it at that moment.
A: That's good, because that's what we were trying for. We never know for sure. The ambiguity at the end is the same for Frankie as it is all the way along. But with the last shot, we realize that Morgan's been writing a letter to [Frankie's] daughter. And we go to that little restaurant, and it looks familiar, and we dolly toward that and it looks a little bit like a cabin—it could be the cabin they discussed. And when we get to the window we see that somebody is in there, but it's a little obscure so we don't know if it's Frankie. Maybe, maybe not. We don't know. So does he go off and become the lost soul the priest predicts he will become, which is probably the case? Or maybe he does return to that little restaurant with great nostalgia for whatever life the two of them had together.

Q: What do you think of women's boxing? Or first, what do you think of boxing?

A: When I was growing up, Joe Louis was the champ, and I admired him. As a boy, I thought it was great stuff. And when I did pictures, I trained. A friend of mine, Al Silvani, was a famous fight trainer. It's an interesting sport. I like it when done well. As far as women, that I don't know. I feel that people should be able to do what they want to do. I guess I'm not as prejudiced as Frankie Dunn, but I thought for a while that maybe women shouldn't be doing the pugilistic type of thing. But I knew a girl who became a woman boxer. She was in Las Vegas and I was working there and I told Silvani to go over and give her a hand, and he did. She did it for a while and then gave it up, wisely so, I suppose. I don't know. Lucia Rijker, who's in the film—she plays the "Blue Bear"—

Q: She's a scary girl!
A: She is. She's like iron. There's a scene in the picture, I said we have to have Lucia for this. And there's this friend of mine who's a referee and a karate champion and all this stuff. And I said, Are you a good ref? Well, you just go in there be a good ref and break 'em up. And he tried, and Lucia just throws him to the mat and the girl she was fighting too. He got up and he was red-faced as could be. And I left it in the picture. But Rijker is that way, and she's a terrific lady. And she's reached a pinnacle of success and adulation in a certain crowd that admires what she's done. She's a terribly fit person and she works very hard and more power to her. I always used to joke on the set, "Can you imagine some poor sap on Sunset Boulevard who grabs her door handle and tries to car jack her? He's going to be surprised." She's just a terrific gal, and she's studying acting. So it worked out perfectly. She could play the part and she helped Hilary a great deal by giving her perspective on what it is to be a woman boxer and on some of the fine points of the art.

Q: This is such a dark film visually, right on the cusp of being too dark to see. It's really gorgeous, but you seldom see an American film that risks being this dark pretty much all the way through.
A: The use of light and darkness in film, for me, is very important. I wanted the film to look like an anytime film. It could have taken place in the thirties or the forties and it's only the cars or what's on the radio that tells you you're in one time and not another. And then I try to design the light and the color to go with the drama. Tom Stern, who has been a gaffer for me for years and is a terrific talent, told me he thought he could get into the Cinematographers Guild, and if he could, would I consider using him. And I said, Let's do it. We got him a lawyer and manipulated

around and got him in the guild. So we used him on *Mystic River* and he did a splendid job. When he was a gaffer I could tell him and the cinematographers he worked for—Jack Green and Bruce Surtees—how I see the look. And a lot of times I do the old John Ford lighting gag. I go around and I shut off lights. Now he's got to the point where he knows, and he says, "Here it is, look at the shot." And he shows it to me with the light on and the light off. And I say, "Okay, leave the light off." Now I could have fiddled around and said we'll shoot it once with the light on and once with it off. But no, I made the decision, and then he got bolder and bolder and I guess I got bold, and we came to this thing.

I kind of like a noir-esque look, especially for this film. And it's nothing more than like a painter saying, I'll splash a little here and a little there, and then seeing that, Oh, I'm oversplashed. The reason I like Tom so much is he's fast and quiet and efficient and so are his two operators, and they're also so ready. Everybody's ready. That's the key for me. They know I'm ready to go at any moment. And the sound guy. I'll just roll my hand and they'll know. Especially with children. Children are brilliant but if you let them know the camera is going, they get self-conscious. And the set is usually so quiet we can just go ahead and start shooting. I've even done that with experienced actors. And then you don't have to have someone yelling "Quiet, quiet," and bells ringing and all that kind of thing.

I remember once I walked on the set for *In the Line of Fire* at MGM. It was the first time in a while that I worked for another director. And there were bells going off. And I said, "What are these bells for? There isn't a fire." And the assistant was yelling, and I said, "Now just relax. If you're yelling, everyone is going to be yelling to get over your yelling. So just talk quietly and everybody will talk quietly along with you."

These are just little tricks that you pick up over the years that work on a certain level. And everybody knows there's no game about it. We don't work long hours, 'cause while we're there we are working. And I always have a good caterer, so everybody has a good lunch. The army travels on its stomach. It's one style. It's not *the* style, but it is one style.

Q: When you started working on the film, did you make a lot of changes in the original script?
A: This is pretty much what it was when I got it. I called Paul Haggis. I didn't know him but I congratulated him and told him his script was very nice, and he asked if I wanted rewrites and I said, "No, but if I need something, I'll call you." I said, "I do make changes along the way." And

he said, "I'll make 'em for you." And I said, "Well, sometimes they're just at the moment when you're adapting to performers and other things." Like when you walk on a set and realize that it would be nicer if the light came from here than there. Those are adjustments made along the way. The script is the same. It's an architecture, but it's not quite drawn to the specs of an architecture. You have to be free with it.

Q: I was wondering about one aspect of Frankie's character. He's a Catholic. He's trying very hard to be a good Catholic. He goes to mass every day. He draws the priest into his soul searching. And that puts what happens at the end in a particular context. It means specifically that he has to go against the Church when he decides to do what he does. But people who are not Catholic or even religious sometimes find themselves in his position and it's every bit as agonizing and complicated as it is for him. I wondered if you ever thought what the story would have been like if religion didn't play such a big part in Frankie's life, or if this was the story you got and you just went all the way with it.

A: It seemed so logical. Frankie Dunn—I figured he's Irish with a Catholic background. I'm not a Catholic, but I understand their dogma on this kind of matter. It just made for a complicated thing. His kind of love/hate relationship with his faith, his uncertainties, I think, plagued him. But I think the key was when he's absolutely desperate, and he goes to the priest and asks to be consoled on this issue. And the priest says, "Leave it with God." And he says, "She's not asking God." And then, the priest says—and I think this is the key to it—"Forget Heaven, forget Hell, forget God, all those things. If you do this you'll be lost somewhere so deep inside that you'll never recover." So the priest even takes it to a level that's emotional and spiritual but not by the Church rule. He's saying that psychologically you'll be damaged to a point that there's no return from. So he even drops the usual discussion that they have when it comes to this sort of thing or abortion issues, or anything else like that. And I think that's one of the things that made it so interesting. It made me think, yes, Frankie should definitely be an Irish Catholic. And I think F. X. Toole [the writer of the short story on which the screenplay is based] is an Irish Catholic. There's some understanding in the writing there that really worked for me. And I liked the priest and I liked the way he operated. He's a wonderful actor [Brian O'Byrne]. Those scenes were all done in one take. He was ready to go and we did them.

Q: Do you want to say anything about dealing with such a hot issue right now when the temper of the country is the way it is and the government seems to think it should make decisions about what I personally think are very private matters? Have you thought about what it means to put this film out there now?

A: You know, I don't think about it. I guess I'm obstinate enough to . . . If it becomes a controversy, that doesn't bother me. Because I think it's thought provoking, no matter what time in history it is, or who you are. I don't care if you're a red state or a blue state. Somebody has had some experience at some point in their life when they have thought about this sort of thing, when they've thought about life and death. And is there a reason now that some people have a dogma against that? Well, people can have a dogma about a lot of things, but then you start thinking about it, and almost anybody, if they start thinking about it, realizes it would be a tough decision, no matter which side you came out on. It would be a tough decision for him to just wait until she dies.

Q: It's so heartbreaking when he says to the priest that selfishly he wants to keep her with him.

A: The thing is not Kevorkian-esque where you do a favor for someone who just comes along and asks you. This is someone he feels very deeply towards. Selfishly, he wants her there and she just wants to leave, and where do you go from there? That's the dilemma.

Q: With the exception of *Mystic River*, your films have increasingly had these very pared down scripts, where certain things we might expect to know are left unanswered, like we never know what caused the rift between Frankie and his daughter. Do you like those kinds of scripts?

A: I do. There's a tendency in moviemaking to treat the audience as if they won't stay with you unless you explain every little thing along the way. I can't tell you how many times I've been asked about what it means in *Mystic River* at the end when Kevin Bacon points his finger at Sean Penn. Does it mean he's going to get him, or does it mean I know and you know and that's a secret we have for life? And I'll say to the guy who asks the question, "What do you think it means?" And he'll say whatever he thinks it is. And I'll say, "Yeah, whatever you think it is, is right." I like it, personally, in movies when there's something left to think about. I'm attracted to that sort of thing. But a lot of scripts are overly expository, or they get to the point where they figure they have to explain, or some executive will say, what happens here? We have to know. Well, they don't have to know anything. They have to think, and why shouldn't they think with you? You provoke certain emotions and you let the imagination take over. To me, that's much more fun. Now that just happens to be an idiosyncrasy of mine. Other people may not feel that way, and that's fine, too. Without using ambiguity to the point where it's boring, if sometimes something is left unsaid, it's much more picturesque in the person's mind than something that's drawn out for you which could be disappointing 'cause you wish it were something else.

Q: I always remember the bit in *The Searchers* where John Wayne comes back from finding the body of the older sister, and he says, "Never ask me what I saw." So, of course, you spend the rest of the movie trying to imagine it.
A: That's one of his brilliant performances and brave, because he wasn't afraid to play the flat-out racism. And when you look at his eyes at that moment you know it wasn't something good that he saw. And you'd almost resent it if he started explaining it. A movie like *Million Dollar Baby* is just a segment of a life, and the other aspects of it—they have to be left in the other life.

Eastwood's *Letters from Iwo Jima*

Terry Gross / 2007

Originally broadcast on *Fresh Air with Terry Gross*, January 10, 2007. Reprinted by permission of WHYY, Inc.

This is *Fresh Air*. I'm Terry Gross.

My guest Clint Eastwood has directed two films about one of the bloodiest battles of World War II, the battle of Iwo Jima. The first film, *Flags of Our Fathers*, showed the battle from the American point of view and told the story behind the famous Pulitzer Prize–winning photo of five Marines planting the flag there. Eastwood's new film, *Letters from Iwo Jima*, describes the battle from the perspective of Japanese soldiers. The Japanese soldiers on Iwo Jima were told to expect to die there, and most of them did. About twenty thousand of the twenty-two thousand Japanese troops on the island were killed in the battle. About seven thousand Americans died there. The Japanese general who was chosen to command the battle, Tadamichi Kuribayashi, developed a strategy of digging underground caves through the island, interconnected by about sixteen miles of tunnels, so that when the Americans invaded, they were attacked by soldiers who remained hidden from view. But the Japanese were outnumbered by the more than seventy thousand Marines who came in over eight hundred ships. The battle lasted thirty-six days. *Letters from Iwo Jima* is on many film critics' ten-best lists, including our critic David Edelstein, who also included Eastwood's *Flags of Our Fathers*.

Clint Eastwood, welcome back to *Fresh Air*. And congratulations on your new film. Did you know that you wanted to make two films, one from the Japanese and one from the American point of view, on Iwo Jima? Or was the second film, the one that was just released, did that occur to you somewhere during the process of working on the first?

Clint Eastwood: It occurred during the process. As we were preparing to do *Flags of Our Fathers*, it occurred to me that the general who was the defender of the island was considered by American generals to be quite clever. And so I just started getting curious about as to what he was like. And so I asked a friend in Japan to send any books that were on him. There were no books in English, but there was a small book about letters that he had written home when he was an envoy in the United States and in Canada in the late twenties and early thirties. And so he had written home and drawn little pictures for his daughter and his son to show them what it was like where he was.

And so I thought, "This is an interesting person," not only the humanity that he had as a father towards his kids but also the fact that he was learning English and learning a lot about our culture at that particular time.

Gross: Is the movie based on letters that he actually wrote during the battle of Iwo Jima?

Eastwood: Yes. The book actually takes it up through letters that he later wrote from Iwo Jima, right up until he wasn't heard from anymore. And then I went through, and we got many articles from magazines and things, though it is not taught—history of this battle is not taught in Japan, there were some articles speculating on some of the people who were on the island at that time. And everything from Olympic champions to regular, working men who were sent over there, with the instructions, "Don't plan on returning."

Gross: Is it not taught in Japan because the battle was such a defeat for the country?

Eastwood: I think so. I think after the war, they didn't teach much about any of the final days of it. A little bit more on Okinawa because there were a lot of civilian casualties there. But on Iwo, which was the first Japanese soil that the Marines invaded when they were taking—because throughout the South Pacific, they were retaking islands that had already been taken and controlled by Japan. And now this was the first Japanese soil, so it became a very important battle for them to defend. They were trying to discourage the Americans from invading the mainland of Japan.

Gross: You know, as an American watching the movie, you're in a very, almost awkward situation. Usually in a war film, the film is told from your country's point of view, if it's an American movie. And, of course, you're rooting for the soldiers and you're rooting for them to, you know, vanquish the other side. But in this film, you become very fond of some of the soldiers and leaders in it—not all of them but some of them. And you don't want them to die. And at the same time, you don't want them to kill the Americans who they're fighting. So you can't have a conventional war film response to this movie.

Eastwood: No, absolutely. It isn't meant to take their side of the story. It's just meant to show that they were in a very tough position by being defenders of a cause that hadn't been working. And the Japanese at that time were under the influence of a military complex that was very aggressive. Had been very aggressive throughout the world, and now they were on the final defense. And so this is just to show their reaction and what their people were like. But what it boils down to is when mothers are losing their sons, mothers—whether they're Japanese or American or whatever nationality—the reaction always has the same pathos.

Gross: Now, you mention that *Letters from Iwo Jima* is loosely based on real letters from the lieutenant general who led the Japanese end of the battle, and he's played in the movie by Ken Watanabe. Did you read those letters yourself?

Eastwood: Well, yeah. I read the ones that were all in the books and everything we could find, and the family furnished us with quite a bit of information. All those letters that Ken Watanabe reads back, most of the information in there is exactly as it was.

Gross: What struck you most about those letters?

Eastwood: Well, the poignancy of a father writing to his children and to his wife about being off at war and about doing this job and wishing he could be with them and wishing he had fixed the kitchen door before leaving and apologizing for not attending to as many things. Talking to his kids about their use of grammar in their letters back. And it was the same as any father in any society.

Gross: It was really interesting to watch how the Japanese military is portrayed in the film. You know, I think most Americans know that there were so-called Kamikaze fighters during World War II who flew planes right into their target and the pilots basically committed suicide in the attack. And you portrayed the kind of emphasis on honor and that killing yourself would be better than surrendering and better in some instances than retreating, as far as the Japanese military higher-ups were concerned.

There's a scene in the movie—and I hope you don't feel I'm giving too much away here—but there's a scene in the movie where several of the Japanese soldiers, knowing that they've lost their end of the battle, consecutively blow themselves up with hand grenades that they've kept. And it's just really kind of shocking and a disturbing scene to watch them kill themselves like this. Can you talk a little bit not only about shooting it but what you had read or heard about this kind of thing happening?

Eastwood: Well, it was quite common, the philosophy at that particular time of committing "seppuku" as they call it, or "hara-kiri," as we—But if you read books, there's a book out called the *Kamikaze Diaries* that's in English, and it's letters also, letters back from these young students who were conscripted into flying. They picked these young college students because they figured they'd give them a cram course in flying where they were only going to fly one way. But most of the letters are quite pathetic because you see there they are writing back and telling their mothers that they really don't want to be doing this and they really don't want to die, and they couldn't resist. The chain of command throughout the Japanese military was very, very strict and very rough, and if you didn't go along with it, you were in deep trouble.

Gross: Could you talk a little bit about shooting that scene in which several of the Japanese soldiers blow themselves up with hand grenades?
Eastwood: Yeah. Well, that actually happened, and we portrayed that, the results of that, in *Flags of Our Fathers*. But in the Mount Suribachi, there was a point where the Japanese that were stationed in that section of the island felt that they were overrun, that there was no hope, and so they just started blowing themselves up. And that's very, very difficult for us to understand from an American philosophy. But they actually did that, and in the book *Flags of Our Fathers*, they account for that sequence. They chronicle that sequence, and it's kind of an amazing thing. And so in the other one, we show them leading up to it and how it came about by a misunderstanding, actually, because General Kuribayashi didn't believe in all that.

The interesting thing that made me want to tell the story about him was that he didn't really believe in suicide attacks and banzai attacks and all these things that were very common for the Japanese soldiers at that time. He believed that being a dead soldier was not being effective at all, so he was a very practical guy. And he came up with all the ideas of tunneling through the island and connecting tunnels that would make a person be able to get away and fight another day.

Gross: The movie starts with the letters of the lieutenant general being dug up on Iwo Jima in 2005. Were the letters actually buried and dug up later?

Eastwood: Well, there were some letters found there, but whether it was done in that exact same form, we're not sure. We're speculating, because nobody really knows exactly how General Kuribayashi died. It was speculated that—there were many stories. One that he died on the island with a PFC in attendance and committed suicide, and another one that he just disappeared. But nobody really knows.

The same with Baron Nishi, who was an Olympic equestrian champion in 1932 at the Olympics in Los Angeles. And nobody knows quite how he died except that it was speculated, and there have been stories written, that he was blinded and he stayed behind in a cave by himself.

Gross: The film opens with shots of Iwo Jima today. Can you describe what it looks like now and what it felt like to be there knowing the casualties in that battle?

Eastwood: Yeah, it's like visiting any battlefield, going to Utah or Omaha Beach and Normandy or any of those battles. And you can almost feel the activity there. The first time you walk out on our Green Beach—the Americans named it Green Beach—which is right at the foot of Suribachi, and you walk out there on that deep black sand, and you start looking out there and visualizing an armada coming in, of American ships, it's quite overwhelming. And you think of all the Marine Corps personnel who suffered casualties on that island. It's an overwhelming experience.

We did that the first trip over there. And then, later on, when you go over there to film and then you film down in the caves, where the hospitals were all built underground in caves, and the places where the troops resided, you wonder how the hell they did it, because it's amazing. The island, there's a lot of geothermal activity, so these caves are immensely, tremendously hot. And so there's just a very humid feeling. In fact, you go into them now, and they don't recommend you stay in there more than fifteen or twenty minutes, but these people had to stay in there for days at a time.

Gross: The cinematography is really—beautiful sounds like the wrong word to use because we're talking about war here. It's not like it's pretty. But the mood, the tone of it just seems so right. A lot of the sequences

are shot in something very close to black and white. I think the color is so subdued it looks almost black and white, although it's very blue-grey more than it is black-white sometimes. But the explosions are in full color. Would you talk a little bit about figuring out what look you wanted the film to have and how you went about getting it?
Eastwood: Well, the film was shot in color, but I sort of de-saturated. We de-saturated it down to the point where it didn't look comfortable color. We didn't—we certainly didn't want the picture to have a Technicolor in the old-fashioned sense, Dorothy and Toto in *The Wizard of Oz* or something. So we wanted to de-saturate it down to where it looked almost close to black and white. The colors were very subdued and, of course, explosions are a little brighter because they're explosions. So it was just a question of choices that we all made to have it have that look, which gave it the non-comfortable feeling of war.

Gross: Because the movie is from a Japanese point of view, the actors in it are largely Japanese. I mean, there are some Americans portrayed as well. And the movie is shot in Japanese. The characters speak Japanese and it's subtitled. So, were most of the actors who you cast English-speaking as well? Were you able to communicate to them in English?
Eastwood: Yeah. Several of them spoke English, but we also had interpreters along for the actors that didn't. And the majority of them did not speak English that well because we brought most of the actors from—there were a few from Los Angeles and New York—but most of them were brought over from Tokyo. And we had interpreters, but emotions are emotions in all languages, and so it wasn't a hard thing to do. But I didn't feel that the picture should be told in English, have Japanese people speaking English because that would definitely feel more movie-movie-like. To me they should be speaking Japanese, except in the scenes where English is the predominant language being used.

Gross: Did you meet survivors of the battle of Iwo Jima from each side?
Eastwood: Yes. Not from the Japanese side so much. There's not too many of them. Out of the twenty-one to twenty-two thousand men that were stationed on the island, only one thousand survived and we're not sure how many of them were combat folks or whether they were Korean conscripted labor. But there were a few, very few. And we didn't get to talk to too many of them, though I've read articles by some of them that are all quite good. But American survivors, I talked to quite a few of them.

Gross: Is there an image that really helped guide you in making *Flags of Our Fathers* from those conversations you had with survivors?

Eastwood: Well, yeah, there is. There's one image that is kind of common, that most of them that were in combat there, they just never really spoke about it too much. They would get together and maybe have Marine Corps celebrations or Marine Corps organizations, but they wouldn't really get into—there's not the gung-ho-ness that you'd think there would be. There was just—it was a tremendous battle. It was intended to be a three- or four-day affair, lasted over a month. And they were pinned down a good portion of the way. When you see an awful lot of your friends are wounded and killed, it's not something you forget easily.

Gross: Have you gotten any reaction yet from Japanese viewers to *Letters from Iwo Jima*?

Eastwood: Yeah. Well, the film has been out there for four weeks now, and it's running very, very well, doing tremendous business in Japan. So the Japanese viewers and Japanese reviewers have been very kind to the film. And I think they like it from an entertainment standpoint, but they're liking it historically as well. I think the younger generation is getting a lot of the answers to curiosity about that battle and what the wartime conditions were for the Japanese soldiers and civilians.

Gross: What about *Flags of Our Fathers*, did that show in Japan?

Eastwood: Yeah. That showed in Japan, too. That ran first, and that did well there, too. But *Letters*, of course, is doing tremendously well there.

Gross: *Flags of Our Fathers* takes a very heroic image, the picture of the soldiers planting the flag at Iwo Jima, and looks at what really happened and how much more ambiguous the story is when you know what really happened. The photo was actually staged after the original flag was given to a congressman, if I remember correctly, who asked for it.

Eastwood: Yeah, I think the secretary of Navy asked for it . . . That's as much as we can get on it.

Gross: And then the men in the photo, at least in the telling of the story in the movie, feel like frauds because the photo was staged, and it's seen as this great heroic moment but they don't feel like it was a heroic moment. What spoke to you about this story?

Eastwood: Well, the picture *wasn't* staged, and that's what makes it so great, is the picture's just people matter of factly trying to put up a flag, but it was a second flag, because they had put up one before that was a smaller one, and they decided to exchange, much like you laid out here. But it was different. They just didn't think too much of it, and three out of the six men who raised the flag in the famous photograph were killed within a week or so of that incident, including even one of the cameramen, the movie cameraman, and so they didn't feel heroic. They just felt they were just doing a job, but all of a sudden, they're brought back and they're being called the heroes, and they're being treated like tremendous stars and being romanced by politicians and society in general to go out on these bond tours. So it's a little tough for them to accept that. It's a big thing to lump on to people who are nineteen or twenty years old and, all of a sudden, be in that kind of commotion.

Gross: Did you see a lot of World War II films in the forties and fifties, and did they have an impact on you?
Eastwood: Yeah. I saw a lot of them when I was growing up and they did have an impact on me. They were exciting, as a kid, to watch war movies, and you're always rooting for somebody, mainly our side, and the enemy was always portrayed as villainous, and our guys were always portrayed as heroic. But those days are gone. I mean that era was more black and white with it all, and that isn't the way war is to somebody else, so it's fun to look at it from different perspectives. Those war pictures were mostly propagandistic. They were selling America as great, and that's where the audience was and that's where it would always be.

Gross: Your view of violence in movies has really changed over the years, and some of your early films were very violent, particularly the Sergio Leone Westerns, like *The Good, the Bad and the Ugly*. Those films almost take a certain pleasure in violence, in film violence. The last few movies that you've made are just—some of them are so much about the costs of violence, whether it's in war or on the street. Was there a turning point in your life where you started to rethink film violence and what you wanted to do with it? I think of the turning point in your movies as maybe being *Pale Rider* and *Unforgiven*, but in terms of what you wanted to do with your gifts when portraying violence onscreen.
Eastwood: Yeah. I think I've been interested in that probably—I think it's just a natural maturing of life, as at some point you start thinking about things a little differently, but that's part of the growing-up process, and I always figured myself, even though I'm in my senior status right

now, I still consider myself a person who's growing up, so you're always changing or thinking of things from a different perspective, and you're looking for stories that think of things from a different perspective. *Unforgiven*, you mentioned, was a man who was haunted by violence, and so we got into that thing where—how it affects you personally, and what it does to your soul. And I think now, in present times, we're looking at World War II, which is easy to look at, but what that has done—what that did to the souls of those men when they came back and how some of them had a hard time adjusting to civilian life after being asked as very young men at an impressionable age to go off and get involved with violent activity.

Gross: I'd like to just ask you about your movie *Million Dollar Baby*, in which you played a boxing coach at a neighborhood gym who reluctantly takes on a woman boxer and ends up caring for her, like a daughter, and as everybody knows, some people on the right accused that film of advocating assisted suicide, and I felt that anybody who had actually seen the film would find it hard to think of the movie as promoting assisted suicide, considering the incredible cost—without getting deep into the plot—the incredible cost that it has for the person who helps. And I'm wondering what the experience was like for you to find a film being, I think, very misinterpreted and used for political effect.
Eastwood: You hit on the most important activity when you say, "Have seen the picture." If you have seen the picture, you look at it a lot differently. I certainly don't advocate assisted suicide. I don't believe in suicide—or assisting—but I can see where a person might get to that. Imaginatively-wise you can see how people might get to that position, and this was an extreme case, but it doesn't mean we were advocating going out and saying, "OK, this should go on all the time." You're always telling extreme cases, but that's what you do when you do a play or a movie. You're always telling some sort of story with extreme dynamics to it, and this—you take the story and you take a person who's lost a relationship with his daughter and has no—and feels terrible about it, and then he finds a relationship with a sort of a surrogate daughter, and then, all of a sudden, tragedy happens, and how does he deal with it? And he doesn't deal with it, and we don't portray the character—that I was portraying—we don't portray him as a person who goes off and lives happily ever after. Obviously, his soul is ripped for the rest of his life. But that's the drama of it all, and you're telling an extreme situation.

Gross: What did it say to you that your movie was used in the way that it was to make points that you didn't think it even made, that it became this kind of talking point?

Eastwood: Well, people interpret things the way they want to interpret them, and you can't do anything about that. The majority of the people got the program, and the majority of the people, whether you're rightist or leftist . . . I don't think anybody, an intelligent audience, feels that different about it in the long run.

Gross: My guest is Clint Eastwood. Earlier in his career, he starred in a trilogy of iconic Westerns—*A Fistful of Dollars*, *For a Few Dollars More*, and *The Good, the Bad and the Ugly*. Each of those Italian films had scores by Ennio Morricone. Morricone also scored several films Eastwood directed. Morricone is now considered one of the most important and influential movie composers of our time. He'll get an honorary Academy Award this year. Next month, he'll make his first American concert appearance. He'll conduct his music at Radio City Music Hall and will also give a private concert at the UN. Before we ask Eastwood about Morricone, here's Morricone's theme for *The Good, the Bad and the Ugly*.

[Soundbite from The Good, the Bad and the Ugly*]*

Gross: Your movies with Sergio Leone had scores by Ennio Morricone; at what point did his music enter into the process for you? Take *The Good, the Bad and the Ugly*. At what point did you hear that really incredible theme that he'd written? Was all of your work done already by the time you heard it?

Eastwood: Well, the first time I heard it was on *Fistful of Dollars*, which I had gone off and made during a hiatus of *Rawhide*, and I did the picture in Europe and then came back, and then they were asking me to come back and do a sequel the following year, and I said, "Well, how about sending me the first one? Let me see what that looks like. Let's see what we've got," because I've been reading about how it's doing well on the foreign box office and everything but I had no idea how it looked. And I came in and, all of a sudden, this score comes on, and I thought, "Wow, this score is really unusual." And unusual is the thing I would say about Ennio Morricone—and I don't know whether it's him or a combination of Sergio Leone, but Sergio was always very interested in music and he was always interested in the framing of sound effects and music in films.

And Morricone was part of those three films, *The Good, the Bad and the Ugly* and *For A Few Dollars More*, and then we used Morricone on *Two Mules for Sister Sara* and *In the Line of Fire*. So over the years, we've spent a lot of time with Morricone's scores.

Gross: Did looking at yourself on screen with his music behind you give you a sense that you didn't have before of how music could change the impact that an image had on the viewer?
Eastwood: Yes. Absolutely. The Leone pictures were very operatic, and Morricone could go flat-out on those with great trumpet solos and all kinds of different sounds and stuff, and he's very clever, very innovative for that particular time especially, and now he's been imitated by many people since then.

Gross: If this is too personal, just let me know. You're in your mid-seventies now and obviously still directing great movies. Is getting older—how does getting older compare to what you expected, say, being in your mid-seventies would be like?
Eastwood: Well, it's a lot better than I thought it would be. I think that getting older is great if you're constantly learning something, you know, providing you have good health and all the things that everybody wishes for. But you know more. You can look at things from more perspectives, and you've seen more in life, and if you enjoy it properly, it can be a nice experience. A lot of people joke about it. Henry Bumstead, who was an associate of mine who just recently passed away in his nineties, he used to always say, "Ah, to be eighty again." So it all depends on where you're looking from. If you're forty, you say, "Oh, thirty wouldn't be bad." Or if you're eighty, seventy looks pretty good. But it's a great learning experience about life, and if you keep it as a learning experience, then it's always fun.

Gross: You have such an iconic face because of the movies that you've been in. I think all of us as we get older we look in the mirror and study how our face has been changing with age, and you know, some people decide, "Oh, well, it's changing. I don't want it to change, so I'll get cosmetic surgery or something." And if you don't, you examine your face changing and you make of it what you will. You know, it's interesting or you regret it or, you know, whatever. What's it been like for you with such an iconic face to watch your face change with age?

[Eastwood laughs]. And to watch it on the large screen, as well as on the mirror, yeah.
Eastwood: I don't think one pays that much attention, you know, because it's all a gradual process, and you're this way and you look this way at this point of life. You're this way, you feel this way at this point of life, whatever it is, and you go on and you enjoy the going on. If you sit there and worry about it and say, "Well, gee, I'll get cosmetic surgery and I'll try to look like I did when I was twenty-eight," that ain't going to happen. All it's going to do is make you look like you have a vanity problem with it, and it's not going to be pleasant when people come up to you and say, "Didn't you use to be so-and-so?" And so it would be kind of an embarrassing moment, so I think people have to just accept things the way they are and move on, move on and say that was another phase. Your thirties were one phase, your forties were one phase, and just keep on going.

Gross: Is cosmetic surgery a problem for you as a director, because so many actors have had, or are having it done, and you can tell, looking at them on a big screen.
Eastwood: It is a problem, because if you're casting a person in a film and you say, "OK, I'd like to cast so-and-so in a part," well, now you have to say, "Could you bring them in?" Before, you could say, "Well, I know his or her work because I've seen him in many pictures and so I don't have to see them. I know how good they are," but now you say, maybe, "Hmm, well, let me see how they are today," because like you say, like you're insinuating here, they may not look the same. They come in and you say, "Geez, they're all cosmetized," if that's a word, and there you go. That's not the look I was expecting. That's not what was in my imagination when I thought of casting that person.

Gross: Are you already working on another movie?
Eastwood: No, not right at the present time. I'm trying to abstain.

Gross: Take a little rest?
Eastwood: Yeah, exactly.

Gross: You probably never expected these two movies to come out as quickly, you know, as close to each other as they did.
Eastwood: Well, they were both sort of distant companions of one another, so it was a way of coming out. Yeah.

Gross: Well, Clint Eastwood, I want to thank you so much for talking with us.

Eastwood: Thank you very much, Terry.

The Quiet American

Geoff Andrew / 2008

Published in *Sight & Sound* 18, no. 9 (September 2008): 17, 21–22. Reprinted by permission of the British Film Institute.

Geoff Andrew: Last time we met, I suggested that your work seemed to be getting closer to Howard Hawks's films in its interest in relationships, place, atmosphere, and so on, rather than plot.
Clint Eastwood: Well, I love Hawks; we're always interested in his characters. And his pacing: *His Girl Friday*—how did he do that? But I guess he had Cary Grant and Rosalind Russell, who were trained to talk like that, whereas nowadays actors try to be more realistic. Those days, actors really pumped it out.

GA: Do you give actors much direction?
CE: I try to direct actors the way I like to be directed. As an actor I like to show what I can do, then be told if something's wrong. So when directing I like to see what actors do and watch it bloom. Sometimes I'll say the pace or something isn't quite right and we'll adjust accordingly. We can talk about things too. For *Changeling*, I gave them stuff about the real case, told them what happened—a lot of what the characters say is what the real people actually said. On *Mystic River* the actors wanted to rehearse. I said go ahead. They didn't want to change the characterizations so I didn't mind. That way they'd be up on the dialogue and on that Boston dialect: "Harvard Yard" and all that!

GA: *Changeling* took forty-two days to shoot; that's fast for a big period movie. You still prefer to work quickly?
CE: I like to move things along. All the directors I used to like when I was growing up were like that, it seems. I only worked with a few—people like Stuart Heisler who came by to do *Rawhide* in their later years. I had

a small part in a William A. Wellman picture; he moved fairly quickly. I gather John Ford and Hawks did that too.

GA: One director I spoke to likened your focus on essentials to Ford's.
CE: I try not to gild it too much. By today's standards Ford didn't do a lot of crazy shots. But when he had Fonda sitting with his feet up on the porch in *My Darling Clementine* or Wayne walking out the door into the prairie in *The Searchers*, that one shot would be impressive and really make something of a scene. Nowadays there's a tendency to do it in six or eight shots instead of just showing one still portrait which you can look at, like some beautiful painting by Velázquez or whoever.

There's no particular director I've consciously followed. Orson Welles once told Merv Griffin on his show that he liked *The Outlaw Josey Wales* a lot because it reminded him of a Hawks movie, and Welles liked Hawks. That was nice, to have a filmmaker from another era looking at your stuff. And Welles really knew how to trick the eye.

GA: Since *Bird*, many of your films have looked much darker than other people's. Why?
CE: A lot of it's in the nature of the story: *Letters from Iwo Jima*, for example, has people living like animals in tunnels underground. But it's also the way I see things—in a noir-esque way I guess! I work very closely with the DoP, and I'll often say "That's too much light!" I just want a sketch, I don't want to see everything. The audience will make up what they see. In the old days they'd have special little lights on a character's eyes. But sometimes you don't want to see the eyes. It's a question of looking *in* at a movie, rather than have it look *out* at you: the audience has to come to a film, be part of it. It's like acting. I've seen a lot of actors throw themselves at the audience, whereas with others you have to go to them a little, put yourselves into them. That makes for a more thoughtful movie.

GA: Restraint was always there in your work as an actor, then you did the same with your direction.
CE: I like the audience to come with me on a trip. I don't want to beg them to come along if they don't want to. If they don't want the trip you're offering, they can go next door to the next complex and see what's on there.

At the end of *The Outlaw Josey Wales* my character just rides off as the sun's coming up. My editor wanted to superimpose an image of the little family Josey had gathered around him so the audience would know he was going to go back to them. I said no, no, we didn't need that. In their minds the audience know he'll eventually go back to the grandmother, the girl, the Indian and the rest; they know because that's what they want. And if they don't want that, it makes no difference anyway!

I grew up with radio, where you'd listen and see pictures in your mind. Later we'd get television series of the shows we'd listened to as children, but the radio shows were always much more interesting, because with them we made the pictures. And everyone has that capability.

GA: You don't appear to feel constrained by genre. You're not afraid to break rules, yet you're not flashy about it. Do you feel different from most of today's directors?
CE: I don't think about that; I hate to get into looking inwards because that means I'm not looking outwards. But it's true I'm probably more influenced by that older tradition when people made a greater variety of films. Nowadays so many decisions about making films are about what's just been out there—the fad of the moment.

To get *Mystic River* and *Million Dollar Baby* made I had to go with hat in hand. Nobody wanted to make them. I took *Mystic River* to people I knew, but even Warner Bros. said "It's so dark." Next I went to them with *Million Dollar Baby*. "It's about a woman in boxing! Nobody'll want to see that!" So I went to Universal and they said, "We've already got a boxing movie." I said, "It's not a boxing movie, that's just the world it's set in. There's more to it than that; it's a father-daughter love story." Then Warner Bros. came back and said, "We don't want you to make this anywhere else, but could you make it on a really austere budget?" So I told them it wouldn't be expensive, and I'd do it like *Play Misty for Me* for no money: they'd pay me a percentage if it made money, and if it didn't, that was fine by me. Same deal as thirty-eight years ago. Anyway, it started slowly and went on to do very well, so we were right on that occasion. We could just as easily have been wrong, I suppose, but at least we're not making a picture because it's part of a trend or because another studio's making something similar across town. That shouldn't be important. You should make what you want to do. When we made *Unforgiven* it was a quiet period for Westerns, but I said, "It's a special story, it'll have its own character." You have to go with what you believe in.

GA: Quite a few of your films have strong female characters, from *Play Misty* and *Breezy* through *Madison County* to *Changeling*.

CE: *Madison County* was a funny picture to do. A friend told me to read the book because she thought I was like the character in it, but when I read it, I thought there was a lot of corny stuff. But at the same time I thought there was something interesting. In the old weepies like the Sirk films there was often someone with some illness or affliction; this had none of that. To me, it was just about a woman leading a kind of boring life then finding some excitement. The book was more about his story, but we made it more about her because she was the one with the dilemma: whether to leave her family or not.

GA: People were surprised at your making that movie, but then you've repeatedly surprised us over the years, from *Breezy* onwards.

CE: Well, even when I took *Play Misty* to Universal—they owned the property but just had it there on the shelf—Jennings Lang said, "Who the hell wants to see Clint Eastwood play a disc jockey?" I said, "You may be right, but it's a good part and there's something about the stalker mentality, and misinterpretation about intent in relationships that's interesting. What do you want me to do? Ten more Westerns?" If I'd stayed working in the genres I became popular in I wouldn't be working today. To do three movies of a certain kind is fine; do seven and that's all you do. At the Cannes press conference, they were asking if I was going to play Dirty Harry again. I said, "At seventy-seven years of age? At some point they throw you out of the police department!" *Dirty Harry* was fun to do and if I said I'd do another Warner Bros. would probably say, "Yeah! Go ahead, here's the check." But I don't just want the pay check. I want to do something that suits me, not something ridiculous.

GA: You've been making a lot of films recently.

CE: I have, and I've no idea why; maybe it's just a streak I was on. With *Mystic River* I'd seen an early critique of the book, so I read it and we went and got it straight away. *Million Dollar Baby* had actually been given to me four years earlier when I was busy with something else, so everything eventually kind of fell into place. *Letters from Iwo Jima* was another example: we were preparing *Flags of Our Fathers*, and at a meeting with [producers] Rob Lorenz and Steven Spielberg, I happened to say, "I've got this other thing I'm thinking about, about a Japanese general. . . ." I'd had a friend send me a book about him. There was very little Japanese material on Iwo Jima, for obvious reasons. But we got what there was and I got this lady to write it. She looked at articles from the postwar years, then put together the story. By the time we were shooting *Flags* in Iceland I had her script, so at weekends I'd work on that, and I got an overall picture of the story from both sides as we went along.

GA: You're now doing pretty much what you want. Do you ever think back to when you were doing bit parts at Universal and RKO, and wonder how on earth you got here?
CE: Oh yeah. When I was doing *Rawhide* I'd think, "What happens if this is the only job I ever get?" The actor's lament: every job's your last. I deferred a lot of the money I was paid for that series, because I thought I probably wasn't going to work for a while. But I followed my instincts, and because I liked Kurosawa and *Yojimbo* a lot that took me to *Fistful* and Leone. When I came back to the States, a director pulled out of a project and that's how I met Don Siegel. One thing just led to another; it's not as if there was some great plan.

GA: Do you ever regret not having taken your political career further?
CE: Not at all. I'd have probably passed away long ago. In my mind it was always only for one term. I was with a group of people having a glass of wine and trying to figure out how to get rid of the administration in Carmel and one guy suggested I do a term. The council seats are for four years and the mayoral term is for two, so I said, "The mayoral thing's shorter, so I could do that." I still made *Bird* and *Heartbreak Ridge* during that period; I just had a second job for a couple of years.

GA: Do you have any unfulfilled ambitions or regrets about your career?
CE: Not really, except I've always loved music and I wish I'd been more disciplined as a child and played more. But the circumstances weren't right at the time, so I'm doing it now. I write and play stuff for my own amusement and have a good time with it. I had quite a knack when I was young—if I'd ground away at it, how far could I have taken it?

Nathan Hale said, "I only regret that I have but one life to give my country." Well, I regret that I have but one life to give myself! But that's all just fantasy, because you wouldn't do all those other things since you wouldn't have the knowledge. Looking back, you fantasize: "Gee, if I'd known when I was six—or twenty, or whatever—what I know now!" But you only know what you know at any particular time and you're constantly learning and changing. That's good, it keeps you going. If you felt you didn't have anything more to take in, your mind would get into a state of senility. Just look at Manoel de Oliveira; he's one hundred but like a man in his sixties! What genes must he have? When I saw him at his tribute, I felt like asking, "What's your diet, sir? What brand of whisky do you drink?"

Changeling Man

In Changeling *Clint Eastwood believes he has found one of America's most shocking stories of brutal crime and corruption, as the director tells Geoff Andrew.*

Brian Grazer brought the project to me and when I was reading it I didn't even know the story was true; I just found it fascinating. So when I heard that it was, I called J. Michael Straczynski, the writer, to ask how much was real, how much a figment of his imagination. He said it was all true. So my producer Robert Lorenz got the *LA Times* and various newspapers of the era and we realized that many of the statements by the police chief, doctors, and city council that were in the script were the real deal. If a police chief nowadays said, "We're going to take criminals off the streets, we're gonna kill 'em on sight," you'd think, "Wow!"—but that's exactly what the guy said!

I was actually living in Los Angeles around that time; my parents moved there in 1934 when I was four. My dad worked in a service station off Highway 101 at Sunset Boulevard. We lived in a little dumpy house with nothing around it apart from other dumpy houses. There was nothing much out at Pacific Palisades then, but now it's all built-up.

We paid a lot of attention to getting right how the city looked then; there were lots of pictures. Downtown LA was much busier and City Hall, which features in the film, was at that time the only really tall building. Now downtown is buried by skyscrapers—they'll regret that if they have an earthquake. Hollywood, Beverly Hills, and Pasadena all seemed way out then, but the red-car system was very efficient. Those streetcars went to Pasadena and Santa Monica and branched out all over the place. The system was still there when I returned to LA in 1953, when I came out of the military and went to the City College, but then someone had the bright idea of taking it out and putting in diesel buses: just what the city didn't need—extra emissions! So we had to recreate the red-car system. Fortunately a few people into nostalgia had kept a few pieces around that they'd restored.

There's always been a glamorous dream about the LA scene. It's in our story, with a kid wanting to get into movies. Because he's read something or heard something on the radio, he thinks he can go there and maybe run across Tom Mix walking down the street! That naivety seems so bizarre now, especially given the corruption our story also deals with. It's like there's something in the air there—LA has gone through quite a few periods when it's been really corrupt and someone has had to come in to straighten it out.

I've dealt with crimes against children before, and that's not unconscious: to me they are the most despicable crimes—stealing people's lives, stealing people's innocence. But when we dealt with what happened at the ranch I didn't want to get too graphic, so we used shadows. I didn't want it to be a horror movie—those scenes are really about the crimes' impact on a boy telling a detective an incredible story.

Even today it's an hour or so's drive from LA to where that ranch was, so imagine what it was like going out there on dirt roads. We went out there too. The house is now in a built-up neighborhood and in many ways it is now as it was then. We didn't see anyone around; even if we had we couldn't have asked if they knew anything about what had happened there because we might have ended up ruining their lives!

We looked at photos in the archives of the two boys in the changeling affair, and Arthur, who the police insisted was Christine's son Walter, really didn't look anything like him. I don't know how they managed it, but they did a hell of a job convincing her she was hallucinating for a while there! There's a picture of Arthur sitting on Christine's lap and they're smiling and it looks like they're having a great old time; evidently the cops had them pose in a photographic gallery. They really went to extremes to put the story of Walter's return over, but she sensed something was wrong and ended up denying he was her son. Still, what's fascinating is that she actually went along with them long enough to take the kid home!

To put their story over the police enlisted the help of the press. It was a long way from today's information age, but there were the *LA Times*, the *Herald*, the *Examiner*, and papers from the smaller towns too, like Hollywood with the *Citizen News*. Now it's a one-newspaper town, of course, and you just wonder how the story would be manipulated today. There'd be many more eyes watching, so maybe it would be more difficult. But we still see amazing things happening. There's creativity in the human mind, but some people use it in the wrong way, to see what they can put over us. You wonder how politicians like Eliot Spitzer in New York ever think they can do all that stuff without anybody knowing. They're nearly always holier-than-thou types too—the hypocrisy!

Do You Feel Lucky, Monk?

Nick Tosches / 2008

Published online as "Web Exclusive," *Vanity Fair*, December 12, 2008, ⟨http://www.vanityfair.com/culture/features/2008/12/eastwood200812⟩. Reprinted by permission of the author.

It's one of those curiosities of human nature. No matter how much we achieve in this world, no matter how much life brings us, there are always regrets and pangs of failure.

"If I've had any regret in life, it was not paying more attention to it and not practice, practice, practice."

That's Clint Eastwood talking, and he's talking about playing the piano. For him, before there were movies, there was the piano.

He was born in San Francisco in 1930. His father was a steelworker and his mother was a factory worker. And there was a piano.

"I started just playing it around the house when I was a little kid. My mother played a little bit. She could read music and stuff. So just bits and pieces. And then I started imitating records and stuff, 'cause she didn't know how to play any jazz or blues particularly. So I just started getting interested in players who were good at it, and one thing led to another."

The players who struck him back then were "Fats Waller and Art Tatum and people like that. And then a lot of the blues pianists that later came along. And I listened to some Dixieland piano players, too. You know, James P. Johnson, the people that date back to that era. And then I listened to a lot of the boogie-woogie piano players of the thirties and forties. Meade Lux Lewis, Albert Ammons, Pete Johnson, stuff like that. And then Oscar Peterson came along. He was just a kid then, or just a very young man, and he started playing out of sight. George Shearing and Oscar Peterson and those guys became very popular in the forties and fifties, so everybody tried to imitate them."

It wasn't until 1955 that Clint made his first film appearance, without credit, as a lab technician in *Revenge of the Creature*. But in the years before and after that inauspicious beginning, he never thought of turning to the piano for a living, though he probably could have done as well on a stage or in a bar with a piano as he did in that lab coat on a soundstage.

"No, I didn't. You know, I had a certain knack when I was very young, but I didn't have very good discipline. I didn't take any piano lessons or anything. We were just on a limited budget and everything. So most of the money I earned from caddying or bagging groceries and stuff was just to go to an occasional movie or something."

By the time of Clint's screen debut, the first wave of rock 'n' roll had come and all but gone. Clint, who was into Robert Johnson and other bygone bluesmen, was into the newer jive as well.

"I did get into rhythm and blues. I love good rhythm and blues. Joe Hunter and Lowell Fulson. Joe Turner, and Wynonie Harris. But I never quite got over into rock 'n' roll too much, it seems."

"You're talking about the late fifties on, the white stuff?"

"Yeah, the white stuff: never. It was sort of a steal from the black stuff, and the black stuff seemed like it had more of the origin."

His love for the flow and flux of this music is evinced in "Piano Blues," the segment he directed for Martin Scorsese's 2003 PBS series, *The Blues*. The piano masters here span those years from boogie-woogie to rhythm and blues, from Jimmy Yancey, born in Chicago in the late nineteenth century, to Fats Domino, born in New Orleans in the early twentieth.

The uncredited lab technician in *Revenge of the Creature* rose, vanished, returned as the Man with No Name, and eventually became the Director with Final Cut. One of the most intriguing examples of Clint's autonomy was *Honkytonk Man*, the 1982 film, directed by and starring him, that drew from elements of the lives of classic country singers such as Jimmie Rodgers and Hank Williams. It was one of those acts of daring, like his recent *Letters from Iwo Jima*, a committed throw of the dice against all commercial odds, that have defined his career as much as his enduring success has.

Six years after *Honkytonk Man*, Clint turned again to music and musicians when he directed Forest Whitaker as jazz revelator Charlie Parker in *Bird*. In preparing to make that movie, he screened a 1979 documentary called *The Last of the Blue Devils*. It was a celebration and reunion of Count Basie, Big Joe Turner, and numerous other characters from the golden age when jazz married rhythm and blues, and it was shot through with archival footage of Charlie Parker and others. Like just about everyone else who's seen *The Last of the Blue Devils*, Clint loved it. He found out that its director, Bruce Ricker, was now producing a documentary about jazz pianist Thelonious Monk, directed by Charlotte Zwerin; and that funds had run dry.

"Well, I always liked Monk," Clint told me. "He came along, he became popular, when I was in my early teens. Nobody could quite figure out what he was doing, but everybody thought he was kind of interesting. Thelonious Monk and Bud Powell and Lennie Tristano and all those guys were all playing at that time. They were all playing around. When they were on tour, you could hear them most anyplace."

Clint bailed out Ricker's *Thelonious Monk: Straight, No Chaser* in the summer of 1987, and it was completed in 1988, the same year Clint finished *Bird*. It was the beginning of a long association between Clint and Ricker, resulting in documentary collaborations such as *Clint Eastwood: Out of the Shadows* and *Tony Bennett: The Music Never Ends*. The most forth-shining of these joint projects was *Eastwood After Hours: Live at Carnegie Hall*.

As Clint said, he didn't practice, practice, practice, but he got to Carnegie Hall all the same, thanks to Ricker, one autumn evening in 1996. The night featured one of the most interesting assemblages in modern music, from Jay McShann to Thelonious Monk Jr., to Phil Ramone, to Joshua Redman; and the show closed with Clint himself at the piano. I told him he looked like he was having a good time.

"I was having a good time. And I picked a tune I played in an assembly when I was in high school—Avery Parrish's 'After Hours'—and I told Jay McShann, I said, 'Look, I don't know how much of this stuff I remember, so you gotta do me a favor. Let me do a couple little stanzas here and then you come in at some point. I'll kinda motion to you when I'm running out of ideas here.' And so he says, 'No problem.'

"All of a sudden, we're playing away, I'm going along, and finally I'm seeing that maybe I'm coming to—I'm overstaying my welcome here. So I look over at Jay, and Jay's backstage, talking away. He's not paying any attention to me. I'm waving like crazy, I'm motioning like crazy, and he's not coming out. And finally, later on, I asked him, 'Jay, where the hell were ya?' He said, 'Well, you seemed to be doing just fine. I thought I'd just let you go ahead and play.'"

Clint and Ricker are now working on a documentary about Dave Brubeck, whom Clint first heard at the Burma Lounge in Oakland in the forties, when the pianist's trio included percussionist Cal Tjader and bassist Ron Crotty.

It comes as no surprise that Clint listens to music every day. "To and from work, I play music in the car; and then sometimes I'll play music that I want to use in the picture. Or I'll get an inspiration about something and I'll sit down and make up something and then I'll put it in the picture as a mock-up score or something."

The theme of *Unforgiven* happened this way. In fact, the themes for most all of his pictures in recent years have happened this way, coming together on his way to and from location. For a quarter of a century, he has worked closely on the scores and soundtracks of his pictures with sax player, arranger, and composer Lennie Niehaus; and Clint himself has been contributing themes since the early eighties, when he wrote one for his daughter Alison, who played his fictional daughter in *Tightrope*. There followed themes for *A Perfect World* and *The Bridges of Madison County* in the nineties, and he has since written music for just about every picture he's made, including the score for his recent *Changeling* and the theme for his even more recent *Gran Torino*, both of which were nominated for Golden Globes.

He has an affinity for some classical composers as well: Brahms, Wagner, Beethoven—especially his third and ninth symphonies—Chopin. "A lot of the pieces I write are sort of Chopin-esque. I think that's one of the biggest influences I have."

When he travels, he often takes an electric piano along with him. "Other times, I'll have a piano put in the room. Yeah, I like to have one in the room."

He himself has two pianos, a Blüthner in LA and an old Chickering in Carmel. It was a serendipity to discover that the Chickering was favored by Thelonious Monk.

"Diana Krall was playing it one night. She was over and she was playing it, and she says this was the preferred piano of Monk. This piano I've got is pretty old and it needs a lot of work."

It seems that he's increasingly trying to make up for that practice he missed as a kid.

"I usually play every day. I'm usually writing something every day. I don't play to perform, though I suppose I could work out some things if I needed to. It's usually just for my own satisfaction and to get material. I'm working on some material now, and I don't know quite where I'm putting it, but I'm working on it."

Clint Eastwood, America's Director: The Searcher

Scott Foundas / 2008

Published in *LA Weekly*, December 18, 2008. Reprinted by permission of *LA Weekly* and the author.

"You've made the first movie of the Obama generation!" exclaimed an audience member, as he rushed up to Clint Eastwood after a recent screening of *Gran Torino*. "Well," the seventy-eight-year-old actor-director replied, without missing a beat, "I was actually born under Hoover." It was an ironic juxtaposition, given that Eastwood's *Torino* character, widowed Korean War vet and former Detroit autoworker Walt Kowalski, has earned comparisons to TV's Archie Bunker, for both his politically incorrect racial epithets and his general hostility toward a modern world that seems to have left him—and his old-fashioned American values— out in the cold. "We could use a man like Herbert Hoover again," Bunker sings at the start of each *All in the Family* episode. But it's change, not nostalgia, that sets the tone in *Gran Torino*, as the belligerent Walt ventures first across the property line and then deeper into the lives of the Hmong immigrant family living next door.

The movie, Eastwood tells me the day after the *Torino* screening, appealed to his own personal philosophy of "never stop learning. If you never stop learning, then you never stop growing as a person, you never stop taking in new information and changing. People ask me, 'Have you changed?' And I say, 'I hope so,' because over ten, twenty, thirty, forty years, you're supposed to change all the time. You're supposed to expand."

That said, *Gran Torino* is hardly one of those rainbow-coalition lessons in tolerance that well-meaning but naive American filmmakers tend to unleash at least once or twice a season—the ones about some randomly connected group of ethnically diverse strangers who take a trip to the Grand Canyon together, or a stuffy New York economist who goes native and starts playing the African drum. Eastwood would no sooner make such a pedantic film about our changing cultural makeup than he would directly address the effects of factory closures on once-prosperous labor meccas like Detroit—even though that too is very much a part of *Gran Torino*. As Manohla Dargis noted recently in the *New York Times*, "Few Americans make movies about this country anymore, other than Mr. Eastwood." But while America is undeniably Eastwood's great subject, as it was for his spiritual mentor, John Ford, he rarely tackles any American issue—social, economic, or otherwise—head-on.

"I go for the sideline effects of it all rather than, 'OK, here we are in the factory that's shutting down,'" Eastwood explains. "The obvious stories, the *Norma Rae* kind of stories, those are hurdles, but they're kind of right out there in front. It's the hurdles that are inside that you have to deal with to make characters interesting, I think."

Interviewing Eastwood can offer a similar education in stealth maneuvers and rear-guard actions. Ask him directly about some seemingly recurring theme in his work—like the way many Eastwood films address the conflict between personal and societal morality—and, at best, you'll get a grudging "I'm attracted to that, I guess."

After directing twenty-nine feature films and acting in more than twice that many, he says there's no grander design to the way he works than simply reading a script and deciding, "OK, this fits with what I want to do next. This is a person I'd like to visit and watch him go through his life."

But Eastwood will allow that, more often than not, those people he chooses to visit are haunted figures with dark and even dangerous pasts, men who have done or witnessed things no man should do or see. He likens Walt Kowalski, traumatized by the atrocities he committed a half-century ago in Korea, to Sanford Clark, the teenage nephew and unwitting accomplice of convicted serial killer Gordon Northcott, whose 1920s killing spree inspired Eastwood's other 2008 release, *Changeling*.

"I looked at a picture of his gravestone—he died at ninety-two—and it says, 'To a loving father and grandfather,'" Eastwood offers. "And you wonder, how the hell did this guy go on to be a loving father and grandfather? How did he bury all that crap? That's a whole story in itself—what his life must have been like, going back after that, having assisted in killing little children. You think, 'God, what could haunt a person any more than that?'"

All of us, Eastwood adds, "have to see a lot of crappy things in a lifetime and you have to deal with them, bury them. Sometimes you get assistance in that; sometimes you don't. The people in *Flags of Our Fathers*: I don't know what those people did. They just told them, 'OK, you're discharged now. The war's over. Go home. Get over it. Forget about it.'"

So, while Eastwood is glad that fans have been telling him how eagerly they're anticipating *Gran Torino* ever since the movie's poster, featuring a vindictive-looking Clint wielding an M-1, started circulating a couple of months ago, he hopes people drawn to the film by its promise of a return to *Dirty Harry*-style vigilantism realize that there's more to the movie than meets the eye. "I wonder if those people will be disappointed—the ones who just want the hard-ass stuff, the rifle in the face and the guns and stuff like that," he says. "You hope if that's what attracts an audience in, it isn't what they're left with. You hope the undercurrent will get to them as well."

It's those undercurrents that have dominated the latter half of Eastwood's filmmaking career, in which images of violence have rarely been offered up for mere titillation or visceral excitement. He points to the scene in the Oscar-winning *Unforgiven* in which the retired gunslinger William Munny (played by Eastwood) and his former partner Ned (Morgan Freeman) gun down a young man with a bounty on his head, who has violently assaulted a frontier-town prostitute. "Afterward, there's that little moment of, 'Jesus, I didn't want to ever do this again,'" Eastwood says. "He had vowed to stay away from that life, but there he is, just because they figured they would go get a little ransom money, and they rationalize it by saying, 'They deserve it anyway.' And that's the way life is."

By way of real-life example, Eastwood mentions the recent incident in which an employee at a Long Island Wal-Mart was trampled to death by several hundred overly eager customers attending the store's post-Thanksgiving sale. "Those people would probably say, 'Well, the guy shouldn't have been in our way,' or, 'The crowd was moving and I had to go with it.' People can rationalize just about anything, but when you really come down to it, the behavior is appalling."

One of *Gran Torino*'s most memorable sequences involves Kowalski giving advice on "how to be a man" to a shy, gang-victimized Hmong teenager (newcomer Bee Vang). It's fitting, because in the forty years since he first donned the Man With No Name's desert poncho, Eastwood has defined a kind of squint-eyed, low-voiced, impermeable macho cool for several generations of moviegoers—and, even in today's fickle youth culture, can still be found gracing the cover of men's lifestyle magazines like *Esquire*. It's a status that Eastwood, like *Gran Torino* itself, both embraces and gently mocks, fully aware of the anachronism of being a "man's man" in our supposedly gender-neutral society.

"The idea that men and women are the same is crazy, because they're not," Eastwood says with a chuckle. "They're equal under the eyes of the law and they're equal in a lot of ways—in fact, women are superior in a lot of ways and men are superior in other ways. So the more we recognize that, the more we can use those superior aspects of the gender. But being a guy now is a strange thing, especially a Caucasian male. Who's the biggest asshole? It's the white guys. You can attack them without hurting anybody's feelings, because they're the buffoons of society at the present time. But I always figure: what the hell, they can take it."

And true to form, Eastwood, who has four Oscars under his belt and is now well past the age at which almost any major star or director has still been actively working, isn't going anywhere just yet. In the spring, he begins production in South Africa on *The Human Factor*, a sports drama set during the first year of Nelson Mandela's presidency, starring his old friend Morgan Freeman as the celebrated leader.

"He's just won the presidency when it starts, and it's about how he unites the country," Eastwood says. "The country is going every which way at that time. All these different groups are at each other's throats. And he takes this really bad white rugby team and takes an interest in them. The blacks can't figure it out: What is he doing with these guys? But then he talks them into winning the World Cup, and they win it. It's sort of a fairy-tale story, but it's one of those truth-is-stranger-than-fiction kind of things. And it shows how brilliant he was, in a way. He knew that if he could make this happen, blacks and whites would come together in genuine enthusiasm."

Which sounds like the second movie of the Obama generation.

Eastwood on the Pitch: At Seventy-Nine, Clint Tackles Mandela in *Invictus*

Scott Foundas / 2009

Published in *LA Weekly*, December 10, 2009. Reprinted by permission of *LA Weekly* and the author.

On a late March morning, the sun sits high in the Cape Town sky, illuminating the trapezoidal monolith of Table Mountain in the distance, while down by the city's busy waterfront, the players of South Africa's national rugby union team—the Springboks—go for a training run. Only the careful observer might notice that, on this particular morning, the team's signature green-and-gold uniforms aren't of the most recent design, and none of the cars passing by on the waterfront thoroughfare bears a model year newer than 1995. Upon closer inspection, he might also notice a familiar if incongruous figure standing off to one side, tall and slender in a golf shirt and chinos, watching the scene transpire on a small, handheld video monitor. After a moment, the figure looks up and almost imperceptibly signals his approval, not with the traditional "Cut! Print!" but rather a small nod of his head and a whispered, "That was good. Let's move on."

It's the twenty-fourth day of filming on Clint Eastwood's *Invictus*, the thirtieth film he has directed in a career that now spans more than a half-century—and, as usual on an Eastwood set, if you didn't know they were shooting a major Hollywood movie here, you'd be none the wiser. No trailers and equipment trucks line the streets—they're parked at a "base camp" a few miles away—and by the time a small crowd of onlookers begins to form, Eastwood has gotten what he needs and is on his way to the next location. Of his storied speed and efficiency—the discipline of a veteran actor who knows that long stretches of waiting around can wear out a performer—Eastwood says it's simply a matter of trusting his instincts. "If you have five answers to choose from on a multiple-choice test, usually your first choice is the right answer," he tells me during a break between shots. Later in the day, Matt Damon, who sports a prosthetic nose, heavily muscled-up physique and a spot-on Afrikaner accent to play the Springboks' captain, François Pienaar, says that working with Eastwood is "the top of the mountain for every department." Then he jokes that he's having such a good time he feels guilty about cashing his paychecks.

"I'll be waiting for my kickback," Eastwood grumbles good-naturedly from his director's chair.

The pace at which Eastwood moves through a movie is the same one with which he greets life itself, as if mindful of the old adage that an idle mind is the devil's playground. In January of this year, on the eve of his seventy-ninth birthday and less than two months before starting the *Invictus* shoot, he was busy promoting *Gran Torino*, which became the highest-grossing film of his career as actor or director. When I showed up in South Africa this spring, Eastwood was several days ahead of the planned *Invictus* shooting schedule. Before postproduction on *Invictus* wrapped earlier this fall, he was already shooting a new film on location in Paris and London. Keeping up with Clint Eastwood, I discover, can be an exhausting task for all but Eastwood himself.

Based on journalist John Carlin's superb nonfiction book, *Playing the Enemy: Nelson Mandela and the Game That Made a Nation*, Eastwood's film returns us to a moment in South Africa's recent past, when the country was taking its first steps as a free nation after forty-six years of segregationist apartheid rule. It was a moment, symbolized by the 1994 election of Mandela (who is played in *Invictus* by Morgan Freeman) as the country's first freely elected president, celebrated the world over. At home, however, there was much work to be done. As Carlin explains in his dense and deeply reported account, Mandela's election was the culmination of a decade-long series of secret negotiations between the future president, the reigning National Party government of F. W. de Klerk, and the leaders of the pro-black African National Congress, designed to bring an end to apartheid while forestalling the civil war that threatened to erupt between extremist groups on both ends of the political spectrum. Still, as Mandela took office, there were those members of the former ruling class who suspected him of being a "terrorist" who wanted to "drive the white man into the sea." Similarly, certain Mandela supporters wished he would do exactly that.

"Don't address their brains, address their hearts" had long been Mandela's personal credo when it came to dealing with his jailers and political opponents. While incarcerated at Pollsmoor Prison in the 1980s, Mandela had boned up on the predominately Afrikaner pastime of rugby in order to work his patented charm offensive on one of the prison's senior officers—a strategy that resulted in Mandela getting a much-desired hot plate for his cell. Now, in a display of the uncanny prescience and insight into human nature that defined his political career, Mandela would again turn to the secular religion of sports as a way of unifying his nascent "Rainbow Nation." With the Rugby World Cup scheduled to be hosted by South Africa in little more than a year's time, he became convinced that the Springboks—who had been banned from international tournament play during the apartheid era—could win the World Cup and, with it, the hearts and minds of the country. The result was an intersection of athletics and politics as dramatic as Jesse Owens's performance at the 1936 Berlin Olympics, or the US hockey team's defeat of the USSR in 1980's so-called "Miracle on Ice."

"He just had some instinct—almost like somebody touched him on the shoulder and said, 'This will work,'" says Eastwood with the awe that seems to creep into people's voices whenever Mandela is mentioned. "How the hell he figured that, I don't know."

Seen from the Cape Town shore, Robben Island might be mistaken for a nature preserve (indeed, it is home to several thousand indigenous penguins, rabbits, and feral cats) or a rustic tourist retreat. As you draw near, however, there is something forbidding about the former leper colony and the jagged limestone rocks that form a natural barricade around it.

The day after my initial visit to the *Invictus* set, the tourist ferry transporting Eastwood and the crew from the mainland is painted with brightly colored human figures raising their hands in gestures of freedom, but the two dozen extras seated nearby, costumed in Robben Island's apartheid-era prison khakis, offer a vivid reminder of the enemies of the state who made this very journey in the hold of the ship, blacked-out portholes obscuring their view. Decommissioned now and preserved as a historical museum staffed mostly by former inmates, a small primary school offering the only evidence of the dwindling local population, Robben Island exudes the haunted air of a Civil War battlefield or a Nazi concentration camp—a monument to inhumanity. It is here, in one of the long, barracks-like buildings dotting the arid landscape, that prisoner number 46664, a.k.a. Nelson Mandela, spent two-thirds of his twenty-seven-year incarceration.

The first of the day's scenes to be shot dramatizes an actual visit to the prison made by the Springboks in May 1995, the day after they had vanquished defending champions Australia in the first match of the World Cup. As the actors file in—most, except for Damon and Eastwood's twenty-three-year-old son, Scott (who is playing the fly half Joel Stransky), actual rugby players cast locally—no acting is needed to express their astonishment at what they see. The spartan cells where Mandela and his fellow prisoners were held measure about fifty square feet—barely large enough for a man of Mandela's size (more than fix feet tall) to extend fully his arms. Mandela's cell, which has been kept in its original condition, contains only a small table, some metallic bowls, a bucket toilet and a folded blanket. (Beds were not introduced until 1974, a decade into his stay.)

Outside in the prison yard, Eastwood, his cinematographer Tom Stern (an Oscar nominee for his work on 2007's *Changeling*) and visual effects supervisor Michael Owens stand in a semicircle discussing several approaches to filming a scene in which Pienaar sees a transparent, ghostly image of Mandela, sitting alone in his cell, reading the William Ernest Henley poem that will eventually give the movie (at this point known only as *Untitled Mandela Project*) its title. Meanwhile, the production designer James J. Murakami (also a *Changeling* Oscar nominee) is dressing the prison yard in sand and limestone for a flashback scene in which Mandela and other prisoners sit chiseling the large rocks into smaller ones—the bane of many a Robben Islander's existence. Helping to set the scene is Derrick Grootboom, an ANC activist and former Robben Island inmate who was arrested in 1986 on charges of sabotage, after lobbing a petrol bomb through the window of a government eviction office in the town of Dysselsdorp. Sentenced to seven years, he remained on Robben Island until the last political prisoners were freed, in 1991.

"There are always good people amongst us," the cheerful Grootboom tells me as we sit on one of the large limestone slabs, recalling one birthday he celebrated behind bars. Although he received no gifts, one of the guards sang him a song, "Jesus Is Love" by the Commodores. "He lifted me up," Grootboom says, staring off into the distance. Now forty-two and recently elected as a judge to the Cape High Court, Grootboom was working as a private prosecutor when the Springboks played their 1995

World Cup Final against New Zealand's undefeated All Blacks and remembers watching the game on television together with his colleagues. "We weren't White, Black, Indian, and Colored," he says, rattling off apartheid's four racial designations. "We were just South Africans." Then came the iconic moment, depicted in Eastwood's film, when Mandela stepped onto the field to greet both teams, wearing a Springbok cap and a replica of Pienaar's No. 6 jersey. "When he went onto the field, wearing that jersey," Grootboom recalls, "he was the epicenter of where the country was going." At that point, it could be argued, the Springboks had won something much more valuable than a gilded trophy.

As morning gives way to afternoon, Freeman arrives on set already in costume, his resemblance to Mandela striking. It was, after all, the president himself who, when asked at a press conference who he thought should play him in a movie, suggested Freeman. Shooting begins, with Freeman and the extras dutifully chiseling away. When Eastwood asks for a second take, Freeman feigns indignation. "Have *you* ever broken stones?" he asks his director. "This is the last time I work for Eastwood!"

From behind the camera, Eastwood shoots his old friend, whom he has directed twice before, a sly grin.

When Eastwood gets the shot to his liking, the crew breaks for lunch, and I find myself seated opposite an extra playing one of the Robben Island jailers—a thick-necked man with an even thicker Afrikaner accent, who tells me he can trace his family's lineage back to South Africa's first Dutch settlers. Afterward, I hop on the wrong transport van and, instead of being taken back to the set, end up on the other end of the island, at the visitor's center, where Freeman and his longtime agent, Fred Specktor, are cooling their heels until Freeman is needed for his next scene. (Specktor, a no-nonsense, old-school Hollywood type, wears a single gold earring in his right ear, similar to the one in Freeman's own—the result of a promise the agent made to the actor when he was trying to sign him as a client.)

Courtly and charming, Freeman tells me about the protracted and ultimately fruitless struggle by which he, his producing partner, Lori McCreary, and a succession of writers attempted to distill Mandela's sprawling 1994 memoir, *Long Walk to Freedom*, into a manageable screenplay. Then Freeman met John Carlin, when the reporter came to Mississippi (where Freeman resides) to report on American poverty for the Spanish newspaper *El País*. Carlin, who knew of Freeman's desire to make a film about Mandela, told him the story of *Playing the Enemy*, which had not yet been published. Freeman, who clearly relishes being a step ahead of the game, had already read Carlin's book proposal as it was making its way around Hollywood. The South African–born screenwriter Anthony Peckham was subsequently hired to hammer out a script. When it came to choosing a director, "My first two choices were Clint Eastwood and Clint Eastwood," says Freeman, who won the 2005 Supporting Actor Oscar for his role as a one-eyed ex-boxer in Eastwood's *Million Dollar Baby*. Asked to elaborate, Freeman says that while many younger, less confident directors second-guess themselves and dither endlessly with their producers around the playback monitor, Eastwood simply "brings the actors in, figures out how to accommodate what they do, and that's it."

With that, we make our way back to the set for Freeman's last shot of the day—another flashback, this time set in the massive limestone quarry where particle dust so deeply penetrated Mandela's eyes that, upon his release, he had to have his tear ducts surgically drained. As the sun dips toward the horizon, Freeman climbs down into the quarry, picks up a shovel—a somewhat difficult feat given that the nerves in his left arm are still regenerating from injuries he sustained in an August 2008 car crash—and starts to dig. When Eastwood signals that it's a wrap for the day, Freeman looks up, wipes his brow, and says with a smile, "When you're doing what you're supposed to be doing in life, you feel good. I'm supposed to be working with Clint Eastwood."

By early August, barely two months after returning from South Africa, Eastwood and his longtime editor, Joel Cox (an Oscar winner for *Unforgiven*), have already finished a fine-cut assembly of *Invictus*, save for some six-hundred visual-effects shots that will be finessed by Michael Owens before the film's December release. At the Warner Bros. lot in Burbank, on the film scoring stage that bears Eastwood's name, a large orchestra is recording the *Invictus* score—a simple piano melody, plus some traditional African choral music and a couple of original songs, most of it written by Eastwood's son Kyle and his partner Michael Stevens (who have worked on the music for Eastwood's last five features). In a testament to the literal and figurative family atmosphere that is a constant around Eastwood's Malpaso Productions, the piano player in the *Invictus* orchestra is one Michael Lang, son of the legendary Jennings Lang, who produced Eastwood's 1971 directorial debut, *Play Misty for Me*. (On the set in South Africa, I also learned that Eastwood's focus puller, Bill Coe, is married to his boom operator, Gail Carroll-Coe, and that their son, Trevor, also works in the camera department as a loader.)

Toward the back of the stage, the senior Eastwood, flanked by Cox and his in-house producer, Rob Lorenz, gives occasional notes on the placement of a cue but mostly nods his approval as sound and image come together before his eyes. Already, there is much discussion about Eastwood's next project, *Hereafter*, which he expects to begin shooting by early fall. Based on an original script by *The Queen* and *Frost/Nixon* writer Peter Morgan, the film links together three stories, each in some way about the border between life and death, this world and the next. (Reuniting with his *Invictus* director, Damon will star as an auto-factory worker who was once a spiritual medium.)

"It's unexplored terrain," Eastwood tells me when I ask what drew him to the material, and indeed, though he has twice cast himself as something like an angel of death, in the existential westerns *High Plains Drifter* and *Pale Rider*, he has never made a film on an overtly supernatural subject. "I liked the way Peter Morgan incorporates real events like the [2004 Indian Ocean] tsunami and the terrorist attacks on London into a fictional story," he continues. "Also, there's a certain charlatan aspect to the hereafter, to those who prey on people's beliefs that there's some afterlife, and mankind doesn't seem to be willing to accept that this is your life and you should do the best you can with it and enjoy it while you're here, and that'll be enough. There has to be immortality or eternal life and embracing some religious thing. I don't have the answer. Maybe there is a hereafter, but I don't know, so I approach it by not knowing. I just tell the story."

Two weeks later, early on a Friday morning, Owens has a batch of effects shots from *Invictus*'s climactic World Cup Final ready for Eastwood's review, and as they look at the footage in a Warner screening room—Owens using a laser pointer to address certain details—what appears on the screen scarcely seems to be computer-generated at all. Mandela's ghostly apparition on Robben Island does, of course, but most of what Owens has created, like the best film editing, will blend so seamlessly into the finished film as to never be noticed by the average filmgoer.

Sweat and dirt have been added to the Springbok uniforms, as have blood and bruises to the players' faces. "Grub 'em all up," Eastwood says enthusiastically, noting that such digital wizardry has alleviated the need for time-consuming makeup touch-ups during shooting. In addition, a film-processing error that had caused the Springboks' green jerseys to appear brown has been corrected, and Johannesburg's Ellis Park Stadium, site of the 1995 World Cup Final, has been digitally aged to remove all signs of the facility's extensive 2008 renovation. Owens, a veteran of George Lucas's Industrial Light & Magic, who first worked with Eastwood on 2000's *Space Cowboys*, acknowledges that there was a steep learning curve involved in bringing the director (who hadn't made an effects-heavy picture since *Firefox* nearly two decades earlier) into the CGI era. Yet Eastwood has made the leap, and Owens has become one more indispensable player on team Malpaso.

"There's a selfishness to it," Eastwood says when I ask him about his well-known loyalty to his collaborators. "They're all people I can depend on. They're people I don't have to start from scratch with just in order to be on the same wavelength with them. They know kind of where I'm headed, and so we just say a few things to each other and we can be sort of minimalistic as far as the intellectual discussion of things."

The next time I see Eastwood is on a brisk, slate-colored morning in early November on *Hereafter*'s London set. A small auditorium in Red Lion Square, near Bloomsbury, has been converted into the fictional Center for Psychic Advancement, for one of several scenes in which Marcus, a twelve-year-old boy from an inner-city housing estate, attempts to contact his twin brother, Jason, who is killed in a car accident earlier in the script. Although Eastwood seems his usually relaxed self, there's a subtle tension in the air brought on by the tight time restrictions governing the use of minors on film sets. Marcus and Jason are played, respectively and sometimes interchangeably, by Frankie and George McLaren, identical twins who have a wise-beyond-their-years pallor reminiscent of Haley Joel Osment in *The Sixth Sense*—a film produced, like Eastwood's, by the husband-and-wife team of Frank Marshall and Kathleen Kennedy.

Unlike Osment, however, who was already a professional child actor with a string of film and TV credits behind him at the time of M. Night Shyamalan's film, the McLaren boys are screen newcomers who have been learning as they go on the set. Eastwood, who has directed children many times before, confides that some days have gone more smoothly than others, and in contrast to the taciturn, hands-off directing style Eastwood favors with stars like Damon and Freeman, these non-pros bring out another side of the actor-turned-director—the patient, nurturing mentor. It's a curious sight indeed, the gruff septuagenarian legend with his arm around the diminutive preteens, literally walking Frankie through the paces of one shot and, a bit later, standing just off camera, breaking down the emotional beats for a close-up in which Georgie must show, without the aid of dialogue, that he is losing faith in yet another sham psychic. "You're starting to think this guy's another phony," Eastwood whispers, then, after getting a reaction he likes, "You're feeling like you want to get up and leave."

As the day nears its end in London, Eastwood and producer Lorenz stand around a computer watching QuickTime videos of the latest effects shots e-mailed by Owens from LA, which is just waking up. Back home, *Invictus* is being fine-tuned for its first press screenings.

When I see *Invictus* in its finished form a week or so later, I'm struck by how effectively Eastwood has managed to capture a sense of Mandela's diplomatic genius while neatly avoiding most of the potholes that have capsized many a Hollywood film about South Africa. In the late eighties and early nineties, as global outrage over apartheid politics grew, movies like *The Power of One* (which also starred Freeman), *Cry Freedom* (about assassinated activist Steve Biko), and *A Dry White Season* (featuring Marlon Brando as a charismatic human-rights attorney) took on the subject, mostly by relying on crusading white interlocutors and offering a heavily stereotyped vision of the apartheid struggle, which one native South African, *Financial Mail* critic Peter Wilhelm, memorably termed "Adolf Hitler versus *The Cosby Show*."

Despite the presence of the Pienaar character—and no shortage of bone-crunching rugby action—*Invictus* is unmistakably told through Mandela's eyes, with keen attention to the skepticism his policies engendered on both sides of South Africa's racial divide (typified by an excellent scene in which the president reprimands his own party members for plotting to abolish the Springbok team colors and logo, seen by many South African blacks as symbols of the apartheid patriarchy). At the same time, Eastwood's film doesn't suffer from the bleeding-heart rush to canonization that pervaded several lesser, made-for-TV Mandela movies. Although it's far from a comprehensive biopic, Eastwood and screenwriter Peckham take pains to show the distance between the public and private Mandela, a man who feels considerably more at ease pouring tea for a former enemy than communicating with his estranged wife and children. It is in precisely this gray zone that Freeman's performance, justly praised by former *New York Times* South Africa correspondent Bill Keller as "less an impersonation than an incarnation," grows large. He manages to play one of history's great men without ever losing sight of the fact that he is, as one of Mandela's bodyguards describes him in the film, "not a saint. He's a man, with a man's problems."

"You've made the first movie of the Obama generation!" So exclaimed an enthusiastic fan upon rushing up to Eastwood after a preview screening of *Gran Torino* (in which Eastwood starred as a racist Korean War vet who rallies to the defense of his embattled Hmong neighbors) late last year—to which the filmmaker gently replied that he had been born under Herbert Hoover. But somewhere in that exchange lies a particular truth about Eastwood, whose recent films have seemed ineluctably of the moment, even as the director has turned toward the past as a way to explain the present. Far be it for this intrinsically classical, unpretentious filmmaker to tackle head-on the wars in Iraq and Afghanistan, but he might give us *Flags of Our Fathers* and *Letters From Iwo Jima*, a double-sided postcard of the "good" war, the young men who fought in it, and the atrocities wrought by each side. While he would surely have equally little interest in making a film directly about the current climate on Capitol Hill, Eastwood might well make one about another divided, economically troubled country pinning its hopes for "change" on its first black leader.

Does that make *Invictus* the second movie of the Obama generation? It just might, even if Eastwood, who tends to hold his own political views close to the vest, is quick to pooh-pooh the parallels. "The material brought that to my attention, but I wasn't trying to sell any American politics in the thing," he tells me when we speak by phone shortly before Thanksgiving. "However," he continues, "Obama is a charismatic young man, and he did talk about change and all this kind of stuff that sounded great. I mean, it sold the nation on him. Whether he's able to deliver the goods or not is another thing."

He then refers to a scene early in *Invictus* when Mandela, out for an early morning walk on the first day of his presidency, sees an Afrikaans newspaper headline that asks: "He Can Win an Election but Can He Run a Country?" In the film, Mandela responds, "It is a valid question." On the phone, Eastwood says, "That's the same question we all probably have about any presidential candidate who wins an election. So far, Obama is having a rough time convincing everybody. Personally, I'm rooting for the guy. I didn't necessarily support him going in, but I'd like to see him succeed because I want the country to succeed. It would be masochistic to do otherwise."

While there are those who will inevitably accuse Eastwood of gilding the lily, of telling one of the few optimistic stories to be plucked from a South Africa that remains rife with despair, the counterproof is right there in *Invictus* itself. For all the celebratory atmosphere of the World Cup Final, the movie ends not with the pomp and circumstance in Ellis Park Stadium or with the crowds of joyous revelers spilling into the Johannesburg streets but rather on the simple, quiet image of the president, seated in the back of his limousine, removing his glasses and massaging the bridge of his nose.

"You see him as a lone figure in the car," Eastwood says. "You can tell he's tired. This is just one hurdle, and you get the feeling he's got a long way to go. You know, he was seventy-five when he took over as president, which is really old, even by today's standards"—curious words coming from a man who, six months shy of eighty himself, seems committed to a more feverish pace of work than ever. "In South Africa, there's still a lot to do after apartheid. There's still tension there, and the crime rate and other things. This was just a start. I don't know how this guy Zuma's going to be," he says of South Africa's newest leader, Jacob Zuma, who took office during the *Invictus* shoot, following a heated power struggle with outgoing President (and Mandela successor) Thabo Mbeki. "You just hope somebody will come and carry the mantle."

Eastwood's words echo something said to me back on Robben Island, by the convict turned judge Derrick Grootboom, who, like many I talked to during my time in South Africa, spoke of a nation still sharply divided along racial and economic lines, where the evil of apartheid has been replaced by an equally insidious form of internecine political warfare. As suggested by the this year's thinly veiled science-fiction allegory *District 9*, much of the country's black population still lives in dire poverty in the townships, an AIDS epidemic rages, and violent attacks on immigrants have become increasingly commonplace. Yet, as Grootboom gazed out over the azure waters of Table Bay on that beautiful spring day, his back turned toward the prison that had stolen five years of his youth, something like hope flickered in his eyes. "We are in our Wild West period right now," he said. "But we are moving quickly into the period where we will realize there is no such thing as 'free for all.' You will see us solidifying the rules, and holding people accountable."

From somewhere behind us, as if to complete Grootboom's thought, comes Eastwood's voice, gently issuing a directive to Freeman and crew: "Action."

Interview with Clint Eastwood: First, Believe in Yourself

Michael Henry Wilson / 2010

Published as "Entretien avec Clint Eastwood: Il faut d'abord croire en soi-même" by Michael Henry in *Positif*, no. 599 (January 2011): 9–13. Reprinted by permission of the author; translated from the French by KC and MHW. Interview conducted on November 30, 2010.

Michael Henry Wilson: What prompted you to make *Hereafter*?
Clint Eastwood: It was the screenplay by Peter Morgan and the intelligence of its structure. I liked the fact that it incorporates authentic events in a fictional story, like the tsunami of six years ago and the terrorist attacks in the London Underground. And I liked the way each of the three stories develops on its own until they eventually mesh. As if destiny brought them together. I had never attempted something like that. Besides, the script touches on the phenomenon of clairvoyance with seriousness and subtlety, without concealing the fact that it attracts quite a few charlatans or crackpots who pretend to make a science of it. Matt Damon's character is a true medium, but he suffers from his gifts instead of profiting from them—to the point that he can't lead a normal life.

Q: In terms of the dramatic structure, one of the challenges is that the movie starts out very strong, then becomes more and more intimate and meditative. People who are expecting a thriller aren't necessarily ready to follow you along the tortuous paths of mourning and pain.
A: I liked the story the way it was. This isn't the first movie to start with a big bang, even though most save it for the end. Anyway, I wasn't striving for the spectacular. It's an intimate story. The tsunami is only one of its components. I think that if Peter Morgan chose this event, which claimed more than two hundred thousand victims, it's because there

were a lot of people who came close to death and survived only by a miracle, for example by clinging to a tree while everyone around them was swept away. In the course of a disaster of this span, there are always multiple individual dramas and some survivors who come back from a near-death experience, like Marie [Cécile de France].

Q: Another misunderstanding comes from the fact that the public is expecting a supernatural dimension, while it's completely absent from the movie.
A: It's not about the occult, it's about the spiritual. That's one of the aspects that immediately fascinated me when I read the script . . . particularly so because the spiritual isn't at all tied to religion, which may have bothered some people. The movie raises questions, but it doesn't claim to resolve them. No one knows what happens on the other side. No one knows before they go there. So the viewer has to think and see how it relates to his own beliefs or experiences. As for me, I'm not certain of anything. I don't know if there is a hereafter. I'm waiting to see it with my own eyes. I'm the kind of person who says, "I'll believe it when I see it."

Q: You are not using fear as a dramatic device. Some reviewers found fault with that. Even the *New Yorker*!
A: I could have made a scary movie if I had wanted to, but that wasn't my intention. Yes, the tsunami is terrifying; but, after that, it's about something else altogether: the child who loses his twin brother, the journalist who sees her career slipping away, the medium who can't establish any relationships with other people. . . . It reminds me very much of *Million Dollar Baby*. The studio [Warner Bros.] was reluctant because they thought a movie on a female boxer wouldn't work at the box office, while it was actually about a father-daughter relationship, which, by the way, was hardly more commercial, because it ended tragically and didn't pass a moral judgment on assisted suicide. Was the hero right or wrong? He disappeared, taking his mystery with him, and the question remain unanswered.

Q: When the boy searches on the Internet, he only finds the dogmatic language of Christian and Islamic preachers. Religion is not able to provide answers to your characters. That was already the case in some of your earlier pictures, notably in *Million Dollar Baby* and *Gran Torino*.
A: They need spiritual comfort, but can't get it from religious institu-

tions. Sometimes they find this solace in their interactions. Here, they find it when they meet Matt's character.

Q: Is this something you've experienced in your personal life?
A: Organized religions have never helped me. I don't discount them, I don't discount anything at all. I have the utmost respect for the people they comfort. The main thing is for everyone to find what works best for them or what helps them to live. But I am always amused by the certainty of those who think they have all the answers. For my part, I don't believe that humanity is privileged to have all the answers. If you're overwhelmed spiritually, don't lose your footing. Don't try to figure everything out. What we are blessed with is our imagination and what it is capable of conceiving. I think you have to believe in yourself first of all.

Q: You have always liked stories where characters encounter each other when nothing has prepared them for it, or even when they should never have met.
A: True. I've always liked that. Here, you have a Frenchwoman who has a privileged position in the media, while the twins, in London, live in a lower-middle-class neighborhood and have a mother who takes drugs. Then there's the medium, who works in San Francisco as a warehouseman but doesn't even know what place he occupies in the world. To each of these characters there corresponds a city and a very distinct environment . . . until they meet and try to communicate what they've experienced.

Q: To mention only some of your unlikely encounters: who could have foreseen that the Walt Kowalski of *Gran Torino* would ever connect with his Hmong neighbors, whom he despises? Or that the Frankie of *Million Dollar Baby* would ever agree to train a waitress who wants to be a boxer?
A: What you are seeing each time is a reticent hero. In *Hereafter*, it's Matt Damon who doesn't want to help others because it makes his own life impossible. In *Million Dollar Baby*, the last thing the old trainer needs is a young female boxer—he never wanted girls in the sport at all. In *Gran Torino*, Kowalski hates everything and everybody; he dislikes his neighbors and his own family; he doesn't like the way his neighborhood, and the world in general, are changing.

Q: Ever since *Midnight in the Garden of Good and Evil*, you have been saying that you don't make movies for the MTV generation or the video game fans. Here again, you take the time to develop the context of each story, to modulate the emotions of every single one of your characters.

A: Obviously, the movie isn't going to be a hit with audiences that are expecting a lot of eye candy. Once the tsunami is over, there's nothing more for them. There aren't any roller coasters at the end! It's a movie for people who want to be transported into a different world and think about what happens to the characters. It's probably more European than American. I've experienced that before. The most glaring example is *A Perfect World*, where an unexpected relationship developed between the criminal and the child he kidnapped. It was strange and ironic, but even with Kevin Costner at the peak of his career, it didn't attract much of a public in this country. What always interests me is how such encounters happen, how relationships develop, how characters mature. If you wanted to make *The Searchers* today, you would probably have a terrible time. The studio would tell you that the action isn't moving forward, that there isn't enough shooting, that it's taking much too much time to find the girl who was abducted by the Indians, that you have to eliminate the racial aspects. . . . They would turn it into a short!

Q: As a matter of fact, the child in *Hereafter* does evoke the one in *A Perfect World*. How did you direct the McLaren twins?
A: Without any problems. Those two kids were terrific. They *were* the characters. They came from the same environment. They weren't actors, they had never been in front of the camera before. Technically, this presented a few minor difficulties, but by the same token, they brought a certain measure of reality. They hadn't been spoiled by the mannerisms people could have taught them. They didn't have any bad habits to overcome. With them, the first take was always good. Kids are born performers. If you let them act naturally, everything will turn out fine. It was the same with the kid in *A Perfect World* [T. J. Lowther], who didn't have any experience, but I selected him immediately after his audition because he was natural.

Q: After the death of the twin brother, the camera rises skyward, as in *Mystic River* when Sean Penn's daughter's body is discovered. Was this a deliberate association?
A: Let's say that it was a deliberate transition after a tragic event, not only to establish distance, but to link up with the plane bringing the

French couple back to Paris. It allows us to pick up the thread of Marie's story again.

Q: What latitude did you give to Cécile de France, who plays her role in French?
A: In the script, her role was written in English. We translated her lines into French. But I told her she was free to modify them so long as it didn't change the dynamics of the scene. For example, for the sequence where she's trying to pitch her book project [on François Mitterand] to the publishers, I encouraged her to express herself in her own way and at her own pace. I would have told her the same thing if the scene had been in English: don't be afraid to improvise as long as the contents of the scene and its rationale are respected. Good actors can do that.

Q: How did you come up with the look of the hereafter, with its blurred silhouettes in a vortex of vivid light?
A: It wasn't described precisely in the script. What guided us were the testimonies of people who have had near-death experiences. I've read quite a lot of them in the course of the years, and met with relatives of some of the people affected. They all speak of a bright white light, and a threshold beyond which there is no fear anymore. In science fiction, you can create the universe you want. But it's much trickier when you have to replicate real experiences. So our visual effects were achieved partly in the studio and partly through computer graphics. There was a lot of CGI in *Space Cowboys*, but it was much more complicated in this movie.

Q: Is it true that you directed the shooting of the tsunami from a surfboard?
A: We were shooting in Maui [one of the Hawaiian Islands]. The main street of Lahaina was our key axis. We were shooting there from all angles in order to have multiple points of view when we added the wave in postproduction. Afterward, I took Cécile into the ocean to film shots of her struggling in the water, then some more with the child and her teddy bear. Tom [Stern] and Stephen [Campanelli] pushed their cameras onto surfboards, and I followed them to find out how that was working. The shots where Cécile is carried away underwater were done in a tank at Pinewood Studio. She spent nine hours in the water there. After that, the sequence was completed with the help of computer graphics. That all required a tremendous amount of preparation. Visual effects are so

expensive that we had to plan everything in advance, down to the tiniest details. My expert was Michael Owens. With him, I made a list of all the indispensable shots, then a list of what was necessary to achieve them. The many amateur videos that were made by tourists at the time of the tsunami in the Indian Ocean [in 2004] helped us a lot. We were able to study every angle in them, and that enabled us to better understand what it means to be caught in the middle of a natural disaster like that.

Q: You yourself had a brush with death during your military service [in 1951], when the plane that was carrying you crashed in the ocean. Were you remembering that at all?
A: Maybe a little, but I was mostly focused on everything that I had to do to make this movie! At the time of the accident in question, I saw a light shining on the shore, and I was determined to swim as far as the beach to save myself—and share a beer with the people there. But when I was younger, I really did almost drown. I must have been four or five years old. One day in Southern California, my father took me out into the surf, and a wave knocked me off his shoulders. I must have floated under water for a moment. I don't remember much from that time in my life, but I do recall precisely the color of the water and the terrifying sensation of being swept away in the current.

Q: In the picture "Dickens's Dream," the author is surrounded by all the characters he invented. Does it ever happen to you, in a dream or even when you're awake, to find yourself haunted by all the characters you have created during your long career?
A: Maybe, sometimes, in my dreams. But they are not necessarily my characters. One of the things I liked a lot about this script is that the American is a blue collar and instead of reading thrillers, he reads Dickens's novels. That's interesting. That reminds me of a character I knew in my youth, when I was working as a lumberjack in Oregon. We were a bunch of guys working in the woods. They were all sort of beefy, but one of them had a thing for flowers. Imagine an elephant in a china shop! He loved to talk about flowers—of all kinds. He even asked me to find some music for a home movie he was making about roses. So I gave him a musical collage, a montage of songs on the theme of flowers!

Q: How did you come to include a piano piece by Rachmaninoff in the British episode?
A: I had written two themes myself: one for Cécile's character, and the

other for Matt's. For the twins, Gennady [Loktionov] and I were looking for something different. He found the right piece in the Second Piano Concerto by Rachmaninoff; a very simple, very sweet piece that we immediately incorporated.

Q: Jacques Tourneur, who had psychic gifts himself, used to say that every filmmaker has to be a little bit of a medium, if only to share the anguish of his characters.
A: He was right. You have to be able to identify strongly with all the characters, whether they are important or not, and even identify with the unpleasant ones. I think we already discussed this quite a bit at the time of *Unforgiven*: I wanted people to be able to identify with Little Bill, Gene Hackman's character. You became attached to him when you watched him building his dream house, even though he was behaving more and more badly in his job as a sheriff. It was similar for my character [William Munny], who, in spite of all his past crimes, was not choked up with remorse. He had convinced himself that his wife had turned him into a decent person—to the point that he remained faithful to her after her death.

Q: You are soon going to tackle a controversial, even monstrous, historical character: J. Edgar Hoover.
A: Brian Grazer [co-producer of *Changeling*] was the one who sent me the project. The script [by Dustin Lance Black] intrigued me because I lived through the time where people were constantly speaking of Hoover and his exploits. He was the head of the FBI for forty-eight years. He was an amazing character from an early age. He began to work for the Justice Department at the age of twenty-four, and was twenty-eight when he was named director of the Bureau. The script flashes back and forward between the period when he was in his twenties and the period when he was in his sixties. Among our actors will be Leonardo [DiCaprio], who will play Hoover, and I hope Judi Dench, for the role of his mother. It's a very interesting story. Will it make a good movie? Will the public want to come and see it? I have no idea!

With *J. Edgar*, Eastwood Again Flexes His Freedom

Scott Bowles / 2011

From *USA Today*, a division of Gannett Co., Inc., November 9, 2011. Reprinted with Permission.

Peanut shells occasionally litter Clint Eastwood's office carpet. Eastwood doesn't eat peanuts. Neither does his staff, which keeps his quarters on the Warner Bros. lot immaculate. The mess belongs to Lola, a squirrel Eastwood lets roam his office and ransack a bag he leaves open on the bottom of a bookcase. She comes through the front door, which Eastwood also leaves open.

Security has tried to evict Lola with traps and pellet guns, Eastwood says. But no one has said a peep to him about the studio policy that bans animals unless they're acting. "If you do something long enough," Eastwood says, surveying his office, which now is free of shells, "people let you do your thing."

The tenet applies to movies, the eighty-one-year-old says. Eastwood has earned a grudging freedom in Hollywood to make his kind of films, which usually run under budget, skip the elaborate effects, and waft to a score Eastwood composes. All are in effect for *J. Edgar*, the controversial biography of former FBI director J. Edgar Hoover that opens in limited release today before a nationwide rollout Friday.

"I guess we make the anti-tent-pole movie," he says. "That's not always the way studios want you to make them, but we do OK."

OK? The guy has won two Oscars, starred in more than sixty films and TV shows and remains Hollywood's most iconic living cop and cowboy. Still, Eastwood, who is considering coming out of acting retirement, barely got 2003's *Mystic River* made. He had to fight to make 2004's *Mil-*

lion Dollar Baby and isn't sure "what people are going to make of this one. But as long as they're talking about it, then you're doing your job."

People will talk. Already, the film's portrayal of Hoover as sexually conflicted has irked some former agents. Two groups campaigned against any suggestion of a sexual relationship with assistant FBI director Clyde Tolson, though Eastwood says he had cooperation from the government and some FBI vets.

J. Edgar also marks the most sexually charged film that the director, an emblem of macho whose credits include *Unforgiven* and *Gran Torino*, has made since his directorial feature debut, 1971's *Play Misty for Me*.

J. Edgar, an intended Oscar contender starring Leonardo DiCaprio as the founding director of the FBI, is less a biopic than an unrequited gay love story. It examines Hoover's long tenure as America's top cop and his relationship with assistant director Tolson (Armie Hammer).

Eastwood grew up on the *Junior G-Men* comic books Hoover helped create in the 1930s, and to prepare for the film, he investigated Hoover like a cop, digging up transcripts, interviewing friends, and consulting an FBI that remains silent on Hoover's sexuality.

But ultimately, Eastwood says, he went on instinct, even asking DiCaprio to ad-lib to intensify the love story.

"Sometimes you just go with your gut and say, 'I can't care what people are going to think,'" Eastwood says. "I don't know if J. Edgar Hoover was gay. I don't really care. But he's a guy shrouded in mystery, which I've always found fascinating."

Whether Eastwood finds it lucrative will be another question. While *Torino* and *Unforgiven* were hits, Eastwood, who also did *Flags of Our Fathers* and *Invictus*, isn't known as a director attuned to focus groups. If anything, Eastwood says, there are too many voices weighing in on what movies get made.

"I understand it, because this has become an expensive business," says Eastwood, who joined it in 1955 with a small role in *Revenge of the Creature*, an installment of the *Creature of the Black Lagoon* series.

"People have a lot invested," he says. "But getting that money back, making that sure-fire hit, has become as important as telling a good story. I'm not that complicated. I still just like a good story."

Eastwood swapped plenty of tales with his parents while growing up in Piedmont, California, when Hoover was making his name chasing gangsters and bootleggers.

"I loved the G-Men and read all the comics I could get my hands on,"

Eastwood says. But the family never discussed reports that began circulating in the 1940s that Hoover was gay.

"And we never talked about anything like cross-dressing," Eastwood says of the rumor that Hoover enjoyed women's clothes. "That wasn't something you talked about at the dinner table back then."

Still, Hoover's legacy fascinated Eastwood, an avid reader and history buff. So when he received the *J. Edgar* script from Dustin Lance Black, who won an Oscar for his *Milk* screenplay, Eastwood responded the way he always does when he sees a script he likes: He went into warp drive.

Few filmmakers shoot more quickly or inexpensively than Eastwood, renowned for using one take, staging few rehearsals, and asking for few script changes. He shot *J. Edgar* in thirty-nine days for $35 million, both roughly half the cost and time of a big-studio release.

"He's very faithful; he works with the same small crew he's worked with for years," DiCaprio, thirty-six, says. "That helps you move incredibly fast. I'm a guy who can ask for quite a few takes, but I never felt when we left a scene that I needed to do it again. You feel artistically safe in his hands."

DiCaprio, too, was fascinated by Hoover. He had done months of research for the John Dillinger biography *Public Enemies* before turning down the role that went to Johnny Depp. After hearing Eastwood had Black's script, DiCaprio called the director to ask to be considered.

Eastwood concedes that he hesitated. "He's a good kid, but everyone is a kid to me now," Eastwood says. "Getting that age right, so we could make him younger or older, was important, and I wasn't sure Leo would look old enough. But he spent five hours in the chair when we had to do makeup. He's a professional. And it doesn't hurt when you've got your story and got a star like Leo. It's harder to say no."

Studios have turned down offers that Eastwood thought they couldn't refuse. After stumbling upon the book *Mystic River* at a Costco in 2002, Eastwood bought the rights to the movie in two weeks. He was ready to shoot in six.

Warner Bros. initially said no. The $25 million movie, execs argued, was too dark and violent and had too depressing an ending. The film earned six Oscar nominations, including best picture and director, and won acting awards for Sean Penn and Tim Robbins. It earned $90 million, the fifth-biggest movie of Eastwood's career.

He says he still met some resistance to 2004's *Million Dollar Baby*, which was nominated for seven Oscars and won Eastwood best director and picture statuettes. The film also earned Hilary Swank a best-actress

Oscar and earned $101 million at the box office. "If *Mystic River* doesn't work, I'm not sure I would have gotten to do *Million Dollar Baby*."

Even *J. Edgar* raised eyebrows at Warner Bros., whose strategy is to focus on high-profile, big-budget films like the *Harry Potter* series and *The Green Lantern*.

Of course, *Potter* is gone and *The Green Lantern* struggled this summer. "I'm not sure how those $100 million movies always work," Eastwood says. "If you paid someone $100 million for a house, you'd probably get a pretty good house. I'm not sure you'd get a good movie."

Black says he was stunned by how hands-off Eastwood was with the script, which calls for Hoover and Tolson to kiss on the mouth and for Hoover to press his late mother's clothes to his body in a tearful scene. "Lance didn't treat it as gay scenes," Eastwood says. "But there was clearly a strong relationship between these men. We wanted natural interactions for them, especially for the time."

One of *J. Edgar*'s most controversial scenes comes during a heated exchange between Hoover and Tolson, who in real life shared a home with Hoover and was his heir. After an on-screen fight that causes Tolson to storm out, Hoover tearfully spits that he loves Tolson.

The line does not exist in the script. Before the scene, Black recalls, Eastwood approached DiCaprio with a suggestion: "Tell Clyde you love him," the director told his star. "Let's make it a very emotional scene." DiCaprio obliged.

Word of the portrayal angered some FBI alums, including the J. Edgar Hoover Foundation and the Society of Former Special Agents of the FBI, which fired off letters to Eastwood.

"There is no basis in fact for such a portrayal of Mr. Hoover," wrote foundation chairman William Branch. The Former Special Agents group wrote Eastwood that the kissing scene "caused us to reassess our tacit approval of your film."

Eastwood isn't surprised by the criticism but says, "A lot of people still haven't seen it yet, so it's hard to have that discussion. And you're never going to please everyone in a movie, even if some executives want to try."

Eastwood says he knew he'd have to make the movie quickly and cheaply to compete with the landslide of films that arrive over the holidays for awards season. He asked stars and crew to join him in taking an undisclosed pay cut.

The crew and cast agreed, including Hammer, who has a personal stake in the film. The great-grandson of oil tycoon and philanthropist

Armand Hammer remembers bitter fights his family had with Hoover's FBI, which considered the Hammer clan a societal menace.

"I took special pleasure in planting a kiss on J. Edgar Hoover's mouth," Hammer says. "I remember (Armand Hammer) laughing, reading in the paper that Hoover said he was a spy. I couldn't get over how they were alike in some ways. I'm sure my grandfather abused power the same way Hoover did. It drove him crazy he couldn't get (Hammer). Those two guys were more birds of a feather than they thought."

While Eastwood chronicles Hoover's pit-bull pursuit of communists and the Mafia, he has always been more interested in the man's personal demons, not his public personae.

The key, he says, was in approaching the film the same way he approached the squirrel, who surprised him one day sitting a foot from the star on his office couch. "You can question what you're doing to death, or you can do things the way you want and know," he says.

Eastwood stretches and heads to the office door, where Lola has led another squirrel to his steps. "She always comes back," Eastwood says. "She knows I'm here, doing my thing."

For Further Reading

Articles

Bogdanovich, Peter. "Hör mir mit dem Showbusiness auf! Die Sache hat mich fast umgebracht." *Süddeutsche Zeitung Magazin*, August 26, 2005, 6–23. Abridged English version: "The Undefeated." *The Word*, December 2005, 72–76.

French, Philip. "'I figured I'd retire gradually, just ride off into the sunset...'" *The Observer*, February 25, 2007. Unabridged audio version: <http://blogs.guardian.co.uk/film/2007/02/my_chat_and_duet_with_clint_ea.html>

Gilbert, Andrew. "Mise en Swing." *Jazz Times*, September 2007, 42–46.

Headlam, Bruce. "The Films Are for Him. Got That?" *New York Times*, December 10, 2008.

Macklin, Tony. "Plant Your Feet and Tell the Truth." *Bright Lights Film Journal*, no. 47, February 2005. <http://www.brightlightsfilm.com/47/clint.htm>

Parkinson, Michael. "Guardian NFT interview: Clint Eastwood." *Guardian*, October 7, 2003.

Ross, Lillian. "Nothing Fancy." *New Yorker*, March 24, 2003, 40–47.

Saada, Nicolas, and Serge Toubiana. "Entretien avec Clint Eastwood: L'Homme de nul part." *Cahiers du cinéma*, no. 549 (September 2000): 26–47.

Schickel, Richard. "The Burden of Heroes." *Time*, October 23, 2006, 44–47.

Books

Beard, William. *Persistence of Double Vision: Essays on Clint Eastwood*. Edmonton: University of Alberta Press, 2000.

Bénoliel, Bernard. *Clint Eastwood*. Revised English edition. Paris: Cahiers du cinéma, 2010. (Masters of Cinema)

Cornell, Drucilla. *Clint Eastwood and Issues of American Masculinity*. New York: Fordham University Press, 2009.

Eastwood, Clint, and Paul Nelson. *Conversations with Clint: Paul Nelson's Lost Interviews with Clint Eastwood, 1979–1983*. New York: Continuum International Pub. Group, 2011.

Eastwood, Clint, and Michael Henry Wilson. *Eastwood on Eastwood*. Revised English edition. Paris: Cahiers du cinéma, 2010.

Engel, Leonard, editor. *Clint Eastwood, Actor and Director: New Perspectives*. Salt Lake City: University of Utah Press, 2007.

Foote, John H. *Clint Eastwood: Evolution of a Filmmaker*. Westport, Conn.: Praeger, 2009.

Frayling, Christopher. *Clint Eastwood*. London: Virgin, 1992.

Gallafent, Edward. *Clint Eastwood: Filmmaker and Star*. New York: Continuum, 1994.

Goldman, Michael R. *Clint Eastwood: Master Filmmaker at Work*. New York: Abrams, 2012.

Plaza, Fuensanta. *Clint Eastwood: Malpaso*. Carmel Valley, Calif.: Ex Libris, 1991.

Schickel, Richard. *Clint Eastwood: A Biography*. New York: A. A. Knopf, 1996.

Vaux, Sara A. *The Ethical Vision of Clint Eastwood*. Grand Rapids, Mich.: William B. Eerdmans Pub. Co., 2012.

Index

Absolute Power, 176
Academy Awards, xvi, 143–44, 163, 215, 233, 239, 252, 254–55
acting and Eastwood: acting for other directors, 65; directing compared to, 20–21; and directing in same film, 21, 56, 65, 123, 126, 133–34, 149, 198; early roles, 4–5, 55–56, 147; enjoyment of, 196; his personality and his roles, 5, 31, 63, 133, 150; preparation, 195–98; studying acting, 5, 100
actors: as directors, 66, 139, 181, 182, 191; Eastwood's recurring use of, 55, 68, 81
adaptations: *The Beguiled*, 130; *The Bridges of Madison County*, 174–75; *Honkytonk Man*, 85; *Letters from Iwo Jima*, 207–8; *Midnight in the Garden of Good and Evil*, 169–70, 174; *The Outlaw Josey Wales*, 32–33
Africa (location, *White Hunter, Black Heart*), 125, 128
African Queen, The, 37, 119, 122, 124; script, 127
age discrimination, 159–60
Agee, James, 127
Aiona, Eddie, 144
Alberta, Canada (location, *Unforgiven*), 142–43
ambiguity, 101, 204–5; in *High Plains Drifter*, 26–28, 46; in *Midnight in the Garden of Good and Evil*, 168, 170–71; in *Million Dollar Baby*, 200; in *Mystic River*, 191, 204
American Film Festival, Deauville, France, xv
Anderson, Bronco Billy, 81
antihero: in *The Beguiled*, 23; in *Bronco Billy*, 82; Eastwood's image as, 21, 31, 58–59, 62–63; in *High Plains Drifter*, 26
anti-Semitism, in *White Hunter, Black Heart*, 126–27
Any Which Way You Can, 42, 51, 65; box office, 54
apartheid, 235–36, 242
Apocalypse Now, 80
archangel, Eastwood characters as, 75, 76, 79
artists, films on, 120, 122, 138, 176
assisted suicide, 203–4, 214–15, 246
audience: disregarding, 84, 117, 123, 134, 136, 153–54; involvement of, 38, 45–46, 47–48, 63, 97; letting audience decide, 117, 204
auteur, Eastwood as, xiv, 51, 56, 137, 197
autonomy, Eastwood's, as a filmmaker, 18, 27, 135, 150, 227, 252
background, characters' lack of, xi, 14, 38, 45–46

259

INDEX

Bacon, Kevin, 181, 191
Barla, Marco, 153, 154
"Barroom Buddies," 99
Barton, Dee, 25
Basie, Count, 99, 227
Battle of San Pietro, The, 121-22
Beethoven, Ludwig van, 229
Beguiled, The, 3, 10-11, 78; antihero in, 23; audience reaction, 22, 117; box-office failure, 22, 62; cinematography, 42; ending, 123; *Play Misty for Me*, compared to, 23; women's roles in, 23, 114
Beguiled, The (Thomas Cullinan), 130
Benjamin, Richard, 59, 65
Berendt, John, 169, 170, 171, 172, 174
betrayal, as a theme, 80
Bird, 112-15, 117-18, 130, 138, 174, 227; budget, 153; casting, 115; cinematography, 125; lighting, 145; music, 113, 129; style, 124
Bitburg, Germany, cemetery incident, 103, 152
Black, Dustin Lance, 251, 254, 255
black actors in Eastwood's films, 87
black audiences, and *Dirty Harry* series, 115
black humor, 78, 86, 92
Blazing Saddles, 55
Block, Wes (character, *Tightrope*), 59-61, 88
blues, 99, 226-27
Bogart, Humphrey, 158, 189
Boise, Idaho (location, *Bronco Billy*), 42, 86
boogie-woogie, 226, 227
Boston, Mass. (location, *Mystic River*), 190
box office: *Any Which Way You Can*, 54; *The Beguiled*, 22; *Bronco Billy*, 40, 53-54, 64, 152; *Dirty Harry* series, 94; Eastwood on, 84; Eastwood's success, 40, 57, 94, 95; *Every Which Way but Loose*, 40, 84, 152; faltering of Eastwood's, 64; *Firefox*, 64; *Gran Torino*, 235; *Honkytonk Man*, 64; *Million Dollar Baby*, 254-55; *Mystic River*, 254; *Play Misty for Me*, 27; *Unforgiven*, 154; Westerns, 110
boxing, 200-201
Boys Don't Cry, 196
Brady Bill, 161
Brahms, Johannes, 229
Branch, William, 255
Brando, Marlon, 110
Breezy, 28-30, 77-78; budget, 29; lighting, 39; locations, 77; promotion, 27
Bridges of Madison County, The, xx, 161-62, 174-76; music, 177; musical theme by Eastwood, 199, 229; novel and film compared, 175, 222; on-set atmosphere, 167; pacing, 177; script, 175; script interventions, Eastwood's, 177
Bridges of Madison County, The (Robert James Waller), 174-75, 222
Bronco Billy, 53-55, 80-82; box office, 40, 53-54, 64, 152; budget, 40, 54-55; cast and crew, 68; cinematography, 42; critical reception, 52, 53, 94, 105; and Eastwood's image, 59, 151; a favorite of Eastwood's, 64, 89; humiliation scene, xv, 44, 54, 69, 82, 94, 101-2; locations, 41-42, 86; promotion, 53; script, 54; script interventions, Eastwood's, 44, 48, 82
Bronco Billy (character), 44, 48, 53, 82, 101-2, 116
Brubeck, Dave, 85, 99, 228
budgets: *Bird*, 153; *Breezy*, 29; *Bronco Billy*,

40, 54–55; Eastwood on, 64–65, 72; *Every Which Way but Loose*, 40, 152; *Honkytonk Man*, 58; *J. Edgar*, 254; learning from the Italians, 5, 72; *Million Dollar Baby*, 221; *Mystic River*, 184, 189, 254; *Play Misty for Me*, 3, 18, 24; Don Siegel and, 72; under, 40, 103, 144, 150, 252; *Unforgiven*, 153
Burton, Richard, 11
Bush, George H. W., 153
Butler, Michael, 36, 82, 151

Cagney, James, 158, 189
Cahiers du cinéma, xv, 95, 136
Calley, John, 184
camera placement, 35, 47–48
Campanelli, Stephen, 249
Cannes Film Festival, xv, 96, 182, 222
Cape Town, South Africa (location, *Invictus*), 234–35
Capra, Frank, 54, 81, 110, 116
career, Eastwood's: critical reassessment, xv–xvi, 95, 105; reviewed, 20–39, 72–92, 101–2, 142–55
Carlile, Clancy, 85
Carlin, John, 235, 238
Carmel, Calif., 5, 29, 87, 147; Eastwood as mayor, 133, 152, 192, 223; location, *Play Misty for Me*, 41, 74
Carnegie Hall, 228
Carroll-Coe, Gail, 239
Carroll-Coe, Trevor, 239
Carter, Forrest, 32–33
casting, 48; *Bird*, 115; black actors, 87; and cosmetic surgery, 217; importance of, 81, 181–82; *J. Edgar*, 254; *Mystic River*, 181, 186; *Play Misty for Me*, 13
Castle Rock Entertainment, 140, 164
Catholicism, in *Million Dollar Baby*, 203

CGI, 239–41, 249–50
Chablis, The Lady, 173
Changeling, 219, 224–25, 231, 237; production design, 224; schedule, 219; score by Eastwood, 229; traumatized child theme, 225
character studies, 173
characters, identification with, 251
child actors, 241, 248
children, crimes against, 179, 190, 225; Eastwood on, 179; as a theme (*see* traumatized child, as a theme)
Chopin, Frédéric, 229
Cimino, Michael, 51, 56, 104
Cinémathèque française, xv
cinematography, 42–44, 77, 166; *The Beguiled*, 42; *Bird*, 125; *Bronco Billy*, 42; desaturated colors, 190, 210–11; *Dirty Harry*, 42; *Letters from Iwo Jima*, 210–11; *Million Dollar Baby*, 201–2; *Mystic River*, 190; *The Outlaw Josey Wales*, 42–43; *White Hunter, Black Heart*, 125. *See also* lighting
City Heat, 59, 65; casting black actors in, 87; soundtrack album, 99
Civil War, U.S., 79, 109, 172
clairvoyance, 245
Clark, Sanford, 231
classical music, 229
Clint Eastwood: Out of the Shadows, 228
Clinton, Bill, 160
Coe, Bill, 239
Colbert, Claudette, 115
Cold War, background in *Firefox*, 83
color timing, xx, 35
Colossus of Rhodes, 66
Columbia Pictures, 115, 119, 140, 154, 164
computer graphics, 239–41, 249–50
Conrad, Joseph, 80

Coogan's Bluff, 77, 149
Cooper, Gary, 101, 116, 158
Cop Killer, 160
cosmetic surgery, 159, 217
Costner, Kevin, 144, 157, 158, 248
costumes: in *The Good, the Bad and the Ugly*, 107; in Westerns, 107
country music, 85, 99, 111, 117
Cox, Joel, 136, 144-45, 152, 200, 239
crimes against children, 179, 190, 225; Eastwood on, 179; as a theme (*see* traumatized child, as a theme)
critics, Eastwood on, 87, 105, 149-50, 168
Crothers, Scatman, 55, 146
Cry Freedom, 242
Cukor, George, xvii
Cusack, John, 170, 172

Daggett, Little Bill (character, *Unforgiven*), 139-40, 251
Daley, Bob, 7, 12, 18, 58; and *The Outlaw Josey Wales*, 32
Daly, Bob (Robert), 111, 153, 166
Damon, Matt, 235, 240
Dargis, Manohla, 231
Davis, Bette, 115
De Sica, Vittorio, 56, 188
Dead Pool, The, 153
death of Eastwood's character, 64, 84
Deauville American Film Festival, xv
Dench, Judi, 251
Depression era: background in *Honkytonk Man*, 85, 86; and Eastwood's childhood, 70-71, 85, 98, 103, 147, 166
Dern, Laura, 159
"Deserve's got nothin' to do with it," 150
DiCaprio, Leonardo, 253, 254, 255
Dickens, Charles, 250

"Dickens's Dream," 250
"Did he fire six shots . . . Do I feel lucky?" (speech), 69-70, 180
directing and Eastwood: and acting in same film, 21, 56, 65, 122-23, 126, 133-34, 149, 198; actors, recurring use of, 55, 68, 81; debut in *Play Misty for Me*, 3-4, 7-10, 19, 23-26, 73-75, 149; directing actors, 48-49, 145-46, 188, 219; directing children, 202, 241, 248; directing sequences for Don Siegel, 19, 20, 73; economy of shooting, 50, 56, 146; influences, 10, 56, 72, 132, 187, 220; interest in, compared to acting, 20-21; on-set atmosphere, 30, 51, 142-43, 167, 188, 199, 202, 234-35; philosophy, 49-51, 104, 124-25, 182-83; *Rawhide* and first ambitions, 20, 49, 72-73; style, 32, 49, 66, 79, 124-25; working fast, 40, 50, 80, 144, 145, 219-20, 254; working with same technical crew, 50-51, 68, 136, 144-45, 166, 254
Directors Guild of America, xiv
Dirty Harry, 11, 45, 101, 180; ad campaign, 23; black actors in, 87; cinematography, 42; Eastwood directing sequences in, xx, 19, 73; fascism, charges of, xii, 94, 149; *Gran Torino*, compared to, 232; political controversy, xii, 86-87, 149-50; racism, accustions of, 87; torture scene, 63; *Unforgiven*, compared to, 154
Dirty Harry (character), 55, 62, 80, 88, 91, 115; Kevin Bacon and, 191; Eastwood identified with, 150; humor, 70; sadness, 37, 101
Dirty Harry series, 80, 91; and black

audiences, 115; box office, 94; dialogue, 69–70; humor in, 86; politics of, 116; popularity, 147, 222; script interventions, Eastwood's, 69–70
disc jockeys, 16, 74
District 9, 244
Dixieland, 226
"Dollars" trilogy, x–xi, 5, 98, 147–48, 215–16. *See also* Leone Westerns
Douglas, Kirk, 100–101
Dry White Season, A, 242
Duck, You Sucker, 67
Dunn, Frankie (character, *Million Dollar Baby*), 194, 195–96, 203–4, 247

Eastwood, Alison, 59, 96, 170, 229
Eastwood, Clint: and aging, 197, 216–17; army service, 100, 121–22, 147, 250; childhood and youth, 70–71, 85, 98–100, 147, 224, 250, 253–54; children, 95–96; early jobs, 147; education, 4, 100; father, 70–71, 98, 147, 166, 226; favorite films, 64, 69, 89; as interview subject, xviii, 58, 131, 231; marriage, 5; mother, 70–71, 226; personality, 58, 95–96, 150, 152; political career, 103, 133, 152, 192, 223; political views, 113, 133, 152–53, 243; private life, 5, 95–96; religious views, 240, 246–47
Eastwood, Kyle, xviii, 5, 96, 239
Eastwood, Maggie, 5, 96
Eastwood, Scott, 237
Eastwood After Hours: Live at Carnegie Hall, 228
Eastwood Scoring Stage, 239
ecological concerns: in *Pale Rider*, 102, 110–11; in *White Hunter, Black Heart*, 126

Edelstein, David, 206
editing: Eastwood on, 49, 90, 129, 183; *Play Misty for Me*, 3; *White Hunter, Black Heart*, 129
Edwards, Blake, 59
Eiger Sanction, The, 30–31, 78–79; betrayal theme, 80; black humor, 78; fatality during shooting, 78; friendship theme, 78
Elephants, 126
Eliot, T. S., 117
Ellington, Duke, 99, 114
endings of films, 21, 38, 41, 111, 123; *The Beguiled*, 123; *Honkytonk Man*, 69, 84, 102; *Million Dollar Baby*, 200; *Mystic River*, 185; open-ended, 45–46; *The Outlaw Josey Wales*, 38, 45–46, 97, 220–21
Escape from Alcatraz, xx, 81, 89, 164
European reception, xv–xvi, 137; *Honkytonk Man*, 64, 105, 116; *A Perfect World*, 248
Evans, Walker, 86
Every Which Way but Loose, 65, 94, 101, 151–52; box office, 40, 84, 152; budget, 40, 152; and Eastwood's image, 51–52, 54, 62, 174; popular success, 53
Executioner's Song, The, 59
exposition: Eastwood's dislike of, 38, 204–5; eliminating, in *A Fistful of Dollars*, 45, 66–67, 97; *Psycho*, 15–16

Fahey, Jeff, 125, 146
family, as a theme, 85
fans, interaction with, 147
fascism, charges of, and *Dirty Harry*, xii, 94, 149
Fatal Attraction, 149

father, absence of the, as a theme, 156
father-daughter relationship, as a theme, xvii, 194–95, 221, 246
Fayard, Judy, xx
FBI, 251, 253
feminism and Eastwood, 95, 114, 152
Fielding, Jerry, 129
Figueroa, Gabriel, 77
Fink, Harry Julian, 70
Firefox, 75, 78–79, 82–84; box office, 64; lighting, 145; locations, 83–84
first takes, 18, 21, 30, 56, 58, 114, 145–46, 203, 248
"First Time Ever I Saw Your Face, The," 17, 19
Fisher, Frances, 154
Fistful of Dollars, A, 5, 21, 96–97, 147–48; critical reception, 93; moral issues, 75; music, 215; script interventions, Eastwood's, 45, 66–67, 97, 108, 148; violence in, 93; and *Yojimbo*, 76, 96, 223
Fitzgerald, F. Scott, 45
Fitzgerald, Maggie (character, *Million Dollar Baby*), 194
Flags of Our Fathers, 206, 209, 212, 222–23, 232, 243; heroism in, 212–13; Japanese reception, 212; locations, 210, 222
Fleming, Eric, 147
Foley, Red, 84
Fonda, Henry, 101, 135
Fonda, Jane, 159
For a Few Dollars More, 98
Ford, John, 50, 56, 102, 132, 135, 150–51, 165; influence on Eastwood, 187, 231; lighting, 202; mise-en-scène, 220; and Don Siegel, 129–30
Foster, Jodie, 139
France, Cécile de, 249

Freeman, Morgan, 175, 194, 196, 232; on Eastwood's direction, 239; as Nelson Mandela, 233, 235, 238–39, 242
friendship, as a theme, 78, 83

Garner, Errol, 25
Gauntlet, The, 35–39, 80, 88, 151; betrayal theme, 80; lighting, 39; script interventions, Eastwood's, 44; violence in, 38–39
Gelmis, Joseph, 19
genre and Eastwood, 100, 151, 193, 221, 222
George, Chief Dan, 33, 43
ghosts, 28, 157
Gillespie, Dizzy, 177
Gleason, Jackie, 102
Golden Globes, 229
golf film project (*Golf in the Kingdom*), 162
Good, the Bad and the Ugly, The, 57, 67, 73, 98; costumes, 107; music, 215; violence in, 213
Gran Torino, 230–33, 242; box office, 235; *Dirty Harry*, compared to, 232; musical theme by Eastwood, 229
Grant, Cary, 219
Grapes of Wrath, The, 50, 56, 98, 152, 174, 176–77
Grazer, Brian, 224, 251
Great Northfield Minnesota Raid, The, 34
Great Train Robbery, The, 102, 110
Green, Jack N., 125, 135–36, 143, 145–46, 166, 202
Green Lantern, The, 255
Gritz, James "Bo," 152
Grootboom, Derrick, 237–38, 244
Group, The, 13
Gulf War, 132–33
gun control, 139, 160–61

INDEX

Hackin, Dennis, 54, 81
Hackman, Gene, 153, 175
Haggard, Merle, 99
Haggis, Paul, 202–3
Hammer, Armand, 255–56
Hammer, Armie, 253, 255–56
Hancock, John Lee, 157, 169–70
Hang 'Em High, 67, 73, 93, 98, 149; and Malpaso's founding, xi, 163
Harden, Marcia Gay, 181
Hartman, Elizabeth, 114
Hartman, Johnny, 177
Hawkins, Coleman, 99
Hawks, Howard, 124, 219, 220; influence on Eastwood, 187; and Don Siegel, 129–30
Haynes, Butch (character, *A Perfect World*), 158–59
Hays Office rules, 21, 108, 124
Heart of Darkness, 80
Heartbreak Ridge, 153
Heaven's Gate, 56
Heims, Jo, 51; and *Breezy*, 29, 77; and *Play Misty for Me*, 15, 24, 73–74
Heisler, Stuart, 219
Helgeland, Brian, 190
Hemingway, Ernest, 95
Henley, William Ernest, 237
Hereafter, 240, 245–51; CGI in, 249–50; location shooting, 241; mise-en-scène, 248–49; music, 250–51; musical themes by Eastwood, 250–51; on-set atmosphere, 241; script, 245; tsunami scene, 249
hereafter, Eastwood's beliefs on, 240, 246
hero: American types, 156; Bronco Billy as, 44, 82; challenge to, 21; Eastwood on, 21, 22; failure of, 22–23; Butch Haynes as, 158; hero and villain,
similarities, 23–24, 148; hero-heroine relationship, 37; in Leone Westerns, 75; lone hero, 59, 85; mysterious hero, 45–46, 61, 97, 108; reticent hero, 247; subversive hero, 76; traditional hero, 46; Josey Wales as, 22
heroism, in *Flags of Our Fathers*, 212–13
High Noon, 75, 76, 110
High Plains Drifter, 26–28, 46–47, 75–76, 107–8, 240; betrayal theme, 80; and *High Noon*, 110; lighting, 47; location, 27, 41, 46–47, 76; location shooting, 27; schedule, 27; television ratings, 89; vengeance theme, 26; and John Wayne, 150
Hirshan, Lenny, 184
His Girl Friday, 219
Hitchcock, Alfred, 124; admired by Eastwood, 10; and *Play Misty for Me*, 16, 18; quoted, 87; transference of guilt theme, 88
Hitler, Adolf, 113
Hoberman, J., 148
Hodenfield, Chris, xx
Hoffman, Dustin, 174
Hog's Breath Inn, 87, 147
Holden, William, 29, 30
Honkytonk Man, 82, 84–86, 94, 102, 120, 138, 227; audience reaction, 64, 84, 116; box office, 64; budget, 58; critical reception, 116; and Eastwood's image, 59; ending, 69, 84, 102; European reception, 64, 105, 116; family theme, 85; a favorite of Eastwood's, 89; and *The Grapes of Wrath*, 152; humor, 102; locations, 86; schedule, 58
Honkytonk Man (Clancy Carlile), 85
Hoover, J. Edgar, 251, 252–54, 255–56
Human Factor, The (working title for *Invictus*), 233. See also *Invictus*

humor, 21, 102; black humor, 78, 86, 92; and Dirty Harry (character), 70; in *Dirty Harry* series, 86; in *The Eiger Sanction*, 78; in *Honkytonk Man*, 102; and Sergio Leone, 66
Huston, Anjelica, 120
Huston, John, 138, 146; and hero of *White Hunter, Black Heart*, 120–22, 124–25, 126–27
Hyams, Joe, 57

Iceland (location, *Flags of Our Fathers*), 222
image, Eastwood's: and aging, 197, 216–17; as antihero, 21, 31, 58–59, 63; appeal of, 31, 68–69; broadening, 61–62, 85; dark side of, 151; evolution of, 90; as fantasy figure, 68–69; and his roles, 51–52, 54, 62, 84, 91, 101–2, 174; private person, compared to, 90, 150
improvisation, 30, 185, 249
In the Line of Fire, 154–55, 164, 176, 197; Kennedy connection, 157; music, 216; on-set atmosphere, 202; script, 144
intrusiveness, avoiding, 66, 182–83
Invictus (working title: *The Human Factor*), 233, 234–44; location shooting, 234–35, 236–39; music, 239; on-set atmosphere, 234–35; schedule, 235; visual effects, 239–41
Iowa (location, *The Bridges of Madison County*), 174
Irving G. Thalberg Memorial Award, 163
It Happened One Night, 36, 115
Italian Westerns, 5, 93, 98, 102, 106–8, 148. *See also* "Dollars" trilogy; Leone Westerns
It's a Wonderful Life, 54
Iwo Jima (location, *Flags of Our Fathers* and *Letters from Iwo Jima*), 210

Iwo Jima, battle of, 206–13; Eastwood meeting survivors, 211–12; flag-raising photograph, 206, 212–13

J. Edgar, 251, 252–56; budget, 254; casting, 254; schedule, 254; script interventions, Eastwood's, 255
jazz: an American art form, 102, 110, 114, 118; and *Bird*, 112–15, 117–18; in *The Bridges of Madison County*, 177; and directing, 117–18; Eastwood's love of, 85, 98–99, 112, 117, 226; and Charlie Parker, 112–13
Joe Kidd, 28, 124
Johnson, James P., 226
Johnson, Robert, 227
Jolly, Pete, 99

Kael, Pauline, 21–22, 145; on *Dirty Harry*, 149
Kamikaze Diaries, 209
kamikaze fighters, 208–9
Kansas Redlegs, 33, 109
Kaufman, Phil, xiv, 31, 33–34, 51, 65–66, 79
Keaton, Buster, 102
Keller, Bill, 242
Kelly's Heroes, 85–86
Kennedy, John F., 148; assassination and *In the Line of Fire*, 144, 157; assassination and *A Perfect World*, 157
Kennedy, Kathleen, 241
Kennedy Center Honors, 185
Kincaid, Robert (character, *The Bridges of Madison County*), 175–76
Korean War, 147
Kowalski, Walt (character, *Gran Torino*), 230, 247
Kral, Irene, 177
Krall, Diana, 229

INDEX 267

Kubrick, Stanley, 146
Kuribayashi, Tadamichi, 206-7, 209-10
Kurosawa, Akira, 96; admired by Eastwood, 76, 223

Lafayette Escadrille, 55-56, 137
LaGravenese, Richard, 175
Lancaster, Burt, 100-101
landscape, in Eastwood's films, 16, 23, 41-42, 125
Lang, Jennings, 222, 239
Lang, Mike (Michael), 99, 239
Last of the Blue Devils, The, 227
Laura, 171
Left-Handed Gun, The, 148
Lehane, Dennis, 189-90
Lenz, Kay, 29, 30
Leone, Sergio: collaboration with Eastwood, 9, 66-67, 107-8, 147-48; death, 149; dedication of *Unforgiven*, 132; differences with Eastwood, 67, 98, 107, 109, 149; and *A Fistful of Dollars*, 45, 66-67, 97, 223; humor, 66; influencing Eastwood, 10, 132; and *The Outlaw Josey Wales*, 108-9; Don Siegel, compared to, 9, 11
Leone Westerns, x-xi, 5, 98, 106-8, 147-48; costumes, 107; critical reception, 148; and Hays Office rules, 108; lighting, 107; music, 106, 215-16; sound, 106-7; style, 106-8; violence in, 148, 213
Letters from Iwo Jima, 206-12, 222-23, 227, 243; cinematography, 210-11; critical reception, 206; Japanese reception, 212; lighting, 220; locations, 210
Lewis, Geoffrey, 55
Lewis, Jerry, 18
lighting: backlighting, 26, 34, 43; *Bird*, 145; *Breezy*, 39; cross-lighting, 34, 43; dark lighting, 34, 135, 145, 190, 201-2, 220; Eastwood on, 34, 135, 145, 201-2, 220; *Firefox*, 145; *The Gauntlet*, 39; *High Plains Drifter*, 47; Leone Westerns, 107; *Letters from Iwo Jima*, 220; like black and white, 135; *Million Dollar Baby*, 201-2; *Mystic River*, 190; *The Outlaw Josey Wales*, 34, 39, 42-43; Bruce Surtees on, 145; *Unforgiven*, 135; and weather, 43-44; *White Hunter, Black Heart*, 135. See also cinematography
Linney, Laura, 181
location scouting, 27, 41-42, 76, 169, 175
location shooting, 20, 48, 77, 103; *Breezy*, 77; *Bronco Billy*, 48; *Hereafter*, 241; *High Plains Drifter*, 27; *Invictus*, 234-35, 236-39; *Mystic River*, 190; *Play Misty for Me*, 18, 25; *Unforgiven*, 142-43; *White Hunter, Black Heart*, 125
locations: *Breezy*, 77; *Bronco Billy*, 41-42, 86; *Firefox*, 83-84; *Flags of Our Fathers*, 210, 222; *High Plains Drifter*, 27, 46-47, 76; *Honkytonk Man*, 86; *Letters from Iwo Jima*, 210; *Midnight in the Garden of Good and Evil*, 169, 172-73; *Mystic River*, 190; *The Outlaw Josey Wales*, 32, 41; *Pale Rider*, 89; *Play Misty for Me*, 41, 74; *White Hunter, Black Heart*, 128
Locke, Sondra, 33, 48, 55, 95
Loktionov, Gennady, 251
London: location, *Hereafter*, 241; location, *White Hunter, Black Heart*, 128
Long Walk to Freedom, 238
Longview, Alberta (location, *Unforgiven*), 142-43
Lorenz, Robert, xvii, 222, 224, 239, 242
Los Angeles, Calif.: location, *Breezy*, 77; location, *Changeling*, 224-25

Los Angeles City College, 4, 100
loss of innocence, 179, 190, 225
Louis, Joe, 201
Lowther, T. J., 248
loyalty, as a theme, 44, 94, 101-2, 194
Lucas, George, 56, 151
Lumet, Sidney, 66

macho-ism, 21-22, 94, 109, 156, 232-33, 253
Mackenna's Gold, 73
MacLaine, Shirley, 11
Magnificent Obsession, 174
Magnum Force, 150
Maguire, Jeff, 144, 154-55
Mailer, Norman, 57, 58, 59, 95, 96, 101
"Make my day," 69, 103, 154
Malkovich, John, 155
Malpaso Company, xiii-xiv, 40, 57-58; and *Bronco Billy*, 54, 81; family atmosphere, 239; formation of, xi, 55, 68, 73, 163; future of, 92; meaning of name, 57; and profits, 58; as a team, 68; at Universal Studios, 7, 163-64; at Warner Bros., 134-35, 163-64
Maltz, Albert, 123
Man with No Name, 45, 93, 97, 107, 148, 232
Mandela, Nelson, 233, 235-36, 238, 242-44; prisoner on Robben Island, 237, 239
Manes, Fritz, 58
Mann, Anthony, 22, 102
market research, 123, 136, 151-52
Marshall, Frank, 241
Matrix Revolutions, The, 189
Maui, 249
Mazzocco, Robert, 152
McCreary, Lori, 238

McLaren, Frankie and George, 241, 248
McPherson, Charles, 129
McShann, Jay, 228
Mercer, Johnny, 172
Midnight in the Garden of Good and Evil, 168-73, 175, 176; European reception, xv; location, 169, 172-73; music, 172; pacing, 173; script and script changes, 169-70
Midnight in the Garden of Good and Evil (John Berendt), 169-70, 174
Milius, John, 22, 51, 150
Million Dollar Baby, 193-205, 222, 254-55; assisted suicide controversy, 203-4, 214-15; awards, 239, 254-55; box office, 254-55; budget, 221; cinematography, 201-2; Eastwood's performance, 193-94, 197-98; ending, 200; father-daughter relationship theme, 194-95, 221, 246; lighting, 201-2; mise-en-scène, 194; score by Eastwood, 199-200; script changes, 202-3
mise-en-scène, 145-46; *Breezy*, 29; Eastwood on, 34-35, 47-49, 75, 123, 128, 220; *Hereafter*, 248-49; *Million Dollar Baby*, 194; *Mystic River*, 187; *Unforgiven*, 135; *White Hunter, Black Heart*, 125
Missouri Breaks, The, 110
Missouri guerrillas, 33
"Misty," 8, 12, 26
Moby Dick (film), 126
Monk, Thelonious, 228, 229
Monk, Thelonious, Jr., 228
Mono Lake, Calif. (location, *High Plains Drifter*), 27, 47, 76
Monterey, Calif., 95; location, *Play Misty for Me*, 41, 74

Monterey Jazz Festival, 24
Montreal Film Festival, 105
moral issues, 31, 75, 109, 158, 231, 246
Morgan, Peter, 240, 245
Morricone, Ennio, 106, 215–16
mountain climbing, 30–31, 78
Muhammad Ali, 82
Mulligan, Gerry, 85, 99
Munny, William (character, *Unforgiven*), 139, 232, 251
Murakami, James J., 237
Museum of Modern Art (New York), xv, 56, 105, 152
music and Eastwood: composing, xviii, 99, 112, 199–200, 229, 250–51; performing, 99–100, 112, 223, 226–29. *See also* jazz
music in films: *Bird*, 113, 129; *The Bridges of Madison County*, 177, 199, 229; *Changeling*, 229; *A Fistful of Dollars*, 215; *The Good, the Bad and the Ugly*, 215; *Gran Torino*, 229; *Hereafter*, 250–51; *In the Line of Fire*, 216; *Invictus*, 239; Leone Westerns, 106, 215–16; *Midnight in the Garden of Good and Evil*, 172; *Million Dollar Baby*, 199–200; *Mystic River*, 199; *Pale Rider*, 99; *A Perfect World*, 229; *Play Misty for Me*, 12, 17, 25–26; *Tightrope*, 99, 199, 229; *Two Mules for Sister Sara*, 216; *Unforgiven*, 199, 229; *White Hunter, Black Heart*, 128–29
My Darling Clementine, 135, 220
mysterious hero, 45–46, 61, 97, 108
Mystic River, 178–88, 189–91, 219, 221, 222, 248; awards, 254; box office, 254; budget, 184, 189, 254; casting, 181, 186; cinematography, 190; ending, 185–86; lighting, 190; locations, 190; mise-en-scène, 187; performances, 182; score by Eastwood, xviii, 199; script, 185; traumatized child theme, 179, 184, 190; vengeance theme, 184
Mystic River (Dennis Lehane), 178–79, 189–90, 222, 254

National Endowment for the Arts, 103
new talent, Eastwood encouraging, 51, 103–4
New York Review of Books, 57, 100, 152
Newman, Paul, 124, 148
Nicholson, Jack, 22, 110
Niehaus, Lennie, 128–29, 200, 229
Night of the Hunter, The, 190
Nishi, Takeichi, 210
Northcott, Gordon, 231

Oakland, Calif., 70, 112, 113, 147, 228
Obama, Barack, 243
O'Byrne, Brian, 203
Of Mice and Men, 176–77
Oglethorpe, James, 172
Oliveira, Manuel de, 223–24
Once Upon a Time in America, 67
Once Upon a Time in the West, 67, 149
Ontario, Ore. (location, *Bronco Billy*), 42, 86
Oscars, xvi, 143–44, 163, 215, 233, 239, 252, 254–55
Osment, Haley Joel, 241
Outlaw Josey Wales, The, 31–35, 79–80, 150; betrayal theme, 80; cinematography, 42–43; ending, 38, 45–46, 97, 220–21; a favorite of Eastwood's, 69, 89; friendship theme, 78; Phil Kaufman replaced as director, 33–34, 65–66, 79; and Sergio Leone, 108; lighting, 34, 39, 42–43;

locations, 32, 41; popular success, 55, 89; schedule, 32; television ratings, 89, 111; and Vietnam War, 79, 109; and Orson Welles, 220
Outlaw Josey Wales, The (Forrest Carter), 32–33
Owens, Michael, 239–41, 250
Oxbow Incident, The, 137–38

pacing, 177, 248
paella trilogy, 5
Page, Geraldine, 6, 114
Paint Your Wagon, 55
Pale Rider, 76, 85, 213, 240; as allegory, 110–11; biblical references, 89; at Cannes Film Festival, 96; and classical Westerns, 102; ecological concerns in, 102, 110–11; location, 89; musical theme by Eastwood, 99; script changes, 82; script interventions, Eastwood's, 89
Parker, Chan, 114
Parker, Charlie "Bird," 112–13, 120, 138–39, 227; Eastwood's memories of, 99, 112–13; historical recordings in *Bird*, 113
Parrish, Avery, 228
Peckham, Anthony, 239, 242
Peckinpah, Sam, 146, 165
Penn, Arthur, 110
Penn, Sean, 181, 187, 191, 254
Perfect World, A, xii–xiii, 144, 156–61; European reception, 248; father, absence of the, theme, 156; Kennedy connection, 157; musical theme by Eastwood, 229; violence in, 156, 160–61; women's roles in, 159
period films, 113
Perot, Ross, 153
Petersen, Wolfgang, 140, 144, 146

Peterson, Oscar, 226
philosophy of filmmaking, Eastwood's, xix, 49–51, 104, 124–25, 182–83
Piano Blues, xviii, 227
Picture Letters from the Commander in Chief, 207–8
Piedmont, Calif., 253
Pienaar, François, 235
Pingitore, Carl, 18
Pink Cadillac, 153
Play Misty for Me, 3–4, 7–10, 12–19, 23–26, 73–75, 222; audience reaction, 56; *The Beguiled*, compared to, 23; box office, 27; budget, 18, 24; casting, 13; critical reception, 19, 94, 149; Eastwood directing and acting in, 126, 149; location shooting, 18, 25; locations, 41, 74; music, 12, 17, 25–26; promotion, 27; *Psycho*, compared to, 15–16, 18; schedule, 18; women's roles in, 23, 114
Playing the Enemy, 235, 238
populism, 87–88
Positif, xv
Post, Ted, xi, 10
Power of One, The, 242
Preminger, Otto, 171
producers: conflicts with directors, 120, 127, 165; Eastwood as producer, 134, 163–67
promotion: *Breezy*, 27; *Bronco Billy*, 53; *Play Misty for Me*, 27; Universal Studios and, 29
Pryor, Richard, 115
Psycho, 15–16, 18, 25
Public Enemies, 254

Quantrill, William Clarke, 33
quest, as a theme, 126

Rachmaninoff, Sergei, 250–51
racism: and *Dirty Harry*, 87; in *The Searchers*, 205; in *White Hunter, Black Heart*, 122
radio, 221
Rashomon, 169
Rawhide, x, 5, 71, 96–97, 100, 107, 147, 166, 223; and Eastwood's first ambitions to direct, 20, 49, 72–73; and Hays Office rules, 108
Reagan, Ronald, 83, 103, 151, 152, 192; quoting from *Sudden Impact*, 95, 103
Reed, Rex, 143
Reflections in a Golden Eye, 126
rehearsals, 18, 30, 58, 126, 198–99, 254; Eastwood on shooting, 30, 114, 145–46; *Midnight in the Garden of Good and Evil*, 172; *Mystic River*, 219
religion, in Eastwood's films, 246–47
Reno, Janet, 160
repertory company, 55
reputation, Eastwood's, reevaluation of, xv–xvi, 95, 105
research, background, 86, 89, 120–21, 172, 254
restraint, 176, 182, 220
revenge, as a theme. *See* vengeance, as a theme
Revenge of the Creature, 147, 227, 253
Reynolds, Burt, 59, 147
rhythm and blues, 227
Richards, Emil, 128–29
Ricker, Bruce, 228
Riesner, Dean, 13, 18, 24, 36, 76
Rijker, Lucia, 201
Ritt, Martin, 66
Robben Island, South Africa (location, *Invictus*), 236–39
Robbins, Tim, 179, 186, 187, 190, 191, 254
Robert Daley Productions, 40

Robinson, Andy, 23
rock 'n' roll, 227
Rodney, Red, 113
Rookie, The, 129, 153
Rubin, Stanley, 119
rugby, 236, 242
Russell, Rosalind, 219

San Francisco, Calif., 147, 226
Sarris, Andrew, 19
Savannah, Ga. (location, *Midnight in the Garden of Good and Evil*), 169, 172–73
Sawtooth Mountains, Idaho (location, *Pale Rider*), 89
schedules: *Changeling*, 219; Eastwood and, 40, 144; *High Plains Drifter*, 27; *Honkytonk Man*, 58; *Invictus*, 235; *J. Edgar*, 254; *The Outlaw Josey Wales*, 32; *Play Misty for Me*, 18
Schickel, Richard, xiv, 154
Schwarzenegger, Arnold, 191
Scorsese, Martin, 227
screenwriting, 183
script interventions, Eastwood's, 65, 82, 183, 202–3; *The Bridges of Madison County*, 177; *Bronco Billy*, 44, 48, 82; *Dirty Harry* series, 69–70; *A Fistful of Dollars*, 45, 97, 108, 148; *The Gauntlet*, 44; *J. Edgar*, 255; *White Hunter, Black Heart*, 119, 125
Searchers, The, 205, 220, 248
self-destructive characters, 69, 102, 116–17, 120, 133, 138–39
Semel, Terry, 153, 166, 169
Shearing, George, 226
Sheen, Charlie, 129
Sherman, William Tecumseh, 172
short on Don Siegel, 9, 19
Shryack, Dennis, 36, 82, 150, 151
Siegel, Don, xi–xii, 65, 223; acting debut

in *Play Misty for Me*, 8, 10, 74; and *The Beguiled*, 10, 130; and budgets, 72; collaboration with Eastwood, 9, 11, 18-19, 20, 149; dedication of *Unforgiven*, 132; directing style, 9, 104; and *Dirty Harry*, 11, 180; and Eastwood's directing compared to, 66; first takes, 21, 56; influencing Eastwood, 10, 56, 104, 129-30, 132; Sergio Leone, compared to, 11; predecessors, 129-30; and producers, 127, 165
Sight & Sound, xvi
Signoret, Simone, 159
Silvani, Al, 201
simplicity in art, 122-23
Sirk, Douglas, 174
Sitting Pretty, 174
Sixth Sense, The, 241
"Smith & Wesson and me," 70
social films, 189
Society of Former Special Agents of the FBI, 255
Soderbergh, Steven, 160-61
sound, xx, 39, 106-7
South Africa: history, 235-36; location, *Invictus*, 234-39, 244
Space Cowboys, 240, 249
Spacey, Kevin, 170, 172
spaghetti Westerns, 5, 93, 98, 102, 106-8, 148. *See also* "Dollars" trilogy; Leone Westerns
Specktor, Fred, 238
Spiegel, Sam, 121, 122, 127
Spielberg, Steven, 151, 161-62, 176, 222
Spitzer, Eliot, 225
spontaneity, 114, 194, 198-99. *See also* first takes; rehearsals: Eastwood on shooting
Springboks, 234, 236, 237, 238

Stanislavsky, Konstantin, 100
Stanley, Frank, 39
Stanwyck, Barbara, 115
Star Is Born, A, xvii
Star Wars movies, 89
stardom and Eastwood, 53, 57, 59, 84, 95, 96, 142, 155
Stark, Ray, 119
Steinbeck, John, 176-77
Stern, Tom, 145, 201-2, 237, 249
Stevens, George, 35
Stevens, Michael, 239
Stinson, Joe, 69
story, importance of the, 61, 66, 98, 138
storyboarding, 26, 75
"Storyteller, The" (short on Don Siegel), 9, 19
Stovall, Red (character, *Honkytonk Man*), 84-85, 91, 102, 176
Straczynski, J. Michael, 224
"Strangers in the Night," 12, 26
Streep, Meryl, 175
stuntmen, 87
stuntwork, Eastwood performing, xx
Sturges, John, 28, 124; influence on Eastwood, 187
Sturges, Preston, 54
Sudden Impact, 87; black humor, 86; commercial potential, 61, 82; critical reception, 94; feminism, 152; popular success, 59; Ronald Reagan quoting from, 95, 103; traumatized child theme, 190
Surtees, Bruce, 18-19, 51, 202; collaboration with Eastwood, 34, 42, 77, 135-36; collaboration with Don Siegel, 42, 77; and *High Plains Drifter*, 47, 77; and *Honkytonk Man*, 86; and *The Outlaw Josey Wales*, 34, 39, 42-43; quoted, 33, 145

Sutherland, Donald, 185
Swank, Hilary, 194, 195–96, 254–55
Sweet and Lowdown, 181
Symbionese Liberation Army, 88

Tarantula, 147
Tatum, Art, 226
Taylor, Elizabeth, 11
technical crew: Eastwood working with same, 50–51, 68, 136, 144–45, 166, 241, 254; *Eiger Sanction*, 78
television style, 108; and film style, 145, 168
terrorist attacks, London, 240, 245
"That's not going to happen," 154–55
Thelonious Monk: Straight, No Chaser, 228
themes: betrayal, 80; family, 85; father, absence of the, 156; father-daughter relationship, xvii, 194–95, 221, 246; friendship, 78, 83; loyalty, 44, 94, 101, 194; quest, 126; transference of guilt, 88; traumatized child, 179, 184, 190, 225; vengeance, 26, 140, 184
Thompson, Jack, 172
Thunderbolt and Lightfoot, 56, 104, 184
Tidyman, Ernest, 27, 75
Tightrope, xiv, 59–63, 88–89, 91, 94; and *Dirty Harry*, 62, 69; and Eastwood's image, 59, 61; family theme, 85; musical theme by Eastwood, 99, 199, 229; transference of guilt theme, 88
tolerance, 171, 173, 230–31
Tolson, Clyde, 253, 255
Tony Bennett: The Music Never Ends, 228
Toole, F. X., 203
Tourneur, Jacques, 251
transference of guilt, as a theme, 88
traumatized child, as a theme, 179, 184, 190, 225
Trouble with the Curve, xiii, xvii

tsunami, Indian Ocean, 240, 245–46, 250
Tuggle, Richard, xiv, 59, 62, 89
Turner, Big Joe, 227
Two Mules for Sister Sara, 11, 77; music, 216

under budget, 40, 103, 144, 150, 252
Unforgiven, 131–33, 139–40, 142–43, 150–51, 174, 180, 221, 251; awards, 143–44, 163; box office, 154; budget, 153; commercial potential, 173–74; and contemporary politics, 132–33; critical reception, 137; dedication, 132; demythifying the West, 140; *Dirty Harry*, compared to, 154; Eastwood directing and acting in, 182; European reception, xv; lighting, 135; location shooting, 142–43; mise-en-scène, 135; musical theme by Eastwood, 199, 229; on-set atmosphere, 142–43, 167; opening scene, 146; title, 138; vengeance theme, 140, 193; violence in, 131–32, 139–40, 146, 153, 157, 160, 213–14, 232
United Artists, 149, 184
Universal Studios: and *Breezy*, 29; and Eastwood's early career, 4–5, 100, 147; headquarters of Malpaso, 7, 151, 163–64; and *High Plains Drifter*, 27; and *Million Dollar Baby*, 221; and *Play Misty for Me*, 24, 25–26, 56, 73–74, 94, 149, 222; promotion, 27, 29

Valdes, David, 142–43, 145, 153, 165
Van Horn, Buddy, 42, 51
Vang, Bee, 232
Velázquez, Diego, 220
vengeance, as a theme, 26, 140, 184, 193
Venora, Diane, 115

Video West, 18
video-assist technology, 18, 234
Vidor, King, 56
Vienna (location, *Firefox*), 83
Viertel, Peter, 119-21, 125, 126, 127
Vietnam War, 148; and *Dirty Harry*, 149; and *The Outlaw Josey Wales*, 79, 109
violence in films, 136-37, 160; Eastwood's evolving views, 179, 213-14; *A Fistful of Dollars*, 93; *The Gauntlet*, 38-39; Leone Westerns, 148, 213; *A Perfect World*, 156, 160-61; *Unforgiven*, 131-32, 139-40, 146, 153, 157, 160, 213-14, 232
violence in society, 156, 160-61
violence on television, 160
visual effects, 239-41, 249-50
Volonté, Gian Maria, 107

Waco, Tex., siege, 160
Wagner, Richard, 229
Wales, Josey (character), 22, 78, 79-80, 109
Waller, Fats, 226
Waller, Robert James, 174-75
Wallis, Hal, 164, 165
Walsh, Raoul, 56, 102, 165; and Don Siegel, 129-30
Walter, Jessica, 13, 23, 24, 30
Warner, Jack, 55, 65, 166-67
Warner Bros.: and *Bird*, 115, 130; and *Dirty Harry*, 150; headquarters of Malpaso, 57, 151, 163, 252; and *Honkytonk Man*, 65, 84; and *J. Edgar*, 255; and *Midnight in the Garden of Good and Evil*, 169; and *Million Dollar Baby*, 221, 246, 254-55; and *Mystic River*, 183-84, 189-90, 221, 254-55; promotion, 164; relationship with Eastwood, xiii, 68, 134-35, 144, 150, 151, 153, 164, 166, 183-84; and *Thunderbolt and Lightfoot*, 184; and *White Hunter, Black Heart*, 119, 130
Watanabe, Ken, 208
Wayne, John, 124, 150, 205
weather, and film production, 34, 43-44, 142-43, 145, 167
Webster, Ferris, 27
Welles, Orson, 220
Wellman, William, xvii, 55-56, 137-38, 220; and Don Siegel, 129-30
Wells, Frank, 150, 151, 184
Westerns, 46, 55, 106-11, 131, 148; an American art form, 102, 110; audience for, 89, 111; classical Westerns, 102; Eastwood's contribution to, 110-11; genre disappearing, 89; and history, 89; Italian Westerns (spaghetti Westerns), 5, 93, 98, 102, 106-8, 148; modern Westerns, 111. *See also* Leone Westerns
Where Eagles Dare, 11
Whitaker, Forest, 115, 227
White Dawn, The, 34
White Hunter, Black Heart, xvi, 119-30; anti-Semitism in, 126-27; cinematography, 125; ecological concerns in, 126; lighting, 135; location shooting, 125; locations, 128; mise-en-scène, 125; music, 128-29; quest theme, 126; racism in, 122; script interventions, Eastwood's, 119, 125; style, 124; women's roles in, 128
Who Framed Roger Rabbit, 130
widescreen composition, 34-35
Wilder, Billy, 165
Wilhelm, Peter, 242
Williams, Jim, 170-72, 173

Wills, Bob, 84, 85, 99
Wilson, John (character, *White Hunter, Black Heart*), 121-24, 126-27, 128
women's boxing, 200-201
women's roles: *The Beguiled*, 23, 114; in Eastwood's films, 37, 95, 114-15, 221; in films of the forties, 115, 159; *A Perfect World*, 159; *Play Misty for Me*, 23, 114; *White Hunter, Black Heart*, 128
World Cup (rugby), 233, 236
World War II films, 213
Worth, David, 42, 51
Wright, Glenn, 144
Wyler, William, 56

Yates, Rowdy (character), 107
Yojimbo, 76, 96, 223
Young, Lester, 99

Zimbabwe (location, *White Hunter, Black Heart*), 128
Zwerin, Charlotte, 228

CPSIA information can be obtained at www.ICGtesting.com
Printed in the USA
BVOW071041121112

304983BV00003B/2/P